WRIGHTSLAW

From Emotions to Advocacy

The Special Education Survival Guide

Peter W. D. Wright

Pamela Darr Wright

Harbor House Law Press, Inc.
Hartfield, Virginia 23071

Wrightslaw: From Emotions to Advocacy – The Special Education Survival Guide
By Peter W. D. Wright and Pamela Darr Wright

Publisher's Cataloging-in-Publication Data
(Provided by Quality Books, Inc.)
Wright, Peter W. D.
    Wrightslaw : from emotions to advocacy : the special education survival guide /
by Peter W.D. Wright & Pamela Darr Wright—1st ed.
    p. cm.
    Includes bibliographical references and index.
    LCCN: 2001091451
    ISBN 1-892320-08-8
    1. Special education—parent participation—United States.
  2. Special education—Law and legislation—United States.
  I. Wright, Pamela Darr. II. Title.
    LC4031.W75 2002   371.9'0973
                                       QBI02-200164

10 9 8 7 6 5 4 3 2

Printing History

Harbor House Law Press, Inc. issues new printings and new editions to keep our books current. New printings include technical corrections and minor changes. New editions include major revisions of text and/or changes. First Edition May 2002.

Disclaimer

The purpose of this book is to educate and inform. While every effort has been made to make this book as complete and accurate as possible, there may be mistakes, both typographical and in content. The authors and Harbor House Law Press, Inc. shall have neither liability nor responsibility to any person or entity with respect to any loss or damage caused, or alleged to be caused, directly or indirectly, by the information contained in this book. If you do not wish to be bound by the above, you may return this book to the publisher for a full refund. Every effort has been made to ensure that no copyrighted material has been used without permission. The authors regret any oversights that may have occurred and are happy to rectify them in future printings of this book.

When You Use a Self-Help Law Book

Law is always changing. The information contained in this book is general information and may or may not reflect current legal developments. This book is designed to provide general information in regard to the subject matter covered. It is sold with the understanding that the publisher and author are not engaged in rendering legal or other professional services. For legal advice about a specific set of facts, you should consult with an attorney.

Bulk Purchases

Harbor House Law Press books are available at quantity discounts for bulk purchases, academic sales or textbook adoptions. For information, contact Harbor House Law Press, P. O. Box 480, Hartfield VA 23071. Please provide the title of the book, ISBN number, quantity, how the book will be used, and date needed.

Toll Free Phone Orders: (877) LAW IDEA or (877) 529-4332   Toll Free Fax Orders: (800) 863-5348

Internet Orders: http://www.harborhouselaw.com

What People Are Saying About
Wrightslaw: From Emotions to Advocacy – The Special Education Survival Guide

"An invaluable, user-friendly resource for parents of children with disabilities! This book is packed with critical information, and provides clear, practical professional guidance that will empower parents with the necessary skills, tools and knowledge for successfully advocating in their child's behalf." – Sandra Rief, author of *How to Reach and Teach ADD/ADHD Children*

"*From Emotions to Advocacy* tips the scales. Everything is here!" – Sue Heath, parent and advocate

"This book will reach the minds and hearts of every parent and advocate. How I wish I had a guide like this when my child entered the system!" – Maureen Reyes, parent and advocate

"Beautifully written, clear-cut . . ." – Linda Morrissey, parent and advocate

"In an-easy-to-follow format, *From Emotions to Advocacy* describes the steps for successful, effective advocacy. This book will help seasoned advocates and parents who are just beginning the advocacy journey." – Melanie Allen, advocate and parent of two special needs children

"This is the bible of special education advocacy for proactive parents . . . like having a trusted, knowledgeable friend to help you every step of the way. *From Emotions to Advocacy* shows you what to do so you do it right the first time!" – Darlene Trousdale, parent and advocate

"*Wrightslaw: From Emotions to Advocacy* should be sent to every parent and issued to every hearing officer. In short, this book is wonderful!" – Sonja Kerr, Esq.

"*From Emotions to Advocacy* is a 'must have' for any parent with a special needs child. It takes away the guesswork and paves an easier road for parents to travel." – Laurie Mix, parent and advocate

"Invaluable for parents who are beginning, and for those who are experienced advocates who need a good reference. Like so many parents, we will always be in your debt." – Catherine Worthington, parent and advocate

"If you read the Wrightslaw books, you will be prepared to successfully advocate for your child." – Joe Jackson, psychologist and advocate

"*From Emotions to Advocacy* is a well-organized parent primer. Congratulations!" – Kathryn Dobel, Esq.

"Pete and Pam Wright accomplish a remarkable feat with their new advocacy book . . . they draw a clear roadmap for parents to follow and make the process understandable and workable. Kudos for accomplishing such a huge task!" – Judy Bonnell, parent and advocate

Acknowledgments

We are grateful to the thousands of parents who contacted us since we established the **Wrightslaw site.** Your letters inspired us to find creative solutions to the problems parents face when they advocate for their children.

We wish to acknowledge the contributions of several individuals who provided ideas for this book.

We thank Minnesota attorney **Sonja Kerr,** New Mexico advocate **Judy Bonnell,** and Indiana advocate **Pat Howey** for their suggestions about using problem resolution worksheets in IEP meetings.

We thank Vermont advocate **Brice Palmer** for his tips about recording meetings and his wise counsel.

We thank **Leonora and Steve Tonks** of Olympia, Washington who helped us synthesize ideas about the parent role and the importance of long-term planning.

We want to acknowledge and thank several people who selflessly gave their time and energy to read and critique portions of the manuscript:

> **Loni Allen,** Family Resource Specialist at Parents Helping Parents in California and advocate for children in the juvenile justice system
> **Judy Bonnell,** parent advocate from New Mexico
> **Larry Goodwin,** parent from Ohio
> **Joe Jackson,** psychologist and advocate for people with disabilities in Virginia
> **Laurie Mix,** parent advocate for her child with ADHD in Washington
> **Linda and Kevin Morrissey,** parent advocates from Connecticut
> **Maureen Reyes,** parent and advocate for her child with multiple disabilities in Texas
> **Law Riskin,** special education teacher in California
> **Darlene Trousdale,** parent and full-time student in California
> **Maggie Wade,** parent advocate in Alaska
> **Catherine Worthington,** parent advocate for her child with multiple disabilities in Florida

We thank **Lynn Trimble,** Phoenix writer, Assistant Editor of *Raising Arizona Kids Magazine,* and mother of three, who carefully edited the entire manuscript and offered many suggestions that we included in the book. Lynn provided advice about time management and taking care of oneself.

We owe a special debt of gratitude to **Suzanne Heath,** a parent from New Hampshire. From the beginning of this project, Sue offered valuable advice about the "ideal parent advocacy manual." Sue read the entire manuscript and offered dozens of suggestions that are included in the final version of *Wrightslaw: From Emotions to Advocacy—The Special Education Survival Guide.*

We thank our copyeditor and proofreader, **Sara Murphy Wright.** Sara continued her work on this book after she was sent to Mississippi on a disaster relief mission. Thanks to Sara, this book is clear, readable, organized, and grammatically correct.

Mayapriya Long designed the cover and layout for *Wrightslaw: From Emotions to Advocacy—The Special Education Survival Guide.*

We thank our creative and resourceful staff, **Debra Pratt** and **Traci Wright,** who make Wrightslaw a warm and wonderful place.

Finally, love and thanks to our families whose patience and support helped us to complete this book.

Dedication

We dedicate this book to you, the parents.

As you shared your struggles and successes, you invited us into your minds and hearts. When you asked questions, you helped us to learn. When you sent thank-you notes, we felt your support.
Thank you.

Contents

Introduction .... **xiii**

From Emotions to Advocacy xiii

Why Advocate? xiv

What You Will Learn xiv

Icons xv

How This Book is Organized xv

A Note to Parents of Section 504 Children xvii

A Note to Special Educators xvii

Section One. Getting Started 1

Chapter 1. Learning About Advocacy 3

Why Advocate? 4

Different Types of Advocates 4

What Advocates Do 5

The Parent's Journey From Emotions to Advocacy 6

Supplies 7

In Summation 7

Chapter 2. Creating Your Master Plan 9

The Need to Plan 9

Elements of a Master Plan 10

Planning for the Future 12

Laura and Steve: Planning 12

Writing Your Master Plan 13

In Summation 16

Chapter 3. The Parent as Project Manager 17

Contractors and Project Managers 17

The Special Education Project Manager 17

Tips: Taking Care of Yourself 19

In Summation 20

Section Two. Advocacy 101 21

Chapter 4. Learning the Rules of the Game 23

The Rules 23
Understanding the School 24
Learning About Your School District 25
Rules of the Game 26
In Summation 27

Chapter 5. Obstacles to Success 29

Obstacles to Advocacy 29
School Obstacles 30
Parent Obstacles 33
Dealing with Difficult People 34
Warning: Common Emotional Traps 40
Your Relationship with the School 40
In Summation 40

Chapter 6. Resolving Parent-School Conflict 41

The Nature of Parent-School Conflict 41
Real Issues: Expense and Control 43
Common Parent-School Problems 44
Tips to Resolve Problems 49
In Summation 51

Chapter 7. Emergency, Crisis, Help! 53

Help! Events That Trigger Crises 53
Crisis Management, Step-by-Step 54
Short-Term Solutions 54
Long Term Planning 55
In Summation 57

Section Three. The Parent as Expert 59

Chapter 8. Evaluations and Your Child's Disability 61

Get a Comprehensive Evaluation 61
Finding Evaluators 62

Understanding Test Results 62
Limitations of School Evaluations 64
Learn About the Disability 64
Learn About Effective Educational Practices 65
In Summation 65

Chapter 9. The File: Do It Right! 67

Document Management System 67
Gather Information About Your Child 67
Organizing the Master File 68
Create Your List of Documents 70
In Summation 72

Chapter 10. Tests and Measurements 101 73

Mike 73
Measuring Growth: Rulers, Yardsticks, and Other Tools 74
Measuring Educational Change: Test Scores 75
Learning About Evaluations 75
Statistics 101 76
The Bell Curve: A Powerful Tool 80
Learning How Test Scores Are Reported 84
In Summation 86

Chapter 11. Tests and Measurements 102 87

Katie 87
Learning About Composite Scores 88
Using Pre- and Post-Testing to Measure Progress 89
Norm-Referenced and Criterion-Referenced Tests 90
Test Categories and Descriptions 97
Charting Test Scores 100
Your Homework Assignment 102
In Summation 102

Chapter 12. SMART IEPs 103

Learning About SMART IEPs 103
Smart IEP Goals and Objectives 104
Present Levels of Performance 105
Legal Definitions: Goals, Objectives and Benchmarks 106
Measuring and Monitoring the Child's Progress 107
Learning to Write SMART Goals and Objectives 108
The SMART Weight Loss Program 108

Mike Trains for the Fitness Test 112
Kevin Learns to Type 112
Megan Learns to Read 113
Non-Goals: Attitude Statements 113
Non-Goals: States of Being 114
Homework Assignment #1: You Learn to Write Goals 115
Homework Assignment #2: You Learn to Write SMART IEP Goals and Objectives 115
In Summation 116

Section Four. Special Education Law 117

Chapter 13. IDEA - Overview and Legislative Intent 119

Legislative Intent 119
The Individuals with Disabilities Education Act of 1997 120
In Summation 120

Chapter 14. IDEA – Section 1400: Findings and Purposes 121

20 U.S.C. § 1400 Congressional Findings and Purpose 121
Wrightslaw Discussion of Findings and Purposes 123
In Summation 124

Chapter 15. IDEA – Section 1401: Definitions 125

20 U.S.C. § 1401 Definitions 125
Wrightslaw Discussion of Definitions 128
In Summation 130

Chapter 16. IDEA – Section 1412: LRE, ESY, Child Find, Private Placement, Assessments 131

20 U.S.C. § 1412 – State Eligibility 131
Wrightslaw Discussion of Child Find, Least Restrictive Environment,
   Private Placements, State and District Assessments 134
In Summation 139

Chapter 17. IDEA – Section 1414: Evaluations, Eligibility, IEPs and Placement 141

20 U.S.C. § 1414(a) Evaluations and Reevaluations 141
Additional Requirements for Evaluations and Reevaluations 143
Wrightslaw Discussion of Evaluations and Eligibility.............................145
20 U.S.C. § 1414(d) Individualized Education Programs 146
Wrightslaw Discussion of Individualized Education Programs (IEPs) and Placement .. 150
In Summation 152

Chapter 18. IDEA – Section 1415: Procedural Safeguards, Due Process, Discipline, etc........ 153

20 U.S.C. § 1415 – Procedural Safeguards 154
Wrightslaw Discussion of Prior Written Notice and Procedural Safeguards Notice ..156
20 U.S.C. § 1415(e), (f), (g), (h), and (i) – Mediation, Due Process Hearings,
    Appeals to Court 157
Wrightslaw Discussion of Mediation, Due Process Hearings, Appeals to Court,
    Attorneys' Fees 161
20 U.S.C. § 1415(k) Placement in Alternative Educational Setting 165
Wrightslaw Discussion of Discipline 170
20 U.S.C. § 1415 (m) Transfer of Parental Rights at Age of Majority 173
Wrightslaw Discussion of Age of Majority 173

Chapter 19. Section 504 of The Rehabilitation Act of 1973 and the Americans with Disabilities Act 175

Wrightslaw Discussion of Section 504, ADA and IDEA 176
Section 504, ADA, High Stakes Testing, Statewide Assessments 178
In Summation 184

Chapter 20. Family Educational Rights and Privacy Act 185

FERPA 185
In Summation 189

Section Five. Tactics and Strategies 191

Chapter 21. The Rules of Adverse Assumptions 193

The Rules of Adverse Assumptions 194
To Avoid Conflict, Prepare for Conflict 197
Proof and Evidence 197
Simple Themes Win Cases 198
In Summation 199

Chapter 22. Creating Paper Trails 201

Why Document? 201
Logs, Journals and Calendars 202
How to Use a Problem Report 205
Handling Telephone Calls 206
In Summation 206

Chapter 23. How to Write Good Evidence Letters 207

Why You Write Letters 207
Strategies: Writing Good Letters 209
Letter Writing Pitfalls 211
Using Strategies in Letters 212
In Summation 218

Chapter 24. Writing the "Letter to the Stranger" 219

The Blame Approach 219
Impact of Angry Letters 220
The Story-Telling Approach 220
Using Persuasive Strategies in Letters 222
Writing "Letters to the Stranger" 223
In Summation 225

Chapter 25. Preparing for Meetings: Taking Control 227

You are a Negotiator 227
Five Rules for Successful Problem Solving 228
Preparing for School Meetings 230
Image and Presentation 235
In Summation 235

Chapter 26. Meeting Strategies: Maintaining Control 237

School Meeting Anxiety 237
Meeting Strategies 238
Common Meeting Problems 240
Use the Problem-Resolution Worksheet 242
Post-meeting Strategies 245
In Summation 245

Chapter 27. In Summation 247

Appendices 249

Appendix A. Appendix A to 34 C.F.R. Part 300 249
Appendix B. Your Rights and Responsibilities Under IDEA 277
Appendix C. Frequently Asked Questions About Special Education, from NICHCY 281
Appendix D. State Departments of Special Education 297
Appendix E. Parent Training Information Centers by State 303
Appendix F. Disabilities Organizations and Information Groups 313

Appendix G. Legal and Advocacy Resources 323

Appendix H. Free Publications 327

Appendix I. Sample Letters to the School 331

Appendix J. Glossary of Special Education and Legal Terms 351

Appendix K. Glossary of Assessment Terms 361

Bibliography 367

Index 369

Introduction

Many parents want to advocate for their child but hold back. If you want to advocate or need to advocate or believe you should advocate for your child but have excuses or reasons why you cannot, this book is for you. We will help you attack obstacles and learn the skills you need to be an effective advocate for your child.

From Emotions to Advocacy

As you read this book, you will experience an array of emotions – from fear, sadness, and anger to excitement, relief, and hope. You will make mental lists of things to do. Write your ideas down on a sheet of paper. Tuck your list into this book and use it as a bookmark. As you learn, your ideas and priorities will change.

You may be tempted to put this book aside and act on your ideas. Try to resist this urge. You have not yet learned what you need to know.

Our advocacy program teaches information and skills, step by step. When you know the information and skills you need to learn, you can make good use of your time. As you complete each step, you will acquire information and polish skills that you will use later.

Skim through the book and the Appendices. When you understand the program, you will know where to focus your energy. You will not allow urgent issues take precedence over important issues.

In the beginning, the process of advocating for your special needs child will feel overwhelming. This is normal. If you follow this program, you will learn how to organize, plan, and use your emotions to become an effective advocate for your child. You will not regret your journey from emotions to advocacy. Because of you, your child's life will change for the better.

Why Advocate?

As the parent of a special needs child, you represent your child's interests. When you negotiate with the school on your child's behalf, you increase the odds that your child will get an appropriate education. You cannot leave this job to others!

Most parents describe the process of negotiating with the school as a frustrating, exhausting ordeal. Some parents throw in the towel. Others prevail. What do effective parent advocates know? What are the secrets of their success?

Effective advocacy comes from research, planning and preparation. Successful advocates know what is important and what is not worth fighting about. When you finish this book, you will have acquired the knowledge and skills you need to be an effective advocate. You will avoid the mistakes that prevent many parents from successfully advocating for their children.

What You Will Learn

On your journey from emotions to advocacy, you will learn about the special education system and issues that make parent-school conflict inevitable. We describe how to learn about your child's disability, how the disability affects your child, and appropriate educational and remediation techniques. You will learn how to measure educational progress, and how to write annual goals and objectives for Individualized Education Programs (IEPs).

We teach you how to use tactics and strategies to prevent problems or resolve problems early. You will learn how to manage your emotions so you do not burn out or throw in the towel.

What This Book is Not About

Wrightslaw: From Emotions to Advocacy–The Special Education Survival Guide does not focus on the needs of children with specific disabilities, nor is this book an in-depth guide to writing Individualized Education Programs (IEPs).

Wrightslaw: Special Education Law (ISBN: 1-8923220-0307) is a legal reference book that includes the full text of the Individuals with Disabilities Act (IDEA), Section 504 of the Rehabilitation Act, the Family Educational Records and Privacy Act (FERPA), implementing regulations, and a casebook of decisions from the United States Supreme Court. You can order *Wrightslaw: Special Education Law* from Harbor House Law Press, Inc. (Toll-free: 877-LAW IDEA) or purchase it online at the Wrightslaw website.

Wrightslaw: SMART IEPs will teach you how to write IEPs that are specific, measurable, use action words, realistic, and are time-limited. Harbor House Law Press will publish SMART IEPs in 2002.

This practical book teaches skills and provides real life examples that make these skills easier to understand and use. Because this book teaches information and skills, we include sample letters, logs, checklists, worksheets, and agendas to make your learning more effective. Even if you have read other books about special education, this book will be an invaluable resource.

Icons

The book includes icons that alert you to Tips, Warnings, Cross-references, and Internet Resources.

☑ Tip

((📢 Warning – Be careful!

📖 Cross-reference

🖱 Internet Resource

How This Book is Organized

Section One is "Getting Started."

You will learn:
- Basic advocacy skills
- Supplies you need to get started
- How to develop a master plan for your child's education
- How to act as your child's special education project manager

Section Two is "Advocacy 101."

In this section, you will learn about:
- Schools as bureaucracies and the rules of the game
- Obstacles to success – school culture, myths, gatekeepers, and emotions
- Common causes of conflict
- Steps you can take to prevent or resolve problems
- Events that trigger parent-school crises

Section Three is "The Parent as Expert."

In this section, you will learn:

- Why you must become an expert about your child's disability and educational needs
- How to organize your child's file, step by step
- How to use information from tests to understand your child's disability
- How to use test scores to monitor and measure your child's progress
- How to write SMART IEP goals and objectives

Section Four is "Special Education Law."

In this section, you will learn about:

- The Individuals with Disabilities Education Act (IDEA)
- Findings and purposes of the IDEA
- Definitions in the IDEA
- Extended school year (ESY), child find, least restrictive environment (LRE), private placements, and statewide assessments
- Evaluations, eligibility, IEPs, and placement
- Prior written notice, procedural safeguards, mediation, due process hearings, appeals, discipline, and age of majority
- Section 504 of the Rehabilitation Act and the Americans with Disabilities Act (ADA)
- Family Educational Records and Privacy Act (FERPA)

Section Five is "Tactics and Strategies."

In this section, you will learn about:

- The "Rules of Adverse Assumptions," proof and evidence, and image and presentation
- How to use logs, calendars, and journals to create paper trails
- How to write effective letters
- How to write a persuasive "Letter to the Stranger"
- How to use problem worksheets, parent agendas, visual aids, and graphs
- Roles of experts
- Pros and cons of tape recording meetings
- How to use problem resolution worksheets and post-meeting thank you letters

Appendices

The book includes several appendices:

- Appendix A to the special education regulations about IEPs, the parental role, and transition
- Frequently asked questions about special education
- Summary of your rights and responsibilities
- State Departments of Special Education by state
- Parent Training Information Centers by state
- Sources of information about disabilities and special education
- Sources of legal information
- Free publications to help you be a more effective advocate for your child
- Sample letters and worksheets that you can tailor to your needs

The book includes glossaries of assessment terms and special education legal terms.

Companion Website

 Visit the companion website for *Wrightslaw: From Emotions to Advocacy - The Special Education Survival Guide* at:

http://www.fetaweb.com/

Fetaweb.com includes articles, checklists, sample letters, charts, and free resources. We encourage you to submit letters, tips and favorite links.

Fetaweb.com will list changes that have occurred since the book was published. We appreciate your comments and suggestions about how we can improve the book.

A Note to Parents of Section 504 Children

If your child has a Section 504 plan and does not receive special education services under the Individuals with Disabilities Education Act, you should read Chapter 19 about Section 504 of the Rehabilitation Act. Next, read Chapters 10 and 11 to learn about your child's test scores. In many cases, Section 504 children are eligible for services under IDEA. Gatekeepers who limit access to special education services often make decisions about eligibility. If you understand your child's test data, you will be in a position to open the door to better services for your child.

A Note to Special Educators

Many parents bring *Wrightslaw: Special Education Law* to school meetings. If school personnel advise the parent that a request is against the law, the parent can use the law book to verify this statement. Some parents bring laptops to meetings and use the *Wrightslaw: Special Education Law CD-ROM* to perform quick searches of the law and regulations.

If emotions are under control on both sides, you will find it easier to work with parents who learn the law. These parents want their children to learn. They expect you to teach their children. When parents organize the file, document events and agreements, and help their teams stay on task, they want to build strong working relationships with school personnel. Everyone wins, especially the children.

Are You Ready?

You cannot loiter in the introduction forever. It's time to learn about special education advocacy! Get a paper and pen so you can write down your ideas. If you are ready to learn, just turn this page.

Section One

Getting Started

Section One is "Getting Started." In Chapter 1, you learn that an advocate speaks, pleads, and argues on behalf of another person. We describe different kinds of advocates for children with disabilities and explain why parents are natural advocates for their children. You learn that advocates gather information, learn the rules of the game, plan and prepare, keep written records, identify problems, and propose solutions. We provide you with a list of supplies you need to get started.

In Chapter 2, you learn that a master plan helps you stay focused, anticipate problems, and prepare for the future. We describe the components of a master plan, including a vision statement, mission statement, goals, strategies, and timelines. You learn how to find and work with independent evaluators and educational consultants. If you are like most parents, you need information and support. We recommend that you join a parent group. Other parents will teach you the rules of the game, help you prepare for meetings, and provide emotional support.

Chapter 3 focuses on the parent as project manager. Project managers organize, plan, monitor progress, anticipate problems, and keep the team focused. Your child's special education is a long-term project. As the parent, you are the logical person to step into the role of special education project manager. We describe the most common reasons why projects fail, and explain the need to make plans, define goals, organize information, and build relationships. You learn about the skills, information and attitude you need to act as your child's special education project manager.

1 | Learning About Advocacy

"If you think education is expensive, try ignorance." — Benjamin Franklin, inventor

In this chapter, you will meet children with disabilities. You will learn that there are different kinds of advocates for children with disabilities and why parents are natural advocates for their children. We provide a quick overview of advocacy skills. Finally, you will discover how advocacy helps parents use their emotions to become empowered.

Marie, a ten-year-old child from Maryland, had several strokes. She uses an electric wheelchair to get around and assistive technology to communicate. When Marie's parents asked their school district for support and services, the district refused, saying, "The Individuals with Disabilities Education Act doesn't apply to your child."

In Indiana, a blind child wanted to attend his neighborhood school. The school district refused and sent Joshua to a residential school for the blind, 25 miles away from home. Josh's parents objected, initiated a special education due process hearing, and prevailed.

Nancy is a bright child with dyslexia. Her New Jersey school district placed her in a special education resource room. Two years passed, but Nancy did not learn to read. Her parents wanted the district to train teachers in effective educational practices so children with dyslexia could be taught to read. The district refused. Nancy's parents advocated for her and prevailed.

In California, the parents of a seven-year-old child with mental retardation wanted their daughter to be educated in a regular classroom. When the school district refused, Rachel's parents spent five years fighting for her right to attend regular classes. After the court ordered the district to support Rachel, so she could attend school with her peers, the school district appealed – all the way to the U. S. Supreme Court. Rachel's parents were her advocates. Today, Rachel Holland is a high school student in regular education classes.

As a first grader in Washington, D.C. public schools, Saundra was misdiagnosed with mental retardation. After 12 years of special education, Saundra was functionally illiterate. Saundra did not have an advocate. "The school system has not given me what I needed," she says. "I feel as though no one really cares."

Why Advocate?

Good special education services are intensive and expensive. Resources are limited. If you have a child with special needs, you may wind up battling the school district for the services your child needs. To prevail, you need information, skills, and tools.

Who can be an advocate? Anyone can advocate for another person. Here is how the dictionary defines the term "advocate":

ad·vo·cate – Verb, transitive. To speak, plead or argue in favor of.

Synonym is support.

1. One that argues for a cause; a supporter or defender; an advocate of civil rights.
2. One that pleads in another's behalf; an intercessor; advocates for abused children and spouses.
3. A lawyer. (*The American Heritage Dictionary of the English Language, Third Edition*)

Special education advocates speak for children with disabilities and special needs who are unable to protect themselves. The advocate performs several functions:

- Supports, helps, assists, and aids
- Speaks and pleads on behalf of others
- Defends and argues for people or causes

Different Types of Advocates

Special education advocates work to improve the lives of children with disabilities and their families. You are likely to meet different types of advocates.

Lay Advocates

Lay advocates use their specialized knowledge and expertise to help parents resolve problems with schools. When lay advocates attend meetings, write letters, and negotiate for services, they are acting on the child's behalf. Most lay advocates are knowledgeable about legal rights and responsibilities. In some jurisdictions, lay advocates represent parents in special education due process hearings.

Educational Advocates

Educational advocates evaluate children with disabilities and make recommendations about educational services. When educational advocates go to eligibility and IEP meetings, they are acting on the child's behalf. Some educational advocates are skilled negotiators. Others are not knowledgeable about special education law or how to use tactics and strategies.

School Personnel

Teachers and special education providers often view themselves as advocates. Teachers, administrators, and school staff may provide support to children and their families. Because they are employed by school districts, it is unlikely that school personnel can advocate for children with disabilities without endangering their jobs.

Parents

Parents are natural advocates for their children.

Who is your child's first teacher? You are. Who is your child's most important role model? You are. Who is responsible for your child's welfare? You are. Who has your child's best interests at heart? You do.

You know your child better than anyone else. The school is involved with your child for a few years. You are involved with your child for life. You should play an active role in planning your child's education.

The law gives you the power to make educational decisions for your child. Do not be afraid to use your power. Use it wisely. A good education is the most important gift you can give to your child.

As the parent of a child with a disability, you have two goals:

- To ensure that the school provides your child with a "free appropriate public education" that includes "specially designed instruction . . . to meet the [child's] unique needs . . ." (20 U.S.C. §1401)
- To build a healthy working relationship with the school.

What Advocates Do

Advocacy is not a mysterious process. Here is a quick overview of advocacy skills.

Gather Information

Advocates gather facts and information. As they gather information and organize documents, they learn about the child's disability and educational history. Advocates use facts and independent documentation to resolve disagreements and disputes with the school.

Learn the Rules of the Game

Advocates take time to educate themselves about their local school district. They know how decisions are made and by whom.

Advocates know about legal rights. They know that a child with a disability is entitled to an "appropriate" education, not the "best" education, nor an education that "maximizes the child's potential." They understand that "best" is a four-letter word that cannot be used by parents or advocates. Advocates know the procedures that parents must follow to protect their rights and the child's rights.

Plan and Prepare

Advocates know that planning prevents problems. Advocates do not expect school personnel to tell them about rights and responsibilities. Advocates read special education laws, regulations, and cases to get answers to their questions.

Advocates learn how to use test scores to monitor a child's progress in special education. They prepare for meetings, create agendas, write objectives, and use meeting worksheets and follow-up letters to clarify problems and nail down agreements.

Keep Written Records

Because documents are often the keys to success, advocates keep written records. They know that if a statement is not written down, it was not said. They make requests in writing and write polite follow-up letters to document events, discussions, and meetings.

Ask Questions, Listen to Answers

Advocates are not afraid to ask questions. When they ask questions, they listen carefully to answers. Advocates know how to use "Who, What, Why, Where, When, How, and Explain Questions" (5 Ws + H + E) to discover the true reasons for positions.

Identify Problems

Advocates learn to define and describe problems from all angles. They use their knowledge of interests, fears, and positions to develop strategies. Advocates are problem solvers. They do not waste valuable time and energy looking for people to blame.

Propose Solutions

Advocates know that parents negotiate with schools for special education services. As negotiators, advocates discuss issues and make offers or proposals. They seek "win-win" solutions that will satisfy the interests of parents and schools.

The Parent's Journey From Emotions to Advocacy

On your journey from emotions to advocacy, you will learn about your child's disability, educational and remedial techniques, educational progress, Individualized Educational Programs (IEPs), and how to artfully advocate.

You will learn how to present your concerns and problems in writing, prepare for meetings, and search for win-win solutions. You will learn how to use your emotions as a source of energy and power, and how to focus on getting an appropriate education for your child.

Supplies

Are you ready to advocate? Here is a list of supplies that will help you get started:

- Two 3-ring notebooks (one for your child's file; one for information about your child's disability and educational information.
- 3-hole punch
- Highlighters
- Package of sticky notes
- #10 Envelopes
- Stamps
- Calendar
- Journal
- Contact log
- Small tape recorder

In Summation

In this chapter, you learned how parent advocates changed the lives of their children with disabilities. You learned about lay advocates and educational advocates, and that teachers and special education staff are limited in their ability to advocate. You learned that parents are natural advocates for their children.

You have an overview of advocacy skills and a list of supplies that will help you advocate. Now you will go one step further and learn about master plans.

Your Notes Here

2 | Creating Your Master Plan

"Failing to prepare is preparing to fail." —John Wooden, UCLA basketball coach

In this chapter, you will learn about planning. We explain how a master plan helps you focus, anticipate problems, and prepare for the future. We describe the five components of a master plan. We discuss how to find and use private sector evaluators and educational consultants. You will learn about the benefits of joining a parent support group or advocacy group.

The Need to Plan

What do you want your child to achieve this year? What are your long-range goals for your child? What do you want your child to be able to do when he or she leaves the public school system? What steps do you need to take to help your child meet these goals?

What are your child's strengths and weaknesses? How does your child's disability affect his or her ability to learn? You need to plan for your child's future.

Can you imagine building a house without a blueprint? You do not know where to situate the house, what types of materials to use, or when to schedule work by subcontractors.

You do not know how large the house will be, how many rooms it will have, or what it will cost to build. You are not aware of obstacles you may encounter, legal requirements, contracts, or permits. Is it reasonable to think that you will figure this out as you go along?

Can you imagine starting a business without a business plan? You have not decided what products you will sell, how you will market your products, or how to fill orders. You do not know what services you should offer.

You have not done research into your market or your competition. You do not know what start-up expenses to anticipate, how much your business will earn, or when you can expect to break even. You do not know about obstacles, legal requirements, or contracts. Is it reasonable to think that you will figure this out as you go along?

Special Education Master Plans

Can you imagine educating a child with a disability without a master plan? You do not know about the child's disability, how the disability affects the child's learning, or how the child needs to be taught. You do not know what services and supports the child needs.

You do not know what steps you should take to ensure that your child receives appropriate services. You do not know if your child is making progress. You are not aware of obstacles you may encounter or how to resolve problems. Is it reasonable to think you will figure this out as you go along?

This year, millions of children with disabilities will spend hundreds of millions of hours in special education classes with no master plans. There is a better way to tackle the job of educating children with disabilities!

Have we sold you on the importance of a master plan? Great!

Planning for Efficiency

Raising a child is hard work. If you have a child who learns differently, has a disability, or has special needs, you work harder and longer. A master plan will help you work more efficiently.

When you have a child with a disability, you battle with insurance companies and schools, negotiate with employers and co-workers for time off, respond to the needs of family members, and deal with the unexpected. As these demands increase, your stress level increases too. It is easy to be sidetracked and forget what is important.

A master plan helps you stay focused, anticipate problems, and prepare for the future. Your master plan includes goals for your child in academic and non-academic areas – hobbies, interests, sports, play, and friendships. Master plans are clear, focused, concise, and flexible.

A master plan is different from an Individualized Educational Program or IEP. The IEP is not a long-term plan. The IEP includes annual goals and short-term objectives that address your child's needs that result from the disability. The IEP focuses on your child's needs now, in the present. The IEP document commits the school to provide agreed-upon services for a period of one year or less.

Elements of a Master Plan

The master plan includes five elements:

- Vision statement
- Mission statement

- Goals
- Strategies
- Timelines

Vision Statement

Your vision statement is a visual picture that describes your child in the future. What does the future hold for your child? Do you see your child as a member of the community? Do you envision your child working at a job and raising a family? What is necessary for your child to be prepared for "employment and independent living?" (20 U. S. C. § 1400(d)) (More about the law later.)

Mission Statement

Your mission statement is a personal statement that describes the reasons you are advocating for your child. Your mission statement reflects your emotional commitment and passion.

☑ **Write your mission statement in positive terms:**

My mission is to obtain a good quality education for my child so my child will have a good life. I will master the information and skills to be an effective advocate.

Make several copies of your mission statement. Put a copy in your child's file, another copy in your journal. You may want to post your mission statement around the house, in places where you will see it – on your refrigerator, by your computer, on the bathroom mirror. Tape your mission statement to the dashboard of your car!

Over the next few weeks, read your mission statement often. This will help you internalize the message. Save your mission statement. In a few months, this sheet of paper will be a reminder about how far you have come. It will be more than a mission statement. It will be your progress report.

Goals

Goals make you stretch, give you direction, and keep you focused when you lose perspective. When you write goals, think about what you need to do to accomplish these goals. Your master plan should include academic and non-academic goals for your child.

☑ **Write your goals as outcomes.**

Assume your child's reading skills are three years delayed. How much progress should your child make toward improving his reading skills this year? How much progress do you expect your child to make next year? When you write a goal, begin the goal with a statement like this: "My child will be able to _____."

What do you expect your child to learn this year? Next year? What do you expect your child to learn by the time he or she moves to the next academic level? What do you expect your child to know by the time he or she leaves the public education system?

Strategies

Strategies help you make decisions, solve problems, and overcome obstacles. Think of strategies as your roadmap.

Timelines

Timelines are statements about what actions need to be completed and when.

Planning for the Future

Imagine your child as a young adult. What do you want for your child? What should your child be able to do? Assume you want your child to have a job and be independent. Your child will need to learn how to be a good worker. How can you approach the goal of helping your child become a good worker?

Break this goal down into behaviors that you can observe: sharing, treating others with respect, listening, offering feedback, following directions, and so forth. For example:

- She shares ideas and information with other people;
- He honors written and verbal agreements;
- She doesn't talk behind other people's backs;
- He doesn't treat co-workers like subordinates;
- She doesn't belittle or talk down to other people;
- He listens to what others say;
- She listens without interrupting;
- He is not abrupt or short with others;
- She provides constructive feedback to others.

 Beware of low goals!

How does planning work in real life? Laura and Steve describe planning for their son, Justin.

Laura and Steve: Planning

Laura and Steve have four children. Fifteen-year old Justin is their youngest child. Justin has autism. Laura and Steve have encountered obstacles in their son's education from the beginning. Today, Justin attends his local high school, takes general education courses, and earns "A's" in art and wood shop. Laura and Steve describe the importance of planning.

Do we have a clear view of what we want for our son? Yes.

We started out, as many parents do, with goals and aspirations for our son. With the diagnosis of autism, we had to modify what we saw as the path for his future.

We had to get through the grieving process before we could look forward to a future for our son. Forming a plan and thinking about possibilities for his future helped us to heal and to adjust our perspective in a positive way. We did not give up our vision; we modified it.

When you have a special needs child, you have to modify your expectations more often. Sometimes there are obstacles you do not see until it is too late.

What keeps me sane? Planning! I cannot emphasize this enough for parents. We make lists of expectations. We write out our goals. We post outcomes of what we want to see happen.

We have a plan for our son. We also have contingency plans. We realize that Justin may never be completely independent. We plan for that too.

Our main goal has always been for Justin to have the most fulfilling life possible. We broke this down into several areas. In the beginning, our goals were very basic – like communicating and cleaning his room. During our modification times, we add to them. Now, some of the goals are:

> *Life skills: cooking; cleaning; personal hygiene*
>
> *Social skills: answer phone; greet people*
>
> *Communication: express wants, needs, desires*
>
> *Job skills: develop talents and interests; identify fields of employment*

Plans are my emotional safety net. I know if things do not go as expected, we have ideas and plans to fall back on. We will make the best of the present situation or make temporary fixes until we can put changes into place.

Now we include the word "functional" in goals. When developing Justin's IEP, we bring a list of outcomes for his life that we developed. When the teachers list a goal, we look to see how it connects with these outcomes and if it is "functional." We also bring our list of educational expectations for the year. I have found that many teachers appreciate a list of ideas.

Writing Your Master Plan

Gathering Information

Begin by gathering information about your child, your child's disability, and how the disability affects your child's ability to learn.

 In Chapter 9, you will learn how to request information about your child from all sources and how to organize your child's file.

Your master plan should include academic and non-academic goals. Begin by writing your goals in non-academic areas:

- Personal hobbies and interests
- Sports and fitness

- Friends and social life
- Family
- Community

As you think about your child's life in these areas, you may discover problems. Is your child inactive? Does your child spend too many hours on the computer or in front of the television? Does your child have friends? Does your child play with other children? Does your child have responsibilities at home? Special interests? Hobbies?

Working with an Independent Evaluator or Educational Consultant

Consult with a private-sector psychologist, educational diagnostician, or consultant to develop goals for your child. Your consultant will give you valuable information and help. Your consultant may:

- Teach you about your child's disability and educational needs
- Provide information about effective teaching and research-based educational practices
- Help you learn about tests, how tests measure educational progress, and how to interpret test results
- Help you design goals, objectives and timeframes
- Evaluate your child's progress toward IEP goals and objectives
- Make recommendations about your child's educational program

Qualities of a Consultant

Look for a consultant who is knowledgeable about your child's disability, child development, and special education. Ideally, your consultant will be available to work with you and your family for the long haul. In addition to making recommendations about your child's educational program, your consultant should attend school meetings to support these recommendations.

Depending on your child's disability and age, you may work with different specialists:

- Psychologists
- Speech-language pathologists
- Educational diagnosticians
- Occupational therapists
- Physical therapists
- Psychiatrists
- Pediatric neurologists
- Therapists and counselors

☑ **To find a consultant, contact medical centers children's hospitals, mental health centers, and clinics. Ask other parents for recommendations.**

Strategies: Finding a Consultant

Contact advocacy groups and organizations that represent individuals with your child's disability and ask them to recommend consultants. Contact private special education schools and ask for their recommended consultants. Before long, you will have a short list of recommendations from different groups and individuals. You will probably find your consultant in this list.

Strategies: Learning From Other Parents

Join a parent support group or advocacy group. How do you find a parent group? Do you know about parent groups in your child's school? Do you know about groups in your community?

 Appendix E lists Parent Training Information groups by state.

When you join a parent support group, you will meet other parents who have traveled down this road. Learn from them. In addition to emotional support, they will teach you the rules of the game.

Look for an active parent group that wants to meet the needs of their members. You may find groups that were established to meet the needs of children who have different disabilities than your child. Do not rule these groups out. Parents of children with disabilities share many common interests and concerns and want to get quality special education services for their children.

If your school district has a special education advisory board, contact a board member and ask about parent groups. If you contact a national or state organization for information, ask if there are local support groups in your community.

 Appendix F lists disabilities organizations and information groups.

When you look for a parent or disability group, think about your interests and needs.

- Do you want emotional support?
- Do you want to meet other families who have a child with a disability?
- Do you want advocacy training?
- Do you want to learn more about your child's disability?
- Do you want to learn about special education issues?
- Do you want to get involved in school reform issues?

Your answers to these questions will help you decide what type of group to join.

Here is how a parent describes the support she receives from other parents:

As parents, we have experienced similar events and emotions. Our children have experienced acts of discrimination. Our hearts have been broken, our senses inflamed.

Each step along this path, we have been supported by other parents, people with disabilities, and advocates. Love for our children brought us together and keeps us together. We have our stories, our experiences, our fears, and our hopes. We need each other.

In Summation

In this chapter, we discussed why plans and strategies are essential to successful advocacy. You learned about master plans and the need to develop goals for your child's future. You learned how to get help from a consultant and the importance of joining a support group.

Do you understand the need for long-term planning? Good! In the next chapter, you will learn about project managers.

3 | The Parent as Project Manager

"A good education is the next best thing to a pushy mother." —Charles Schulz, cartoonist

In the last chapter, you learned that your child's special education is a long-term project and that you need a master plan. In this chapter, you will learn about project managers who organize, plan, monitor progress, anticipate problems, and keep the team focused. As your child's parent and advocate, you are the logical candidate for this job. We describe the attitude, knowledge, and skills you need to act as your child's special education project manager.

Contractors and Project Managers

If you build a house, you may have a general contractor manage the project. Contractors manage schedules, deal with people, anticipate problems, and ensure that jobs are done. Contractors are project managers.

In the business world, project managers plan, organize, monitor progress, and ensure that projects are completed. Project managers remove obstacles and resolve conflicts between people. On long, complicated projects, project managers are invaluable.

The Special Education Project Manager

As the parent of a child with a disability, you have learned that you need to make long-range plans for your child. Schools do not make long-term plans for students. Although your child may have a case manager, this individual is not responsible for your child's education after your child leaves the public school system. If your child has an Individualized Educational Program (IEP), the IEP addresses your child's needs for one year or less.

You are the constant factor in your child's life. You represent your child's interests. If your child does not receive an appropriate education and master the skills necessary to be an independent, self-sufficient member of the community, you will deal with the outcome.

In the last chapter, Laura and Steve described how they planned for their son Justin. Here is how Laura and Steve describe their role:

As his parents, we are the bottom line. We must make decisions for Justin until he can decide for himself.

The educators, aides, psychologists, specialists, and doctors are resources to help him progress along the path of life. We look to them for expertise in their fields. We do not expect them to answer all the questions and deal with all the problems our son faces.

If you are like most parents, you do not have training in project management. Many parents learn about special education by jumping in. Sometimes, parents jump from the frying pan into the fire!

When you learn project management skills, you will be a more effective advocate. Set aside time to organize information about your child, make long-term plans, write goals with timelines, and build working relationships with school personnel. Here is the job description for a special education project manager.

Learns New Information

The special education project manager learns about the child's disability and how the disability affects the child's ability to learn. The manager does research about effective special education practices.

The special education project manager knows that the most common reasons why projects fail are:

- Lack of planning
- Fuzzy goals
- Team members who do not know what is expected of them
- Team members who do not get the training and support they need
- Team members who feel over-burdened and under-appreciated

The project manager knows that conflict is inevitable when people with different interests and perspectives work together, and that unresolved conflict causes good plans to fail. The project manager is aware of school obstacles and parent obstacles that can derail plans and cause small problems to erupt into major crises.

Masters New Skills

Your child's special education is a team project. A team makes decisions about your child's special education program and placement. At team meetings, the project manager identifies problems and offers solutions. The project manager uses facts and objective data to support requests, monitor progress, and persuade school officials to provide the services and supports the child needs.

The project manager gathers and organizes information in the child's file and keeps the file up to date. The manager maintains a contact log and writes follow-up letters after meetings, conversations, agreements, and events.

Builds Relationships

The project manager establishes good working relationships with people on the child's team. Acting as a coach, planner, and motivator, the project manager helps the team stay focused.

The project manager is organized, flexible, open to new ideas, and willing to learn. The manager understands the importance of keeping emotions under control and treating others with respect.

The manager tactfully educates teachers and other school personnel about the child's disability and how the child learns. The project manager knows that the child's teachers are usually not the problem and supports the teachers' need for training. When teachers receive better training, they can do a better job.

Takes Care of Self and Family

Raising a special needs child can be overwhelming. If you are not careful, special education can consume your life. Many parents drive themselves until they are exhausted and burned out.

Pace yourself. Listen to tapes about time management. Use a schedule to gain control of your life. Spend time with friends or family to re-charge your batteries and regain a healthy perspective. See Table 3-1 for more tips about taking care of yourself and your family.

Table 3-1	*Tips: Taking Care of Yourself*

▷ Set aside time with your partner. Use email or voicemail to stay in touch.

▷ Schedule one-on-one time with each child. Write the child's name by a date on the calendar. Let the child pick the place and activity.

▷ Master the art of the short escape. Visit a local attraction for an afternoon or a local resort for a weekend. Short escapes will help you unwind.

▷ Nurture friendships. Make time to go to the movies, have meals, exercise, or take walks with friends.

▷ Ask friends for help. Tell friends or family when you need help with child-care and errands.

▷ Find another parent whom you can contact when you are worried and need encouragement.

▷ Share child-care with another family. Pick times each week when you can help the family and when they can help you. You will each have someone to contact when you need a break.

Continued

▷ Help others. If you spend one hour a month helping others, this will help you keep your problems in perspective. You will know that you are not alone.

▷ Set aside a block of time to do special education tasks (i.e., making phone calls and filing documents). If you stick to a schedule, special education will not consume your life.

▷ Simplify. Get rid of clutter. Your home will be more relaxing and peaceful.

▷ Take the phone off the hook. When you need quiet time, turn your phone off for a few hours.

▷ Take care of your health. Schedule and keep appointments with doctors. If you feel anxious or depressed, see a mental health professional.

In Summation

In this chapter, you learned about project managers. Your child needs a project manager who can plan, organize, and monitor progress. Project managers meet with people, anticipate problems, remove obstacles, and help the team focus. You learned about the attitude, knowledge, and skills required for the successful candidate for this job.

Are you willing to act as your child's special education project manager? Good! Let's move on to the next chapter where you will learn about the rules of the game.

Section Two

Advocacy 101

In the first section of *Wrightslaw: From Emotions to Advocacy–The Special Education Survival Guide,* you learned advocacy basics, the need to create master plan for your child's special education, and the role of the special education project manager. You are ready to move on to Advocacy 101.

Chapter 4 is "Learning the Rules of the Game." You will learn about gatekeepers, special education teams, and one-size-fits-all (OSFA) programs. When you learn the rules of the game, you will be a more effective advocate and negotiator for your child.

Chapter 5 will teach you about "Obstacles to Success." School obstacles include myths, rules, and school culture. Lack of information, isolation, and emotions are obstacles for parents. You will learn about personality styles and how to deal with difficult people. When you recognize obstacles, you can take steps to minimize or prevent problems.

Chapter 6 is "Creating and Resolving Parent-School Conflicts." When you understand the real reasons for conflict, you will understand why parent-school conflict is normal, predictable, and inevitable. We describe the most common reasons for conflict and recommend strategies you can use to resolve problems. When you use these strategies, you are more likely to resolve your problem without damaging your relationship with the school.

Chapter 7 is "Emergency, Crisis, Help!" If you are like many parents, emotions are your Achilles heel. In this chapter, you will learn how problems can erupt into crises. We explain common pitfalls and describe the steps parents should take in a crisis. If you use the short-term and long-term strategies in this chapter, you will improve your odds for a good outcome.

4 | Learning the Rules of the Game

"In the first place, God made idiots. That was for practice. Then he made school boards."
—Mark Twain, writer

As you begin to advocate for your child, you need to learn about school systems and how your district resolves problems and makes decisions. In this chapter, you will learn that your district is a bureaucracy with rules, customs and traditions and a chain of command. You will learn about Gatekeepers and One-Size-Fits-All (OSFA) special education programs.

When you learn the rules, you will be a more effective advocate and negotiator for your child. It's time to learn the rules of the game!

The Rules

"Those who play the game do not see it as clearly as those who watch."
— Chinese Proverb

Do you remember your first weeks on a new job? During those weeks, you felt insecure and uneasy. You did not know what to expect. You did not know how problems were handled and how decisions were made in this new environment. The fear of the unknown made you feel anxious.

In time, you found answers to your questions. When you learned what to expect, you felt comfortable. Your anxiety dropped.

When you begin to advocate, expect to feel anxious and insecure. As an outsider, you do not know how problems are solved and how decisions are made. As with new job jitters, your anxieties are caused by the fear of the unknown. During your first school meetings, expect to feel insecure and anxious. These jitters are normal reactions to your new role and the unfamiliar environment. As you gain experience, you will know what to expect and you will feel less anxious.

Understanding the School _____

What do you know about your child's school? What do you know about your school district? How are parents of children with disabilities perceived by the teachers at your child's school? How are parents of children with disabilities viewed in your school district? Who wields power in your school district? When you have answers to these questions, you will be able to advocate effectively for your child.

If you are like many parents, school meetings are confusing and frustrating. When you ask questions, your don't get answers.

Your child's team is a small part of a large system. School districts have a chain of command. If you have an unusual request, your child's school team may not have the authority to grant your request. An invisible administrator may be the person who answers your request.

School Bureaucracy Rules

Bureaucracies are created to fulfill missions. The mission of public schools is to provide a standardized education to all children. Public schools offer a standardized curriculum that children are expected to learn.

Schools are modeled after factories. The principal runs the school building, teachers provide the labor, and children are the raw material. Parents are outsiders. Power flows from the top. Teachers and parents do not have the authority to make decisions that involve a commitment of resources.

Special Education Rules

When you advocate for your child, you will learn about special education rules. You will learn about gatekeepers and one-size-fits-all (OSFA) programs. When you understand how the special education system operates and how decisions are made, you will be a more effective advocate.

Gatekeeper Rules

When you advocate, you are likely to meet gatekeepers. Gatekeepers limit the number of children who have access to special education services and limit the services children can receive. If you have health insurance through an HMO or managed care firm, you know about gatekeepers.

Gatekeepers may tell you that your child is not entitled to:

- An evaluation
- Any change in the IEP
- More services
- Different services

The Gatekeeper's job is to say "No!" One of your jobs is to persuade the gatekeeper that your child's situation is different and requires a different approach.

"We Can't Make Exceptions"

School districts have elaborate systems of rules that govern how decisions are made and by whom. When you try to develop an appropriate program for your child, you may run into the "We can't make exceptions" rule. "We can't make exceptions" is related to "We have never done that before." When you prepare and plan, you can defeat both arguments.

"One-Size-Fits All" (OSFA) Programs

Many school districts have standardized "One-Size-Fits-All" (OSFA) special education programs. If your district is creative, you may have two program options: OSFA #1 and OSFA #2. In a typical OSFA program, decisions about the child's program and placement are based on the child's disability category or label, not on the child's unique needs.

If you have a four-year-old child with autism, your child's program and placement may be the school's standardized OSFA preschool program for all children with autism. If your child has dyslexia, the child's program and placement is likely to be the district's standardized ~~ram for all children with learning disabilities.

What is wr~

The ~ ed to provide each child with an individualized special
~ ut child's unique needs. Standardized OSFA programs
~ ue needs. Schools design OSFA programs for the
~ em.

Individu~

~ nsive and more difficult to administer. If you
are try~ ram for your child, expect to run into
resistance~ that uses categories and labels to make
decisions. h~ vail.

When pare~ ign appropriate individualized programs. What is t~ ow what their child needs, and they
know how the syste~ of the game.

[handwritten note: full inclusion for a child is appropriate to acquire social skills after necessary]

Learning About Your S~

What do you know about y~ charge? What is the
school's perception of parents of c~ negotiate and advocate,
you need to know the answers to th~

Learning About School Climate

Climate is a term that describes the learning environment created by teachers and administrators. What is the climate of your child's school?

If your child's school has a positive climate, you will be encouraged to play an active role in your child's education. Teachers and parents build healthy working relationships.

Learning About School Teams

If you are like many parents, you may not realize that your child's school team has invisible members whom you may never meet. These invisible members are school administrators who have the power to make decisions about special education programs.

If you request a special education program that is different from the district's standardized program, the team may not have the authority to grant your request. The team has to consult with invisible members who make these decisions. These invisible members may not know you or your child.

Who are your invisible team members? How will these people respond to your request?

Rules of the Game

To negotiate on your child's behalf, you need to be able to analyze your strengths and weaknesses and the school district's strengths and weaknesses. You need to learn the rules of the game. What are these rules?

Table 4-1	*Ten Reasons Why Schools Say No!*

1. The school does not want to change long-standing procedures.
2. The school does not want to make exceptions to existing policies or practices.
3. The school is afraid of setting a precedent.
4. The school does not have the staff to meet the child's needs.
5. The staff is not trained to meet the child's needs.
6. The school does not have a program to meet the child's needs.
7. The school is committed to their one-size-fits all service delivery models.
8. The school believes the services your child needs are too expensive.
9. The school is overwhelmed by the complexity of your child's needs.
10. The school does not understand the legal requirement to provide your child with an individualized program.

If you know the rules of the game, you are on time for meetings. You prepare. You present your concerns and problems in writing. You work to develop "win-win" solutions to these problems. You keep your emotions under control and shake hands at the end of the meeting. You take steps to protect the parent-school relationship.

When parents do not know the rules of the game, they show up late for meetings. Some assume that school personnel always make good decisions about educating their children with disabilities. Others fight battles over issues they cannot win. Some lose their tempers, throw down the bat and go home. When parents do not know the rules of the game, they do not understand the need to protect the parent-school relationship.

When you negotiate for your child, you will prevail on some issues. You will not always prevail. You need to identify your key issues and those issues that are less important. If the school refuses to negotiate on an important issue, you do not give up. You find other ways to tackle the problem and get your child the services he or she needs.

If you keep an open mind, you will learn from experience. After each school meeting, think about what you learned. When you have negative experiences, remember that you can learn from these bumps in the road.

As a parent, you represent your child's interests. If you do not represent your child's interests, no one else will. Special education is expensive. Resources are limited. School personnel act as gatekeepers, and limit access to expensive services.

These are the rules of the game.

In Summation

In this chapter, you learned about the rules of the game. You learned that schools are governed by rules and chains of command. You learned that invisible team members make important decisions. When you learn the rules, you will be a more effective advocate for your child.

In the next chapter, you will learn about obstacles to success. These obstacles include myths, emotions, and school culture. When you recognize these obstacles, you can prevent problems.

Your Notes Here

5 | Obstacles to Success

"Nothing in the world is more dangerous than sincere ignorance and conscientious stupidity."
—Martin Luther King, civil rights activist

In this chapter, we describe obstacles you may encounter as you advocate for your child. When you recognize obstacles, you can take steps to prevent problems. You will learn about school obstacles, including inaccurate information, myths, and school culture. We will describe common parent obstacles including isolation, lack of information, and emotions.

You will learn to recognize personality styles, from Pit Bulls to Wet Blankets, and strategies you can use to deal with difficult people. We describe emotional traps you need to avoid. This chapter ends with strategies to help you build a working relationship with school personnel.

Obstacles to Advocacy

When you advocate for your child, common obstacles include inaccurate information and myths about how children learn. You are likely to get conflicting answers to your questions.

Inaccurate Information

Never assume that legal advice or information you receive from school personnel is accurate. In most cases, school people who offer legal advice have not read the law. Their advice is based on information they received from sources within the school system.

Here are a few examples of inaccurate information and bad advice that parents and teachers receive.

From parents:

"I was told my child is not eligible for services because he is passing."

"My child is in fifth grade and can't read. The IEP team will not include a goal about teaching my child to read. They said IEP goals must relate to the curriculum."

"When I asked the district to evaluate my child, they said they don't have enough staff."

"The IEP team said they are not allowed to provide one-on-one speech therapy because this would violate the inclusion law."

Is this information accurate? No!

From teachers:

"Children who have ADHD are not eligible for special education. Maybe we can offer an accommodations plan."

"Some of my students need services in the summer. My supervisor says it is against the law to tell parents about extended school year services."

Is this information accurate? No!

Many people who offer legal advice have not read the law. Their advice is based on what they heard at a conference, read in an article, or overheard in the teacher's lounge.

Myths

Here are some common myths about how children learn:

"He has dyslexia. He will never learn to read." (Special education teacher)

"She is mentally retarded. She will be happier in a special class with other mentally retarded children." (Special education director)

"He has a disability. He will never be able to pass the state tests." (School psychologist)

Issues about who learns, who does not learn, and why children have trouble learning are not as simple as these statements lead you to believe.

If you have high expectations for your child, do not be surprised if the school views you as unrealistic and advises you to lower your expectations.

In 1953, educators told Pete Wright's parents: *"You need to lower your expectations for Peter. He is not college material. College is not a realistic goal for him."* Pete Wright is a successful attorney and co-author of this book.

Twenty-five years later, special educators told Pete Wright: *"You need to lower your expectations for Damon. He wants to go to law school. This is not a realistic goal for him."* Today, Damon is a successful trial lawyer.

If you have a child with a disability, teach your child to work hard and persevere. Because you are your child's role model, you must work hard and persevere too!

School Obstacles

Rich and Beth's four-year-old son has autism. If Alex receives intensive early intervention, he may be able to attend regular education classes in two or three years.

Rich and Beth are willing to sacrifice to ensure that Alex gets the help he needs. When they asked the school for help, they encountered resistance. The school placed Alex in a self-contained preschool class for a few hours a week. This is how Rich described the IEP meeting:

"They placed Alex in a self-contained class with disabled children because they think he will learn and imitate other children. Alex has autism! He does not notice other children. He will not learn by imitation. I thought we were partners in this process."

School Culture

School culture acts as an invisible wall that prevents parents and school staff from working together. When you advocate for your child, you need to understand the power of school culture.

When you recognize school culture, you will feel less frustrated. You will understand that school culture is not unique to you, your child, your school, your school district, your state, or region. As Pete says, *"The children's names and dates of birth change, but the facts and issues remain the same."*

Beliefs, Perceptions, & Attitudes

School culture includes beliefs, perceptions, and attitudes shared by people who work in schools–educators, school psychologists, administrators, and other personnel.

Beliefs affect the decisions we make and the actions we take. While beliefs may not be expressed openly, they have an enormous impact on relations between parents and school personnel, and influence how decisions are made for children with disabilities.

Still not sure you understand what "school culture" means? Try this exercise.

Think back to your childhood. Visualize the elementary school you attended. School culture is the unspoken feeling that "this is how things are done around here." You sensed it when you walked toward the school. You smelled it when you walked through the doors. You heard it when bells rang and lockers slammed. Schools are different. Nothing feels like "The School." Here are three examples of school culture.

5,000 Evaluations: Same Conclusion

Why do children have learning and behavior problems? To answer this question, a psychologist named Galen Alessi analyzed 5,000 evaluations by school psychologists to determine the importance of five factors: inappropriate curriculum, ineffective teaching, ineffective school management practices, inadequate family support, and child-based problems. He asked:

- Is the child misplaced in the curriculum, or does the curriculum include faulty teaching routines?
- Is the child's teacher not implementing effective teaching and/or behavioral management practices?

- Are the principal and school administrators not implementing effective school management practices?
- Are the parents not providing the home-based support necessary for effective learning?
- Does the child have physical and/or psychological problems that contribute to learning problems?

Dr. Alessi's findings will not surprise many parents of children with disabilities:

- Inappropriate curriculum was never mentioned as a factor.
- Ineffective teaching was never mentioned as a factor.
- Ineffective school management practices were never mentioned as factors.
- Parent and home factors were cited as problems in 10-20 percent of the evaluations.
- Child factors were cited in 100 percent of the evaluations.

When Dr. Alessi asked the school psychologists about their one-sided evaluations, they explained that they were not allowed to mention school related factors. Informal school policy or school culture required them to limit their findings to child and family factors.

How Principals View Children with Learning Problems

As school leaders, principals shape school culture. How do principals view children with learning problems? Researchers studied the attitudes of principals in elementary schools where large numbers of children were retained and referred to special education.

The principals did not have a positive view of young children with problems, nor did they believe schools were responsible for providing these children with help. The principals believed that children's learning problems were due to social and economic factors, including single parent homes and dysfunctional families. They believed that disadvantaged children were immature and slow learners.

Children who entered school with limited educational experiences were perceived as intellectually limited. Because the school did not provide enrichment or tutoring, many of these children failed. Eventually, the children were retained or referred to special education.

Belief: Parents are the Problem

This is how one insider describes the school's perspective of parents of children with disabilities:

"School personnel believe that on a subconscious level, parents of disabled children are disappointed or embarrassed by their children's disabilities. This disappointment or embarrassment is expressed by the parent demanding that the school take responsibility for fixing the problem."

Belief: We are the Experts

As you advocate for your child, you must understand that school personnel believe they are the experts about children and learning. Most believe they know what is best for your child. Although you have observed your child in hundreds of situations, many educators believe that because you are emotionally involved, you are incapable of knowing what your child needs.

What can you do to change these beliefs and attitudes? Nothing! You cannot change the beliefs of others.

Obstacles Within the System

As your child's advocate, you will negotiate with your school district. As you learned in the last chapter, school districts are bureaucracies. Let's take a closer look at schools.

In schools, rules govern how things are done. Because school bureaucracies depend on rules, it is difficult for school personnel to devise creative solutions to problems.

Schools have clear lines of authority. In most districts, power flows from the school board to the superintendent and administrative staff, then to principals and teachers. Teachers are at the bottom in power, pay, prestige, and autonomy.

Principals run the school building. Teachers educate the children. Because there are clear boundaries between positions, a teacher will not run the school while the principal is away.

Public schools are the education providers for all children. The mission of public schools is to provide students with a standardized education. Standardized educational programs are not individualized, nor are they designed to meet the unique needs of the child with a disability.

Parents are outsiders. School districts rarely solicit or accept advice from parents when they design special education programs. Most decisions are based on economics, tradition, and convenience.

Parent Obstacles

If you are like most parents, your obstacles include lack of information, isolation, and emotions. In the last chapter, we advised you to join a parent support group. When you take this step, you will begin to deal with the isolation and lack of information obstacles.

Emotions

As a parent, emotions may be your Achilles Heel. To be an effective advocate, you must control your emotions and use them as a source of energy.

How do you process the fact that your child has a disability? How do you deal with your fears that the disability may prevent your child from leading a productive, independent life?

If you are like many parents, when you learn that your child has a disability, you turn to school personnel and medical specialists for help. If your school district does not provide your child with appropriate services, you get frustrated and angry. If you believe your child was damaged, you are likely to feel angry and betrayed. Once broken, trust is hard to mend.

Anxiety and Intimidation

One father, a businessman who specializes in marketing and sales, describes his feelings about school meetings:

"There is something about this team business where you sit around a big table, and it's just you on one side, and six or seven school people on the other side. I always feel intimidated when I go to meetings."

"I feel like I did when I was eight years old and had to go to the principal's office. I was in trouble then and it feels like I'm in trouble now!"

Your school experiences will affect your feelings about schools, teachers, and school meetings. Many parents feel intimidated at school meetings. School teams often include several school representatives and one parent. Given these dynamics, anxiety is a normal reaction.

Pity and Over-protectiveness

As a parent, you may feel helpless as you watch your child struggle. Resist the urge to step in and take over. If you give in to this urge, you will do things for your child instead of teaching your child how to do things on his or her own. Your child may learn that helplessness is a useful tactic.

If you are tempted to lower your expectations, remember that your child will internalize your expectations and beliefs. If you feel sorry for your child, your child will sense this. Your child's self concept will change.

A vicious cycle will begin: low expectations lead to low achievement, which leads to lower expectations, which lead to even lower achievement. For many children with disabilities, negative beliefs are more disabling than their original problems.

Help your child to be strong and resilient.

Dealing with Difficult People

Personality conflicts crop up when people with different interests and personalities work together. These conflicts are draining, distracting, and can derail you from your goal. We will look at several personality styles, how to recognize them, and strategies you can use to work with them without getting angry, sidetracked, or throwing in the towel.

- Pit Bulls and Bullies
- Know-it-Alls and Experts
- Conflict Avoiders
- Wet Blankets
- Snipers
- Complainers

If you understand personality styles , you are less likely to take offense. As you learn about these personality styles, you will discover that they are familiar. You may even recognize yourself! If you discover your personality style, you will learn about the impact you have on others.

Behavior as Communication

One purpose of behavior is to communicate. People also use behavior to gain control of others. Most people are not aware of the impact their behavior has on others. If you have a personality clash with a school person, you need to:

- Control your emotions
- Minimize the negative impact of the conflict
- Work toward your mutual interests

Your goal is neither to passively take abuse, nor to change people. You need to:

- Recognize personality styles
- Understand the meaning of behavior
- Use this information to work more effectively with difficult people

When you analyze, plan, and prepare, you put your brain in charge of your emotions.

Pit Bulls and Bullies

Pit Bulls are aggressive, forceful people. If they cultivate a smooth image, they often rise to positions of power and authority. Pit Bulls have strong opinions about what people should do and strong needs to prove that their view of the world is right.

If you have a difference of opinion with a Pit Bull, expect him to take this personally. Pit Bulls are impatient people with quick tempers. They get angry when people do not do what they believe should be done.

Pit Bulls believe they are right. Because they believe they are right, they believe that their bad behavior is justified – you made them behave badly. Pit Bulls have little respect for people who lack confidence.

Strategies: Dealing with Pit Bulls and Bullies

When you deal with a Pit Bull, you may feel overwhelmed, confused, and afraid. Stand up for yourself. Do not back down or blow up.

When a Pit Bull explodes, give him time to run out of steam. Say, "Mr. Jones, you interrupted me." Do not worry about being polite.

Do not argue or attack. Do not demean the Pit Bull or his position. Express your views or perceptions about the issue. Maintain eye contact.

"In my opinion..."

"My experience has been different..."

Do not fight to win. Pit Bulls are expert fighters – they cannot back down or give in. If you win a battle, you are likely to lose the war. If the Pit Bull feels defeated, he will look for another battle to win.

If you let a Pit Bull push you around, he may become a Bully. The Bully will view you as worthless and believe you deserve to be squashed.

Stand up to the bully and he will be your friend. After you express your perspective, prepare to bury the hatchet. If the Pit Bull cannot overwhelm you, he may respect you. Pit Bulls want respect from people whom they view as strong. Make it clear that you do not intend to question their authority but you believe your perception has value.

"I know you are the principal. What you say goes. But I have some ideas that would make things work better."

Know-it-Alls and Experts

When you attend meetings with school personnel, you will meet Know-it-Alls who will tell you what to do and how to solve your problems. Their unsolicited advice and patronizing attitudes may cause you to feel irritated and resentful.

Many Know-it-Alls *are* knowledgeable. They view themselves as experts and do not realize how they appear to others. Know-it-Alls are persistent people who will fight until they prevail.

Strategies: Dealing with Know-it-Alls

When you deal with a Know-it-All, try to get the person to consider alternative views. If you attack their expertise, they will view this as a personal attack. Do not confront them. When confronted, they will get defensive and will fight to prove they are right.

Use Facts and Information

Because Know-it-Alls *are* knowledgeable, facts and information are important to them. Use facts and information to support your requests. Review your information and check your facts for accuracy.

Ask questions. Listen. Do not interrupt. Paraphrase their points. Show that you appreciate their knowledge.

"Let me make sure I understand. I think I heard you say . . ."

Use 5 W's + H + E questions to raise issues. When you ask questions, the Know-it-All may take another look at their assumptions. Use questions to move from abstract proposals to specific details.

- Specifically, how will this happen?

- How do you see this program working a year from now?

- What steps will the school take to implement the IEP?

- When?

- Who will take each step?

- What can we expect our child to learn within the next three or four months?

Acknowledge their competence. Defer to them as The Experts. Take a subordinate role.

If you take these steps deliberately and choose to deal with them in this manner, you will not feel diminished. You understand the rules of the game. You are in control. You will feel less helpless and angry.

 Most school personnel cannot accept parents as experts about their children. If you try to assume an expert's role, you will be caught up in an endless "no-win" power struggle.

Conflict Avoiders

When you deal with school personnel, you will meet Conflict Avoiders. Conflict Avoiders are pleasant, supportive people who want to help. Most are good listeners.

Conflict Avoiders dislike making decisions. After a meeting with a Conflict Avoider, you may believe that the person made a decision in your favor. Weeks pass and nothing changes. You request another meeting. Your Conflict Avoider listens, apologizes, and mentions unforeseen delays.

You have learned that your school district is a bureaucracy. In bureaucracies, people must make decisions about how to allocate scarce resources: money, labor, and time. When Conflict Avoiders have decision-making authority, they realize that any decision will disappoint or upset someone. Decision-making is painful for them so they procrastinate until the need to make a decision passes.

Conflict Avoiders are difficult to deal with because they cannot or will not tell you that they are procrastinating. You believe they agreed to your proposal. When nothing changes, you will feel let down.

Strategies: Dealing with Conflict Avoiders

Discover Reasons for Avoidance

Make it easy for the Conflict Avoider to tell you about conflicts or reservations that are preventing them from making a decision. Reassure them that you can take bad news. Pay attention to indirect words, hesitations, and omissions that signal resistance.

Help Solve Problems

After you clarify issues, help the person look at the facts, make a list of solutions, and prioritize the solutions. Help the Conflict Avoider solve the problem by making a decision.

Provide Support

Give Conflict Avoiders support after they make decisions. After making decisions, Conflict Avoiders often have buyer's remorse. Buyer's remorse describes the doubts and concerns that kick in after the person makes a decision. If you do not address these issues, you may discover that the Conflict Avoider revoked the decision!

If you see signs of anger or withdrawal, take your decision off the table until things cool off.

Wet Blankets

"It won't work. They won't let us do that."

When you deal with people who work in a bureaucracy, you will meet Wet Blankets. Wet Blankets respond negatively to any attempt to solve a problem. They see obstacles as impassable barriers. Wet Blankets feel disappointed, bitter, and hopeless. Their negativity is contagious.

Strategies: Dealing with Wet Blankets

When you deal with Wet Blankets, it is important to understand their sincere belief that nothing will change or improve. At some point, they were bitterly disappointed and concluded that people who have power do not care about them. They feel angry and defeated.

Don't Argue, Listen

If you get into a debate about issues, Wet Blankets dig in. They sincerely believe they are right. At some point, Wet Blankets were burned. They do not trust the system. If you listen to their complaints, you may learn about potential problems and pitfalls.

Ask Questions

Ask 5 W's + H + E questions. When you ask questions, you clarify your belief that you are dealing with problems that have solutions. You understand that there are obstacles but do not believe that the problem cannot be solved.

Snipers

Snipers are masters of the sneak attack, often delivered with a smile. If you have a run-in with a Sniper, you will feel pinned down by digs and sarcasm. Like Pit Bulls, Snipers have strong feelings about how other people should think and act. Their behavior is based on feelings of superiority and a desire to control.

Snipers get away with bad behavior because they understand that most people want to avoid scenes. The Sniper seeks revenge without responsibility. Deal with them as you do Pit Bulls.

Complainers

Complainers are irritating, exhausting and hard to ignore. They view themselves as blameless, innocent, and perfect and have strong views about how things should be. When reality does not fit their view, they believe this is someone's fault and blame others when things go wrong.

Complainers believe they are powerless. When they encounter obstacles, they believe powerful people must remove these obstacles. They complain so powerful people will pay attention, take action and solve problems.

"I've brought this to your attention. That is all I can do. Now, it is up to you."

Usually, complainers are placated, ignored or avoided. If you do not right their wrongs, Complainers feel angry and self-righteous. There is often a kernel of truth to their complaints. If you have a desire to help others, you may find yourself trapped by a Complainer.

Strategies: Dealing with Complainers

When you deal with Complainers, listen, acknowledge, and interrupt. Listen to their complaints. Acknowledge that you heard the complaints. Interrupt to set limits on their complaints. When you deal with Complainers:

- Interrupt to get control
- Sum up facts without comment or apology
- Do not agree
- Shift to problem solving
- Ask for their complaints in writing

Warning: Common Emotional Traps

When you advocate for your child, you need to be aware of common emotional traps and pitfalls:

- Self pity. If you find yourself asking, "Why does it have to be so hard?" or "Why can't things be different?" you are falling into the self-pity trap.
- Resistance. If you use passive-aggressive behavior to defeat them, you also defeat yourself.
- Temper tantrum. If you blow up, you prove that they were right about you!
- Quitting. OK, you quit. Now what?

Your Relationship with the School

Your goal is to develop a businesslike relationship with the staff at your child's school. To accomplish this goal, you need to recognize the power of school culture, myths, and misinformation.

Be careful about sharing information about your personal life or your feelings with school staff. If you share personal information, you may give ammunition to people who will blame you for your child's problems.

If you disagree with school staff, do not show your anger. If you lose your temper, you give ammunition to school personnel who look down on parents. Do not waste your time and energy getting mad or thinking about how you can get even. If you are feeling sorry for yourself or brooding about injustice, contact your support group or a special education friend.

Focus your energy in a positive direction—on solving problems. Use your emotions as a source of energy. Focus on what is important—getting an appropriate education for your child.

In Summation

In this chapter, you learned about obstacles you may encounter, including inaccurate information, myths and beliefs, and school culture. We described emotional obstacles for parents, including fear, anxiety and intimidation. You learned about the dangers of pity and helplessness.

You learned about personality styles and strategies you can use to deal with difficult people. We offered information about how to structure your relationship with the school.

In the next chapter, you will learn about conflict and why conflict between parents and schools is normal and inevitable. You will learn strategies to deal with common parent-school problems.

6 | Resolving Parent-School Conflict

"If you only have a hammer, you see every problem as a nail." —Abraham Maslow, psychologist

In this chapter, you will learn why conflict between parents and schools is normal and inevitable. We will discuss the impact that beliefs, perceptions, and interests have on conflict and identify six issues that increase parent-school conflict. You will learn about the high cost of conflict, including loss of trust, damaged relationships, and emotional and financial stress.

You will learn that your goal is to build a healthy working relationship with the school. If you build a working relationship with the school, it will be easier to negotiate for special education services and supports. This does not mean you will never have conflict!

The Nature of Parent-School Conflict

"I am so frustrated! The IEP team did not meet with us in good faith. The team members did not read the new private sector evaluations on our son. How can an IEP team make recommendations about a child's special education when they do not read the evaluations about the child?"

Conflict between parents and schools is not new. For 150 years, public schools decided who could attend school and who had to stay home. During these years, the schoolhouse doors were closed to many children with disabilities.

When Congress passed Public Law 94-142 in 1975, they knew about the tradition of excluding children with disabilities from school. For the special education law to work, this tradition had to end. Congress added procedural safeguards to the law. The purpose of procedural safeguards is to protect the rights of children and the interests of their parents.

 You will learn about procedural safeguards in Section 4.

When Congress re-authorized the Individuals with Disabilities Education Act (IDEA) in 1997, they found that the implementation of the law was impeded by low expectations and the failure of schools to use research-based, proven methods of teaching and learning.

The reauthorized IDEA focuses on improving educational results and accountability. Congress strengthened the role of parents to ensure that families have meaningful opportunities to participate in their children's education. The child's parents and school officials must make all decisions about the child's special education program. This shared responsibility for decisions about how to educate children with disabilities makes conflict inevitable.

Beliefs, Perceptions and Interests

Conflict occurs when people have different beliefs, perceptions, and interests.

Beliefs are issues about which you feel strongly. Beliefs are based on emotions. Your beliefs affect your perceptions.

Perceptions are your thoughts about an issue or problem. When you disagree with your spouse about who is responsible for housework or how your earnings should be spent, you and your spouse have different perceptions and opinions about these issues.

Interests are your needs, desires, concerns, and fears. The strongest interests involve basic human needs—security, recognition, and control over one's life.

Conflict is not bad. Problems arise when people do not know how to handle conflict. Game-playing, vague communications, and hidden agendas happen because people are uncomfortable with conflict. Unresolved conflict carries a high price tag, from damaged relationships, betrayal, and mistrust, to financial and emotional stress.

When Interests Conflict

Assume you have a dispute with the school about your child's special education program. You ask for more help or different help. The school refuses because they believe they are providing enough help. You get angry because you believe the school is not doing enough for your child. The school personnel get angry because they believe you do not appreciate their efforts on your child's behalf.

Both sides believe they are right. These beliefs may drive you and the school to take positions based on the assumption that you are right. When you believe you are right, it is very hard to compromise.

You want the school to provide your child with a special education program that is individualized and effective. You want your child to benefit from special education. You believe the current program is damaging your child. You fear that if your child does not master basic skills, your child will not be an independent, productive adult.

What do you know about the school district's interests? What are their concerns and fears? What do they want? You know that your school district is a bureaucracy. Your school district fears change, loss of control, and loss of face.

Real Issues: Expense and Control _____

If you look closely at disputes between parents and schools, you will find that most disputes are actually about expense and control. Most special education disputes fall into four categories. (See Table 6-1)

Expense of Individualized Programs

Good special education services are intensive, individualized and expensive. Many parent-school disputes are actually about how to allocate scarce resources, not about the official "presenting problem."

Parents and schools have different objectives. As the parent of a child with a disability, you want your child to receive an individualized special education program that meets your child's unique needs. Individualized programs are labor-intensive and expensive.

Table 6-1	*Common Issues in Special Education Disputes*

Eligibility
The child has educational problems that suggest a disability. The school has not found the child eligible for special education, perhaps by using a "discrepancy formula" to deny eligibility.

Failure to Provide an Appropriate Education
The child's IEP is supposed to be individualized to meet the child's unique needs. Many districts offer "One size fits all" programs that do not meet the child's needs.

Failure to Implement the IEP
The child has an IEP that includes a commitment to provide services. The school is not providing the services and supports in the IEP.

Inappropriate Discipline
The child has behavior problems caused by the disability. The school has a "zero tolerance" discipline policy. Although the child's behavior is a result of the disability, the school suspends or expels the child.

Loss of Control

Teachers and special education service providers are the designated education experts. When you actively advocate on your child's behalf, your assertiveness may cause some school personnel to feel threatened. When the school views a parent as a threat, school personnel often try to limit that parent's ability to advocate.

Common Parent-School Problems

Here are six common parent-school problems and strategies you can use to resolve these problems.

Problem: Different Views of the Child

"When I go to meetings, they never say anything good about my daughter."

If you are like many parents, you feel sad about the school's perception of your child. You view your child as an individual with unique qualities and abilities. When you offer information about your child's skills and interests, the school ignores, discounts, or rejects your information. If the school does not observe a skill or behavior, it does not count.

You may believe the school must see your child as an individual before there can be agreement on the services your child needs. The school may believe you are a single-minded emotional parent who is incapable of making rational decisions about your child's educational program.

Strategies: Different Views of the Child

If you and the school have different views of your child, try to narrow the gap.

Write a letter that describes your child and what you want for your child. Your letter should be factual and polite. Send copies of this letter to the regular members of your child's team. Ask that your letter be included in your child's file.

 You will learn how to write effective letters in Chapters 23 and 24.

If you feel offended by disparaging comments about your child, mention this in your letter. Explain that these comments focus on your child's weaknesses only, not on your child's abilities, strengths, aspirations, and needs. Stick to the facts. Do not try to make people feel guilty.

Problem: Lack of Information

If you are like many parents, when you learned that your child had a disability, you felt lost. You did not know what to do or where to turn. When you entered the world of special education, you felt overwhelmed.

In the beginning, you spent time learning about your child's disability. Later, you learned how the disability affects your child's learning and how your child needs to be taught. As you learned, you had more questions. You may have questions about your child's progress, special education program and placement, or the instructional methods used to educate your child.

What happens if the school cannot or will not answer your questions? What happens if your child's teacher says, *"I really shouldn't tell you this but..."* or *"You can't tell anyone I told you this but..."*

You begin to listen for evasions. You spend more time talking with the teacher who said, "*I really shouldn't tell you this but . . .*"

As you become aware of the imbalance of knowledge and information, you feel anxious and frustrated. "*They know the rules. We do not. We are at a disadvantage. How can we advocate for our children?*"

If you do not get straight answers, you will turn to people outside the system for answers. You will use the Internet, participate in online chats, and join listservs. When you get answers to your questions from outside sources, you will feel differently about the school.

After conversations with the teacher, you may realize that invisible strangers are making decisions about your child's special education program. Your perspective will change.

Strategies: Lack of Information

If you have a problem getting the school team to hear you, write a parent agenda for the next meeting. Your parent agenda should include your perceptions, your concerns and problems, and your proposed solutions. Keep your agenda short — one or two pages are usually best.

 In Chapter 25, you will learn how to write and use a parent agenda.

A few days before the meeting, send your parent agenda to the team members. Assume that no one will read the agenda before the meeting. Some people will lose it; others will forget about it. Do not take offense. Bring extra copies of your parent agenda to the meeting.

When you present a written document to the school team, you make it more difficult for the team to ignore your concerns or overlook your comments. Your agenda will become part of your child's educational file. If you continue to have problems with the school, your agenda is evidence of your attempts to resolve problems.

Problem: Lack of Options

If you have questions about your child's progress, placement, program, or instructional methods that the school cannot answer, you may view this as proof that something is wrong. Despite the requirement to provide your child with a program tailored to his or her unique needs, most schools do not offer many program options.

You may view this lack of options as evidence that the school does not understand your child's needs. New thoughts crowd into your mind, "*Something is wrong with the services my child is receiving.*" You try to push these unwanted thoughts away.

Although school districts should involve parents in program planning, few do so. Districts that involve parents learn that parents offer fresh ideas and creative solutions. When parents are involved in planning, they are more committed to making the solutions a success.

If you express concerns about your child's program or placement, the smart school district will ask, "*What do you want for your child?*" Smart districts do not say, "*We don't do that.*"

Strategies: Lack of Options

If you have a problem with limited program options, write a letter to the school team. Explain that you understand the district is supposed to provide a program that meets your child's needs. You are requesting information about all program options that are available. Advise that you need this information before you can make an informed decision about an appropriate program for your child. You appreciate their help. The tone of your letter should be polite.

Never use the word "best" or the terms "maximum potential" or "most appropriate."

Eliminate these words from your vocabulary. Ask your consultant or private sector expert not to use these terms in reports or evaluations.

By law, your child is **not entitled to the "best" program,** nor to a program that maximizes the child's potential. If you ask for the "best" program, your words will come back to haunt you. Your child is entitled to an appropriate program, no more, no less.

You will learn about the words "best" and "appropriate" in Chapters 15 and 16.

Problem: Hidden Issues

"*I should not be made to feel guilty because my child needs services, or that my child's services are expensive.*"

The school is required to provide your child with a special education program that is tailored to your child's unique needs. By law, these services must be free – "at no cost to child's parents."

Schools act as gatekeepers. When schools provide special education services that are tailored to the unique needs of the child, the school must commit personnel and financial resources.

Assume you request an unusual or expensive program at the next IEP meeting. At the end of the meeting, you realize the team did not respond to your request. Perhaps someone changed the subject. What happened? The IEP team could not admit that they did not have the authority to approve your request.

According to the IDEA, the IEP team that includes the child's parents makes all decisions about the child's special education program and placement. In fact, if you request an unusual or expensive program, the decision is likely to be made by an administrator who does not know you or your child and did not attend the meeting.

No one will tell you this! The IEP team may pretend that you did not make a request. The team leader may suddenly cancel the meeting. The school may claim that the IEP meeting was not really an IEP meeting.

Strategies: Hidden Issues

Hidden issues cause tremendous confusion and mistrust. The simplest strategy is to put your request in writing. When you write your post-meeting thank you letter, explain that you made a request about your child's program that the team did not address. Ask for a response to your request. (To see how one parent handled this, read Jim Manners' letter in Chapter 24 about Writing Letters to the Stranger.)

Problem: Feeling Devalued

"My child's school doesn't value children with disabilities enough to help them prepare for life. Prepare them for placement in a sheltered workshop—that's enough."

Several factors make conflict between you and the school more likely:

- When you are lied to
- When important information is withheld from you
- When you are patronized
- When you sense hidden issues or agendas
- When you feel devalued

School personnel also feel devalued. Several factors make conflict with parents more likely:

- When you do not share your concerns with the school
- When you request a due process hearing without trying to work things out
- When school personnel sense that you have hidden agendas or issues
- When they feel devalued

Strategies: Feeling Devalued

You must learn how to disagree without devaluing the other side. If you feel devalued, do not react. Include a factual description of what happened in a letter or post-meeting thank you note. Express your hope that this will not happen again. *Do not discuss your feelings.* The tone of your letter should be polite.

Problem: Poor Communication and Intimidation

"The IEP team leader was rude and condescending. She monopolized the meeting, interrupted us when we tried to talk, and misstated our position."

Common parent-school communications problems include:

- Lack of follow-up
- Misunderstandings
- Intentional vagueness
- Intimidation

When schools bring large numbers of school personnel to meetings, they are usually trying to intimidate parents or prepare their witnesses for a due process hearing. When parents request a service or program and the school responds by scheduling another meeting without responding to the parents' original request, the school is trying to wear the parents out.

Strategies: Poor Communication and Intimidation

When conflict reaches this degree of intensity, the parent-school relationship is polarized. Both sides feel angry and betrayed. If your district uses bullying tactics, this ensures that you will feel betrayed and lose trust. Bullying makes conflict inevitable. There are no simple solutions to these problems.

If the school is unwilling to resolve problems, you are at a crossroads. To secure the services your child needs, you may have to engage in litigation. Litigation has significant risks. If you prevail and force the school to accept your solution, as occurred in civil rights litigation in our country, you may win a victory that takes years to implement. (Example: Massive resistance after the U. S. Supreme Court decision in *Brown v. Board of Education*.)

You are left with the option of extending an olive branch, while protecting yourself and your child and preparing for litigation. Throughout this book, you will learn how to use tactics and strategies to build healthy working relationships with school personnel. If you use these strategies, you can often cause a positive shift in your relationship with the school.

Table 6-2	*How Special Education Disputes Are Resolved*

1. Informally, in IEP meetings and private meetings

2. Complaint to the state education agency.

3. Mediation

4. Due process hearing.

5. Appeal to court.

Problem: Loss of Trust

"We know that our child was damaged by the school. We do not know how severe or enduring the damage will be. Often, our feelings of betrayal are so strong and bitter that we will never trust again."

If you lose trust, your belief that the school knows how to help your child changes to a belief that the school does not know how to help your child or does not want to help your child.

When you lose trust, you feel insecure and anxious. You may believe that your child has been damaged. Is the damage permanent? From your perspective, the people you trusted violated your trust. If you feel betrayed, or you view the school relationship as worthless, you are in crisis. In the next chapter, we will help you deal with a school crisis.

If conflict is inevitable, what can you do? Hide? Duck? Fight?

Strategies: Loss of Trust

If you discover that your spouse committed adultery, you will suffer loss of trust. You will feel betrayed. Special education disputes involve similar emotions, including loss of trust and betrayal.

In marital conflict, some relationships heal and become stronger. Other relationships terminate. The child's life may improve because the parents reconcile or because the parents divorce. The child's life may worsen after the parents reconcile because of continuing discord. The child's life may improve because the parents' relationship is healthier. How conflict affects the child depends on how adults handle the conflict.

When communication breaks down, this may lead to litigation or to improved relationships. To improve relations, the parent will have to take the first step and extend the olive branch. Yet, the parent must also anticipate that litigation may be necessary to resolve ongoing problems.

Tips to Resolve Problems

How do you resolve work schedule problems with your co-workers? You negotiate. How do you resolve financial problems with your partner? You negotiate. How do you resolve problems with your school? You negotiate.

Negotiate to Resolve Problems

When you negotiate, you put yourself in the shoes of the other side and answer questions like these:

- Perceptions: How do they see the problem?
- Interests: What do they want?
- Fears: What are they afraid will happen if they give me what I want?
- Positions: What is their bottom line?

If you have a dispute with the school, you have two goals: to resolve the issue and to protect the parent-school relationship. In parent-school disputes, emotions run high on both sides. Your emotions and the emotions of school personnel merge with the issue, leading to anger, mistrust, and bitterness. When this happens, relationships are polarized and a good outcome is less likely.

Table 6-3	**Five Golden Rules for Negotiators**

1. Listen more than you talk.

2. Ask 5 Ws + H + E questions to clarify the perspective and position of the other side.

3. Storytelling reduces resistance. Make requests by telling the child's story.

4. Make situations informal. Meet in different places. If things are tense, bring food that smells good.

5. Treat other people with respect.

If you have a problem with school personnel, remind yourself that you are dealing with people. People are emotional. When people feel emotional, it is difficult for them to think about new solutions to problems.

Never Underestimate the Importance of "Face"

Some parents initiate litigation because they want the school to admit their failures. Do not do this!

You have learned that your school district is a bureaucracy. Bureaucracies cannot admit that they did not or cannot fulfill their mission. If you confront the school with evidence that they failed, they will attempt to save face by claiming that:

- The child is really making progress. (We did not fail.)
- The child is choosing not to learn. (The child failed.)
- The child's problems are due to poor parenting. (You failed.)

Many disputes boil down to positions taken to save face. If you seek a "win-lose" solution to your dispute with you as the winner, you do not understand the importance of face. You risk losing the issue *and* destroying your relationship with the school.

☑ **Try to resolve disagreements and problems early.**

Table 6-4	**Four Deadly Sins for Negotiators**

1. Blaming and shaming

2. Criticizing and finding fault

3. Sarcasm, scorn and ridicule

4. Judging, patronizing and bullying

In Summation

In this chapter, you learned that parent-school conflict is normal and inevitable. We described the impact of beliefs, perceptions, and interests on conflict. We identified issues that cause conflict and provided simple strategies that you can use to resolve conflict before things get out of hand.

Your Notes Here

7 | Emergency, Crisis, Help!

> "In Chinese, the word crisis is composed of two characters. One represents danger and the other represents opportunity."   —John F. Kennedy, President

In the last chapter, you learned that parent-school conflict is normal, predictable and inevitable. In this chapter, you will learn how to manage a crisis. We will describe typical parent-school crises that cause parents to seek outside help. You will learn that the crisis has two sides: danger and opportunity. We will describe how to avoid common pitfalls and will provide strategies you can use to weather a crisis.

Help! Events That Trigger Crises

Here are common events that trigger crises and requests for help from parents. The school:

- Placed the child in a less desirable program, despite objections by the parents;
- Refused to change the child's program and placement, despite recommendations from a private sector professional that the program is not appropriate;
- Refused to consider or include private sector test results and recommendations in the child's IEP;
- Refused to provide accommodations and modifications so the child failed high-stakes tests;
- Decided the child is not learning disabled but is emotionally disturbed or mentally retarded, and unilaterally changed the child's label and placement;
- Decided the child is not emotionally disturbed, but has a conduct disorder and is not eligible for special education services;
- Decided the child is not mentally retarded, but is a slow learner and is not eligible for special education services;
- Caused the child to be arrested at school and suspended or expelled the child for behavior that is related to the child's disability;
- Sent the child home because they do not have an appropriate program and do not want the child in school;

- Insisted that inclusion means all special education services must be delivered in the classroom;
- Terminated the child from special education because the child did not benefit from the only program they offer;
- Terminated the child from special education after the child's IQ scores dropped because there is no longer a severe discrepancy between the child's ability and achievement scores;
- Refused to provide necessary services because these services are expensive or would establish a precedent.

Three factors increase the chances of a crisis:

- The school makes a unilateral decision;
- The school ignores information from others, including professionals and parents;
- The decision or action may harm the child.

In a crisis, you will feel frightened, confused, guilty, angry, and helpless. Your common sense and good judgment vanish. What should you do? During a crisis, your first response is likely to be a big mistake!

Crisis Management, Step-by-Step

"It's not whether you get knocked down. It's whether you get up again."
—*Vince Lombardi, football coach*

A crisis hits! What should you do?

For the first few days, do nothing. You are feeling helpless and emotionally overwhelmed. If you believe you must do something, resist this urge!

Do you start a fight when you have no ammunition? No! Do you start a fight before you know where the high ground is? No! You do not start a fight until you have a good chance of prevailing.

Short-Term Solutions

Think. Regroup. Analyze the issues. Gather information. Locate the high ground. Think about how to solve the problem. Plan a strategy so you can take the hill and prevail, without firing a shot.

Use your energy to prepare. Focus on short-term solutions and long-range planning. In a crisis, you need to:

- Control your emotions.
- Remove your child from the middle.
- Make long-range plans.

Control Your Emotions

Keep your emotions under control! Do not obsess about unfairness. If you allow yourself to obsess about unfairness or revenge, you will make mistakes.

Be careful about revealing your feelings to school personnel. If you share your feelings, the school will perceive you as emotional and vulnerable. If you discuss your personal problems, you are likely to appear to be more problem-ridden than you are.

Spend your time and energy thinking, planning, and preparing. When you prepare, it is more difficult to make mistakes. Put your emotions in your backpack. Use your emotions as a source of energy to keep you moving, step-by-step, to high ground.

Remove Your Child from the Middle

Children who are embroiled in battles between their parents and their school are similar to children in custody battles. As they travel back and forth between the two sides, they are in the middle.

Many children assume that parent-school problems are their fault. You may explain the situation to your child but you should not allow or encourage the child to take sides.

Long-Term Planning

A crisis is an opportunity. The crisis forces you to face reality. You realize that you must take steps to change your child's educational situation. You need to do long-term planning.

Begin a Program of Self-Study

You need to learn about the law, your child's disability, how your child learns, and how your child should be taught. Where do you begin? Join one or two special education organizations for one year. Immerse yourself in information about disabilities, educational remediation techniques, legal rights and responsibilities, and tactics and strategies.

📖 For a list of disabilities organizations and information groups, see Appendix F.

🖱 For websites for disabilities organizations and information groups, visit the companion site to this book at http://www.fetaweb.com/

Join a Support Group

Get help from other parents. Look for a support group or advocacy group in your community. Members of the group will provide information, recommend experts, offer support, and alleviate the sinking feeling that you are fighting this battle alone.

📖 For advice about how to find a support group, read Chapter 2.

Learn About Legal Rights and Responsibilities

You need to learn about your legal rights and responsibilities. Read and re-read the Individuals with Disabilities Education Act (IDEA). Use a highlighter. Attach sticky notes on those pages that relate to your child's situation.

There are dozens of good legal research sites on the Internet.

FindLaw is an encyclopedic law site. http://www.findlaw.com/

Versuslaw offers full-text access to appellate state and federal decisions, including decisions from the U. S. Supreme Court. http://www.versuslaw.com/

Wrightslaw is a special education law and advocacy site. http://www.wrightslaw.com

Learn About Special Education

You need accurate information about your child's disability and appropriate educational techniques. When you use the Internet, you can find answers to many of your questions.

Visit the fetaweb.com site for resources. http://www.fetaweb.com/

Get Advocacy Information From Your State

Contact the Special Education Division of your **State Department of Education.** Ask for a copy of your state special education laws, regulations, and guidelines. Request all material about special education, IEPs, and Section 504 programs. Visit the site maintained by your state department of education.

For contact information for your state Department of Education, see Appendix D.

Your state has an independently operated and funded **Protection and Advocacy Office.** Protection and Advocacy Offices are not associated or affiliated with state Departments of Education. Request the publications about special education, IEPs, and parent rights and responsibilities from your state P & A office.

http://www.protectionandadvocacy.org/

Contact your state **Parent Information and Training Center.**

For a list of state Parent Information and Training Centers with contact information, see Appendix E.

Request Your Child's Records

Request a complete copy of your child's cumulative and confidential files from your child's school and from the administrative office where the special education department is located. Request a copy of your child's records from all agencies and individuals that may have information about your child.

📖 You will learn how to request this information and organize your child's file in Chapter 9.

Get a Comprehensive Evaluation

Get a comprehensive evaluation of your child from an independent expert in the private sector. The purpose of this evaluation is to identify your child's problems and develop a plan to address these problems. Before you can make wise decisions about your child's special education program, you need accurate diagnostic information about the child's disability, strengths, weaknesses, and needs.

At this point, many parents say . . .

"But the school is supposed to test my child . . ."

"I want an independent evaluation and I want them to pay for it!"

If the school arranges and pays for an independent evaluation, you should expect this evaluation to support the school's position. You need accurate diagnostic information about your child's problems from an evaluator who is independent of the school district. With this information, you will be able to develop solutions to problems.

You are likely to have to pay for this evaluation. View the evaluation as an investment in your child's future. A comprehensive evaluation will give you a roadmap for the future.

☑ **Many universities have child development clinics and education and psychology departments that will evaluate your child at low or no cost.**

Examine Your Beliefs

Examine your beliefs about your child and your child's disability. Do you feel sorry for your child? Do you feel guilty about your child's problems? When you tried to protect your child from painful experiences, did you become over-protective? Will pity, guilt, and over-protectiveness help your child grow up into an emotionally healthy adult?

If your child has a disability, your child learns differently. Your child must be taught differently. When your child is taught correctly, your child can and will learn. Conditions that are disabilities in large classroom environments often have powerful, corresponding strengths. When the child learns to channel these qualities, they can be assets.

In Summation _____

In this chapter, you learned how to manage a crisis with the school. We described events that trigger school crises. You learned crisis management techniques, including the need to control your emotions, remove your child from the middle, and begin a program of self-study. You learned about the steps you should take in long-term planning.

Section 3 is "The Parent as Expert." In this Section, you will learn about tests and evaluations, how to organize your child's file, what test data means, how to measure educational progress, and SMART IEPs.

Your Notes Here

Section Three

The Parent as Expert

As a parent, you negotiate with the school on your child's behalf. To be an effective negotiator, you need to be an expert about your child. You need to know about:

- Your child's disability
- Your child's educational needs
- Your child's educational progress

In Chapter 8, "Evaluations and Your Child's Disability," you will learn about comprehensive evaluations. We explain the limitations of testing by the school. We provide strategies you can use to learn about your child's disability and effective educational practices.

Chapter 9 is "The File: Do It Right!" In this chapter, you will learn how to organize your child's file. The process of organizing your child's file will help you understand your child's disability and educational history. When your child's file is organized, you will be prepared for the next school meeting.

In Chapter 10, "Understanding Tests and Measurements 101," you will learn about the normal distribution of data and how to use the bell curve to measure educational progress. In this chapter, you will learn about percentile ranks and standard scores, composite scores, and subtest scatter.

Chapter 11, "Understanding Tests and Measurements 102," will teach you how to use pre- and post-tests to measure your child's progress. You will learn about norm referenced and criterion referenced tests, standard deviations, and standard scores. You will learn how to convert standard scores into percentile ranks, and percentile ranks into standard scores. When you analyze your child's test scores and understand what the scores mean, you will be able to develop an appropriate program for your child.

If the school develops an inadequate IEP for your child, your child will not receive an appropriate education. Chapter 12 teaches you about SMART IEPs that are specific, measurable, use action words, are realistic, and time-limited. You will learn how to use present levels of performance to write measurable goals and objectives about what your child will learn and be able to do.

8 | Evaluations and Your Child's Disability

"Parents have become so convinced that educators know what is best for children that they forget that they are the experts." —Marian Wright Edelman, educator

In this chapter, you will learn about the comprehensive evaluation and how to use information from the evaluation to design an appropriate educational program. You will learn how to do research about your child's disability, educational needs, and your legal rights and responsibilities.

Help! My son has dyslexia. He can barely read and write. The school will not put anything in his IEP about teaching him how to read and write. What can I do?

Help! My daughter has a cochlear implant. She can listen and speak. The school placed her in a class with deaf children where they are teaching her sign language and lip reading. What can I do?

Help! The school took my son out of special education. He is failing. When I asked them to put him back in special education, they said he does not qualify. What can I do?

Many parents feel powerless in their dealings with their school. Although you may feel powerless, *you are not powerless*. The best antidote to helplessness is information. Knowledge is power!

Get a Comprehensive Evaluation

Until you know where you are and where you need to go, you cannot develop a master plan. A useful master plan for your child's special education uses information about your child's present levels of functioning. When you have accurate information, you can develop realistic goals and objectives.

Base your master plan on a comprehensive evaluation of your child by an expert or experts who are independent of your school district. You cannot always rely on the school district to do a quality evaluation of your child.

Finding Evaluators

You want to find an evaluator who is knowledgeable about your child's disability. Evaluators work in the private sector, in university medical centers, children's hospitals, and child development centers. To find an evaluator, contact advocacy groups organizations and private special education schools. Ask other parents for recommendations.

 For information about finding and working with consultants or evaluators, review Chapter 2.

You want to establish a good working relationship with the evaluator or consultant. If possible, interview two or three individuals. When you schedule an appointment to meet with an evaluator, explain that you are looking for an independent professional who can evaluate your child, help you design an appropriate educational program for your child, and monitor your child's progress in the program.

☑ **If possible, look for an evaluator who can work with you and your child for several years.**

Understanding Test Results

If you are like many parents, when you read an evaluation, you feel confused. Ask the evaluator to give you all scores as standard scores, percentile ranks, grade equivalents and age equivalents. Schedule a follow-up appointment in a week or two.

Make two or three extra copies of the evaluation. File the original report in your child's Master File. Use a copy as you study. Read the evaluation several times. Make margin notes. Use a highlighter on your copy. Do not write on or mark the original document. As you read and re-read the evaluation, make a list of questions you have about the test results and what the test scores mean.

When you return for the follow-up session, bring this list of questions. Ask the evaluator to explain the test data and help you understand the educational implications of the data. For example:

Does the data explain your child's difficulties in the classroom?

Does the data explain your child's difficulty learning new skills?

What does the data tell you about educational approach that should be used to teach your child?

If you are like many parents, school personnel may have told you that you cannot expect your child to make progress because your child has a disability. In most cases, this is simply not true. If a special needs child receives intensive, individualized instruction, the child may make more than one year of progress in an academic year. When this happens, the child is "closing the gap."

Your child may need intensive, individualized instruction to acquire skills. Think about Helen Keller. Helen Keller was blind and deaf. What happens to children with multiple handicaps who are enrolled in special education programs? Helen Keller was fortunate. Her teacher was Anne Sullivan. Anne Sullivan used intensive, individualized direct instruction techniques to teach Helen Keller the skills she needed to be an independent, self-sufficient adult.

Ask the evaluator to help you design a plan for your child's special education. Where should you start? Of the problems identified in the evaluation, what problems are most important? What needs should be addressed first? Does the child have communication problems that are affecting the child's ability to acquire other skills? Should the child's communication problems be addressed first?

Does the child have deficiencies in social skills? Is the child's inability to relate to others a primary deficit? Does the child have psychological problems that are causing social problems? Does the child have psychological problems because her educational skills are not being remediated?

What skills should be addressed now? What skills can wait? What skills may improve after the child receives remediation in basic reading, writing, arithmetic and spelling skills? The only way to answer these questions is by a comprehensive evaluation.

How do you translate test results into a master educational plan? What is your child's most important educational need? What specific educational services does the child need now? How often should the child receive these services?

Assume your eight year-old-son has autism. The evaluator identifies speech and language problems as your child's most important need. What services does he need now? How frequently? In what setting? Does he need a 20-minute group speech session once a week? Does he need 30 minutes of one-on-one speech therapy three times a week? Does the evaluator recommend a particular technique?

Assume your daughter is in sixth grade. Her reading skills are at the second grade level. The evaluator identifies her most important need as the acquisition of reading skills. What type of remediation program does she need to bring her reading skills up to the level of her peers?

Assume the evaluator recommends this as an appropriate goal for your daughter:

In one academic year, the child's reading skills will increase by two years, from the second grade level to the fourth grade level, with progress measured twice a year on an individual standardized test.

To meet this goal, the child requires one-on-one remediation 60 minutes a day from a teacher who is specially trained in the remediation of children who have severe reading disabilities.

If your child meets this goal, you will use new data to update your child's performance levels. You will revise the goal so the child's skills continue to improve as measured by test data.

Limitations of School Evaluations

Assume your child was evaluated by the school district. You cannot rely on school testing to design your master plan.

According to a report from The Council of Exceptional Children, teachers say that school evaluations do not provide the information they need to design instruction, including information about children's achievement, learning styles and learning patterns. (Check the Bibliography for the citation of this report)

In some cases, school assessments were too narrow to provide an accurate picture of the child's abilities. In other cases, teachers received computer score sheets of composite intelligence and achievement test scores that were useless in designing instruction.

Your independent evaluator should conduct a comprehensive evaluation, including intelligence and educational achievement testing. The evaluator should observe your child's responses and do additional testing to identify specific areas of weakness. If possible, the independent evaluator should observe the child in the classroom. The child should be evaluated in all areas that affect learning (i.e., hearing, physical therapy, speech-language therapy, occupational therapy, academic skills remediation).

After the comprehensive evaluation is completed, you may need help to translate the test results and data into an appropriate educational program for your child. Many parents work with an educational consultant who is trained to design special education programs.

 See Chapter 2 for information about educational consultants.

Learn About the Disability

If you followed the suggestions at the end of Chapter 1, you purchased two large 3-ring notebooks. Use one notebook for your child's Master File. Use the other notebook for information about your child's disability, educational techniques, and advocacy information.

Learn from Organizations

As you gather information, begin with organizations that deal with your child's disability. Appendix F is a comprehensive list of organizations, associations and clearinghouses.

 For links to organizations, visit www.fetaweb.com /

Learn from the Treatment Team

Get information about your child's disability from your child's doctor, psychologist, and other members of the treatment team. Ask for patient information pamphlets and recommended reading. Members of your child's treatment team should be able to answer questions about your child and can be an excellent resource.

Learn from School Personnel

You may learn about your child's needs from school personnel. Although some school personnel may not be willing to help, most knowledgeable educators will help you understand your child's educational needs.

When you take these steps—join a special education organization, do research, get information from your child's treatment team and special educators, you will soon be knowledgeable about your child's disability and needs.

 Although the Internet can be a great resource, some web sites and listserv posts contain inaccurate information and bad advice that encourages acrimony between parents and schools.

Learn About Effective Educational Practices

To gather information about how your child learns, read books and articles, get information from special education associations, your child's doctor and treatment team, and special education professionals. Use the Internet to find answers to questions.

In Summation

Lack of accurate information is a big obstacle for most parents. When you follow the steps in this chapter, you will learn about your child's disability and effective special education practices. You are becoming an expert.

As you gather and organize the information about your child into a master file, you may be surprised at what you learn. We guarantee that organizing your child's file will give you a new perspective about your child's disability and educational history. In the next chapter, you will learn how to organize your child's file the right way!

Your Notes Here

9 | The File: Do It Right!

"Do the hard jobs first. The easy jobs will take care of themselves."
—Dale Carnegie, motivational speaker

As the parent of a child with a disability, you know the special education system generates mountains of paper. Some information is important so you are afraid to throw anything away. The mountain of paper grows higher every year. What do you do with it? How do you organize this information?

You need a simple, foolproof document management system. In this chapter, you will learn how to organize your child's file. After you organize the information about your child into a file, you will have a clearer understanding of your child's disability and educational needs.

Document Management System

Think about the last school meeting. Did the IEP team members have a complete copy of your child's file? Did you have a complete copy of your child's file? How can the IEP team make decisions about your child's special education program if they do not have complete, accurate information about your child?

Schools keep records in different places. Information and reports are misplaced. When you organize your child's file, you will have all the information about your child in one place. With our document management system, you can track your child's educational history. When you use this parent-tested system, you can quickly locate any document in your child's file.

When you take your organized file to the next school meeting, you will understand the power of getting organized. You will gain a sense of control.

Gather Information About Your Child

Follow these steps to get information about your child.

Make a Master Provider List

Make a list of all individuals and agencies that may have information or records about your child. Your list should include the names and titles of all professionals who have provided medical or mental health treatment services, including doctors, therapists, and other health care providers. Include their addresses, telephone and fax numbers, and email addresses. Maintain your list by category of service rendered, e.g., medical, educational, psychological evaluations.

Request Your Child's Records

Send a letter to the individuals and agencies on your list and request a copy of your child's records. Explain that your request relates to a school issue and the need to secure an appropriate education for your child. Ask if you should expect to pay a photocopying fee and what this fee will be. Your letters should be neat and convey a professional image.

📖 **See Appendix I for sample letters to request records from health care providers.**

If you do not receive a response within ten days, send a short letter explaining that you requested information ten days ago and have not received a response. Attach a copy of your original letter to the second request letter. Ask if you can do anything to expedite the request. Offer to visit the office to help copy the information. Be polite. Appendix I includes a sample second request for information letter.

☑ **Make photocopies of all letters for your file.**

Request Your Child's Educational Records

Write a letter to the school and request a complete copy of your child's entire cumulative file and confidential file, omitting nothing. You want copies of all evaluations, records, correspondence, and other documents the school has about your child. Use a word processor for your letter. Expect to pay a reasonable photocopying fee.

📖 **Appendix I includes sample letters to request educational records.**

Send one letter to the principal of your child's school and one letter to the director of special education. If you do not know the director's name and address, call the main office of the school district and request this information. If your child does not attend a public school, send the letter to the principal of the last public school your child attended.

Before you mail these letters, sign them and make copies of the signed letters for your Master File. Log the letters into your contact log.

Organize the Master File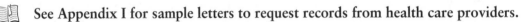

You will organize and file all information about your child in three-ring notebooks. Gather all documents that relate to your child. Bring all paper in boxes, file folders, and bags together in one place. Begin by organizing the documents by year.

☑ Do not skip this section, even if you have organized your child's file.

Step 1: Date All Documents

With a pencil, lightly write the date of each document in the lower right corner of the first page (Example: 11/09/02).

☑ **Use a soft lead pencil when you date the documents. You may need to erase your notations later.**

Before long, mail will roll in from your requests. Using a pencil, lightly date each document in the lower right hand corner. Date everything - evaluations, reports, correspondence, report cards, and medical reports.

When you find duplicate documents, compare the duplicates, decide which document has the best photocopy quality, and use this as your master. Put the duplicates in a box. You will not need them for your notebook. Do not throw them away. You may need to provide copies to other people later.

☑ **Do not write on original documents. You may need copies of these documents later.**

Work samples provide useful information about your child's skills. Include a few samples of your child's schoolwork.

Many parents say that when they organize documents, they begin to read and are sidetracked. Force yourself to stick with this job until you finish. Do not stop to read the documents. Just date and organize! Lightly pencil the date on the bottom right corner of the first page.

Step 2: File All Documents in a Three-Ring Notebook

Hole-punch, then file all dated documents in a large three-ring notebook. When you hole-punch, be careful that you do not destroy important signatures or dates. When documents are formatted horizontally, hole-punch on the top edge.

File all documents in chronological order, oldest document on top and newest document at the end. Some parents use the child's birth certificate as the first document in the file. The last document is the most recent piece of information. This may be a report card, IEP, or letter from the school.

☑ **Do not put documents in clear plastic envelopes. If you are in a meeting and need to find a document in the file, removing documents from plastic envelopes takes too long.**

Do not file documents by category (i.e., IEPs, psychological evaluations, correspondence, etc.). If you file documents by category, your system will fail. Assume you have a comprehensive letter written by a child psychologist three years ago. The Eligibility Committee and the IEP team used the psychologist's letter. Is this document a letter? A report? An evaluation?

Trying to figure out categories is confusing and time-consuming. If your system is confusing and difficult, it will fail. Use our parent-tested system. You have better things to do with your time!

Step 3: Read the Master File for the "Big Picture"

After you complete Step 2, read your child's Master File from beginning to end. When you read the information chronologically, you will see the big picture.

At the beginning of this chapter, we mentioned the mountains of paper generated by the special education system. After reports are written, they are filed away. Few people will read or review this information again. Because there is no master plan, no one looks at the big picture.

Instead of looking at the forest, parents and school staff focus on the bark of the trees. When you organize your child's file, you will see the forest, perhaps for the first time. You will understand. Many parents say that making a neat, organized, chronological Master File is a powerful educational experience.

Table 9-1	*Four Rules for Organizing the File*

1. Do not write on your original documents.

2. Do not use a marker or highlighter on your original documents.

3. Do not release your original documents to anyone.

4. Keep your notebook current.

Create Your List of Documents

You have dated the documents and filed them in chronological order, oldest document on top, most recent on the bottom. Now you need to create your Master Document List. When you organize documents chronologically and generate your Master Document List, you can compress your child's history into a few pages. You can locate any document in seconds.

☑ **If you want to make a note on a document in your Master File, write on a sticky note that you attach to the document.**

To create your Master Document List, make a table with four columns. If you are using a word processing program, insert a four-column table. If you are not using a computer, draw a table with four columns on several sheets of paper. Label the columns: Date, Author, Type, and Significance. (Table 9-2 shows you how to format your list)

Enter each document by date, author, and type. Leave the Significance column blank. Attach sticky notes to all pages in your Master File that have test scores (i.e., the Wechsler Intelligence Test and Woodcock Johnson Tests.)

Table 9-2	Format for Master Document List		
Date	Author	Type	Significance

☑ **If you use a word processing program, the program can sort the list by date, author, or type of document.**

When you use a word processing program, you can change the font to highlight test data and other important information. You make it easier to find important information. To see how a Master Document List looks, look at Table 9-3.

✍ **Download a Master Document List from the Fetaweb site: www.fetaweb.com/**

When you organize your child's file, you will learn about your child's disability and educational history. This is an important step in becoming an expert. When you finish this job, you will have a clearer understanding of your child's educational needs.

Table 9-3	Sample Master Document List		
Date	Author	Type	Significance
7/16/01	Cannon	Psychological Evaluation	School evaluation. **WISC-III IQ** above avg. **WJ-R**: Reading, writing skills 3 years delayed.
8/23/01	Center Elementary School	IEP	Placed in resource program. Progress will be 80% on teacher made tests and observations.
5/14/02	Collins	Educational Evaluation	School evaluation with **WJ-R, TOWL, K-ABC.** No gain in reading and writing skills. Percentile ranks dropped.
6/6/02	Center Elementary School	Report Card	B's in Reading and Writing. Promoted to next grade.
9/10/02	Stein	Psychiatric Evaluation	Severely **depressed**. Anti-depressant meds ncreased. MD recommends psychiatric hospitalizaton.
10/14/02	Barton	Educational Evaluation	Private sector evaluation. **WRAT & WIAT.** Child illiterate; requires 1:1 direct instruction.
11/5/02	Stein	Discharge Summary	Severe depression from school failure, poor academic skills; needs remediation.

You do not need to complete the "Significance" column yet. When you learn more about evaluations and test scores, you will recognize important information in documents.

In Summation

In this chapter, you learned how to organize your child's file. The process of organizing this information helps you understand your child's disability, history, and educational needs. You created a Master Document List that will enable you to find a specific document quickly and easily.

To be an expert, you need to learn how to identify your child's needs and how to measure your child's educational progress. This information is in your child's test scores. It is time to learn about tests and measurements.

10 | Tests and Measurements 101

"If something exists, it exists in some amount. If it exists in some amount, it is capable of being measured."   —Descartes, philosopher

To be a successful advocate, you must learn about tests and measurements—statistics. Statistics allow you to measure your child's progress or lack of progress (regression) using numbers.

In this chapter, you will learn how to use statistics to measure change. You will learn about the bell curve and how to use the bell curve to measure educational progress. You will learn about percentile ranks and standard scores, composite scores, and subtest scatter.

Mike

Assume you have an eleven-year-old child who is in the sixth grade. In third grade, Mike was found eligible for special education services as a child with a specific learning disability. He has not made much progress in reading, spelling, or writing since he entered special education three years ago. Mike is angry and depressed and says, "I hate school."

You are afraid. What if Mike never masters the basic academic skills? What kind of future will he have?

At the next IEP meeting, you share your concerns about Mike's lack of progress. You want the school to provide a different program. The IEP team disagrees. One member says Mike is getting all the help he needs. Another member says your expectations are too high. The psychologist says if you do not accept Mike's limitations, you will damage him.

The IEP team offers accommodations and modifications for his special education program. They want to reduce his assignments and give him "talking books." They do not propose to teach Mike to read, write, spell, and do math. You know what is happening. The IEP team is lowering the bar.

What can you do? How can you get the IEP team to listen? How can you persuade the IEP team to develop a different educational program for Mike? You need to learn what Mike's test scores mean and how to chart these scores.

Before you can develop an appropriate special education program, you must understand your child's strengths and weaknesses. When you understand your child's test scores, you can use a computer or graph paper to create progress or regression graphs.

The principles of tests and measurements are not difficult to learn. You use statistics in many areas of life. When you read these two chapters, you will discover that you already know many of these concepts.

Pollsters use statistics to measure attitudes and preferences. Reporters use statistics to measure change or lack of change. If you read articles about economic and social changes, politics, or the weather, you are reading about statistics.

Plan to read these two chapters about tests and measurements several times. When you study, make notes. You will encounter some terms and concepts that are new to you—standard deviations, standard scores, grade equivalents, and age equivalents. You are likely to be familiar with other terms like percentiles and averages.

When you master this information, you will understand your child's test scores. You will be able to use information from objective tests to make decisions about your child's special education program. You may find that your expertise exceeds that of many special education team members. You will have the tools you need to change your child's life. When you go to the next school meeting, you will be glad you did your homework!

You will be able to answer questions like these:

- How is your child functioning, compared with other children the same age?
- How is your child functioning, compared with others in the same grade?
- How much educational progress has your child made since the child was last tested?
- If your child receives special education, has your child progressed or regressed in the special education program?
- If your child's age and grade equivalent test scores have increased, has your child made progress when compared to the peer group?

When you learn about tests and measurements, you will be able to compare test results and measure your child's progress.

Measuring Growth: Rulers, Yardsticks, and Other Tools

How do you measure your child's physical growth? You measure growth with a measuring tape and scales. You measure how much the child's height increases in inches, and how much the child's weight increases in pounds over a period of months and years.

You use simple tools to monitor your child's physical growth. Even if we present this information in millimeters and kilograms, you know that when your child's height and weight increase, your child is growing. With a table or formula, you can easily convert this information into inches and pounds.

Assume that one year ago, your child was five feet, three inches tall. One year later, your child is five feet, six inches tall. There are several ways you can report this information. You can say that your child was sixty-three inches tall one year ago, and is now sixty-six inches tall. You can say that your child was 5.25 feet tall and is now 5.5 feet tall. You can say that one year ago, your child was 160 centimeters tall and is now 168 centimeters tall. You can even say that one year ago, your child was 1.75 yards tall, and is now 1.83 yards tall!

If you measure your child at regular intervals, you can create a chart or graph that tracks changes in your child's height and weight. You can use growth charts at the doctor's office to compare your child's growth with the growth of the average child.

Measuring Educational Change: Test Scores

Your child's educational growth can be measured and charted in a similar fashion. Although the tools you use to measure educational growth are different, the principles are the same. How do you measure educational growth and change? Instead of a tape measure and a set of scales, you use psychological and educational achievement test scores.

You can begin with the standardized educational achievement tests that school districts administer to students. Although standardized educational achievement tests are general measures, they provide useful information. Standardized educational tests are similar to medical screening tests. Standardized tests may suggest that the child has a problem, and that additional individual testing should be completed to diagnose the child's problem and develop a treatment plan.

The process of identifying a child's disability unfolds in a similar manner. Schools are required to use a variety of individually administered tests to determine if the child has a disability and if the disability adversely affects educational performance. The child is usually evaluated by two or more individuals (e.g., a school psychologist, educational diagnostician, speech-language evaluator, occupational therapist, etc.).

Learning About Evaluations

As a parent, you need answers to questions about your child's disability and educational needs. How does your child's disability affect learning? What specific areas are affected? How serious are your child's problems? What are your child's strengths and weaknesses?

Does your child need special education? What academic skills need to be remediated? How will you know if your child is making progress? How much progress is sufficient? You will find answers to these questions in the tests and evaluations administered to your child.

Overcoming Fears

"I'm just a parent. I did not finish college. The people who tested my kid went to school for years. I can't understand this stuff!"

Some parents believe they cannot understand test results. If you believe you cannot understand tests, it is time to change your beliefs.

Perhaps you are reading this book because your child is performing poorly in school or has been identified with learning problems. Perhaps your child believes that he or she cannot learn to read, write, spell, or do arithmetic. **Your child needs to overcome these beliefs. So do you!**

Learning What Tests Measure

Tests do not always measure what they appear to measure. For example, in an assessment of a child's reading skills, different tests measure different types of reading skills: oral reading, silent reading, reading comprehension, word recognition, or word attack skills.

The Woodcock Reading Mastery Test – Revised (WRMT-R) is a commonly used educational achievement test. The Woodcock Reading Mastery Test includes one subtest that measures the child's ability to read aloud and pronounce isolated words out of context. This is a word identification test, not a measure of global reading skills. The child's score on this subtest may be adversely affected by speech or word finding problems.

On another reading test, the child reads a passage of text aloud (oral reading), and then answers questions. The child's score is based on the accuracy of words read aloud and the child's understanding of the passage read.

On a different test, the child reads a passage of text and answers multiple-choice questions about the passage. The child's score may measure the child's ability to eliminate answers that are presented in multiple-choice format, i.e., the child's reasoning ability, not reading skills. Some children can discern the context based on a few words. Other children have excellent word recognition skills but cannot interpret the words in a body of text or passage.

You need to know what tests measure and how tests are administered.

Statistics 101

When you learn a new subject, you must also learn new words and concepts. At first, these terms and concepts may be confusing. Be patient. These terms will soon be familiar to you.

You Use Statistics to Measure and Describe Relationships

You use statistics to measure things and describe relationships between things, using numbers. Let's look at a simple topic that is familiar to many people – your car's gas consumption.

When you describe your car's gas mileage, you can make any of the following statements:

- My gas tank is half full
- My gas tank is half empty
- My tank is at the fifty percent mark
- I have used eight gallons
- I have eight gallons left in my tank
- My odometer shows that I will need to fill the tank in 150 miles
- My odometer shows that I've traveled 150 miles since I last filled the tank

Each of these statements accurately describes your car's gas consumption.

You Use Statistics to Make Decisions

When should you fill your gas tank? You know your gas tank holds sixteen gallons of gas. Your gas gauge shows that the tank is less than half full. You have been driving in the city. You will be driving on the highway for the rest of the day. You have used an exact amount of gas. An exact amount of gas remains in your tank.

There are several ways to describe this—gallons used, gallons remaining, miles driven, miles to go, percentage left, and so forth. With this information, you calculate that your car averages between seventeen and twenty-three miles to a gallon of gas, depending on driving conditions.

You Use Statistics to Measure Change

Using this data, you can also measure change. If you compare your car's present mileage to the mileage you obtained before a tune-up, you can measure miles per gallon before and after the tune-up. You can measure the impact of the tune-up on your car's gas consumption.

Let's look at another way that we use tests and measurements. Assume you went to the doctor a few months ago because you were feeling weak and tired. Your doctor asked questions about your symptoms and ordered some lab tests. After reviewing your test results, the doctor explained that your blood glucose level was moderately elevated.

To reduce your blood glucose level, the doctor developed a treatment plan that included changes in your diet and a daily program of exercise.

After one month, you returned for a follow-up visit. The doctor ordered another round of lab tests. If your blood glucose level had returned to normal, you probably did not require additional treatment. If your blood glucose level remained elevated, you may need treatment that is more intensive. When you measure change after an intervention with *"appropriate objective criteria and evaluation procedures"* (34 C.F.R. §300.346), you and your doctor can make rational decisions about your health.

You can use statistics to compute your car's gas consumption, make medical decisions, and measure your child's growth. You can also use statistics to measure educational progress. When you measure educational growth or progress, as when you measure gas consumption or glucose levels, you can report the same information in different ways.

Because educational test results are reported in different formats and compared in different ways, you need to understand all the different scoring methods that are used to measure and evaluate progress, including:

- Age equivalent scores (AE)
- Grade equivalent scores (GE)
- Standard scores (SS) and standard deviations (SD)
- Percentile ranks (PR)

When you learn to use statistics, you will be able to measure your child's progress or lack of progress in an educational program. Regression is the term for lack of progress. You need to recognize educational regression, a common problem in special education.

You Use Statistics to Compare

You can use statistics to evaluate how one child performs, when compared to other children who are the same age or in the same grade.

Let's look at one component of physical fitness in a group of elementary school students. Our group or sample consists of 100 fifth grade students. The children are enrolled in a physical fitness class to prepare them for the President's Physical Fitness Challenge. We will assume that the average chronological age (CA) of this group is exactly ten years, zero months (CA=10-0). The children are tested in September, at the beginning of the school year.

To qualify as physically fit, each child must meet several goals. Push-ups are used to measure upper body strength. Each child must complete as many push-ups as possible within a specified time. The child's raw score is the number of push-ups the child completes. Raw score is a term for the number of items correctly answered or performed.

After all the students complete the push-up test, we list their scores. Here are the results:

- Half of the children completed 10 push-ups or more.
- Half of the children completed 10 push-ups or fewer.
- The average child completed 10 push-ups.
- The average or mean number of push-ups completed by this group of fifth graders is 10.
- Half of the children scored above the mean or average score of 10.
- Half of the children scored below the mean or average score of 10.
- Fifty percent of the children scored 10 or above.
- Fifty percent of the children scored 10 or below.

When we analyze the children's scores, we see patterns:

- One-third of the group completed between 7 and 10 push-ups.
- One-third of the group completed between 10 and 13 push-ups.
- Two-thirds of the group scored between 7 to 13 push-ups.
- Half of the group (50 percent) completed between 8 and 12 push-ups.
- The lowest scoring child completed one push-up.
- The highest scoring child completed 19 push-ups.
- The remaining one-third completed fewer than seven or more than 13 push-ups.
- Nearly all the children—96 out of 100—completed between 4 and 16 push-ups.

This information is presented in Table 10-1.

Table 10-1 | *Push-Up Scores and Percentile Ranks*

Push-ups	Percentile Rank
19	99
18	99
17	99
16	99
15	98
14	91
13	84
12	75
11	63
10	50
9	37
8	25
7	16
6	9
5	5
4	2
3	1
2	1
1	1

These test results provide us with a sample of data. We can use this data to compare the performance of an individual child to the entire group. In making these comparisons, the data will allow us to identify an individual child's strengths or weaknesses when compared to the peer group of fifth graders.

If we use the same push-up test for children in other grades, we can compare our original group of fifth graders to other groups – older children, younger children, children who attend different schools. If we gather enough information or data, we can compare our original group of fifth graders – or an individual child within that group – to a national population of children whose upper body strength was tested by their ability to do push-ups.

The Bell Curve: A Powerful Tool

In nature, characteristics are distributed along theoretical curves. For our purposes, the most important curve is the normal distribution or bell curve. Because the percentages along the bell curve are well known and researched, the bell curve is our frame of reference.

Why is the bell curve such a powerful tool? When you use the bell curve, you can compare scores, measure progress, and measure effectiveness. You can compare one child to others and you can compare groups.

You Can Make Comparisons

Using the bell curve, you can draw a visual map or graph that provides additional information. You can use the bell curve to see where a single child scores when compared to the peer group. You can compare one child's score on an arithmetic test in terms of the number of correct answers to the average number of correct answers by children of the same age.

When you compare the push-up scores of children who attend different schools, you can learn whether the physical fitness of children, as measured by their ability to do push-ups, varies between schools, neighborhoods, states, or countries.

You Can Measure Effectiveness

When you use the bell curve, you can measure the effectiveness of a class or program. Assume you want to know if the physical fitness class is effective for the group of fifth graders. You ask, "Did the children's fitness levels improve?" How will you answer this question?

To measure the effectiveness of the fitness class, you measure the children's fitness before they begin the class and after they complete the class. If the fitness class has been effective in improving physical fitness, you will see individual and group improvement. If the program is effective, the children's ability to perform fitness skills will improve measurably over time. In this example, improved physical fitness is assessed with "appropriate objective criteria and evaluation procedures . . ." (34 C.F.R. §300.346) (This is the federal regulation about IEPs.)

You Can Measure Progress

The bell curve allows you to measure progress. Before you can use the bell curve, you need to know how the bell curve is designed.

On the bell curve, the bottom or horizontal line is called the X-axis. In the sample of fifth graders, the X-axis represents number of push-ups. An up-and-down or vertical line would be the Y-axis. In this sample, the Y-axis represents the number of children who earned a specific score. The highest point is ten. Most of the children completed ten push-ups.

Figure 10-1 | ***Bell Curve: Number of Push-ups***

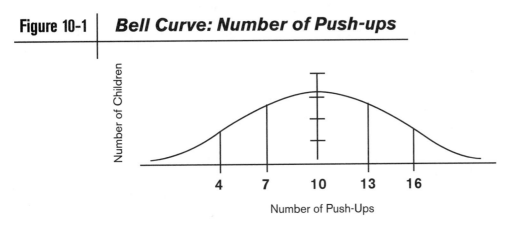

As you see in Figure 10-1, the midway point on the X-axis equals a score of 10 push-ups. Because more children completed 10 push-ups than any other number, the highest point on the bell curve represents a score of 10. The second most frequent scores were 9 and 11, followed by 8 and 12. This pattern continues to the far ends of the bell curve. In the sample, the ends occurred at 1 and 19 push-ups.

You Can Compare Scores

You can use the bell curve to compare one child's score to the scores achieved by other members of the child's peer group. Figure 10-2 is a bell curve with the push-up scores of our fifth graders.

Figure 10-2 | ***Bell Curve with Push-up Scores and Percentiles***

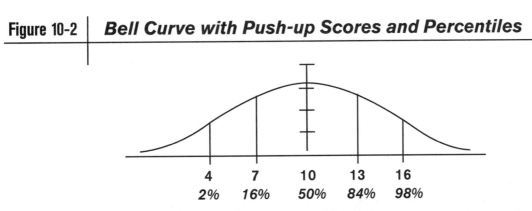

Amy completed 10 push-ups. Her raw score is 10. You know that the raw score describes the number of items correctly answered or performed. Amy performed 10 push-ups. Her raw score of 10 places her in the middle of the class. Half of the children in Amy's class did 10 push-ups or more. Half of the children did 10 push-ups or less. Amy's score places her at the 50th percentile. The term for an individual's percent level is percentile rank (PR). Amy's percentile rank is 50 (PR=50).

Erik did 13 push-ups. When you look at the bell curve in Figure 10-2, you see that Erik's score of 13 places him at the 84th percent level. Erik's percentile rank is 84 (PR=84). Erik's ability to do push-ups places him in the 84th position out of the 100 fifth graders tested on the measure of upper body strength.

Sam completed seven push-ups. His raw score of 7 places him at the (bottom) 16 percent. Sam's percentile rank is 16 (PR=16). In the sample of 100 fifth grade children, 84 children earned higher scores than Sam.

Larry completed six push-ups. You convert his raw score of 6 to a percentile rank of 9 (PR=9). You know that 91 children scored higher and eight children scored lower than Larry in upper body strength, as measured by the ability to do push-ups.

Oscar completed two push-ups. His raw score of 2 places him in the bottom 1 percent of our group of fifth graders (PR=1).

Nancy's raw score of 17 places her in the top 99 percent. You know that Nancy scored at the 99th percentile rank (PR=99).

You can see the relationship between the number of push-ups completed and the child's percentile rank (PR) in Table 10-2.

You Can Compare One Child to Many

When you use the bell curve, you can compare one child's score to those of a group of children. You can compare a single child's progress or regression to the progress of

Table 10-2 | *Push-Up Scores of Fifth Grade Students*

Child's Name	Raw Score	Percentile Rank
Oscar	3	1
Larry	6	9
Sam	7	16
Amy	10	50
Erik	13	84
Frank	15	95
Nancy	17	99

others in the child's peer group. The bell curve allows you to compare one child's score to the scores earned by older children, younger children, children in different grades, or children who attend different schools.

Let's see how this works. You will measure the children's upper body strength, as measured by the number of push-ups they can perform. You decide to expand your study to include all children in the elementary grades, from Kindergarten through fifth grade. You will assume that the average chronological age of elementary school children is eight years, zero months (CA=8-0 years).

You Can Compare Groups

After you test the third graders and analyze the data, you find that the average or mean score of the third graders is six push-ups. The average third grade child (who is 8 years old) can do six push-ups.

You ask, "How can we compare children in different groups?" Look at Larry, a member of the original group of fifth grade students. Although the average fifth grader performed 10 push-ups, Larry completed only six push-ups. You convert Larry's raw score of six to a percentile rank of 9 (PR=9).

When you compare Larry's performance to that of all elementary school students, you see that Larry is functioning at the level of the average third grader who is eight years old. This means that Larry's age equivalent score is 8 years, zero months (AE=8-0) and his grade equivalent score is third grade, zero months or beginning third grade (GE=3-0).

Find Amy in Table 10-2. When Amy was tested, she was a 10-year-old fifth grade student. Amy scored 10 push-ups, which is the mean for her peers. Amy's grade equivalent score is fifth grade (GE=5-0). Her age equivalent score is 10.0 years (AE=10-0).

Find Frank in Table 10-2. You see that Frank has a raw score of 15 push-ups. His raw score of 15 converts to a percentile rank of 95 (PR=95). Frank's score looks great, until you learn that Frank was "held back" three times! Although Frank is in the fifth grade, he is 13 years old.

You need this information about Frank's age to analyze his performance. Frank's raw score is 15. The average raw score for eighth graders (who are 13 years old) is 15. Frank has a grade equivalent score of 8th grade (GE = 8.0). His age equivalent score is 13 years (AE = 13-0).

At age 13, Frank was included in the sample of fifth graders whose average age was 10. When compared to other fifth graders, Frank scored at the 95th percentile rank (PR) level. When you compare Frank to other children in his expected grade, he scored at the 50th percentile rank. His achievement is in the average range. If you compare Frank's performance to children who are three years younger, does this provide an accurate picture of his physical fitness? No.

Frank helps you understand two important issues. First, you see that Frank performs at a superior level when compared with other children in his grade. Second, you see that Frank performs at an average level when compared with children who are the same age.

Many children with disabilities are held back or retained between kindergarten and first grade. This practice is based on the mistaken belief that early school problems are due to immaturity and will resolve if the child has an extra year to mature. In some districts, school personnel describe this practice of holding children back as "readiness." In fact, the child is retained. If your child received a year of "readiness," make sure your child's achievement levels are described as age equivalent scores, not grade equivalent scores.

Learning How Test Scores Are Reported

To understand what test data means, you need to know how scores are reported. Test scores are reported as:

- Percentile ranks
- Age equivalents
- Grade equivalents
- Raw scores
- Scale scores
- Subtest scores
- Standard scores

 To learn assessment terms, refer to the Glossary of Assessment Terms in Appendix K.

Although Frank's performance is superior for his grade, it is average for his age. If you did not know Frank's grade and age, you could easily have misinterpreted Frank's achievement.

Learning About Raw Scores

The child's raw score is the number of push-ups completed. Assume you want to get an overall fitness score for a child. To get an overall or composite score, you measure three skills: sit-ups, push-ups, and a timed 50-yard dash. The overall fitness score includes the child's scores on these three skills.

Learning About Scale Scores

Next, develop a weighting system to convert each child's raw score to a scale score. After you convert the raw scores to scale scores, you can compare each of the three scores to each other (push-ups, sit-ups, 50-yard dash). How can you convert raw scores into scale scores?

One way to convert scores is to use a rank order system. In a rank order scoring system, the child who scores highest in an event (most push-ups, most sit-ups, fastest run) receives a scale score of 100. The lowest scorer receives a scale score of 1. The remaining 98 children receive their respective "rank" as their scale score.

After the children's raw scores are converted into scale scores, it is easy to compare an individual child's performance to the group, or to all children who are of the same age or in the same grade. You can easily compare one child's performance at different times, i.e., before and after the fitness class.

☑ **Scores on standardized norm-referenced tests are reported as standard scores, percentile ranks, age equivalent scores, and grade equivalent scores.**

Learning About Composite Scores

After you develop a composite score, the child's raw scores on the different fitness subtests have less significance. This is what happens in educational and psychological tests.

Most educational and psychological tests are composed of several subtests. The scores on these subtests are combined to develop composite scores. When you rely solely on composite scores for information, you can run into problems.

Learning About Subtest Scatter

Subtest scatter is the difference between the highest and lowest subtest scores. If you find a significant amount of subtest scatter on a test, this suggests that the child has areas of strength and weakness that need to be explored. How do you know if there is significant subtest scatter?

Most subtests have a mean or average score of 10. Most children score + 3 to - 3 points from the mean of 10, so most children will score between 7 and 13.

Assume Ann was evaluated on a test that includes 10 subtests. On three subtests, she earned a score of nine. On four subtests, she earned a score of ten. On three subtests, she earned a score of eleven.

On the 10 subtests, Ann scored between 9 and 11. Subtest scatter is the difference between the highest and lowest scores. Ann's subtest scatter is 2 (11 – 9 = 2). Ann's subtest scatter is minimal. Her overall composite score is 10.

Assume that Brandon is evaluated on the same test. On four subtests, Brandon scored 10; one three subtests, he scored 16; on three subtests, he scored 4. Brandon's composite score is 10. He performed average on four subtests, very well on three subtests, and very poorly on three subtests. When you compute the difference between his highest and lowest subtest scores, you find that Brandon's subtest scatter is 12 (16 - 4 = 12).

Brandon's composite score of 10 is average. Is Brandon an average child? Because Brandon's subtest scores demonstrated significant subtest scatter, you need to know more about his weak and strong areas.

You need to understand your child's disability and how the disability affects your child's learning. You need to know what skills need to be strengthened and what strengths can be harnessed to help remediate the child's weaknesses. Tests and measurements will give you answers to these important questions.

In Summation

In this chapter, you learned about the bell curve, percentile ranks and standard scores, composite scores, and subtest scatter. You should re-read this chapter from time to time.

In the next chapter, you will learn how to use pre- and post-tests to measure progress. We describe norm-referenced and criterion-referenced tests, standard deviations, and standard scores. You will learn how to chart your child's scores and how to create progress graphs.

11 | Tests and Measurements 102

> "Underlying all assessments are a respect for children and their families, and a desire to help children. A thorough assessment should allow us to learn something about the child that we could not learn from simply talking to others about the child, observing the child, or reviewing the child's records."   —Jerome Sattler, psychologist

In this chapter, you will learn about composite scores and how to use pre- and post-tests to measure progress. You will learn about norm-referenced and criterion-referenced tests, standard deviations, and standard scores. You will learn how to convert standard scores into percentile ranks, and how to convert percentile ranks into standard scores.

You will learn what the subtests of the Wechsler Intelligence Test for Children measure. You will learn how to chart out test scores, how to use a computer to create progress and regression graphs, and how to incorporate objective scores in your child's IEP

Katie

Katie is a fourteen-year old ninth grader who is failing several subjects. Katie is angry and sullen, and wants to quit school. Katie's desperate parents take her to a child psychologist. Before the psychologist diagnoses Katie's problems and develops a treatment plan, she administers a complete comprehensive psychological and educational testing battery to Katie.

When the psychologist meets with Katie and her parents to discuss the evaluation results, she explains that Katie scored two standard deviations above the mean on the Similarities subtest of the Wechsler Intelligence Test for Children, Third Edition (WISC-III). She says Katie scored two and a half "standard deviations" below the mean on the spontaneous writing sample of the Test of Written Language, Third Edition (TOWL-III).

What do these test scores mean? Do they explain Katie's academic problems? Do they account for her moodiness and dislike of school?

You will learn more about Katie in this chapter. When you finish this chapter, you will understand the significance of Katie's two scores and you will know why Katie's self-esteem plummeted.

Learning About Composite Scores

School evaluators often use composite or cluster scores as the sole basis to determine eligibility and educational progress. Using composite scores as the sole basis to determine eligibility and progress is inappropriate and leads to poor decisions.

Test results on children are often reported as composite scores. The Wechsler Intelligence Scale for Children, Third Edition (WISC-III) is the most commonly administered test of ability. Psychologists often provide three Wechsler Intelligence Quotient (IQ) scores: Verbal IQ (VIQ), Performance IQ (PIQ), and Full Scale IQ (FSIQ).

These IQ scores are composite scores. The Verbal and Performance IQ scores are composites of five subtests, each of which measures a different area of ability. The Full Scale IQ is a composite of the Verbal and Performance IQ, so it is a composite of ten subtest scores. IQ scores that fall between 90 and 110 are within the average range, that is, between the 25th and 75th percentiles.

The Woodcock-Johnson Psycho-Educational Battery - Revised (WJ-R) and the newer Woodcock-Johnson III (WJ III ACH) are the most commonly administered individual educational achievement tests. The Woodcock-Johnson tests include several mandatory and optional subtests. These subtests are combined into composite or cluster scores. The third edition of the Woodcock-Johnson Tests includes an educational achievement portion identified by the three letters, "ACH." Similarly, the cognitive portion of the test battery, known as the Woodcock-Johnson III Tests of Cognitive Abilities is identified by "COG."

What do you know about composite scores and subtest scatter in your child's evaluations? If you rely on composite or cluster scores and do not examine your child's subtest scores, you may overlook significant strengths and serious weaknesses.

Katie is the 14-year-old you met at the beginning of this chapter. On the Wechsler Intelligence Scale for Children-III (WISC-III), Katie earned a Full Scale IQ of 101. You know that IQ scores between 90 and 110 are "average." If the only information you had was Katie's Full Scale IQ score, you would assume that Katie's IQ of 101 placed her in the "average range" of intellectual functioning. Is Katie an "average" child?

You learned that Katie's Verbal IQ is 114 and her Performance IQ is 86. If you subtract the Performance IQ score from the Verbal IQ score, you find a 28-point difference between Katie's Verbal and Performance scores.

If you did not have these two IQ scores, you might view Katie as an "average" child — and you would be mistaken. In fact, because Katie's test scores had an unusual amount of scatter, many psychologists would not report Katie's Full Scale IQ score because it is not a valid indicator of her intellectual abilities.

Katie's Verbal IQ score of 114 translates into a percentile rank of 82 (PR=82). Her Performance IQ of 86 converts to a percentile rank of 18 (PR = 18). When you look at Katie's scores as percentile ranks, you see a fluctuation of 64 points (82 –18 = 64) between her verbal and performance abilities. We will look more closely at Katie's test scores shortly.

When Apparent Progress Means Actual Regression

If you are like many parents, you do not know if your child is making real progress. You use statistics to make medical decisions and develop treatment plans. Health care professionals use objective tests to diagnose medical problems. Medical interventions are assessed with objective tests. In the last chapter, you saw how pre- and post- tests are used to make decisions about continuing, terminating, or changing a medical treatment plan.

You should apply these principles to special education decisions and planning. Use objective tests to diagnose the child's educational problems. The team of parents and school staff should develop an IEP that includes measurable goals and objectives. After a specified time, the child's progress is measured with objective tests. When you compare test results, you will know if your child is learning and making progress.

Using Pre- and Post-Testing to Measure Progress

Pre- and post-testing allows us to measure educational benefit or regression. Using scores from pre- and post-testing, we can create graphs to visually demonstrate a child's progress or regression.

To see how pre- and post-testing work, we will revisit our fifth grade fitness class. On the first test, Erik's score of 13 push-ups placed him in the top 84 percent of the group. At the end of the fitness class, the children were re-tested. Erik completed 14 push-ups on the post-test. Did Erik make progress? Yes and no.

The average performance of the fifth graders improved by two push-ups, from a raw score of 10 to a raw score of 12 push-ups. Erik's raw score improved by 1, from 13 to 14 push-ups. Erik's age equivalent and grade equivalent scores increased slightly over the first testing but his position in the group dropped from the 84th to the 75th percentile level. Although Erik is still ahead of his peers, he regressed slightly when compared to his prior rating within the peer group.

What about Sam? In Chapter 10, you learned that Sam completed seven push-ups. On the post-test, Sam's performance improved from a raw score of 7 to a raw score of 8. Sam's age equivalent and grade equivalent scores increased slightly but his position in the peer group dropped from the 16th to the 9th percentile rank. Sam continues to fall behind his peers.

Assume we test Sam again when he returns to school in the fall. We will have three sets of data (beginning 5th grade, end 5th grade, beginning 6th grade). If Sam's percentile rank continues to drop, he is regressing. How long will it take Sam to recoup the skills he lost during the summer? Regression and recoupment are key issues in determining the child's legal right to extended school year services (ESY).

Norm-Referenced and Criterion-Referenced Tests

Most educational achievement tests are norm-referenced or criterion-referenced. When we use a norm-referenced test, we analyze progress or regression by measuring changes in the child's position within the group, i.e., the norm.

When we evaluated our original group of fifth graders, we compared each child's performance to the norm group of fifth graders. Erik (raw score of 13, percentile rank of 84) and Sam (raw score of 7, percentile rank of 16) were referenced or compared to the norm group of fifth graders. We computed each child's change in position, i.e., progress or regression.

We also referenced the criteria of number of push-ups completed. A criterion-referenced test determines whether a specific criterion is met, without reference to a norm group. Assume that the criterion for success is eight push-ups. When Sam was tested at the beginning of the year, he completed seven push-ups. Sam failed to reach the criterion for success of eight push-ups. Assume that Sam received a year of physical fitness remediation. At the end of the year, Sam completed the eight push-ups. Did Sam meet the criterion for success? It depends.

Definitions for success change over time. The answer to this question depends on whether the criterion for success changes when children are one year older.

If you rely on criterion-referenced measures, you can be misled about whether your child is making progress or falling behind the peer group. When you use a criterion-referenced test, you need to know the criterion for success.

Learning About Standard Deviations

To understand test scores, you need to know the mean and standard deviation of the test. On most educational and psychological tests, the mean is 100 and the standard deviation is 15 (Mean = 100, SD = 15). On the smaller subtests within these educational and psychological tests, the mean is 10 and the standard deviation is 3 (Mean = 10, SD = 3).

For definitions of assessment terms, check Appendix K.

Average scores do not deviate far from the mean. As scores fall above or below the mean, they are a certain value or distance from the mean – for example, 1 or 2 standard deviations from the mean.

The mean is 0 (zero) standard deviations from the mean. The next markers on the bell curve from left to right are -1 and +1 standard deviations from the mean, followed by 2 standard deviations from the mean. Figure 11-1 shows standard deviations and the relationship to percentile ranks and standard scores.

Figure 11-1 | *Bell Curve: Standard Deviations and their Relationship to Percentile Ranks and Standard Scores*

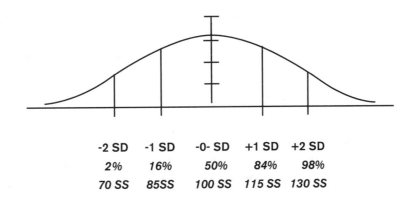

-2 SD	-1 SD	-0- SD	+1 SD	+2 SD
2%	16%	50%	84%	98%
70 SS	85SS	100 SS	115 SS	130 SS

In our original push-up test, the mean was 10 push-ups and the standard deviation (SD) was three push-ups. The push-up example in Chapter 10 uses scores that are the same as subtest scores on most educational and psychological tests.

On subtests, one standard deviation above the mean is 13 (10 + 3 = 13). One standard deviation below the mean is 7 (10 - 3 = 7). (See Figure 11-1)

One standard deviation above the mean is always at the 84 percent level (PR = 84). If a child scored 13 on a subtest, the child scored at the 84th percentile. One standard deviation below the mean is always at the 16 percent level (PR = 16). If a child scores 7 on a subtest, this score is at the 16th percentile. (See Figure 11-1)

Two standard deviations above the mean are always at the 98 percent level (PR = 98). Two standard deviations below the mean are always at the 2 percent level (PR = 2). (See Figure 11-1)

When you look at your child's test scores, you may find that the child scored one standard deviation below the mean on a test or subtest. If the score is one standard deviation below the mean, the child's percentile rank is 16.

Review the Wrightslaw Quick Rules of Tests in Table 11-1.

Table 11-1	*Wrightslaw Quick Rules of Tests*

All educational and psychological tests based on the bell curve report their scores as standard scores and percentile ranks. To interpret test results, you need to know the mean and the standard deviation of the test. Most tests use a mean of 100 and a standard deviation of 15.

When educational and psychological tests use standard scores (SS) with a mean of 100 and a standard deviation of 15, a standard score of 100 is at the 50th percentile rank (PR). A standard score of 85 is at the 16th percentile rank. A standard score of 115 is at the 84th percentile rank.

When educational and psychological tests use subtest scores with a mean of 10 and a standard deviation of 3, a subtest score of 10 is at the 50th percentile rank.

A subtest score of 7 is at the 16th percentile rank; a subtest score of 13 is at the 84th percentile rank.

A standard score of 100 is at the 50th percentile rank. One-half of children will fall above and one-half will fall below the mean at the 50th percentile, which is represented as a standard score of 100.

Two-thirds of children will score between + 1 and - 1 standard deviations from the mean.

Two-thirds (68 percent) of children will score between the 84th and 16th percentile ranks. (84 minus 16 = 68)

Half of 68 percent is 34 percent. When you subtract 34 percent from the mean of 50 percent, you have 16 percent. When you add 34 percent to the mean of 50 percent, you have 84 percent.

A standard deviation of -1 is at the 16th percentile. A standard deviation of 0 is at the 50th percentile. A standard deviation of +1 is at the 84th percentile.

A standard score of 85 is at the 16th percentile. A standard score of 100 is at the 50th percentile. A standard score of 115 is at the 84th percentile.

A standard deviation of -2 is at the 2nd percentile. A standard deviation of +2 is at the 98th percentile.

A standard score of 70 is at the 2nd percentile. A standard score of 130 is at the 98th percentile.

A standard score of 90 is at the 25th percentile. A standard score of 110 is at the 75th percentile.

One-half (50 percent) of children will score between the 75th and 25th percentiles (75 minus 25 = 50).

One-half of children will have standard scores between 90 and 110, which is within the "average range."

Learning About Standard Scores

Assume that at an IEP meeting, the school psychologist said your child had a standard score of 85 in reading and a standard score of 70 in written language. If you are like many parents, you may feel relieved. You assume these scores mean your child is "passing". Many parents believe standard scores are like grades, with 100 as the highest score and 0 as the lowest. Standard scores are not like grades!

In standard scores, the average or mean score is 100 with a standard deviation of 15. An "average child" will earn a standard score of 100. If the child scores 1 standard deviation above the mean, the child's standard score is 115 (100 + 15 = 115). If the child scores 1 standard deviation below the mean, the child's standard score is 85 (100 - 15 = 85).

Because a standard score of 115 is 1 standard deviation above the mean, it is always at the 84 percent level. Because a standard score of 85 is 1 standard deviation below the mean, it is always at the 16 percent level. A standard score of 130 (+2 SD) is always at the 98 percent level. A standard score of 70 (-2 SD) is always at the 2 percent level.

If your child has a standard score of 85 in reading, your child is functioning at the 16th percentile. If your child's standard score is 70 in written language, your child is functioning at the 2nd percentile. This information is summarized in Wrightslaw's Quick Rules of Tests. (Table 11-1)

Do you remember Katie? On the Wechsler Intelligence Scale (WISC-III), Katie earned a Full Scale IQ of 101. You learned that Katie's "average" Full Scale IQ score was misleading when you learned that her Verbal IQ score was 114 and her Performance IQ score was 86.

Katie's psychologist also found that Katie scored 2 standard deviations above the mean on the Similarities subtest of the Wechsler Intelligence Scale for Children, 3rd Revised (WISC-III). What does this mean?

You know if a score is 2 standard deviations above the mean, the score was 16, which is at the 98th percentile. The Similarities subtest of the WISC-III measures intellectual reasoning ability. If Katie scored 2 standard deviations above the mean on the Similarities subtest, her reasoning ability is at the 98th percentile.

The psychologist also found that Katie had a standard score of 68, more than 2 standard deviations below the mean, on the spontaneous writing sample of the Test of Written Language, Third Edition (TOWL-III). A score that is more than 2 standard deviations below the mean is lower than the 2nd percentile. If Katie's standard score is 68, her ability to spontaneously produce a writing sample is at the 1st percentile.

When we introduced Katie to you, we asked two questions:

- Do Katie's test scores explain the academic problems Katie is having?
- Do Katie's test scores help us understand her moodiness and dislike of school?

Table 11-2 | *Conversion Table: Standard Scores and Percentile Ranks*

Standard Score	Subtest Score	Percentile Rank
145	19	>99
140	18	>99
135	17	99
130	16	98
125	15	95
120	14	91
115	13	84
110	12	75
109	–	73
108	–	70
107	–	68
106	–	66
105	11	63
104	–	61
103	–	58
102	–	55
101	–	53
100	10	50
99	–	47
98	–	45
97	–	42
96	–	39
95	9	37
94	–	34
93	–	32
92	–	30
91	–	27
90	8	25
89	–	23
88	–	21
87	–	19
86	–	18
85	7	16
80	6	9
75	5	5
70	4	2
65	3	1
60	2	<1
55	1	>1

Katie's reasoning ability is at the 98th percentile. Her ability to convey her thoughts in writing is below the 1st percentile. If Katie is very bright but cannot convey her ideas or knowledge on written assignments and tests, would you expect her to feel frustrated and stupid? Do you understand why Katie is angry, depressed, and wants to quit school?

The results of most educational and psychological tests are reported in standard scores. You need to learn how to convert standard scores into percentile ranks. You can use Table 11-2 to convert standard scores into percentile ranks and percentile ranks into standard scores.

Learning About Subtest Scores

On the Wechsler Intelligence Scale for Children, the Verbal and Performance IQ scores are composites or averages of different subtests, with each subtest measuring different abilities.

When we presented Katie's test results, you learned that variation among the subtest scores (subtest scatter) is a valuable source of information. Look at Katie's Wechsler subtest scores in Table 11-3.

On the Wechsler Intelligence Scale for Children, subtest scores range from a low score of 1 to a high score of 19. Wechsler subtest scores have a mean of 10 and a standard deviation of 3. A subtest score of 7 is one standard deviation below the mean (-1 SD). By using the Conversion Table (Table 11-2), you can convert a subtest score of 7 to a percentile rank of 16 (PR = 16).

Table 11-3	**Katie's Subtest Scores on the Wechsler Intelligence Scale, 3rd Edition (WISC-III)**

Verbal Subtests	Score	Performance Subtests	Score
Information	10	Picture Completion	6
Similarities	16	Coding	4
Arithmetic	11	Picture Arrangement	10
Vocabulary	13	Block Design	12
Comprehension	12	Objective Assembly	7
(Digit Span)	8	(Symbol Search)	6
		Verbal IQ = 114	
		Performance IQ = 86	
		Full Scale IQ = 101	

When you look at Katie's subtest scores, you see that she has significant subtest scatter, from a high score of 16 on Similarities (98th percentile) to a low score of 4 on Coding (2nd percentile). You know that subtest scatter is the difference between the highest and lowest subtest scores. Subtract the lowest score of 4 (Coding) from the highest score of 16 (Similarities). Katie's subtest scatter is 12 (16 – 4 = 12).

You need to know what these subtests measure. When we discussed Katie's subtest scores earlier, you learned that the Similarities subtest is correlated with abstract reasoning ability. The Coding subtest measures visual-perceptual mechanics. Jerome Sattler describes the Coding subtest as "an information processing task that involves the discrimination and memory of visual pattern symbols." He also explains "A child with visual defects or specific motor disabilities may be penalized on this subtest. Generally, do not give the subtest to a child with either of these disabilities. If you give it, do not count it in the final score." He also notes that a left handed child is often penalized on the Coding subtest because the child will "have to lift his hand repeatedly during the task to view" the tested items. The right-handed child does not.

Katie's could excel in discussions of complex literature in an honors English class because of her reasoning abilities but she could not write what she knows. Since Katie could not write what she knew, she was placed in slow-paced remedial classes. Because her abilities were untapped, Katie concluded that she was stupid and wanted to quit school.

When you look at Katie's scores, you see that (Digit Span) and (Symbol Search) scores are in parentheses. On the WISC-III, the Digit Span, Symbol Search and Mazes subtest scores are not included in the Verbal, Performance and Full Scale IQ scores. These subtests are used for other composite scores.

Table 11-4	**Wechsler Intelligence Scale for Children-III (WISC-III)** **Subtests** (Source: The Psychological Assessment Resources, Inc.)

Subtest	Ability Measured
Information	Factual knowledge, long-term memory, recall
Similarities	Abstract reasoning, verbal categories and concepts
Arithmetic	Attention and concentration, numerical reasoning
Vocabulary	Language development, word knowledge, verbal fluency
Comprehension	Social and practical judgment, common sense
Digit Span	Short-term auditory memory, concentration
Picture Completion	Alertness to detail, visual discrimination
Coding	Visual-motor coordination, speed, concentration
Picture Arrangement	Planning, logical thinking, social knowledge
Block Design	Spatial analysis, abstract visual problem-solving
Object Assembly	Visual analysis and construction of objects
Symbol Search	Visual-motor quickness, concentration, persistence
Mazes	Fine motor coordination, planning, following directions

☑ When subtest scores are in (parentheses), the scores are not computed in the composite score.

Test Categories and Descriptions

Tests administered to children fall into several categories: intellectual or cognitive tests; educational achievement tests; projective personality tests, questionnaires and surveys; speech and language tests; and neuropsychological tests.

☞ **For information about tests, check the *Test Locator* on the ERIC site: www.ericae.net/.**

The *Test Locator* is a joint project of the ERIC Clearinghouse on Assessment and Evaluation, the Library and Reference Services Division of the Educational Testing Service, the Buros Institute of Mental Measurements at the University of Nebraska in Lincoln, the Region III Comprehensive Center at GW University, and Pro-Ed test publishers. This site has information on more than 10,000 tests and research instruments. After you review the material at ERIC/AE, visit the test publisher's website for more information about a specific test.

Two of the most commonly used tests for children are the Wechsler Intelligence Scale for Children (WISC-III) and the Woodcock-Johnson achievement tests. The Psychological Corporation publishes the Wechsler Intelligence Scale for Children

☞ **The Psychological Corporation site: www.psychcorp.com/.**

The Riverside Publishing publishes the Woodcock-Johnson Tests. Riverside Publishing site: www.riverpub.com/

By the time you read this chapter, new versions or editions will have replaced some of these tests. Like the law, tests are always changing.

Intellectual or Cognitive Tests

The most commonly used intellectual or cognitive tests are the Wechsler Intelligence Scale for Children, Third Edition (WISC-III) and the Stanford-Binet Intelligence Scale – Fourth Edition (SB:FE).

Wechsler Intelligence Scale for Children (WISC-III)

The WISC-III provides an estimate of the child's level of functioning. The Full Scale IQ is a measure of general intelligence, scholastic aptitude, and readiness to master school skills. The Verbal Scale measures verbal comprehension and the ability to process verbal information. The Performance Scale measures perceptual organization, the ability to think in visual images and interpret visual information quickly. Table 11-4 lists the thirteen Wechsler subtests with a brief statement about what each subtest measures.

The child's scores can be affected by many factors, including motivation, cultural opportunities, and attention span.

When psychologists interpret scores, they should consider other information, including previous or current assessment results, the child's developmental and educational history, health, and other situational factors.

If there is a significant difference between the Verbal and Performance IQ Scales, the Full Scale IQ may not accurately represent the child's level of functioning. Some experts believe that the WISC-III is not the best test to evaluate children who function at very high or very low levels.

Stanford-Binet, Fourth Edition (SB:IV)

The Stanford-Binet includes 15 subtests that measure verbal reasoning, abstract/visual reasoning, quantitative reasoning, and short-term memory. Some experts believe the Stanford-Binet (SB:IV) is not the best test to assess giftedness.

 When a child's IQ score declines, this is usually because a head injury, tumor, test scoring error, or an inappropriate education.

Educational Achievement Tests

Educational achievement tests measure the academic skills children acquire through instruction – reading, mathematics, spelling, writing, vocabulary, science and social studies.

Screening Tests

There are two types of achievement tests: screening tests and comprehensive tests. Screening tests assess reading, math, and spelling frequently with just one subtest per skill area. Screening tests are brief tests used to determine whether the child should be evaluated on a comprehensive test. Examples of screening tests are the Wide Range Achievement Test – 3 (WRAT-3) and the Wechsler Individual Achievement Test – Screener (WIAT – Screener).

Comprehensive Achievement Tests

Comprehensive achievement tests assess three or more subject areas. Examples include the Wechsler Individual Achievement Test – Comprehensive Test (WIAT) with 8 subtests and the Woodcock-Johnson III Tests of Achievement (WJ III ACH) with 23 subtests. The three subject areas evaluated in most educational achievement tests are reading, writing and mathematics.

Comprehensive tests are divided into two categories: multiple-subject tests and single-subject tests. School psychologists and special educators are more likely to use multiple-subject tests that provide information about the basic skills of reading, writing and mathematics.

Other frequently administered educational achievement tests include the Kaufman Test of Educational Achievement (K-TEA) and the Peabody Individual Achievement Test (PIAT-R).

Single-Subject Tests

Single-subject tests include several subtests that measure different skills in one broad area. Single-subject tests allow the evaluator to obtain more information about the child's strengths and weaknesses in a specific area.

The Woodcock Reading Mastery Tests-Revised (WRMT-R) includes six subtests that measure different reading skills. The KeyMath-Revised test includes 13 subtests that measure basic math concepts, operations, and applications. The Gray Oral Reading Test, Third Edition (GORT 3) is a single subject test that focuses on the ability to read a passage of text aloud.

Personality Tests

Children experience frustration and unhappiness when they cannot succeed in school. Personality tests are designed to assess the child's mental state, degree of anxiety, and areas of stress.

Personality tests can show that a child who is viewed as "emotionally disturbed," is often a reasonably healthy child who is intensely frustrated because of chronic school failure.

Projective personality tests include:

- Children's Apperception Test (CAT)
- Draw-a-Person (DAP)
- House-Tree-Person (H-T-P)
- Kinetic Family Drawing
- Thematic Apperception Test (TAT)

Objective personality tests include:

- Minnesota Multiphasic Personality Inventory for Adolescents (MMPI-A)
- Millon Adolescent Clinical Inventory (MACI)

Behavior Rating Scales

Surveys and questionnaires provide norm-reference data about the child's behavior, how the child sees himself or herself, and how parents and teachers view the child.

Commonly administered questionnaires include the Conners' Rating Scales and the Vineland Adaptive Behavior Scales (VBAS). Conner's includes questionnaires for parents and teachers that focus on attention, impulsivity, and social problems associated with ADHD. The Vineland focuses on communication, daily living skills, socialization, and motor skills.

Speech and Language Tests

Commonly used speech and language tests include:

- Test of Language Development (TOLD-3)
- Clinical Evaluation of Language Fundamentals–Third Edition (CELF-3)

- Peabody Picture Vocabulary Test-Revised (PPVT-3)
- Test of Written Language (TOWL-3)

Neuropsychological Tests

Neuropsychological tests assess specific neurological issues that affect learning. Children who have difficulty processing information and have significant scatter may benefit from a neuropsychological evaluation. A comprehensive neuropsychological evaluation can be especially valuable if a child's eligibility for special education is disputed.

Charting Test Scores

Assume that three years ago, your child was tested with the Woodcock Johnson Psychoeducational Battery (WJ-R). In word identification, your child scored at the 10% level. In passage comprehension, the child scored at the 60% level. The child's composite reading score was 35%.

Recently, your child was reevaluated with the same form of the Woodcock-Johnson test. On word identification, your child scored at the 5% level. On passage comprehension, the child scored at the 45% level. The child's composite reading score was 25%.

With these test results, you may conclude that your child needs a different, more intensive reading remediation program. The school may refuse because your child's composite reading score falls within the "average range." What can you do?

Creating Progress and Regression Charts

You can use test scores to create progress or regression graphs or charts. If you use a computer that has a spreadsheet program like Microsoft Excel, the program has a wizard that creates graphs.

Graphs of your child's test scores are important tools. Use pre- and post-test scores to make graphs of progress or regression. You can use the same data to make different types of graphs and charts. When you use a computer to make graphs, it is easy to change the display mode for your graphs (i.e., line and bar, portrait and landscape) Try different modes to find one that has a strong visual impact.

Visit the Fetaweb.com site to view a PowerPoint presentation about graphs

When parents use graphs, they can often convince school personnel that the child needs a more intensive remediation program. The school may provide these services. On occasion, schools have reimbursed parents who paid for these services.

☑ **For more information about reimbursement, see 20 U. S. C. § 1412a(10) in Chapter 16 and the *Burlington* and *Carter* cases in *Wrightslaw: Special Education Law.***

Table 11-5	*Parent's Homework Assignment*

1. Read these chapters about tests and measurement several times.

Use a highlighter or make margin notes to help you learn the information.

2. Make a list of all tests that have been given to your child. Arrange the list in chronological order.

Look for test results as standard scores and percentile ranks. Test scores may be reported as "ranges" (i.e., high-average, low-average) or as grade equivalent or age equivalent scores. If standard scores are not included in the evaluation, ask the school to provide this information. When you request your child's test data as standard scores, the school should comply with your request.

3. List all tests given more than once.

Using your list, make a new list of all tests that have been given more than once. The repeated tests will probably include the Wechsler Intelligence Scale, the Woodcock-Johnson, the Wechsler Individual Achievement Tests (WIAT), and/or the Kaufman Educational Achievement Tests.

4. Convert the standard scores into percentile ranks.

Make a list of the standard scores on the first test. Using the conversion chart in Table 11-2, convert the standard scores to percentile ranks. Make a list of the standard scores from the most recent test. Convert these standard scores to percentile ranks.

5. Compare scores.

When you compare the test results, you should know if your child is catching up (being remediated), staying in the same position, or falling behind (regression)

6. Make graphs of scores.

Find areas where your child has regressed or made minimal progress. Chart these test results. If you have a computer, software programs like MS Excel and PowerPoint have "wizards" that will help you set up your graphs. With these software programs, you can make dramatic visual presentations of the test data. If you do not have a computer, you can use graph paper and colored markers to make graphs.

7. Consult with an independent expert.

Make an appointment to meet with the independent psychologist or educational diagnostician who evaluated your child. Gather your information – your list of test scores, the standard score/percentile rank conversion chart, the bell curve chart, and your child's evaluations – and take the information to your meeting.

Ask the private sector expert to use the bell curve chart with standard scores, standard deviations and percentile ranks to teach you about your child's test scores. Make a copy of the bell curve chart. If possible, it will be useful to tape-record the session so you can review it later along with the bell curve chart and test scores.

Using Test Scores in Your Child's IEPs

Assume that your child's IEP includes a keyboarding goal. The IEP goal purports to "measure" the child's progress by "teacher observation" with an 80 percent success rate. How can you write an IEP goal for keyboarding that includes objective scores?

By December 2001, the child will type 15 words-per-minute, with one word-per-minute deducted for each error, on a 5-minute timed typing test of text.

By June 2002, the child will type 30 words-per-minute, with five words per minute deducted for each error, on a 5-minute timed typing test of text.

This goal includes "Appropriate objective criteria and evaluation procedures and schedules, for determining, on at least an annual basis, whether the short-term instructional objectives are being achieved." (34 C.F.R. Section 300.346). You will learn more about IEP goals in Chapter 12.

Your Homework Assignment

Read your Homework Assignment in Table 11-5. After you make a list of tests given to your child, select tests that have been given more than once. Using the Conversion Table (Table 11-2), convert the repeated test scores from standard scores to percentile ranks. When you compare these scores, you should be able to tell if your child is making progress or regressing.

In Summation

In this chapter, you learned how to use pre- and post-tests to measure progress. You learned about norm-referenced and criterion-referenced tests, standard deviations, and standard scores. You learned how to convert standard scores into percentile ranks, and percentile ranks into standard scores.

You learned what the subtests of the Wechsler Intelligence Test for Children measure. You learned how to chart test scores and how to create progress graphs. You learned how to include test scores in your child's IEP. You finished your Homework Assignment.

In the next chapter, you will learn about SMART IEPs that are specific, measurable, use action words, are realistic, and time-limited. You will learn how to use your child's test scores to write present levels of performance and how to write measurable goals and objectives.

12 | SMART IEPs

"If you're not sure where you're going, you're liable to end up someplace else. If you don't know where you're going, the best made maps won't help you get there."

—Robert Mager, psychologist, writer, educator

If you are like many parents, you feel anxious and insecure at IEP meetings. What do you know? What can you offer? What should you do?

Some parents believe that if they are not educators, they have nothing of value to offer in planning their child's educational program. Other parents realize that their child's IEP is not appropriate but do not know how to resolve the problem. Diane belongs to this group. She told us:

I do not think my son's IEP is appropriate. The only goal is 'Commitment to academic success.' I imagine 'Commitment to academic success' is appropriate for all students. If 'Commitment to academic success' is not appropriate, what should I propose?

How are measurable goals, objectives, and benchmarks defined? Can you give me an example of a well-written IEP? (Diane, parent of 15-year-old special education student)

Diane represents countless parents who are confused about IEP goals and objectives. If you are the parent of a child with a disability, you are probably confused too.

How do you write IEP goals and objectives? Do you agree with Diane when she says, "Commitment to academic success is not an appropriate goal?"

Learning About SMART IEPs

The term SMART IEPs" describes IEPs that are specific, measurable, use action words, are realistic and relevant, and time-limited.

S   Specific

M   Measurable

A   Use Action Words

R   Realistic and relevant

T   Time-limited

Let's examine each of these concepts.

Specific

SMART IEPs have specific goals and objectives. Specific goals and objectives describe each behavior and skill that will be taught, and define each skill or behavior in ways that are observable and measurable.

Measurable

SMART IEPs have measurable goals and objectives. Measurable goals and objectives allow you to assess the child's progress. When you use measurable goals and objectives, you know when a goal is reached and when a skill is mastered. If you establish a goal to lose 25 pounds, you will use scales to measure your progress.

Action Words

SMART IEPs use action words like: "The child will be able to . . . "

Realistic and Relevant

SMART IEPs have realistic, relevant goals and objectives. SMART goals and objectives address the child's unique needs that result from the child's disability. SMART IEP goals are not based on district curricula, state or district tests, or other external standards.

Time-limited

SMART IEP goals and objectives are time-limited. Time-limited goals and objectives enable you to monitor progress at regular intervals.

Assume your child is learning to type. Here is a SMART goal for typing:

At the end of the first semester, Mark will touch-type a passage of text at a speed of 20 words per minute, with no more than 10 errors, with progress measured on a five-minute timed test.

At the end of the second semester, Mark will touch-type a passage of text at a speed of 40 words per minute, with no more than 5 errors, with progress measured on a five-minute timed test.

Smart IEP Goals and Objectives

Begin by analyzing your child's present levels of performance. The present levels of performance describe "areas of need arising from the child's disability." The present levels of performance tell you what the child knows and is able to do.

Using information from the present levels of performance about what your child knows and is able to do, write a statement about what the child will learn and be able to do. Your SMART goal will focus on performance and observable behavior. Break the goal down into objectives that describe what the child will learn and be able to do. Focus on performance and observable behavior.

Present Levels of Performance

The present levels of educational performance include data from objective tests, including "criterion-referenced tests, standard achievement tests, diagnostic tests, or any combination of the above." (*Appendix A*, Question 1)

If your child has reading problems, the present levels of performance should include reading subtest scores. If your child has math problems, the present levels of performance should include math subtest scores.

The federal special education regulations describe how IEPs should be developed:

In developing each child's IEP, the IEP team shall consider:

(i) The strengths of the child and the concerns of the parents for enhancing the education of their child;

(ii) The results of the initial or most recent evaluation of the child; and

(iii) As appropriate, the results of the child's performance on any general State or district-wide assessment programs.

The IEP must include:

(1) A statement of the child's present levels of educational performance, including

(i) How the child's disability affects the child's involvement and progress in the general curriculum (i.e., the same curriculum as for nondisabled children); or

(ii) For preschool children, as appropriate, how the disability affects the child's participation in appropriate activities . . ." (See Chapter 17 about IEPs)

When you read *Appendix A* to the special education regulations (see Appendix A to this book), you will learn that:

In assessing children with disabilities, school districts may use a variety of assessment techniques to determine the extent to which these children can be involved and progress in the general curriculum, such as criterion-referenced tests, standard achievement tests, diagnostic tests, other tests, or any combination of the above.

The purpose of using these assessments is to determine the child's present levels of educational performance and areas of need arising from the child's disability so that approaches for ensuring the child's involvement and progress in the general curriculum and any needed adaptations or modifications to that curriculum can be identified. (*Appendix A*, Question 1)

The term "**performance**" describes what the child can do. What are your child's present levels of performance? Do you know what your child's standard scores, percentile rank, grade equivalent and age equivalent scores mean? (If you completed the Homework Assignment in Chapter 11, you will be able to answer these questions.)

Definitions: Goals, Objectives and Benchmarks

You have learned that your child's IEP must include measurable annual goals, benchmarks and short-term objectives. Let's define these terms.

Goal: ambition, aim, mark, objective, target

Objective: something toward which effort is directed: an aim, goal, or end of action

Benchmark: point of reference from which measurements may be made; something that serves as a standard by which others may be measured or judged; a standardized problem or test that serves as a basis for evaluation or comparison (*Merriam-Webster's Collegiate Dictionary*)

Legal Definitions: Goals, Objectives and Benchmarks

Your child's IEP must include "a statement of measurable annual goals, including benchmarks or short-term objectives" that relate to "meeting the child's needs that result from the child's disability . . ."

How do the law and regulations define these terms?

Objectives: short-term objectives break "the skills described in the annual goal down into discrete components."

Benchmark: a benchmark describes "the amount of progress the child is expected to make within specified segments of the year . . . benchmarks establish expected performance levels that allow for regular checks of progress within specified segments of the year." (*Appendix A*, Question 1)

Generally, benchmarks establish expected performance levels that allow for regular checks of progress that coincide with the reporting periods for informing parents of their child's progress toward achieving the annual goals. (*Appendix A*, Question 1)

☑ Read *Appendix A* before IEP meetings.

Appropriate Goals and Objectives: Acquiring Basic Skills

IEP goals and objectives should focus on the acquisition of basic skills. What are basic skills? Basic skills help the child become independent and self-sufficient:

- Be able to communicate
- Acquire social skills; be able to interact with other people
- Be able to read

The child must learn to communicate. Most children will communicate by expressive and receptive speech. Some children use assistive technology to communicate. The child must learn social skills so he or she can interact with other people. In addition to communication and social skills, the child must learn to read. Generally, between Kindergarten and third grade, children learn to read. After third grade, children read to learn.

IEP goals and objectives should:

- Meet the child's needs that result from the disability;
- Enable the child to be involved in and progress in the general curriculum;

- Meet the child's other educational needs that result from the child's disability. (*Appendix A*, Introduction)

You use benchmarks and short-term objectives to assess your child's progress. Your child's progress should be assessed objectively and often. When you assess performance, you observe whether your child has mastered a skill or can perform a task.

Your child's IEP must include "a statement of measurable annual goals, including benchmarks or short-term objectives, related to—

(i) meeting the child's needs that result from the child's disability to enable the child to be involved in and progress in the general curriculum; and

(ii) meeting each of the child's other educational needs that result from the child's disability. (34 C.F.R. § 300.347(a)(2). (See Chapter 17 for the law about IEPs)

Measuring and Monitoring the Child's Progress

The law requires IEP teams to write "measurable annual goals, including benchmarks or short-term objectives." Measurable goals enable you to know if your child is making progress.

The IEP team:

(2) must develop either measurable, intermediate steps (short-term objectives) or major milestones (benchmarks) that will enable parents, students, and educators to monitor progress during the year . . . (*Appendix A*, Question 1)

Advising the Parent About Child's Progress

Did you know that the school must inform you about your child's educational progress at regular intervals? In fact, your child's IEP must include:

A statement of –

(i) How the child's progress toward the annual goals . . . will be measured; and

(ii) How the child's parents will be regularly informed (by such means as periodic report cards), at least as often as parents are informed of their nondisabled children's progress, of –

(A) their child's progress toward the annual goals, and

(B) the extent to which that progress is sufficient to enable the child to achieve the goals by the end of the year. (*Appendix A*, Question 1)

Reviewing and Revising the Child's IEP

Your child's IEP team must meet at least once a year to "review the child's educational progress." As your child grows and changes, your child's educational needs also change. The IEP should be revised as often as necessary. You can request a meeting to revise the IEP at any time.

The IEP team must revise the child's IEP to address —

(i) any lack of expected progress toward the annual goals . . . and in the general curriculum, if appropriate . . . (34 C.F.R. § 300.343(c)(2))

Learning to Write SMART Goals and Objectives

Are you still confused about SMART IEP goals and objectives? If you believe a parent cannot develop SMART goals and objectives, it is time to change your beliefs!

Change the facts. Assume that like many parents, inactivity and stress have caused you to gain weight. This extra weight came on gradually — so gradually that you did not realize how much weight you had gained until you went to the doctor for a checkup. When you weighed in, you discovered that you gained 50 pounds since your last checkup three years ago!

Your doctor has more bad news. You are "borderline diabetic" and your blood pressure is high. You must lose weight and change your lifestyle. If you do not take action, you are at risk to develop serious health problems within the next few years. When you go back to work, you think about what the doctor said. What can you do? You have been on fad diets. You lost weight but the loss was always temporary. When you went off the diet, you gained even more weight. You are worried and distracted. Fifty pounds!

Your friend Marie asks, "What's wrong?" You explain. Marie tells you that several of her friends used the Weight Watchers® Program to lose weight. She explains that Weight Watchers is not a crash-diet or fad. You hit the Internet and find the Weight Watchers web site.

When you explore the Weight Watchers site, you learn that their weight loss programs are based on sound research. Their medical advisors include specialists in endocrinology, diabetes, nutrition, clinical and health psychology, and exercise physiology.

The SMART Weight Loss Program

You decide to use WeightWatchers® as the basis of a SMART Weight Loss Program that is tailored to your unique needs as an overweight, stressed-out parent. Your SMART Weight Loss Program will include long-term goals and short-term objectives that are specific, measurable, use action words, are realistic, relevant, and time-limited.

Present Levels

You are 5 feet, 5 inches tall and weigh 190 pounds. Your doctor wants you to lose 50 pounds. You check the height-weight chart on the Weight Watchers site at www.weightwatchers.com. According to this chart, you should weigh between 138 and 144 pounds. You check the Body Mass Index (BMI) to find out how much weight you should lose. You plug your height (5 feet, 5 inches) and weight (190 pounds) into the Body Mass Index (Table 12-1).

TABLE 12.1 | *Body Mass Index (Courtesy of Weight Watchers International)*

Number	Interpretation
19 or under	Is considered underweight. A weight loss plan is not suggested.
20 to 25	Is the healthy range for adults
26-30	Is considered overweight – people in this range are at an increased risk for disease.
30 or more	Is considered obese – people in this range are at a great risk for disease.

Your BMI is 32. A number of 30 or more "is considered obese – people in this range are at great risk for disease."

Measurable Goals and Objectives

If you lose 50 pounds, you will weigh 140 pounds. When you plug "140 pounds" into the Body Mass Index, the BMI is 23. A number between 20 and 25 is "in the healthy range for adults." You are on the right track.

You learn that WeightWatchers® uses a "1-2-3 Success Plan." With the "1-2-3 Success Plan," your first goal is to lose 10% of your present weight in 12 weeks. This sounds like a good plan.

Long-term Goal: I will lose 50 pounds in nine months.

Short-term Objective: I will lose 19 pounds (10% of my present weight) in 12 weeks.

Are your goals and objectives specific, measurable, use action words, realistic, relevant, and time-limited? Yes!

An independent observer can quickly look at the data and determine if you are progressing toward your goal. The independent observer can assess and understand the data without interviewing you or Weight Watchers' staff. Subjective feelings and beliefs about progress have no place in our own Weight Watchers' IEPs.

Because it is important to measure progress objectively and often, you attend WeightWatchers® meetings once a week. Every week, a coach measures your weight and teaches you strategies to help you meet your goal. Because your weight is measured objectively, you know exactly how much weight you have lost and how much weight you have to lose. This is criterion-referenced data, not norm-referenced data. The criteria for success are to lose 19 pounds in 12 weeks.

Revising Your Goals and Objectives

Assume you lose 19 pounds in 12 weeks. At the end of 12 weeks, you weigh 171 pounds. You need to lose 31 pounds to reach your goal of 140 pounds. If you continue at the rate of 1.5 pounds a week, you will reach your goal in about 20 weeks. You revise your goal:

Long-term Goal: I will lose 31 pounds in 20 weeks.

Short-term Objective: I will lose 16 pounds in 10 weeks. At the end of 10 weeks, my weight will be 155 pounds.

You are successful. In 10 weeks, you weigh 155 pounds. To reach your goal of 140 pounds, you must lose 15 pounds. You revise your goal again.

Goal & Objective: I will lose 15 pounds in 10 weeks. At the end of 10 weeks, my weight will be 140 pounds.

Are your goals and objectives specific, measurable, use action words, are realistic, and time-limited? Yes!

You designed the SMART Weight Loss Program to measure your progress objectively and often. When you broke your long-term goal down into short-term objectives, you gained control over the process. When you met the first objective of losing 10% of your body weight in 12 weeks, you realized that you could complete this weight loss program successfully.

You used SMART IEP principles to develop a SMART Weight Loss Program. Your SMART Weight Loss Program includes specific, measurable, active, realistic, time-limited goals and objectives.

Using Objective Data

When a doctor develops a treatment plan for a sick child, the doctor uses objective data from diagnostic tests. Medical specialists use objective data to measure the effectiveness of treatment plans. You want your doctor to use objective data to analyze the effectiveness of a treatment program, not subjective feelings and beliefs.

Your child's IEP is similar to a medical treatment plan. The IEP includes:

- Present levels of performance from objective tests and assessments
- Measurable goals and objectives
- A plan to address the child's educational problems
- A statement of how the child's progress will be measured

Making Decisions

You are a member of your child's IEP team. The IEP team must identify and define your child's problems before the team can develop an appropriate educational plan.

The IEP team will gather information from different sources. This information may include observations of your child in different environments, including the home and classroom. This information includes objective test data that describes your child's problems, the severity of the problems, and measure your child's progress or lack of progress.

Let's look at a medical problem to see how progress should be assessed. Your son John complains that his throat is sore. His throat is red. His skin is hot to the touch. He is sleepy and lethargic. When you take John to the doctor, his temperature is 104 degrees. Lab tests show that John has an elevated white count. A strep test is positive. According to these tests, John has a strep infection.

Your doctor uses this objective test data to develop a treatment plan. When you return for a follow-up visit, the doctor is likely to order more tests. You need objective tests to know if John's infection is under control. Similarly, you need objective tests to know that your child is acquiring reading, writing and arithmetic skills.

Measuring Progress

Jay is an eight-year-old boy who received special education services for two years, beginning in kindergarten. Jay's parents felt that he was not learning how to read and write like other children his age. The school personnel assured the parents that Jay was making progress.

After two years, a child psychologist in the private sector tested Jay. While Jay's abilities were in the average to above average range, his reading and language skills were at the kindergarten level. Despite two years of special education, Jay had not learned to read or write.

When a teacher says a child is making progress, the teacher is offering an opinion based on subjective observations. In many cases, teacher opinions and subjective observations are not accurate. If you have concerns about your child's progress, get independent testing of your child's reading, writing, and mathematics skills by an expert in the private sector. These test results will tell you if your child is making progress.

Is your child receiving passing grades? Can you rely on grades to measure progress? No. Grades are not objective assessments of progress. Many factors influence grades, including effort, attendance, behavior, and attitude.

You say, "The IEP for my child does not include objective measures of progress. How can the IEP be written differently? How can I tell if my child is actually making progress?"

Mike Trains for the Fitness Test

Change the facts. Your eight-year-old son, Mike, is upset because he did not pass the President's Physical Fitness Test. He wants to pass the test next year and asks for your help.

To pass the President's Physical Fitness Test, your child must meet specific criteria. Your child's performance on fitness skills is measured objectively. You check Mike's scores. He ran the 50-yard dash within the specified time. He completed only 12 out of an expected 25 sit-ups and could not complete a single pull-up.

You and Mike know what he needs to do to qualify for the President's Physical Fitness Award. You help him design a SMART training program with goals and objectives that target his weak areas (i.e. sit-ups, pull-ups) and maintain or improve his running ability.

When Mike takes the Fitness Test, his performance on the test is measured objectively. His running speed over a specified distance is measured with a stopwatch. His ability to do the required number of sit-ups and pull-ups is measured by counting. Because these measurements are objective, anyone who observes Mike will know if he meets the criteria for the Physical Fitness Award. The observer will focus on the outcome of the educational program, not the process of Mike's program.

Kevin Learns to Type

Let's look at a goal that evaluates the child's progress subjectively. We will revise the goal to make it a SMART goal that is specific, measurable, uses action words, is realistic and relevant, and time-limited. Kevin will learn to type.

The school's proposed IEP says that Kevin will acquire keyboarding skills. Kevin's progress will be assessed by "Teacher Judgment," "Teacher Observation" or "Teacher-made Tests" with a score of "80%" as the criteria for success. The school's goal does not include words per minute or an error rate.

After we revise the goal to make it specific, measurable, active, realistic, relevant, and time-limited, the goal reads:

By the end of the first semester, Kevin will touch-type a passage of text at a rate of 15 words per minute with no more than 10 errors on a 5-minute test.

By the end of this academic year, Kevin will touch type a passage of text at a rate of 35 words per minute with no more than five errors on a 5-minute test.

Megan Learns to Read

Meet Megan, a fifth grader who has not learned to read. Megan's reading decoding skills are at the 10th percentile level. How will Megan's parents know if she is benefiting from the special education program? If Megan receives an appropriate education, her scores on reading subtests will improve.

According to Megan's SMART IEP goal:

> *After one year of specialized instruction, Megan will be able to decode words at the 25th percentile level as measured by the decoding score of the Gray Oral Reading Test-Diagnostic (GORT-D).*

When Megan's reading skills reach the 25th percentile level, she is making progress. Her progress will be measured with standardized tests. Megan's next IEP will include new goals and objectives to bring her reading skills up to the level of her peers.

Non-Goals: Attitude Statements

Earlier in this chapter, Diane asked if "commitment to academic success" was an appropriate goal. IEPs often include attitude statements (i.e., "have a good attitude," "display a cooperative spirit," or "develop healthy peer relationships").

You cannot measure an attitude. An attitude is a state of mind that exists within an individual. Attitudes are not measurable, nor are attitudes observable to outsiders.

You must be able to describe an outcome to know if the goal has been met. How will you know if an attitude goal is met? Can you measure Johnny's "better attitude?" No. Can you observe "commitment to academic success?" No.

Perhaps we agree that Johnny has a better attitude. On what do we base our opinions? Dr. Robert Mager, author of books about goal analysis and measuring educational outcomes, explains that we base our opinions on circumstantial evidence.

We use circumstantial evidence to decide if Johnny's attitude has improved. If Johnny displays behaviors that we associate with a good attitude, we conclude that Johnny's attitude has improved. Examples: Johnny smiles often. Johnny stopped yelling at the teacher and his classmates. Johnny offers to help others. These are concrete observations, not subjective beliefs.

Strategies: How to Deal with Attitude Goals

Assume that the IEP team proposes an "attitude goal" for your child's IEP. What can you do? If you tell the team that they cannot measure an attitude, they may conclude that you have a bad attitude!

Use the **Columbo Strategy**. Ask questions —"5 Ws + H + E" questions. (Who, What, Why, Where, When, How, and Explain.) Tell the school staff that you are confused. You want to ask a stupid question. (Do you see why we call this the "Columbo Strategy?")

Ask, "How will we **know** that Johnny has a better attitude?"

From the team members' comments, you can make a list of **behaviors**. What behaviors will they observe? Who will observe these behaviors? When? How often? As you continue to ask questions, the team members will make statements that describe observable behavior—circumstantial evidence.

Assume your son Johnny has behavior problems in class. The IEP team proposes to change Johnny's behavior. You agree that this is an appropriate goal. You have concerns about the educators' ability to devise clear goals and objectives. What can you do?

Use the Columbo Strategy. Ask questions. What is Johnny doing? How often? When? Ask more questions. Listen attentively to the answers. You may observe that your team begins to describe observations of your child's behavior. If you use "5 Ws + H + E" questions skillfully, you may be able to help school personnel shift from feelings and beliefs to facts and observations.

Assume the teacher says, "Johnny pinches his classmates at least two times an hour." Good! Now you have data. You have Johnny's present levels of performance in pinching to use as a starting point.

You ask, "What change in Johnny's pinching behavior do we seek?"

The teacher may say, "Johnny should never pinch anyone." While this may be true, you cannot measure improved behavior until you have a starting point (present level of performance) and a goal to measure progress.

After some discussion, the team formulates this goal: "During the next two weeks, Johnny will pinch classmates no more than once every two hours." Now you have a goal that allows you to measure changes in Johnny's pinching behavior.

Anticipate resistance from educators if you criticize abstract goals and request observable goals and objectives. When you encounter resistance, use this strategy suggested by Dr. Mager.

Ask the resistant person to describe the child's negative, undesirable observable behaviors. Make a list of these negative observable behaviors that need to be changed. When you finish your list, turn the list around and use the list to describe desired positive behaviors. These positive behaviors are "circumstantial evidence" that can be used to determine that the goal has been reached.

Non-Goals: States of Being

Public school IEPs often include goals that cannot be measured. Examples: to appreciate music, to understand weather, to have a better attitude, to develop a love of reading, to show respect for authority.

Non-Goal: The student will appreciate classical music.

To accomplish this non-goal, the student will listen to classical music three hours a day, for one month. How can you assess "appreciation of classical music?" How will independent observers know if the student appreciates classical music? The goal focuses on a state of being. You cannot measure a state of being.

Non-Goal: The student will understand the workings of a gasoline combustion engine.

Do you want the student to understand a gasoline combustion engine? How will you know if the student understands the workings of a gasoline combustion engine?

Do you want the student to be able to repair a gasoline combustion engine? Do you want the student to be able to take an engine apart and put it back together? Do you want the student to be able to diagnose a malfunctioning engine?

Homework Assignment #1: You Learn to Write Goals

1. Make a list of statements that describe what you expect your child to know (knowledge) and what you expect your child to be able to do (performance).

2. Select one statement. Write one goal that is specific, measurable, uses action words, is realistic and relevant, and is time-limited. Use words that describe the intended outcome. For example, "Mary will be able to . . ."

3. Write the performances that will show that your child has mastered the goal. As you read these statements, you see how they become more specific:

- My child will learn to read.
- My child will learn to read at the fifth grade level.
- After one year of individualized tutoring an hour a day, my child will read at the fifth grade level.
- After one year of individualized tutoring an hour a day in the acquisition of reading skills, my child will read at the fifth grade level, as measured by the global composite score of the GORT 3 (Gray Oral Reading Test, Third Edition)

4. Your independent consultant or evaluator can give you reasonable timeframes for remediation. Do not set your goals too low.

Homework Assignment #2: You Learn to Write SMART IEP Goals and Objectives

1. Go through the most recent testing on your child. Make a list of your child's educational achievement scores in reading, writing, mathematics, and spelling.

2. Revise your list and write child's skills in objective measurable terms. Use data from tests (i.e., percentile ranks, standard scores, grade- or age-equivalent scores).

3. List your child's skills as present levels of performance. Example: "My child reads a passage of text orally at the 10th percentile level as measured by the GORT 3."

4. After one year of special education, where should the skill be? Write this statement as a measurable goal. For example:

> *By May 15 [one year later], my child will be able to read a passage of text orally at the ___ [insert the appropriate increased percentile or grade equivalent level] as measured by the Gray Oral Reading Test.*

Earlier in this book, we described the hierarchy of skills that children must acquire:

* Be able to communicate
* Be able to interact with other people; acquire social skills
* Be able to read

Most children with disabilities have reading problems. In this chapter, you learned how to measure reading skills objectively. In your child's case, you need to focus on the skills your child needs to acquire. These skills may include communication, social interactions with others, academic skills, or other areas affected by your child's disability. You need to determine how you can objectively measure the child's present levels of performance and how to describe future levels of performance.

To learn more about goals, objectives and benchmarks that are appropriate for your child, you must learn about your child's disability. You must learn how to objectively measure changes in skill levels. When you master these tasks, you will be able to write measurable goals and objectives.

 This chapter is an abbreviated version of information from *Wrightslaw: SMART IEPs,* scheduled for publication in 2002.

 The SMART IEPs book will have a companion site: www.smartieps.com/

In Summation

In this chapter, you learned about SMART IEPs that are specific, measurable, use action words, are realistic and relevant, and time-limited. You learned how to use present levels of performance to write measurable goals and objectives. It's time to learn about special education law.

Section Four

Special Education Law

"So you want to convince others of the justice of your case? Research it, learn it, live it, prepare it. Prepare your argument. Write out your thoughts."

– Gerry Spence, trial lawyer, author

As the parent of a child with a disability, you need to learn how to do legal research. If the school says, "The law says we cannot do what you ask us to do," you need to research the issue independently. After you read the statute, the regulation, and a case or two, you will know what the law says the school can and should do. Knowledge gives you power.

To understand a legal issue, you should study three types of law:

- Statutory law
- Regulatory law
- Judicial decisions, also known as case law

Read the statute first. Next, read the federal regulation and your state regulation. The regulation usually expands on the statute. Then, read cases that interpret your issue. After you read the statute, regulations, and cases, you will understand the law about your issue. Do not rely on legal advice provided by school personnel or articles written by others. In this book, you will read the law. In the beginning, this is more difficult than having the law interpreted for you. As you read, the law will begin to fit together in your mind. When you know how the law is organized, you can find sections or regulations that are relevant to your situation.

Each chapter in this Section begins with a short introduction, followed by selected portions of the statute. Following the statute is a Wrightslaw discussion of the law that includes regulations that explain the statute. You will read about the most important laws governing the education of children with disabilities, including:

- The Individuals with Disabilities Education Act
- Section 504 of the Rehabilitation Act
- The Americans with Disabilities Act
- The Family Educational Rights and Privacy Act

The Individuals with Disabilities Education Act includes four sections:

- Part A is about findings, purposes and definitions
- Part B is about eligibility, evaluations, IEPs, due process hearings, and discipline
- Part C focuses on the needs of infants and toddlers with disabilities
- Part D is about grants, research, and training programs

This book focuses on parts of five statutes in the IDEA that are most important for parents: Section 1400, Section 1401, Section 1412, Section 1414, and Section 1415. Many of the statutes about infants and toddlers in Part C are identical to the statutes in Part B.

Each chapter is cross-referenced with *Wrightslaw: Special Education Law* (ISBN: 1-892320-03-7), the legal reference book that includes the Individuals with Disabilities Education Act of 1997, Section 504 of the Rehabilitation Act, the Family Educational Rights and Privacy Act (FERPA), implementing regulations, and decisions in special education cases by the U. S. Supreme Court. *Wrightslaw: From Emotions to Advocacy - The Special Education Survival Guide* is a tactics and strategies book that includes a primer of special education law. *Wrightslaw: Special Education Law* is a legal reference book that includes tactics and strategies.

☑ **When you cross-reference, you create a system that allows you to find information quickly.**

As you read the statutes in this book, skim through your state special education regulations. Write the page number of your state regulation in this book and in *Wrightslaw: Special Education Law*. Cross-reference your state regulations by logging in relevant pages of *Wrightslaw: Special Education Law*.

13 | IDEA – Overview and Legislative Intent

> "In these days, it is doubtful that any child may reasonably be expected to succeed in life if he is denied the opportunity of an education."
>
> —*Brown v. Board of Education*, 347 U.S. 483 (1954)

In this chapter, you will learn about the factors that led Congress to enact the special education law in 1975 and the most recent amendment in 1997. You will also learn about statutory law, regulatory law, case law, and the Supremacy Clause.

Legislative Intent

On November 19, 1975, Congress enacted Public Law 94-142, also known as **The Education for All Handicapped Children Act of 1975.**

In May 1972, this legislation was introduced after several:

. . . landmark court cases establishing in law the right to education for all handicapped children . . .

In 1954, the Supreme Court of the United States (in *Brown v. Board of Education*) established the principle that all children be guaranteed equal educational opportunity.

In these days, it is doubtful that any child may reasonably be expected to succeed in life if he is denied the opportunity of an education. Such an opportunity . . . is a right which must be made available to all on equal terms.

Congress described the high social and economic costs that society paid for failing to provide an appropriate education:

Yet, the most recent statistics provided by the Bureau of Education for the Handicapped estimated that of the more than 8 million children . . . with handicapping conditions requiring special education and related services, only 3.9 million such children are receiving an appropriate education. 1.75 million handicapped children are receiving no educational services at all, and 2.5 million handicapped children are receiving an inappropriate education.

The long-range implications of these statistics are that public agencies and taxpayers will spend billions of dollars over the lifetimes of these individuals to *maintain such persons as dependents and in a minimally acceptable lifestyle. With proper education services, many would be able to **become productive citizens**, contributing to society instead of being **forced to remain burdens**. Others, through such services, would **increase their independence**, thus **reducing their dependence** on society.*

There is no pride in being forced to receive economic assistance. Not only does this have negative effects upon the handicapped person, but it has far reaching effects for such person's family.

*Providing educational services will ensure against persons needlessly being **forced into institutional settings**. One need only look at public residential institutions to find thousands of persons whose families are no longer able to care for them and who themselves have received no educational services. Billions of dollars are expended each year to maintain persons in these subhuman conditions . . .*

*Parents of handicapped children all too frequently are **not able to advocate the rights of their children** because they have been **erroneously led to believe that their children will not be able to lead meaningful lives** . . .*

It should not . . . be necessary for parents throughout the country to continue utilizing the courts to assure themselves a remedy . . .

The Individuals with Disabilities Education Act of 1997

Congress amended the Individuals with Disabilities Education Act several times since 1975. On June 4, 1997, Congress amended the Individuals with Disabilities Education Act again (IDEA-97).

The amended statute is in Volume 20 of the United States Code (U.S.C.), beginning at Section 1400. The special education regulations are in Volume 34 of the Code of Federal Regulations (C.F.R.), beginning at Section 300.

Following each statute and discussion, you will see a reference to the Code of Federal Regulations. The United States Code and the Code of Federal Regulations are available in libraries, on the Internet, and in *Wrightslaw: Special Education Law.*

Each state has special education statutes and regulations that must be consistent with federal law. State laws may not diminish or reduce the rights of special education children but may provide children with more rights and protections. The rules of procedure vary from state to state. When state law conflicts with federal law, federal law is supreme, pursuant to the Supremacy Clause of the U. S. Constitution.

In Summation

In this chapter, you learned about the legislative history of the special education law. In the next chapter, you will learn about the Findings and Purposes of the Individuals with Disabilities Education Act.

14 | IDEA– Section 1400: Findings and Purposes

"If the children are untaught, their ignorance and vices will in future life cost us much dearer in their consequences than it would have done in their correction by a good education."   —Thomas Jefferson

This section of the Individuals with Disabilities Education Act describes Congressional findings about educating children with disabilities and the purposes of the special education law. If you are advocating for a child with a disability, you should read these sections several times.

20 U.S.C. § 1400 Congressional Findings and Purpose

(c) Findings.

(1) Disability is a natural part of the human experience and in no way diminishes the right of individuals to participate in or contribute to society. Improving educational results for children with disabilities is an essential element of our national policy of ensuring equality of opportunity, full participation, independent living, and economic self-sufficiency for individuals with disabilities.

(2) Before the date of the enactment of the Education for All Handicapped Children Act of 1975 (Public Law 94-142)

(A) the special educational needs of children with disabilities were not being fully met;

(B) more than one half of the children with disabilities in the United States did not receive appropriate educational services that would enable such children to have full equality of opportunity;

(C) 1,000,000 of children with disabilities in the United States were excluded entirely from the public school system and did not go through the educational process with their peers;

(D) there were many children with disabilities throughout the United States participating in regular school programs whose disabilities prevented such children from having a successful educational experience because their disabilities were undetected; and

(E) because of the lack of adequate services within the public school system, families were often forced to find services outside the public school system, often at great distance from their residence and at their own expense.

(3) Since the enactment and implementation of the Education for All Handicapped Children Act of 1975, this Act has been successful in ensuring children with disabilities and the families of such children access to a free appropriate public education and in improving educational results for children with disabilities.

(4) However, the implementation of this Act has been **impeded by low expectations, and an insufficient focus on applying replicable research** on proven methods of teaching and learning for children with disabilities.

(5) Over 20 years of research and experience has demonstrated that the education of children with disabilities can be made more effective by

(A) having **high expectations** for such children and ensuring their **access in the general curriculum** to the maximum extent possible;

(B) **strengthening the role of parents** and ensuring that families of such children have meaningful opportunities to participate in the education of their children at school and at home;

(C) coordinating this Act with other local, educational service agency, State, and Federal school improvement efforts in order to ensure that such children benefit from such efforts and **that special education can become a service for such children rather than a place where they are sent;**

(D) providing appropriate special education and related services and aids and supports in the regular classroom to such children, whenever appropriate;

(E) supporting high quality, **intensive professional development for all personnel** who work with such children in order to ensure that they have the skills and knowledge necessary to enable them

(i) to meet developmental goals and, to the maximum extent possible, those challenging expectations that have been established for all children; and

(ii) to be prepared to lead productive, independent, adult lives, to the maximum extent possible;

(F) providing incentives for whole school approaches and pre-referral intervention to reduce the need to label children as disabled in order to address their learning needs; and

G) focusing resources on teaching and learning while reducing paperwork and requirements that do not assist in improving educational results.

. . .

(d) Purposes. The purposes of this title are:

(1) (A) to ensure that all children with disabilities have available to them a **free appropriate public education** that emphasizes special education and related services **designed to meet their unique needs and prepare them for employment and independent living;**

(B) to ensure that the **rights** of children with disabilities and parents of such children **are protected;** and

(C) to assist States, localities, educational service agencies, and Federal agencies to provide for the education of all children with disabilities;

(2) to assist States in the implementation of a statewide, comprehensive, coordinated, multidisciplinary, interagency system of **early intervention services** for infants and toddlers with disabilities and their families;

(3) to ensure that educators and parents have the necessary tools to improve educational results for children with disabilities by supporting systemic change activities; coordinated research and personnel preparation; coordinated technical assistance, dissemination, and support; and technology development and media services; and

(4) to assess, and ensure the effectiveness of, efforts to educate children with disabilities.

Wrightslaw Discussion of Findings and Purposes

When we feel overwhelmed by a daunting task that lies before us, it helps to look at the progress we have made. When the special education law was enacted in 1975, less than half of all children with disabilities were receiving an appropriate education. More than one million children with disabilities were completely excluded from school.

When Congress amended the law in 1997, they focused on the need to improve educational results for children with disabilities as "an essential element of our national policy of ensuring equality of opportunity, full participation, independent living, and economic self-sufficiency for individuals with disabilities."

Low Expectations and Failure to Use Proven Methods

Congress found that implementation of the law has been impeded by low expectations and the failure of schools to use proven methods of teaching and learning for children with disabilities. Congress concluded that the education of children with disabilities would be more effective by having high expectations for the children and providing them with access to the general curriculum.

Role of Parents Strengthened

To ensure that families could participate in the education of their children at school and at home, Congress strengthened the role of parents. Congress emphasized the need to provide school personnel with "high quality, intensive professional development."

☑ **Stop. Back up to Section 1400(d) about the "Purposes" and mark it in this book so that you can find it quickly.**

Schools are required to provide all children with disabilities with a free appropriate public education that:

- Is designed to meet their unique needs
- Prepares them for employment and independent living

This is the most important part of IDEA. Refer to § 1400(d)(1)(A) frequently. Re-read it now.

📖 **For the full text of Section 1400, without omissions, see *Wrightslaw: Special Education Law* at pages 1-10, 19-24. The key regulation, 34 C.F.R. § 300.1, is at page 139.**

In Summation

In this chapter, you learned about the findings and purposes of the special education law. In the next chapter, you will learn definitions of key terms.

15 | IDEA–Section 1401: Definitions

"Loyalty to a petrified opinion never broke a chain or freed a human soul." – Mark Twain, author

In this chapter, you will learn the legal definitions of nine (out of thirty) terms from the special education statute. This chapter will help you understand, apply, and use these terms as used in the statute.

20 U.S.C. § 1401 Definitions

Except as otherwise provided, as used in this Act:

(1) **Assistive Technology Device.** The term 'assistive technology device' means any item, piece of equipment, or product system, whether acquired commercially off the shelf, modified, or customized, that is used to **increase, maintain, or improve** functional capabilities of a child with a disability.

(2) **Assistive Technology Service.** The term 'assistive technology service' **means any service that directly assists a child** with a disability in the selection, acquisition, or use of an assistive technology device. Such term includes:

(A) the evaluation of the needs of such child, including a functional evaluation of the child in the child's customary environment;

(B) purchasing, leasing, or otherwise providing for the acquisition of assistive technology devices by such child;

(C) selecting, designing, fitting, customizing, adapting, applying, maintaining, repairing, or replacing of assistive technology devices;

(D) coordinating and using other therapies, interventions, or services with assistive technology devices, such as those associated with existing education and rehabilitation plans and programs;

(E) training or technical assistance for such child, or, where appropriate, the family of such child; and

(F) training or technical assistance for professionals (including individuals providing education and rehabilitation services), employers, or other individuals who provide services to, employ, or are otherwise substantially involved in the major life functions of such child.

(3) Child with a disability.

(A) In general. The term **'child with a disability'** means a child

(i) with mental retardation, hearing impairments (including deafness), speech or language impairments, visual impairments (including blindness), serious emotional disturbance (hereinafter referred to as 'emotional disturbance'), orthopedic impairments, autism, traumatic brain injury, other health impairments, or specific learning disabilities; and

(ii) **who, by reason thereof,** needs special education and related services.

(B) Child aged 3 through 9. The term **'child with a disability'** for a child aged 3 through 9 may, at the discretion of the State and the local educational agency, include a child

(i) experiencing developmental delays, as defined by the State and as measured by appropriate diagnostic instruments and procedures, in one or more of the following areas: physical development, cognitive development, communication development, social or emotional development, or adaptive development; and

(ii) **who, by reason thereof,** needs special education and related services.

(8) Free appropriate public education. The term 'free appropriate public education' means special education and related services that –

(A) have been provided at public expense, under public supervision and direction, and without charge;

(B) meet the standards of the State educational agency;

(C) include an appropriate preschool, elementary, or secondary school education in the State involved; and

(D) are provided in conformity with the individualized education program required under section 1414(d).

(22) Related services. The term 'related services' means **transportation,** and such developmental, corrective, and other supportive services (including speech language pathology and audiology services, psychological services, physical and occupational therapy, recreation, including therapeutic recreation, social work services, counseling services, including rehabilitation counseling, orientation and mobility services, and medical services, except that such medical services shall be for diagnostic and evaluation purposes only) as may be **required** to assist a child with a disability **to benefit** from special education, and **includes the early identification and assessment** of disabling conditions in children.

(25) Special education. The term 'special education' means **specially designed instruction,** at no cost to parents, to meet the **unique needs** of a child with a disability, including

(A) instruction conducted in the classroom, in the home, in hospitals and institutions, and in other settings; and

(B) instruction in physical education.

(26) Specific learning disability –

(A) **In general.** The term 'specific learning disability' means a disorder in one or more of the basic psychological processes involved in **understanding or in using language,** spoken or written, which disorder may manifest itself in imperfect ability to listen, think, speak, read, write, spell, or do mathematical calculations.

(B) **Disorders included.** Such term includes such conditions as perceptual disabilities, brain injury, minimal brain dysfunction, **dyslexia,** and developmental aphasia.

(C) **Disorders not included.** Such term does not include a learning problem that is primarily the result of visual, hearing, or motor disabilities, of mental retardation, of emotional disturbance, or of environmental, cultural, or economic disadvantage.

(29) Supplementary aids and services. The term 'supplementary aids and services' means aids, services, and other supports that are provided in **regular education classes** or other education related settings to enable children with disabilities to be educated with nondisabled children to the maximum extent appropriate in accordance with section 1412(a)(5).

(30) Transition services. The term 'transition services' means a **coordinated** set of activities for a student with a disability that

(A) are designed within an **outcome oriented process,** which promotes movement from school to post school activities, including post secondary education, vocational training, integrated employment (including supported employment), continuing and adult education, adult services, independent living, or community participation;

(B) are based upon the individual student's needs, taking into account the student's preferences and interests; and

(C) include instruction, related services, community experiences, the development of employment and other post school adult living objectives, and, when appropriate, acquisition of daily living skills and functional vocational evaluation.

Wrightslaw Discussion of Definitions

For the parent of a child with a disability, the most important definition is "child with a disability." Your child's classification under the IDEA as a "child with a disability" controls your child's eligibility for special education, as described in the Individuals with Disabilities Education Act.

Eligibility for Special Education

Having a disability does not qualify the child for special education under the IDEA unless the child also "by reason thereof, needs special education and related services."

 Wrightslaw: Special Education Law at page 25; 34 C.F.R. § 300.7 at page 140.

The child must meet both criteria before the child is eligible for a free appropriate public education under the IDEA. To understand this concept, "**who, by reason thereof,** needs special education and related services," re-read the definition of **special education** and **related services**.

If you have difficulty with these terms, please understand that lawyers, legal scholars, and judges are struggling with these terms too. Depending on their backgrounds, different individuals will interpret words, phrases and statutes differently.

Children with attention deficit disorder (ADD) and attention deficit hyperactive disorder (ADHD) are often classified as Other Health Impaired (OHI). Many children with ADD/ADHD also have written language disorders and other problems that should make them eligible for services under the IDEA. If this child has a written language disability, the child may be classified with specific learning disability, in addition to Other Health Impairment. (Note: In Section §1412(a)(3)(b), you will learn that children do not need to be classified or labeled before they can receive special education services.)

Special Education

The statute defines special education as "specially designed instruction . . . to meet the **unique needs** (of a child) . . . including instruction in the classroom, in the home . . . and in other settings . . ."

Although instruction must be specially designed to meet the child's unique needs, the law does not require that this specialized instruction be provided at the school. For example, the child may receive special education as individualized one-on-one tutoring after school. Schools are not required to provide special education in self-contained or resource classes.

 Wrightslaw: Special Education Law at page 29; 34 C.F.R. § 300.26 at page 145.

Related services

Related services are services that "may be **required** to assist a child with a disability to benefit from special education . . ." Related services include transportation and may include tutoring. The key is that related services may be **required** to help the child "benefit from special education."

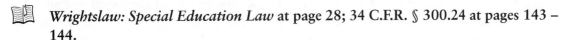 *Wrightslaw: Special Education Law* at page 28; 34 C.F.R. § 300.24 at pages 143 – 144.

Supplemental aids and services

Supplemental aids and services are provided in **regular** (not special) education classes to enable the child to be educated with nondisabled children. Supplemental aids and services include support in regular education as opposed to related services that are provided in special education.

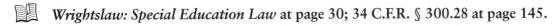 *Wrightslaw: Special Education Law* at page 30; 34 C.F.R. § 300.28 at page 145.

Specific learning disability

The term "specific learning disability" is addressed in several statutes and regulations about evaluations and eligibility. The presence or absence of a learning disability is often erroneously determined by the spread or "discrepancy" between the child's IQ score and educational achievement score. No statutory authority supports these "discrepancy models." Although the federal regulations mention discrepancy issues, the regulations do not define discrepancy formulas.

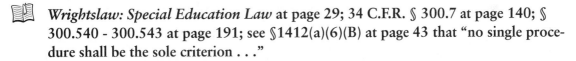 *Wrightslaw: Special Education Law* at page 29; 34 C.F.R. § 300.7 at page 140; § 300.540 - 300.543 at page 191; see §1412(a)(6)(B) at page 43 that "no single procedure shall be the sole criterion . . ."

Assistive technology

Assistive technology devices and services are ways to level the playing field for children with disabilities who may learn differently or have special needs.

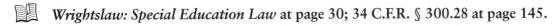 *Wrightslaw: Special Education Law,* pages 24 – 25; 34 C.F.R. §§ 300.5 and 300.6 at pages 139 - 140.

Transition services

Transition services are essential for the child's successful transition from special education to regular education and from school to work and/or higher education. Transition services are also crucial for the young child's successful move from preschool and early intervention programs to special education and general education classes.

Wrightslaw: Special Education Law at page 31, 34 C.F.R. § 300.29 at page 145 and *Appendix A*, page 215-217.

Free appropriate public education (FAPE)

The term free appropriate public education (FAPE) has been litigated extensively since the IDEA was enacted. This term continues to drive most special education litigation. The child with a disability is not entitled to the "best" education, nor to an education that maximizes the child's potential, nor to the "most appropriate" education. The child is entitled to a "Free Appropriate Public Education" (FAPE).

 Wrightslaw: Special Education Law at page 27; 34 C.F.R. § 300.13 at page 132; and §§ 300.300 - 313 about "FAPE" at pages 163 – 166; also the U. S. Supreme Court decision in *Board of Education v. Rowley*, beginning at page 305. In *Rowley*, the U. S. Supreme Court discussed FAPE, "best" and "maximizing potential."

 Eliminate the word "best" from your vocabulary! If an evaluator uses the term "best" in a report or evaluation, this may cause your child not to receive the services he or she needs.

In Summation

In this chapter, you learned the definitions of terms that are litigated frequently. When Congress passes legislation that includes vague terms, this is usually because the legislators could not agree on definitions that were acceptable to all sides. By using vague terms, they ensured that the courts would define the terms. This is true in many areas of law.

To understand the definitions that may affect your child's situation, read the statute. Definitions and legal terms are often ambiguous and must be interpreted in light of the purposes of the IDEA. You may find it helpful to re-read Section 1400(c) and (d) now. In the next chapter, you will learn about child find, least restrictive environment and mainstreaming, extended school year, private placements, and state and district assessments or "high-stakes testing."

16 | IDEA–Section 1412: LRE, ESY, Child Find, Private Placement, Assessments

"Most schools function – with stunning efficiency – to stop real learning."
—George Leonard, author

To be eligible for federal funds, the states must provide the U. S. Department of Education with assurances that they have policies and procedures in effect to ensure that all children with disabilities receive a free appropriate public education. Although Extended School Year (ESY) is not cited in an IDEA statute, the special education regulations that interpret Section 1412 clarify ESY. This chapter includes legal requirements about:

- Expelled students entitlement to FAPE
- Extended school year (ESY)
- Requirements about "child find" systems
- Least restrictive environment
- Private school placements
- State and district assessments

20 U.S.C. § 1412 State Eligibility

(a) **In general.** A State is eligible for assistance under this part for a fiscal year if the State demonstrates to the satisfaction of the Secretary that the State has in effect policies and procedures to ensure that it meets each of the following conditions:

(1) **Free Appropriate Public Education.**

(A) **In general.**

A free appropriate public education is available to all children with disabilities residing in the State **between the ages of 3 and 21**, inclusive, **including** children with disabilities who have been suspended or expelled from school.

. . .

(3) Child Find.

(A) In general.

All children with disabilities residing in the State, including children with disabilities attending private schools, regardless of the severity of their disabilities, and who are in need of special education and related services, are **identified, located, and evaluated** and a practical method is developed and implemented to determine which children with disabilities are currently receiving needed special education and related services.

(B) Construction.

Nothing in this Act requires that children be **classified by their disability** so long as each child who has a disability listed in section 1401 and who, by reason of that disability, needs special education and related services is regarded as a child with a disability under this part.

. . .

(5) Least Restrictive Environment.

(A) In general.

To **the maximum extent appropriate**, children with disabilities, including children in public or private institutions or other care facilities, are educated with children who are not disabled, and special classes, separate schooling, or other removal of children with disabilities from the regular educational environment **occurs only when the nature or severity** of the disability of a child is such that education in regular classes with the use of **supplementary** aids and services cannot be achieved satisfactorily.

(6) Procedural Safeguards.

(A) In general

Children with disabilities and their parents are afforded the procedural safeguards required by section 1415.

(B) Additional Procedural Safeguards.

Procedures to ensure that **testing and evaluation materials and procedures** utilized for the purposes of evaluation and placement of children with disabilities will be selected and administered so as **not to be racially or culturally discriminatory.** Such materials or procedures shall be provided and administered in the child's **native** language or mode of communication, unless it clearly is not feasible to do so, **and no single procedure shall be the sole criterion** for determining an appropriate educational program for a child.

. . .

(10)(C) Payment for Education of Children Enrolled in Private Schools Without Consent of or Referral by the Public Agency.

Payment for education of children enrolled in private schools without consent of or referral by the public agency.

(i) In general. Subject to subparagraph (A), this part does not require a local educational agency to pay for the cost of education, including special education and related services, of a child with a disability at a private school or facility if that agency made a free appropriate public education available to the child and the parents elected to place the child in such private school or facility.

(ii) Reimbursement for private school placement. If the parents of a child with a disability, who previously received special education and related services under the authority of a public agency, enroll the child in a private elementary or secondary school without the consent of or referral by the public agency, a court or a hearing officer may require the agency to reimburse the parents for the cost of that enrollment if the court or hearing officer finds that the agency had not made a free appropriate public education available to the child in a timely manner prior to that enrollment.

(iii) Limitation on reimbursement. The cost of reimbursement described in clause (ii) may be reduced or **denied** (I) if (aa) at the most recent IEP meeting that the parents attended **prior to removal of the child from the public school,** the parents did not inform the IEP team that they were rejecting the placement proposed by the public agency to provide a free appropriate public education to their child, including stating their concerns and their intent to enroll their child in a private school at public expense; or (bb) **10 business days** (including any holidays that occur on a business day) **prior to the removal of the child from the public school, the parents did not give written notice to the public agency** of the information described in division (aa); (II) if, prior to the parents' removal of the child from the public school, the public agency informed the parents, through the notice requirements described in section 1415(b)(7), of its intent to evaluate the child (including a statement of the purpose of the evaluation that was appropriate and reasonable), but **the parents did not make the child available for such evaluation;** or (III) upon a judicial finding of unreasonableness with respect to actions taken by the parents.

(iv) Exception. Notwithstanding the notice requirement in clause (iii)(I), the cost of reimbursement may not be reduced or denied for failure to provide such notice if (I) the parent is illiterate and cannot write in English; (II) compliance with clause (iii)(I) would likely result in physical or serious emotional harm to the child; (III) the school prevented the parent from providing such notice; or (IV) the parents had not received notice, pursuant to section 1415, of the notice requirement in clause (iii)(I).

. . .

(17) Participation in Assessments.

    (A) In general.

    Children with **disabilities are included in general State and district wide assessment programs,** with appropriate accommodations, where necessary. As appropriate, the State or local educational agency

(i) develops guidelines for the participation of children with disabilities in alternate assessments for those children who cannot participate in State and district wide assessment programs; and

(ii) develops and, beginning not later than July 1, 2000, conducts those alternate assessments.

Wrightslaw Discussion of Child Find, Least Restrictive Environment, Private Placements, State and District Assessments

According to Section 1412(a)(1)(A) of the IDEA, children "with disabilities who have been suspended or expelled" are entitled to continue to receive services.

For articles and resources about discipline, visit the Wrightslaw site: www.wrightslaw.com/

Extended School Year

Federal regulation Section 300.309 states that children with disabilities may be entitled to Extended School Year (ESY) services.

 *Wrightslaw: Special Education Law* at page 42; 34 C.F.R. §§ 300.121 - 300.122 at pages 146 – 148; ESY regulation, § 300.309 at page 165.

Several ESY cases are available on the Wrightslaw site, including one of this author's cases, *Lawyer v. Chesterfield County* which caused Virginia public schools to rewrite their procedures regarding Extended School Year services for children with disabilities.

Child Find

In Section 1412(a)(3)(A) and (B), you learned that states must implement "child find" policies and procedures that ensure that all children with disabilities are identified, located and evaluated, even if these children are advancing from grade to grade or passing.

When you read this statute and the accompanying regulation, you will learn that children do not have to be classified by disability to receive special education services. The statutory language is clear:

> *"Nothing in this Act requires that children be classified by their disability so long as each child who has a disability listed in section 1401 and who, by reason of that disability, needs special education and related services is regarded as a child with a disability under this part."*

When schools spend time quibbling over labels, this leads to delays in providing services. This new addition to the law is intended to correct for that practice.

 Wrightslaw: Special Education Law at pages 42 – 43; 34 C.F.R. § 300.125 at page 148 - 149.

Least Restrictive Environment

In Section 1412(a)(5)(1) you learned about the term "**least restrictive environment.**" "Inclusion" is not mentioned in the statute. However, the IDEA requires schools to educate children with disabilities in the least restrictive environment. The LRE concept is often called **mainstreaming** or inclusion. Because children's needs differ, school districts are required to offer a "**continuum of alternative placements.**"

Mainstreaming

School districts often tell parents that the law requires them to mainstream a child, even when the child needs individualized instruction that cannot be delivered in the regular classroom environment. When you read the law, you will see that the law takes a commonsense approach to this issue. While children should be mainstreamed "to the maximum extent appropriate," they can be removed from regular classes for special education if this is necessary for them to learn.

Assume your child has a learning disability that affects her ability to read and write. Your child also has auditory memory problems. Is it likely that your child can receive individualized instruction in the quiet environment necessary to learn new sounds in a typical classroom of 20 or 30 students?

If the child's basic skills are impaired, the child requires one-on-one direct instruction to acquire these skills. Examples of one-on-one educational approaches include ABA/Lovaas Therapy for children with autism and Orton-Gillingham approaches for children with dyslexia. One-on-one remediation with ABA/Lovaas or Orton-Gillingham approaches cannot be accomplished in a mainstream setting. If the child is receiving instruction in the basic skills of speaking and reading, it is appropriate for the child to be "segregated" during this instruction.

If we expect children with disabilities to be members of mainstream society, the children should be members of the mainstream society of their peers. However, children must be taught basic skills. If the child needs intensive, one-on-one remediation, it is appropriate to deliver this instruction in a one-on-one or small group setting. When the child learns new skills, the child's needs change. Full inclusion is often necessary for a child to acquire appropriate social skills. Parents must perform a balancing test based on the need for the child to acquire specific skills in the hierarchy of communication, social skills, and reading as discussed earlier in this book.

When least restrictive environment, inclusion, and mainstreaming issues have been litigated, appellate courts have applied different standards. Shannon Carter's parents withdrew her from the public school special education program and placed her in a private special education boarding school. For three years, Shannon was educated exclusively with other dyslexic children. When the case was litigated before the U. S. Court of Appeals for the Fourth Circuit, the court held:

> The school district suggests that the Act's preference for "mainstreaming" handicapped students justifies its IEP and makes the public school placement superior to Trident, which educates only children with disabilities. The Act's mainstreaming policy, however, is of no avail to the school district here. Under the Act, mainstreaming is a policy to be pursued so long as it is consistent with the Act's primary goal of providing disabled students with an appropriate education. Where necessary for educational reasons, mainstreaming assumes a subordinate role in formulating an educational program. In any event, the Act's preference for mainstreaming was aimed at **preventing schools from segregating handicapped students from the general student body**; the school district has presented no evidence that the policy was meant to restrict parental options when the public schools fail to comply with the requirements of the Act.

Florence County appealed this decision to the U. S. Supreme Court on other grounds. Later, the U. S. Supreme Court issued a unanimous ruling for Shannon Carter.

All decisions in *Florence County School District IV v. Carter* are on the Wrightslaw website.

Wrightslaw: Special Education Law at page 43; 34 C.F.R. § 300.130 at page 149; §§ 300.305-300.307 at page 164; and 300.550-300.556 at pages 192-193.

Testing and Evaluation Materials

In Section 1412(a)(6)(B), you learned that testing and evaluation methods and materials may not be racially or culturally discriminatory. This concept is repeated in the evaluation procedures part of the statute. Despite clear language of the statute, testing often reflects racial and cultural differences that affect the child's label and subsequent educational program. Schools must administer tests in the child's native language. No single procedure shall be the sole criterion for determining an appropriate educational program.

Many school districts use discrepancy formulas to deny eligibility for children with learning disabilities and ADD/ADHD, despite language in the statute that "no single procedure" (i.e., a mathematical determination of eligibility based on test score spread) "shall be the sole criterion."

§ 1414(b)(2) and (3) below and *Wrightslaw: Special Education Law* at page 43, 34 C.F.R. § 300.129, and 300.143 at pages 149 and 153.

Reimbursement

If the school district fails to provide your child with FAPE, and you secure an appropriate special education for your child in a private setting, you may be entitled to reimbursement for the costs of the private school or therapy. In some parts of the country, these cases are called "*Carter* cases" because they are similar to Shannon Carter's case.

The U. S. Supreme Court decisions in **Carter** (*Florence County School Dist. IV v. Carter*, 510 U.S. 7, (1993)) and **Burlington** (*Burlington v. Dept. of Ed. of Mass.*, 471 U.S. 359, (1985)) authorize reimbursement to parents, subject to certain conditions.

If parents plan to request reimbursement for a unilateral private placement, or for therapy, private tutoring, ABA/Lovaas/Discrete Trial Therapy, the parent must give the school district clear notice of their intentions at the last IEP meeting or by letter delivered ten business days before the child's removal from the public school.

 Wrightslaw: Special Education Law at page 44-45; 34 C.F.R. § 300.403; and §§ 300.450-300.462 at pages 173-176.

High Stakes Testing

According to Section 1400(a)(17), children with disabilities are to be included in the state and district assessments that may be used to determine graduation. Many children with disabilities have not been taught reading, writing, spelling and arithmetic skills that "prepare them for employment and independent living" or allow them to pass statewide assessments.

Before the Individuals with Disabilities Education Act was amended, public schools often excluded children with disabilities from state and district assessments which prevented these children from receiving regular high school diplomas. These new requirements about including children with disabilities in state and district testing are ways to make schools accountable. A benefit is that remediation during the early elementary school years should increase.

If the child does not acquire basic skills, or the child has other disabilities, the child may need accommodations or modifications on high stakes tests. After the statute was amended to require schools to include children with disabilities in high stakes tests, litigation about accommodations and modifications has increased.

 Wrightslaw: Special Education Law at page 48; and 34 C.F.R. §§ 300.138-300.139 at page 151.

In December, 2000, the Office of Civil Rights of the U. S. Department of Education issued a report about high stakes testing entitled *The Use of Tests as Part of High-Stakes Decision-Making for Students: A Resource Guide for Educators and Policy-Makers*. The report relies heavily on the *Standards for Educational and Psychological Testing* (known as the "*Joint Standards*"). OCR reports that "many policy-makers and educators are unaware of the test measurement standards" of the *Joint Standards*. The OCR report explained that:

> *Examples of high-stakes decisions affecting students include: student placement in gifted and talented programs or in programs serving students with limited-English proficiency; determinations of disability and eligibility to receive special education services; student promotion from one grade level to another; graduation from high school and diploma awards; and admissions decisions and scholarship awards.*
>
> . . .
>
> *Is it ever appropriate to test [elementary or secondary] students on material they have not been taught? Yes, if the test is used to find out whether the schools are doing their job. But if that same test is used to hold students "accountable" for the failure of the schools, most testing professionals would find such use inappropriate. It is not the test itself that is the culprit in the latter case; results from a test that is valid for one purpose can be used improperly for other purposes.*
>
> . . .
>
> *Used appropriately, tests can provide important information about a student's knowledge to help improve educational opportunity and achievement. However, as said by the National Research Council's (NRC's) Board on Testing and Assessment, "no single test score can be considered a definitive measure of a student's knowledge."*
>
> . . .
>
> *Policy-makers and the education community need to ensure that the operation of the entire high-stakes decision-making process does not result in the discriminatory denial of educational opportunities or benefits to students.*
>
> . . .
>
> *Sometimes scores from a test used for graduation purposes are used to provide remediation instruction for students who do not pass the test. In this case, "[s]chools that give graduation tests early . . . assume that such tests are diagnostic and that students who fail can benefit from effective remedial instruction . . . Using these test results to place a pupil in a remedial class or other intervention also involves a prediction about the student's performance—that is, that as a result of the placement, the student's mastery of the knowledge and skills measured by the test will improve. Thus, evidence that a particular treatment (in this case, the remedial program) benefits students who fail the test would be an appropriate part of the test validation process*
>
> . . .
>
> *Neither a test score or any other kind of information can justify a bad decision. Research shows that students are typically hurt by simple retention and repetition of a grade in school without remedial and other instructional support services. In the absence of effective services for low-performing students, better tests will not lead to better educational outcomes.*

. . .

Furthermore, federal laws generally require the inclusion of students with disabilities in state- and districtwide assessment programs, except as participation in particular tests is individually determined to be inappropriate for a particular student. Assessment programs should provide valuable information that benefits students, either directly, such as in the measurement of individual progress against standards, or indirectly, such as in evaluating programs. Given these benefits, exclusion from assessment programs, unless such participation is individually determined inappropriate because of the student's disability, would generally violate Section 504 and Title II. If a student with a disability will take the systemwide assessment test the student must be provided appropriate instruction and appropriate test accommodations.

The report explains that failure to achieve a certain score on a high stakes test could lead to disparate treatment and discriminatory outcomes. Yet, failure to administer such tests to children with disabilities is also a violation because this does not permit measurement of the individual's progress against standards. In other words, testing is valuable, but the outcomes and subsequent use of test data, such as denial of a high school diploma, may be discriminatory. Such discrimination is a violation of Section 504 of the Rehabilitation Act and Title II of the Americans with Disabilities Act.

For articles and resources about high stakes testing, visit www.wrightslaw.com/ and www.fetaweb.com/

In Summation

In this chapter, you learned that states must provide the U. S. Department of Education with assurances that they have policies and procedures to ensure that all children with disabilities receive a free, appropriate education.

You learned that schools must provide FAPE to suspended and expelled students who are eligible for services under the IDEA and that your state must have a "child find" system. You learned about least restrictive environment (LRE), mainstreaming and inclusion, private school placements, and high stakes testing. In the next chapter, you will learn about evaluations, reevaluations, eligibility criteria, Individualized Educational Programs (IEPs), IEP teams, and placement decisions.

Your Notes Here

17 | IDEA–Section 1414: Evaluation, Eligibility, IEPs, and Placement

"The greatest danger for most of us is not that we aim too high and we miss, but that we aim too low and we reach it."   —Author unknown

In this chapter, you will learn about evaluations, re-evaluations, eligibility, Individualized Educational Programs (IEPs), IEP teams, and placement decisions.

A Wrightslaw discussion of evaluations and eligibility follows the statute about evaluations. A Wrightslaw discussion of IEPs, IEP teams, and placement decisions follow the statute about IEPs. Except for the "Purposes" section of the law, Section 1414(d) is the most important area of law for you to read and understand. Evaluations are used to determine your child's eligibility for services and termination of services. Data from evaluations are used in the present levels of performance in your child's IEPs. There are two meetings described in the law, eligibility meetings and IEP meetings. In some areas of the country, one or both of these two meetings are called an ARD or MDT meeting or report. The initials usually describe "Assessment/Admission, Review, Discharge" and "Multi-Disciplinary Team" meetings and report. They are simply either the eligibility or IEP meetings, the reports, or both, dependent upon the terminology in your state.

Appendix A to the federal regulations uses a frequently asked questions (FAQs) format to clarify the law about IEPs, transition, high stakes testing, and other issues. (Appendix A to the Regulations is Appendix A to this book.)

20 U.S.C. § 1414(a) Evaluations and Reevaluations

(1) Initial Evaluations.

(A) In general.

A State educational agency, other State agency, or local educational agency shall conduct a full and individual initial evaluation, in accordance with this paragraph and subsection (b), before the initial provision of special education and related services to a child with a disability under this part.

(B) Procedures.

Such initial evaluation shall consist of procedures

(i) to determine whether a child is a child with a disability (as defined in section 1401(3)); and

(ii) to determine the educational needs of such child.

(C) Parental Consent.

(i) In general. The agency proposing to conduct an initial evaluation to determine if the child qualifies as a child with a disability as defined in section 1401(3)(A) or 1401(3)(B) shall obtain an informed consent from the parent of such child before the evaluation is conducted. Parental consent for evaluation shall not be construed as consent for placement for receipt of special education and related services.

(ii) Refusal. If the parents of such child refuse consent for the evaluation, the agency may continue to pursue an evaluation by utilizing the mediation and due process procedures under section 1415, except to the extent inconsistent with State law relating to parental consent.

(2) Reevaluations.

A local educational agency shall ensure that a reevaluation of each child with a disability is conducted

(A) if conditions warrant a reevaluation or if the child's parent or teacher requests a reevaluation, but at least once every 3 years; and

(B) in accordance with subsections (b) and (c).

(b) Evaluation Procedures.

(1) Notice. The local educational agency shall provide notice to the parents of a child with a disability, in accordance with subsections (b)(3), (b)(4), and (c) of section 1415, that describes any evaluation procedures such agency proposes to conduct.

(2) Conduct of Evaluation. In conducting the evaluation, the local educational agency shall

(A) use a variety of assessment tools and strategies to gather relevant functional and developmental information, including information provided by the parent, that may assist in determining whether the child is a child with a disability and the content of the child's individualized education program, including information related to enabling the child to be involved in and progress in the general curriculum or, for preschool children, to participate in appropriate activities;

(B) **not use any single procedure as the sole criterion** for determining whether a child is a child with a disability or determining an appropriate educational program for the child; and

(C) use technically sound instruments that may assess the relative contribution of cognitive and behavioral factors, in addition to physical or developmental factors.

(3) **Additional Requirements.** Each local educational agency shall ensure that

(A) tests and other evaluation materials used to assess a child under this section

(i) are selected and administered so as **not to be discriminatory on a racial or cultural basis;** and

(ii) are provided and administered in the child's **native language** or other mode of communication, unless it is clearly not feasible to do so; and

(B) any standardized tests that are given to the child

(i) have been validated for the specific purpose for which they are used;

(ii) are administered by trained and knowledgeable personnel; and

(iii) are administered in accordance with any instructions provided by the producer of such tests;

(C) the child is assessed in **all areas of suspected disability;** and

(D) **assessment tools and strategies that provide relevant information that directly assists persons in determining the educational needs of the child are provided.**

(4) **Determination of eligibility.**

Upon completion of administration of tests and other evaluation materials

(A) the determination of whether the child is a child with a disability as defined in section 1401(3) shall be made by a **team** of qualified professionals **and the parent** of the child in accordance with paragraph (5); and

(B) a copy of the evaluation report and the documentation of determination of eligibility **will be given to the parent.**

(5) **Special rule for eligibility determination.**

In making a determination of eligibility under paragraph (4)(A), a child shall not be determined to be a child with a disability if the determinant factor for such determination is lack of instruction in reading or math or limited English proficiency.

§ 1414(c) Additional Requirements For Evaluations and Reevaluations

(1) **Review of existing evaluation data.**

As part of an initial evaluation (if appropriate) and as part of any reevaluation under this section, the IEP Team described in subsection (d)(1)(B) and other qualified professionals, as appropriate, shall

> **(A) review existing evaluation data on the child, including evaluations and information provided by the parents of the child,** current classroom based assessments and observations, and teacher and related services providers observation; and

> (B) on the basis of that review, and input from the child's parents, identify what additional data, if any, are needed to determine

> (i) whether the child has a particular category of disability, as described in section 1401(3), or, in case of a reevaluation of a child, whether the child continues to have such a disability;

> (ii) **the present levels of performance and educational needs of the child;**

> (iii) whether the child needs special education and related services, or in the case of a reevaluation of a child, whether the child continues to need special education and related services; and

> (iv) **whether any additions or modifications** to the special education and related services are needed to enable the child **to meet the measurable annual goals** set out in the individualized education program of the child and to participate, as appropriate, in the general curriculum.

(2) Source of Data. The local educational agency shall administer such tests and other evaluation materials as may be needed to produce the data identified by the IEP Team under paragraph (1)(B).

(3) Parental Consent. Each local educational agency shall obtain **informed parental consent,** in accordance with subsection (a)(1)(C), **prior to conducting any reevaluation** of a child with a disability, except that such informed parent consent need not be obtained if the local educational agency can demonstrate that it had taken reasonable measures to obtain such consent and the child's parent has failed to respond.

(4) Requirements if additional data are not needed.

If the IEP Team and other qualified professionals, as appropriate, determine that no additional data are needed to determine whether the child continues to be a child with a disability, the local educational agency

> (A) shall notify the child's parents of (i) that determination and the reasons for it; and (ii) the right of such parents to request an assessment to determine whether the child continues to be a child with a disability; and

> (B) **shall not be required to conduct such an assessment unless requested to by the child's parents.**

(5) Evaluations before change in eligibility. A local educational agency shall evaluate a child with a disability in accordance with this section before determining that the child **is no longer** a child with a disability.

Wrightslaw Discussion of Evaluations and Eligibility

You have learned that the school must conduct a full evaluation before the child can be found eligible for special education. The parent must consent to this evaluation and subsequent reevaluations. In sections 1414(b)(1), (2), (3), (4), and (5) and sections 1414(c)(1), (2), (3), (4), and (5) you learned that the school district must describe to the parent "any evaluation procedures" that the agency proposes to conduct.

The purpose of evaluations is not limited to eligibility decisions. Evaluations are used to "gather information . . . that provide(s) information . . . in determining . . . the present levels of performance and educational needs of (your) child . . . and (determine) whether any additions or modifications to the special education and related services are needed to enable the child to meet the measurable annual goals . . ." set out in the IEP.

Before the IDEA was amended, parents were often excluded from eligibility determinations. The amended statute requires parents to be included in eligibility meetings. The school must consider information provided by the parent, including evaluations from private sector evaluators. If the school proposes to terminate the child from special education, the school must reevaluate the child before they can make this decision.

If you do not understand your child's test data, you will not be able to play an active role in planning your child's educational program.

Understanding your child's test data is more important than understanding the law.

To measure your progress on a trip, you use an odometer, speedometer, and watch. When you use these devices, you can tell where you are going and when you will arrive at your destination. The same principles apply to your child's acquisition of basic skills. You can measure basic skills.

Review and analyze your child's test data before IEP meetings.

Wrightslaw: Special Education Law at pages 59-61; 34 C.F.R. § 300.320-300.321 at page 166; 34 C.F.R. § 300.530-300.536 and 34 C.F.R. § 300.540-300.543 at pages 189-191.

Visit www.fetaweb.com for PowerPoint and Excel charts of test data that you can modify.

§ 1414(d) Individualized Education Programs ——————

(1) Definitions.

As used in this title:

(A) Individualized education program.

The term 'individualized education program' or 'IEP' means a written statement for each child with a disability that is developed, reviewed, and revised in accordance with this section and that includes

(i) a statement of the child's **present levels of educational performance**, including (I) how the child's disability affects the child's involvement and progress in the general curriculum; or (II) for preschool children, as appropriate, how the disability affects the child's participation in appropriate activities;

(ii) a statement of **measurable annual goals, including benchmarks or short-term objectives,** related to

(I) meeting the child's needs that result from the child's disability to enable the child to be involved in and progress in the general curriculum; and

(II) meeting each of the child's other educational needs that result from the child's disability;

(iii) a statement of **the special education and related services and supplementary aids and services** to be provided to the child, or on behalf of the child, and a statement of the **program modifications or supports for school personnel** that will be provided for the child

(I) to advance appropriately toward attaining the annual goals;

(II) to be involved and progress in the general curriculum in accordance with clause (i) and to participate in extracurricular and other nonacademic activities; and

(III) to be educated and participate with other children with disabilities and nondisabled children in the activities described in this paragraph;

(iv) an explanation of the extent, if any, to which the child **will not participate with nondisabled children** in the regular class and in the activities described in clause (iii);

(v)

(I) a statement of any individual **modifications in the administration of State or districtwide assessments** of student achievement that are needed in order for the child to participate in such assessment; and

(II) if the IEP Team determines that the child will not participate in a particular State or districtwide assessment of student achievement (or part of such an assessment), a statement of (aa) why that assessment is not appropriate for the child; and (bb) how the child will be assessed;

(vi) the projected **date for the beginning of the services** and modifications described in clause (iii), and the anticipated **frequency, location, and duration of those services** and modifications;

(vii)

(I) beginning at **age 14, and updated annually, a statement of the transition service needs** of the child under the applicable components of the child's IEP that focuses on the child's courses of study (such as participation in advanced placement courses or a vocational education program);

(II) beginning **at age 16** (or younger, if determined appropriate by the IEP Team), **a statement of needed transition services** for the child, including, when appropriate, a statement of the interagency responsibilities or any needed linkages; and

(III) beginning at least one year before the child reaches the **age of majority under State law**, a statement that the child has been informed of his or her rights under this title, if any, that will transfer to the child on reaching the age of majority under section 1415(m); and

(viii) a statement of

(I) **how the child's progress toward the annual goals described in clause (ii) will be measured;** and

(II) how the child's parents will be regularly informed (by such means as periodic report cards), at least as often as parents are informed of their nondisabled children's progress, of (aa) their child's progress toward the annual goals described in clause (ii); and (bb) the extent to which that progress is sufficient to enable the child to achieve the goals by the end of the year.

(B) Individualized education program team.

The term 'individualized education program team' or 'IEP Team' means a group of individuals composed of

(i) the **parents** of a child with a disability;

(ii) at least **one regular education teacher of such child** (if the child is, or may be, participating in the regular education environment);

(iii) at least **one special education teacher**, or where appropriate, at least one special education provider of such child;

(iv) a **representative** of the local educational agency who

(I) is **qualified** to provide, or supervise the provision of, specially designed instruction to meet the unique needs of children with disabilities;

(II) is **knowledgeable** about the general curriculum; and

(III) is knowledgeable about the **availability of resources** of the local educational agency;

(v) an individual who can **interpret the instructional implications of evaluation results**, who may be a member of the team described in clauses (ii) through (vi);

(vi) at the discretion of the parent or the agency, **other individuals** who have knowledge or special expertise regarding the child, including related services personnel as appropriate; and

(vii) whenever appropriate, **the child** with a disability.

(2) Requirement that Program Be in Effect.

(A) **In general. At the beginning of each school year,** each local educational agency, State educational agency, or other State agency, as the case may be, **shall have in effect, for each child with a disability in its jurisdiction, an individualized education program,** as defined in paragraph (1)(A).

(B) **Program for child aged 3 through 5.** In the case of a child with a disability aged 3 through 5 (or, at the discretion of the State educational agency, a 2 year old child with a disability who will turn age 3 during the school year), **an individualized family service plan** that contains the material described in section 1436, and that is developed in accordance with this section, may serve as the IEP of the child if using that plan as the IEP is

(i) consistent with State policy; and

(ii) agreed to by the agency and the child's parents.

(3) Development of IEP.

(A) **In general.** In developing each child's IEP, **the IEP Team,** subject to subparagraph (C), **shall consider**

(i) the strengths of the child and the concerns of the parents for enhancing the education of their child; and

(ii) **the results of the initial evaluation or most recent evaluation** of the child.

(B) **Consideration of special factors.** The IEP Team **shall**

(i) **in the case of a child whose behavior impedes his or her learning or that of others, consider,** when appropriate, strategies, including **positive behavioral interventions, strategies, and supports to address that behavior;**

(ii) in the case of a child with limited English proficiency, consider the language needs of the child as such needs relate to the child's IEP;

(iii) in the case of a child who is blind or visually impaired, provide for instruction in Braille and the use of Braille unless the IEP Team determines, after an evaluation of the child's reading and writing skills, needs, and appropriate reading and writing media (including an evaluation of the child's future needs for instruction in Braille or the use of Braille), that instruction in Braille or the use of Braille is not appropriate for the child;

(iv) consider the communication needs of the child, and in the case of a child who is deaf or hard of hearing, consider the child's language and communication needs, opportunities for direct communications with peers and professional personnel in the child's language and communication mode, academic level, and full range of needs, including opportunities for direct instruction in the child's language and communication mode; and

(v) consider whether the child requires assistive technology devices and services.

(C) **Requirement with respect to regular education teacher.** The **regular education teacher of the child,** as a member of the IEP Team, **shall,** to the extent appropriate, **participate in the development of the IEP** of the child, including the determination of appropriate positive behavioral interventions and strategies and the determination of supplementary aids and services, program modifications, and support for school personnel consistent with paragraph (1)(A)(iii).

(4) Review and Revision of IEP.

(A) **In general.** The local educational agency shall ensure that, subject to subparagraph (B), the IEP Team

(i) **reviews** the child's IEP periodically, but **not less than annually** to determine whether the annual goals for the child are being achieved; and

(ii) **revises** the IEP as **appropriate to address**

(I) any lack of expected progress toward the annual goals and in the general curriculum, where appropriate;

(II) the results of any reevaluation conducted under this section;

(III) information about the child **provided to, or by, the parents,** as described in subsection (c)(1)(B);

(IV) the child's anticipated needs; or

(V) other matters.

(B) Requirement with respect to regular education teacher. The regular education teacher of the child, as a member of the IEP Team, **shall,** to the extent appropriate, **participate** in the review and revision of the IEP of the child.

(5) Failure to Meet Transition Objectives.

If a participating agency, other than the local educational agency, fails to provide the transition services described in the IEP in accordance with paragraph (1)(A)(vii), the local educational agency shall reconvene the IEP Team to identify alternative strategies to meet the transition objectives for the child set out in that program.

. . .

(f) Educational Placements. Each local educational agency or State educational agency shall ensure that the **parents** of each child with a **disability are members of any** group that makes **decisions on the educational placement** of their child.

Wrightslaw Discussion of Individualized Education Programs (IEPs) and Placement

The IEP drives your child's educational program. Generally, a well-drafted IEP with **clear, quantifiable goals and objectives** will lead to a successful program. Relying on a vague, inaccurate IEP is like relying on an inaccurate map when you are lost in the woods–it is easy to get lost. If you do not have a well-written IEP, it will be easy for you and your child's teachers to get off-track.

Definition of the IEP

The statute defines the **Individualized Education Program (IEP)** as a written statement that includes several required components. The IEP must include the child's present levels of educational performance, information about how the disability affects the child's involvement and progress in the general curriculum. For preschool children, the Individualized Family Service Plan (IFSP) should include information about how the disability affects the child's participation in appropriate activities.

 Section 1414(d)(1)(A))

Required Components of the IEP

Your child's IEP must include a statement of the **measurable annual goals** that focus on meeting your child's needs that result from the disability. The IEP must include **benchmarks and/or short-term objectives.**

The IEP must also include a statement of the special education, related services, and supplementary aids and services that the school will provide. Your child's IEP should also include program modifications and support for school personnel.

☑ Remember the definition of special education in 20 U.S.C. § 1401(25)

Your child's IEP must include the projected **date** when special education services will begin, and must describe the **frequency, location,** and **duration** of the services and modifications. Your child's IEP must explain the extent to which your child will not be educated with nondisabled children.

The IEP should also include accommodations and modifications in state and district assessments. The IEP must include a statement about how your child's progress will be measured and how you will be regularly informed of your child's progress or lack of progress.

Assume your child is in the eighth grade, has an average IQ, and is reading at the 4th grade level. With fourth grade reading skills, your child cannot be involved in or progress through the general curriculum. To be consistent with the purpose of IDEA, given these facts, the school must teach your child to read. The school must also provide subject matter material by other means (i.e., books on tape).

In Section 1414(d) (2), you learned that your child's IEP **must be in effect at the beginning of each school year.** The IEP team must consider whether your child requires assistive technology devices and services. In Section 1400(d) (3), you learned that the IEP team must consider the child's strengths and the parent's concerns for enhancing the child's education. The team must also consider the results of the most recent evaluation.

Transition Planning in Your Child's IEP

When your child reaches the age of 14, the IEP team must consider the child's transition from special education to advanced placement courses, vocational education, higher education, and employment. If other participating agencies fail to provide transition services in the IEP, Section 1414(d)(5) requires the IEP team to reconvene and identify alternative strategies.

Members of Your Child's IEP Team

Section 1414(d)(1)(B) establishes that your child's IEP Team includes the parent, at least one of your child's regular education teachers, at least one special education teacher, a representative of your school district, and a psychologist or educational diagnostician who can interpret the educational implications of evaluation results. Your child may be a member of the IEP team.

At the discretion of the parent or school district, your child's IEP team may include other individuals who have knowledge or special expertise about your child.

Behavior Issues in Your Child's IEP

If your child displays behavior that impedes your child's learning or the learning of others, the school district must include **positive behavioral interventions**, strategies, and supports to address this behavior.

Reviewing and Revising Your Child's IEP

The IEP team must review and revise your child's IEP at least once a year. The IEP team must revise your child's IEP more often to address lack progress, reevaluation results, or information provided by the child's parents. Are the goals and objectives being met? If not, how should your child's program be changed?

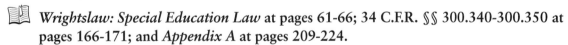 *Wrightslaw: Special Education Law* at pages 61-66; 34 C.F.R. §§ 300.340-300.350 at pages 166-171; and *Appendix A* at pages 209-224.

Making Decisions About Your Child's Placement

Section 1414(f) establishes that the child's parents must be "members of any group that makes decisions on the educational placement of their child."

Wrightslaw: Special Education Law at page 66, 34 C.F.R. § 300.501 at page 178.

Parent Input in the IEP

You must understand your child's test data before you can have meaningful input into your child's IEP. Because your child's IEP is based on **present levels of functioning**, it is important that you know your child's skill levels. Your child must be assessed in all areas of suspected disability. The IEP team must consider the results of the initial evaluation or the most recent evaluation, private sector evaluations, and information provided by the child's parent.

In Summation

In this chapter, you learned about evaluations, evaluation procedures, and requirements for evaluations. You learned about the required components of your child's IEP, IEP team members, transition planning, assistive technology, and the need to revise your child's IEP if the child is not making sufficient progress.

In the next chapter, you will learn about the procedural safeguards that were established to protect the rights of parents and children and to resolve parent-school disputes. These safeguards include prior written notice, procedural safeguards notice, the right to review records and the right to an independent evaluation. Safeguards include ways to resolve disputes, including mediation, due process hearings, and appeals to State or Federal court.

18 | IDEA–Section 1415: Procedural Safeguards, Due Process, Discipline, etc.

"... whether the IEP and the FAPE requirements were put there out of mistrust of the parents, or out of mistrust of school authorities. It seems to me they were put there to make sure that the school authorities did not give the disabled child second-rate treatment. "

– Transcript of Oral Argument, statement by Supreme Court Justice, *Florence County School District IV. v. Shannon Carter* (October 6, 1993)

In Section 1415, you will learn about prior written notice, procedural safeguards notice, mediation, due process hearings, statutes of limitation, appeals, discipline, and age of majority.

Legal disputes are usually analyzed in terms of **substance** and **procedure**. In criminal law, was the confession voluntary or was the confession made after the defendant was held incommunicado and not allowed to talk with an attorney? (Procedural issue.) Regardless of whether there was a confession, did the defendant commit the crime? (Substantive issue.) Do fingerprint evidence, eyewitness testimony, and DNA evidence establish guilt? (Substantive issue.) Is the defendant a juvenile or adult? (Procedural issue.)

If the school convenes an IEP meeting and deliberately excludes the child's parent, does this invalidate the IEP? (Procedural issue.) Is an IEP that offers four months of gain in reading skills after one year of special education invalid? (Substance, see *Carter.*) In most states, judges have held that procedural breaches must cause an actual loss of educational opportunity to the child before the procedural breach is legally sufficient to affect the outcome of the case.

IDEA is like other laws, with rules of procedure and issues that relate to substance. In some factual scenarios, these two issues merge. Substantive issues usually involve evaluations, eligibility and the child's IEP. Procedural issues focus on notice, timelines, the right to review records, remedies if the school district fails to obey the law, mediation, due process, discipline, and resort to courts.

Unless your child is labeled with an emotional disturbance, behavior disorder, or ADD/ADHD, is facing suspension or expulsion, or is at risk for suspension, you are advised to skip §1415(k) about "Placement in Alternative Educational Setting." This long, confusing section includes detailed rules about suspending and expelling children with disabilities.

Subsection 1415(b) is about records and the responsibilities of the school district and parent to provide notice to one another. Subsections 1415(c) and (d) address Prior Written Notice and the Procedural Safeguards Notice. A Wrightslaw discussion follows the section on notices and documents.

Subsections 1415(e), (f), (g), (h), (i), and (j) are about mediation, due process hearings, appeals to court, attorney's fees and "stay put." A discussion of mediation and litigation follows. Subsection 1415(k) focuses on discipline of children with disabilities. You do not need to study this section unless your issue concerns possible disciplinary matters. A Wrightslaw discussion follows.

20 U.S.C. § 1415 – Procedural Safeguards

(a) Establishment of Procedures. Any state educational agency, State agency, or local educational agency that receives assistance under this part shall establish and maintain procedures in accordance with this section to ensure that children with disabilities and their parents are guaranteed procedural safeguards with respect to the provisions of free appropriate public education by such agencies.

(b) Types of Procedures.

The procedures required by this section shall include:

(1) an opportunity for the parents of a child with a disability to **examine all records** relating to such child and to **participate in meetings** with respect to the identification, evaluation, and educational placement of the child, and the provision of a free appropriate public education to such child, and to obtain an **independent educational evaluation** of the child;

. . .

(3) **written prior notice** to the parents of the child **whenever** such agency

(A) **proposes to initiate or change**; or

(B) **refuses to initiate or change**; the identification, evaluation, or educational placement of the child, in accordance with subsection (c), or the provision of a free appropriate public education to the child;

(4) procedures designed to ensure that the notice required by Paragraph (3) is in the native language of the parent, unless it clearly is not feasible to do so;

(5) an opportunity for **mediation** in accordance with subsection (e);

(6) an **opportunity to present complaints** with respect to any matter relating to the identification, evaluation, or educational placement of the child, or the provision of a free appropriate public education to such child;

(7) procedures that **require the parent** of a child with a disability, or the attorney representing the child, **to provide notice** (which shall remain confidential)

(A) to the State educational agency or local educational agency, as the case may be, in the complaint filed under paragraph (6); and

(B) **that shall include**

(i) the name of the child, the address of the residence of the child, and the name of the school the child is attending;

(ii) a **description of the nature of the problem** of the child relating to such proposed initiation or change, including facts relating to such problem; and

(iii) **a proposed resolution of the problem** to the extent known and available to the parents at the time;

(8) procedures that require the State educational agency to develop a model form to assist parents in filing a complaint in accordance with paragraph (7).

(c) Content of Prior Written Notice. The notice required by subsection (b)(3) shall include

(1) a **description of the action** proposed or refused by the agency;

(2) an **explanation of why the agency proposes or refuses to take the action;**

(3) **a description of any other options that the agency considered** and the reasons why those options were rejected;

(4) **a description of each evaluation procedure, test, record, or report the agency used** as a basis for the proposed or refused action;

(5) **a description of any other factors** that are relevant to the agency's proposal or refusal;

(6) **a statement that the parents of a child with a disability have protection** under the procedural safeguards of this part and, if this notice is not an initial referral for evaluation, the means by which a copy of a description of the procedural safeguards can be obtained; and

(7) sources for parents to contact to obtain assistance in understanding the provisions of this part.

(d) Procedural Safeguards Notice.

(1) In general. A copy of the procedural safeguards available to the parents of a child with a disability **shall** be given to the parents, at a minimum

(A) **upon initial referral** for evaluation;

(B) **upon each notification of an individualized education program meeting** and upon **reevaluation** of the child; and

(C) **upon registration of a complaint** under subsection (b)(6).

(2) Contents.

The procedural safeguards notice **shall include a full explanation of the procedural safeguards,** written in the native language of the parents, unless it clearly is not feasible to do so, and **written in an easily understandable manner,** available under this section and under regulations promulgated by the Secretary relating to

(A) independent educational evaluation;

(B) prior written notice;

(C) parental consent;

(D) access to educational records;

(E) opportunity to present complaints;

(F) the child's placement during pendency of due process proceedings;

(G) procedures for students who are subject to placement in an interim alternative educational setting;

(H) requirements for unilateral placement by parents of children in private schools at public expense;

(I) mediation;

(J) due process hearings, including requirements for disclosure of evaluation results and recommendations;

(K) State level appeals (if applicable in that State);

(L) civil actions; and

(M) attorneys' fees.

Wrightslaw Discussion of Prior Written Notice and Procedural Safeguards Notice_____

Examine Records

The school district must give you the opportunity to examine all records and to obtain an independent educational evaluation of your child.

Prior Written Notice

If the school district proposes to initiate or change, or refuses to change the identification, evaluation, or educational placement of your child, the district must provide you with **prior written notice.** Prior written notice must explain the district's rationale, describe other options that were considered, and describe the evaluation, test, record, or report that was used as the basis for their action. Prior written notice must be written so it is easily understood.

Many courts have held that a violation of a rule of procedure does not automatically mean that the parent prevails in subsequent litigation. The procedural violation must cause loss of educational opportunity before this affects the outcome of a case.

 Wrightslaw: Special Education Law at pages 67-68; and 34 C.F.R. §§ 300.501, 300.502 at pages 178-179. For the content of notice, see pages 68-69; and 34 C.F.R. §§ 300.503, 300.504 at pages 179-180.

Complaint Resolution: Mediation, Due Process Hearings, Appeals to Court

You are learning that the IDEA includes rules of procedure about resolving complaints, including mediation, due process hearings, and appeals to state or federal court. Before you request a due process hearing, you should be familiar with the federal statute and regulations and your state special education statute and regulations about due process hearings.

A due process hearing is usually a formal, contested, adversarial trial. Special education cases are similar to medical malpractice cases, with battles of expert witnesses, and the emotions of bitterly contested divorce cases with child custody and equitable distribution issues.

 Before you request a due process hearing, read the Rules of Adverse Assumptions in Chapter 21.

20 U.S.C. § 1415(e), (f), (g), (h), and (i) – Mediation, Due Process Hearings, Appeals to Court

(e) Mediation.

(1) **In general.** Any State educational agency or local educational agency that receives assistance under this part shall ensure that procedures are established and implemented **to allow parties** to disputes involving any matter described in subsection (b)(6) **to resolve such disputes through a mediation process** which, at a minimum, shall be available whenever a hearing is requested under subsection (f) or (k).

(2) Requirements.

Such procedures shall meet the following requirements:

(A) The procedures shall ensure that the mediation process

(i) is **voluntary** on the part of the parties;

(ii) **is not used to deny or delay** a parent's right to a due process hearing under subsection (f), or to deny any other rights afforded under this part; and

(iii) is conducted by **a qualified and impartial mediator who is trained in effective mediation techniques.**

(B) A local educational agency or a State agency may establish procedures to require parents who choose not to use the mediation process to meet, at a time and location convenient to the parents, with a disinterested party who is under contract with

(i) a parent training and information center or community parent resource center in the State established under section 1482 or 1483; or

(ii) an appropriate alternative dispute resolution entity; to encourage the use, and explain the benefits, of the mediation process to the parents.

(C) The State shall maintain a list of individuals who are qualified mediators and knowledgeable in laws and regulations relating to the provision of special education and related services.

(D) **The State shall bear the cost of the mediation process,** including the costs of meetings described in subparagraph (B).

(E) Each session in the mediation process shall be scheduled in a timely manner and shall be held in a location that is convenient to the parties to the dispute.

(F) **An agreement** reached by the parties to the dispute in the mediation process **shall be set forth in a written mediation agreement.**

(G) **Discussions** that occur during the mediation process **shall be confidential and may not be used as evidence** in any subsequent due process hearings or civil proceedings and the parties to the mediation process may be required to sign a confidentiality pledge prior to the commencement of such process.

(f) Impartial Due Process Hearing.

(1) In general. Whenever a complaint has been received under subsection (b)(6) or (k) of this section, the parents involved in such complaint shall have an opportunity for an impartial **due process hearing,** which shall be conducted by the State educational agency or by the local educational agency, as determined by State law or by the State educational agency.

(2) Disclosure of evaluations and recommendations.

(A) In general. At least **5 business days prior to a hearing** conducted pursuant to paragraph (1), **each party shall disclose to all other parties all evaluations** completed by that date and recommendations based on the offering party's evaluations that the party intends to use at the hearing.

(B) Failure to disclose. A hearing officer **may bar any party that fails to comply with subparagraph (A) from introducing the relevant evaluation or recommendation** at the hearing without the consent of the other party.

(3) Limitation on conduct of hearing.

A hearing conducted pursuant to paragraph (1) may not be conducted by an employee of the State educational agency or the local educational agency involved in the education or care of the child.

(g) Appeal.

If the hearing required by subsection (f) is conducted by a local educational agency, any party aggrieved by the findings and decision rendered in such a hearing may appeal such findings and decision to the **State educational agency**. Such agency shall conduct an impartial review of such decision. The officer conducting such review shall make an independent decision upon completion of such review.

(h) Safeguards.

Any party to a hearing conducted pursuant to subsection (f) or (k), or an appeal conducted pursuant to subsection (g), shall be accorded

(1) the **right to be accompanied and advised by counsel and by individuals with special knowledge or training** with respect to the problems of children with disabilities;

(2) the **right to present evidence and confront, cross examine, and compel the attendance of witnesses;**

(3) the **right to a written,** or, at the option of the parents, electronic verbatim **record of such hearing;** and

(4) the right to **written,** or, at the option of the parents, electronic **findings of fact and decisions** (which findings and decisions shall be made available to the public consistent with the requirements of section 1417(c) (relating to the confidentiality of data, information, and records) and shall also be transmitted to the advisory panel established pursuant to section 1412(a)(21)).

(i) Administrative Procedures.

(1) In general.

(A) Decision made in hearing. A decision made in a hearing conducted pursuant to subsection (f) or (k) shall be **final,** except that any party involved in such hearing may appeal such decision under the provisions of subsection (g) and paragraph (2) of this subsection.

(B) Decision made at appeal. A decision made under subsection (g) shall be final, except that any party may bring an action under paragraph (2) of this subsection.

(2) Right to bring civil action.

(A) **In general.** Any party aggrieved by the findings and decision made under subsection (f) or (k) who does not have the right to an appeal under subsection (g), and any party aggrieved by the findings and decision under this subsection, **shall have the right to bring a civil action** with respect to the complaint presented pursuant to this section, which action may be brought in **any State court** of competent jurisdiction **or in a district court of the United States** without regard to the amount in controversy.

(B) Additional requirements. In any action brought under this paragraph, the court

(i) shall receive the records of the administrative proceedings;

(ii) shall hear additional evidence at the request of a party; and

(iii) basing its decision on the preponderance of the evidence, shall grant such relief as the court determines is appropriate.

(3) Jurisdiction of district courts; attorneys' fees.

(A) In general.

The district courts of the United States shall have jurisdiction of actions brought under this section without regard to the amount in controversy.

(B) Award of attorneys' fees.

In any action or proceeding brought under this section, the court, in its discretion, **may award reasonable attorneys' fees** as part of the costs to the parents of a child with a disability who is the prevailing party.

(C) Determination of amount of attorneys' fees.

Fees awarded under this paragraph shall be based on rates prevailing in the community in which the action or proceeding arose for the kind and quality of services furnished. No bonus or multiplier may be used in calculating the fees awarded under this subsection.

(D) Prohibition of attorneys' fees and related costs for certain services.

(i) Attorneys' fees may not be awarded and related costs **may not be reimbursed** in any action or proceeding under this section for services performed subsequent to the time of a **written offer of settlement** to a parent if

(I) the offer is made within the time prescribed by Rule 68 of the Federal Rules of Civil Procedure or, in the case of an administrative proceeding, at any time more than ten days before the proceeding begins;

(II) the offer is not accepted within 10 days; and

(III) the court or administrative hearing officer finds that the relief finally obtained by the parents is not more favorable to the parents than the offer of settlement.

(ii) **Attorneys' fees may not be awarded relating to any meeting of the IEP Team** unless such meeting is convened as a result of an administrative proceeding or judicial action, or, at the discretion of the State, for a mediation described in subsection (e) that is conducted prior to the filing of a complaint under subsection (b)(6) or (k) of this section.

(E) Exception to prohibition on attorneys' fees and related costs.

Notwithstanding subparagraph (D), an award of attorneys' fees and related costs may be made to a parent who is the prevailing party and who was substantially justified in rejecting the settlement offer.

(F) Reduction in amount of attorneys' fees.

Except as provided in subparagraph (G), whenever the court finds that

(i) the parent, during the course of the action or proceeding, **unreasonably protracted** the final resolution of the controversy;

(ii) the amount of the attorneys' fees otherwise authorized to be awarded unreasonably exceeds the hourly rate prevailing in the community for similar services by attorneys of reasonably comparable skill, reputation, and experience;

(iii) the time spent and legal services furnished were excessive considering the nature of the action or proceeding; or

(iv) **the attorney representing the parent did not provide to the school district the appropriate information in the due process complaint in accordance with subsection (b)(7);** the court shall reduce, accordingly, the amount of the attorneys' fees awarded under this section.

(G) Exception to reduction in amount of attorneys' fees.

The provisions of subparagraph (F) shall not apply in any action or proceeding if the court finds that the State or local educational agency unreasonably protracted the final resolution of the action or proceeding or there was a violation of this section.

(j) Maintenance of Current Educational Placement.

Except as provided in subsection (k)(7), during the pendency of any proceedings conducted pursuant to this section, unless the State or local educational agency and the parents otherwise agree, the **child shall remain in the then current educational placement of such child,** or, if applying for initial admission to a public school, shall, with the consent of the parents, be placed in the public school program until all such proceedings have been completed.

Wrightslaw Discussion of Mediation, Due Process Hearings, Appeals to Court, Attorneys' Fees

Mediation

Mediation is a process that allows parties to resolve their dispute without litigation. If entered into in good faith, mediation can lead to a "win-win" resolution of the complaint.

The mediator must be impartial and trained in mediation techniques. Good mediators do not need to be knowledgeable about special education law and practice. The mediator is not an arbitrator. Arbitrators must issue rulings in favor of one party or the other.

Mediation is a two-way street. Both sides must be prepared to discuss their differences frankly, without the presence of lawyers. The mediator's role is to **help the parties express their views and positions**, and to help the parties hear and understand these views and positions. Before entering mediation, both parties should understand their rights and the law.

Mediators should not take sides. **The mediator's job is to facilitate communication.** Some poorly trained mediators think their role is to explain the law and force a settlement, even if this means the mediator must take sides. If mediators are not properly trained and supervised, their personal and professional biases will have a negative impact on the mediation process. This will destroy trust on both sides and send cases to litigation.

Confidentiality

Confidentiality is vital to the success of mediation. Discussions and admissions by the parties are confidential. Without confidentiality, the purpose of mediation would be to gain a tactical advantage in subsequent litigation.

In law, **settlement discussions are usually confidential.** If a case is not settled, information from settlement discussions may not be used or disclosed in a subsequent trial. Any attempt to use confidential information from mediation or settlement discussions could lead to adverse consequences if the case were to end up in State or Federal Court.

Preparing for Mediation

If you have a dispute with the school, you need to learn how to resolve disputes and develop win-win solutions to problems. Two resources are *Getting to Yes* by Roger Fisher and *Getting Past No* by William Ury (see Bibliography).

 Wrightslaw: Special Education Law at pages 69-70, 34 C.F.R. § 300.506 at page 181.

 For articles about mediation, visit Wrightslaw at www.wrightslaw.com/ and Fetaweb at www.fetaweb.com/

Statute of Limitations

The time limit for requesting a due process hearing varies. In some states, you may have one or two years to request a due process hearing to remedy a problem, seek reimbursement for a private placement, or other relief. In some states, the statute of limitations (also known as a limitations of actions) may require that you request a hearing within 60 days of the incident, issue, or IEP meeting that triggered the dispute.

Each law may have a different statute of limitations. If different laws were violated, different statutes of limitation may affect a set of facts. Failure to comply with the statute of limitations usually results in waiving your rights. Courts do not protect parties who have rights and waive them.

Learn the statutes of limitations in your state. The statutes may be in your state special education regulations or they may be based on a specific case.

To learn the statutes in your state, talk to an attorney in your state who specializes in special education law. Get a copy of your state special education regulations. If you do not find the statutes of limitations in your state regulations, contact the person at the state department of education who monitors due process hearings and ask about the statute of limitations in your state.

Due Process Hearings

Parents and school district resolve disagreements and disputes about special education issues through due process hearings. Due process hearings are conducted differently in different states, and even within the same state. In some states, due process hearings are called Fair Hearings.

There are two systems of due process hearings. In a **two-tier system,** the due process hearing is held at the local level. The losing party may appeal to the State Educational Agency. The SEA appoints an independent Review Officer who issues a decision. The losing party at the review level may appeal to State or Federal Court. In states that adopted a **one-tier system,** the due process hearing is held by the State education agency (SEA). The losing party may appeal directly to State or Federal court.

Before you request a due process hearing, you must understand and apply the **Rules of Adverse Assumptions** to your situation. Due Process Hearings are complicated legal procedures. Do not expect to represent yourself.

 Read Chapter 21 about the Rules of Adverse Assumptions

Do not rely on school personnel or school testing. You will need independent evaluations and independent witnesses. Prepare as though you will not be able to testify at your due process hearing. If you develop **a paper trail** and secure competent independent experts from the private sector, you will be in a strong position if a due process hearing is necessary to resolve your issue. When you take these steps, you increase the odds that you will not need a due process hearing.

Exhibits

Most state regulations require each party to **disclose and provide a copy of all exhibits and the names of all witnesses** to the other party at least one week before the hearing. Failure to comply may result in dismissal of the case.

Your exhibit list may include:

- Letters, journals, logs
- Evaluations and reports
- Research, journal articles, book chapters
- Other documents that are relevant to your case

Many U. S. District Courts have adopted a rule that **all evidence must be submitted at the due process hearing** and no evidence may be submitted to the District Court Judge. An exception may be "after-discovered" evidence.

Hearing Officers and Administrative Law Judges

The quality of hearing officers varies around the country. In some states, hearing officers are employees of other school districts. In one state, hearing officers must have a high school diploma and cannot be employed by the school district. You will not be surprised to hear that parents in these states believe hearing officers who are school district employees are biased in favor of school districts.

In some states, hearings are conducted by Administrative Law Judges. Some people believe hearing officers should be attorneys. Other people believe that attorneys are rigid, and conduct hearings as legal proceedings with the burden of proof on parents.

If you are involved in a due process hearing, the personality, temperament, biases, and life experiences of your hearing officer or Administrative Law Judge will have a significant impact on the outcome of your case.

"Stay Put"

The requirement to maintain the current educational placement is called **"stay put."** If the parent objects to the school district's plan to change a child's program, placement, or eligibility status, and requests a special education due process hearing, the child must **"stay put"** in the placement that preceded this proposal.

However, this rule does not prevent the parent from removing the child from a public school placement and enrolling the child in a private special education school.

 See the statute discussed in § 1412(a)(10). See U. S. Supreme Court decisions in *Burlington* and *Carter* in *Wrightslaw: Special Education Law,* pages 323 and 343 respectively.

Attorneys' fees

The court may award attorneys' fees to the parents if they are the prevailing party. No attorneys' fees will be awarded for IEP meetings unless the IEP meeting is convened as the result of a due process hearing. School board counsel will assert that the IEP meeting was not the result of the pending litigation.

If the school district makes a written settlement offer more than ten days before the hearing that is the same as, or similar to, the relief received through litigation, and the parent rejects this offer, the parent loses all entitlement to attorneys' fees. Special education attorneys rarely represent parents on "contingency" arrangements since the outcome is rarely a large financial verdict, but instead relates to educational services. If the school settles in accordance with the "ten day written settlement offer" in the statute, then the parents are not entitled to reimbursement for attorneys' fees.

Exhaustion of Administrative Remedies

You cannot bring a special education dispute or complaint about an issue related to the Individuals with Disabilities Education Act directly to federal court until you exhaust your administrative remedies. The rare exception is sufficient proof that exhaustion would be futile.

Due process hearings are not meetings held to resolve misunderstandings. Due process hearings are similar to trials. In most cases, parents and school districts have retained counsel. The parents are entitled to a written verbatim record or transcript of the hearing.

Our system of justice is based on the adversarial approach. Under adversarial theory, the truth will come out in a dispute. Most due process hearings include opening statements, submission of evidence with specific rules about admissibility, rules about direct and cross-examination, and closing statements. For witnesses, going through cross-examination can be a brutal experience.

Successful Outcomes

Ultimately, your success in a hearing will depend on the law and facts, the preparedness of the attorneys, and the life experiences of the hearing officer, Administrative Law Judge, or other decision-maker. The pre-existing beliefs and opinions of the decision-maker are more controlling of outcome than the facts and the law. This is true in most litigation and is not unique to special education disputes.

 Wrightslaw: Special Education Law at pages 71-74; and 34 C.F.R. § 300.507-300.514 at pages 182-184.

20 U.S.C. § 1415(k) Placement in Alternative Educational Setting

☑ Skip Subsection 1415(k) unless you are dealing with a discipline issue. This part of the statute evolved from Congressional compromises with vague words and standards that courts may be resolved over the next decade. At press time Congress was considering changes to this subsection.

(1) Authority of school personnel.

(A) **School personnel under this section may order a change in the placement** of a child with a disability

(i) to an appropriate interim alternative educational setting, another setting, or suspension, **for not more than 10 school days** (to the extent such alternatives would be applied to children without disabilities); **and**

(ii) **to an appropriate interim alternative educational setting** for the same amount of time that a child without a disability would be subject to discipline, but **for not more than 45 days if (I) the child carries or possesses a weapon to or at school, on school premises,** or to or at a school function under the jurisdiction of a State or a local educational agency; **or (II) the child knowingly possesses or uses illegal drugs** or sells or solicits the sale of a controlled substance while **at school** or a school function under the jurisdiction of a State or local educational agency.

(B) Either before or not later than 10 days after taking a disciplinary action described in subparagraph (A)

(i) **if the local educational agency did not conduct a functional behavioral assessment and implement a behavioral intervention plan for such child before the behavior that resulted in the suspension described in subparagraph (A), the agency shall convene an IEP meeting** to develop an assessment plan to address that behavior; or

(ii) if the child already has a behavioral intervention plan, the IEP Team shall review the plan and modify it, as necessary, to address the behavior.

(2) Authority of hearing officer. A hearing officer under this section may order a change in the placement of a child with a disability to an appropriate interim alternative educational setting for not more than 45 days if the hearing officer

(A) determines that the public agency has demonstrated by substantial evidence that maintaining the current placement of such child is substantially likely to result in injury to the child or to others;

(B) considers the appropriateness of the child's current placement;

(C) considers whether the public agency has made reasonable efforts to minimize the risk of harm in the child's current placement, including the use of supplementary aids and services; and

(D) determines that the interim alternative educational setting meets the requirements of paragraph (3)(B).

(3) Determination of setting.

(A) In general. The alternative educational setting described in paragraph (1)(A)(ii) shall be determined by the IEP Team.

(B) Additional requirements. Any interim alternative educational setting in which a child is placed under paragraph (1) or (2) shall

(i) be selected so as to enable the child to continue to participate in the general curriculum, although in another setting, and to continue to receive those services and modifications, including those described in the child's current IEP, that will enable the child to meet the goals set out in that IEP; and

(ii) include services and modifications designed to address the behavior described in paragraph (1) or paragraph (2) so that it does not recur.

(4) Manifestation Determination Review.

(A) In general. If a disciplinary action is contemplated as described in paragraph (1) or paragraph (2) for a behavior of a child with a disability described in either of those paragraphs, or if a disciplinary action involving a change of placement for more than 10 days is contemplated for a child with a disability who has engaged in other behavior that violated any rule or code of conduct of the local educational agency that applies to all children

(i) not later than the date on which the decision to take that action is made, the parents shall be notified of that decision and of all procedural safeguards accorded under this section; and

(ii) **immediately, if possible, but in no case later than 10 school days after the date on which the decision to take that action is made, a review shall be conducted of the relationship between the child's disability and the behavior subject to the disciplinary action.**

(B) Individuals to carry out review. A review described in subparagraph (A) shall be conducted by the IEP Team and other qualified personnel.

(C) Conduct of review. In carrying out a review described in subparagraph (A), the IEP Team may determine that the behavior of the child was not a manifestation of such child's disability only if the IEP Team

(i) first considers, in terms of the behavior subject to disciplinary action, all relevant information, including (I) evaluation and diagnostic results, including such results or other relevant information supplied by the parents of the child; (II) observations of the child; and (III) the child's IEP and placement; and

(ii) then determines that (I) in relationship to the behavior subject to disciplinary action, the child's IEP and placement were appropriate and the special education services, supplementary aids and services, and behavior intervention strategies were provided consistent with the child's IEP and placement; (II) the child's disability did not impair the ability of the child to understand the impact and consequences of the behavior subject to disciplinary action; and (III) the child's disability did not impair the ability of the child to control the behavior subject to disciplinary action.

(5) Determination that behavior was not manifestation of disability.

(A) In general. If the result of the review described in paragraph (4) is a determination, consistent with paragraph (4)(C), that the behavior of the child with a disability **was not a manifestation of the child's disability,** the relevant disciplinary procedures applicable to children without disabilities may be applied to the child in the same manner in which they would be applied to children without disabilities, **except as provided in section 1412(a)(1).**

(B) Additional requirement. If the public agency initiates disciplinary procedures applicable to all children, the agency shall ensure that the special education and disciplinary records of the child with a disability are transmitted for consideration by the person or persons making the final determination regarding the disciplinary action.

(6) Parent appeal.

(A) In general.

(i) If the child's parent disagrees with a determination that the child's behavior was not a manifestation of the child's disability or with any decision regarding placement, **the parent may request a hearing.**

(ii) The State or local educational agency shall arrange for an **expedited hearing** in any case described in this subsection when requested by a parent.

(B) Review of decision.

(i) In reviewing a decision with respect to the manifestation determination, the hearing officer shall determine whether the public agency has demonstrated that the child's behavior was not a manifestation of such child's disability consistent with the requirements of paragraph (4)(C).

(ii) In reviewing a decision under paragraph (1)(A)(ii) to place the child in an interim alternative educational setting, the hearing officer shall apply the standards set out in paragraph (2).

(7) Placement during appeals.

(A) In general. When a parent requests a hearing regarding a disciplinary action described in paragraph (1)(A)(ii) or paragraph (2) to challenge the interim alternative educational setting or the manifestation determination, the child shall remain in the interim alternative educational setting pending the decision of the hearing officer or until the expiration of the time period provided for in paragraph (1)(A)(ii) or paragraph (2), whichever occurs first, unless the parent and the State or local educational agency agree otherwise.

(B) Current placement. If a child is placed in an interim alternative educational setting pursuant to paragraph (1)(A)(ii) or paragraph (2) and school personnel propose to change the child's placement after expiration of the interim alternative placement, during the pendency of any proceeding to challenge the proposed change in placement, the child shall remain in the current placement (the child's placement prior to the interim alternative educational setting), except as provided in subparagraph (C).

(C) Expedited hearing.

(i) **If school personnel maintain that it is dangerous for the child to be in the current placement** (placement prior to removal to the interim alternative education setting) during the pendency of the due process proceedings, the local educational agency may request an expedited hearing.

(ii) In determining whether the child may be placed in the alternative educational setting or in another appropriate placement ordered by the hearing officer, the hearing officer shall apply the standards set out in paragraph (2).

(8) **Protections for children not yet eligible for special education and related services.**

(A) **In general.** A child who has not been determined to be eligible for special education and related services under this subchapter and who has engaged in behavior that violated any rule or code of conduct of the local educational agency, including any behavior described in paragraph (1), may assert any of the protections provided for in this subchapter if the local educational agency had knowledge (as determined in accordance with this paragraph) that the child was a child with a disability before the behavior that precipitated the disciplinary action occurred.

(B) **Basis of knowledge.** A local educational agency shall be deemed to have knowledge that a child is a child with a disability if

(i) **the parent of the child has expressed concern in writing** (unless the parent is illiterate or has a disability that prevents compliance with the requirements contained in this clause) to personnel of the appropriate educational agency that the child is in need of special education and related services;

(ii) the behavior or performance of the child demonstrates the need for such services;

(iii) **the parent of the child has requested an evaluation of the child pursuant to section 1414 of this title;** or

(iv) the teacher of the child, or other personnel of the local educational agency, has expressed concern about the behavior or performance of the child to the director of special education of such agency or to other personnel of the agency.

(C) **Conditions that apply if no basis of knowledge.**

(i) **In general.** If a local educational agency does not have knowledge that a child is a child with a disability (in accordance with subparagraph (B)) prior to taking disciplinary measures against the child, the child may be subjected to the same disciplinary measures as measures applied to children without disabilities who engaged in comparable behaviors consistent with clause (ii).

(ii) **Limitations.** If a request is made for an evaluation of a child during the time period in which the child is subjected to disciplinary measures under paragraph (1) or (2), the evaluation shall be conducted in an expedited manner. If the child is determined to be a child with a disability, taking into consideration information from the evaluation conducted by the agency and information provided by the parents, the agency shall provide special education and related services in accordance with the provisions of this subchapter, except that, pending the results of the evaluation, the child shall remain in the educational placement determined by school authorities.

(9) Referral to and action by law enforcement and judicial authorities.

(A) Nothing in this subchapter shall be construed to prohibit an agency from reporting a crime committed by a child with a disability to appropriate authorities or to prevent State law enforcement and judicial authorities from exercising their responsibilities with regard to the application of Federal and State law to crimes committed by a child with a disability.

(B) An agency reporting a crime committed by a child with a disability shall ensure that **copies of the special education and disciplinary records of the child are transmitted** for consideration by the appropriate authorities to whom it reports the crime.

(10) Definitions. For purposes of this subsection, the following definitions apply:

(A) **Controlled substance.** The term 'controlled substance' means a drug or other substance identified under schedules I, II, III, IV, or V in section 202(c) of the Controlled Substances Act (21 U.S.C. 812(c)).

(B) **Illegal drug.** The term 'illegal drug'

(i) means a controlled substance; but

(ii) does not include such a substance that is legally possessed or used under the supervision of a licensed health-care professional or that is legally possessed or used under any other authority under that Act or under any other provision of Federal law.

(C) **Substantial evidence.** The term 'substantial evidence' means beyond a preponderance of the evidence.

(D) **Weapon.** The term 'weapon' has the meaning given the term 'dangerous weapon' under paragraph (2) of the first subsection (g) of section 930 of title 18, United States Code.

Wrightslaw Discussion of Discipline

☑ **Unless your child is facing suspension or expulsion, or is at risk for discipline problems, skip this section.**

School personnel can initiate short-term suspensions or changes in placement without the authority of a Hearing Officer under (k)(1). For a longer change in placement, the school must obtain an order from a Hearing Officer, pursuant to (k)(2).

Suspensions for up to 10 days

If a child brings a weapon or illegal drugs to school, the child can be suspended for ten days and placed in an alternative setting for 45 days, without an Order from a Hearing Officer.

If the child did not carry a weapon or illegal drugs to school, the school may suspend the child for up to ten days and/or send the child to an alternative setting ten days.

Suspensions for more than 10 days

For a longer placement in an interim alternative setting, the school must obtain an ORDER from an independent Hearing Officer before placing the child in the interim alternative setting for up to 45 days.

Behavioral Intervention Plan

If the school does not conduct a functional behavioral assessment and fails to devise a behavioral intervention plan before an incident, the school must convene an IEP meeting to develop a behavioral intervention plan. If the IEP team has a behavioral intervention plan in place, the school must convene an IEP meeting to review and perhaps to modify this plan to address the child's behavior problems.

If the IEP team decides that the child's behavior is not a manifestation of the disability, the child may be treated as a regular education child, subject to 20 U.S.C. § 1412(a)(1). Remember: 1412(a)(1) requires that a "free appropriate public education is available to all children with disabilities residing in the State between the ages of 3 and 21, inclusive, including children with disabilities who have been suspended or expelled from school."

School Must Provide FAPE

Regardless of whether the child's behavior was or was not related to the disability, the school may not deny educational services to the child with a disability.

If the school suspends or expels a child with a disability for behavior that is not related to the disability, the school must continue to provide the child with a free, appropriate public education. This requirement has led to a proliferation of "alternative educational settings."

Put Your Concerns in Writing

If you are concerned that your child has a disability, special needs, or learns differently, you should put your concerns in writing. Describe the disability and how, in your opinion, it adversely affects educational performance. If you report your concerns orally, for the purposes of law and litigation, you said nothing. Follow up your conversations, meetings, and telephone calls with letters that restate what you discussed and your concerns.

Courts do not have sympathy for individuals who know they have rights, fail to protect their rights, and complain that their rights were violated. Individuals who complain that their rights were violated must be able to prove that they took reasonable steps to protect themselves, and despite these steps, their rights were violated.

Medications and Controlled Substances

According to this definition, over-the-counter medications (i.e., aspirin, ibuprofen, and antacids) are not controlled substances. If your child has Ritalin that was prescribed by a doctor, the school may not expel or suspend your child. But if your child tries to sell or distribute a drug, your child faces sanctions that are described in the beginning of this section under (k)(1) and (k)(2).

Using "zero tolerance" anti-drug policies, many school districts have labeled over-the-counter-medication as "drugs," branded children as drug violators, and expelled children from school. Using "zero tolerance" policies where punishments do not fit the crime, schools are suspending and expelling children for bringing penknives and cracker-jack toys to school.

Zero tolerance policies require that children from kindergarten through 12th grade receive harsh punishments, often for minor infractions that pose no threat to safety. Compelling research indicates that these "get-tough" disciplinary measures fail to meet sound educational principles. In many cases, their application defies commonsense.

The Harvard Civil Rights Project reported that:

Unfortunately, zero tolerance policies that prescribe automatic and/or harsh punishments undermine the ability of teachers and administrators to form trusting relationships with students, and ultimately, these policies transmit negative messages about fairness, equity, and justice. As a result, many students are further alienated from the educational process, and behavioral problems meant to be remedied are, instead, exacerbated.

 For information about zero tolerance and the Harvard Civil Rights Project, see Appendix H.

Under zero tolerance policies, a Virginia school district expelled a child who brought a one-inch, plastic toy replica of a gun to school. According to the IDEA, a toy is not a weapon. A child with a disability who receives services under the IDEA is protected from these abuses. A child who is protected from discrimination under Section 504 is not protected.

The discipline section of the IDEA is under attack in Congress. After this book is published, Congress may modify the statute. If your child is facing suspension or expulsion, you need to have a current copy of the law. Your state department of education should be able to provide you with the current state law and regulations about discipline.

 Wrightslaw: Special Education Law at pages 75-79, 34 C.F.R. §§ 300.519, 300.529 at pages 185-189.

20 U.S.C. § 1415 (m) Transfer of Parental Rights at Age of Majority

(1) **In general.** A State that receives amounts from a grant under this part may provide that, when a child with a disability reaches the age of majority under State law (except for a child with a disability who has been determined to be incompetent under State law)

(A) the public agency shall provide any notice required by this section to both the individual and the parents;

(B) all other rights accorded to parents under this part transfer to the child;

(C) the agency shall notify the individual and the parents of the transfer of rights; and

(D) all rights accorded to parents under this part transfer to children who are incarcerated in an adult or juvenile Federal, State, or local correctional institution.

(2) **Special rule.** If, under State law, a child with a disability who has reached the age of majority under State law, who has not been determined to be incompetent, but who is determined not to have the ability to provide informed consent with respect to the educational program of the child, the State shall establish procedures for appointing the parent of the child, or if the parent is not available, another appropriate individual, to represent the educational interests of the child throughout the period of eligibility of the child under this part.

Wrightslaw Discussion of Age of Majority

Unless a child is determined to be incompetent, when the child reaches the age of majority, the rights accorded to the parent will transfer to the child. Most states have established procedures so that parents can continue to represent the interests of their adult children.

For more information about this issue and the forms that your adult child can sign to give you permission to advocate on behalf of your child, contact your state department of education. (Appendix D is a listing of all state departments of education.)

 Wrightslaw: Special Education Law at page 79-80 includes suggested language for a form. See also federal regulation 34 C.F.R. § 300.517 at page 185.

Your Notes Here

19 | Section 504 of The Rehabilitation Act of 1973 and the Americans with Disabilities Act

Morality cannot be legislated but behavior can be regulated. Judicial decrees may not change the heart, but they can restrain the heartless. — Martin Luther King, civil rights activist

In this chapter, you will learn about Section 504 of the Rehabilitation Act and the Americans with Disabilities Act, as contrasted with the Individuals with Disabilities Education Act (IDEA).

The key portion of **Section 504 of the Rehabilitation Act** at 29 U. S. C. § 794 states:

Section 794. Nondiscrimination under Federal grants and programs

(a) Promulgation of nondiscriminatory rules and regulations

No otherwise qualified individual with a disability in the United States, as defined in Sec. 705(20) of this title, shall, solely **by reason of her or his disability, be excluded from the participation in, be denied the benefits of, or be subjected to discrimination** under any program or activity receiving Federal financial assistance or under any program or activity conducted by any Executive agency or by the United States Postal Service . . .

The **Americans with Disabilities Act**, as it applies to public entities, is identical. Subchapter II, Part A, of the Americans with Disabilities Act at 42 U. S. C. § 12132 and § 12133 states:

Section 12132. Discrimination

Subject to the provisions of this subchapter, no qualified individual with a disability shall, **by reason of such disability, be excluded from participation in or be denied the benefits of the services, programs, or activities of a public entity, or be subjected to discrimination by any such entity.**

Section. 12133. Enforcement

The remedies, procedures, and rights set forth in section 794a of title 29 shall be the remedies, procedures, and rights this subchapter provides to any person alleging discrimination on the basis of disability in violation of section 12132 of this title.

The language of ADA tracks Section 504 and explains that the remedies, procedures and rights under the ADA are the same as under the Rehabilitation Act. Except for accessibility of buildings, and modifications and accommodations in testing, Section 504 and ADA provide few protections and limited benefits to children with disabilities.

Wrightslaw Discussion of Section 504, ADA and IDEA

Section 504 is a civil rights law. The purpose of Section 504 is to protect individuals with disabilities from discrimination for reasons related to their disabilities. ADA broadened the agencies and businesses that must comply with the non-discrimination and accessibility provisions of the law.

Unlike IDEA, Section 504 and ADA do not ensure that a child with a disability will receive an individualized educational program that is designed to meet the child's unique needs and provide the child with educational benefit, so the child will be prepared for "for employment and independent living."

Eligibility

The child who has a disability or impairment does not automatically qualify for special education services under the IDEA. If the child has a disability but does not need special education services, the child will not qualify for special education and related services under the IDEA but may receive protections under Section 504 of the Rehabilitation Act.

To be eligible for protections under Section 504, the child must have a physical or mental impairment. This impairment must substantially limit at least one major life activity. Major life activities include walking, seeing, hearing, speaking, breathing, learning, reading, writing, performing math calculations, working, caring for oneself, and performing manual tasks. The key is whether the child has an "impairment" that "substantially limits . . . one or more . . . major life activities."

Section 504 requires an evaluation that draws information from a variety of sources. Section 504 does not require a meeting before a change in placement.

Protection from Discrimination

Section 504 protects children with disabilities from discrimination. It is important to understand that if your child does not receive special education services under

IDEA, your child does not have the procedural protections that are available under the IDEA statute.

Accommodations and Modifications

Under Section 504, the child with a disability may receive accommodations and modifications that are not available to children who are not disabled. These accommodations and modifications are also available under IDEA.

Confusion about Benefits and Rights

Some parents and educators believe that under IDEA, the child must be placed in special education classes but that if the child has a 504 plan, the child may remain in the regular classroom. For these reasons, parents often assume that Section 504 is more desirable. This is incorrect. "Special education" under IDEA is not a place or placement.

The child who receives Section 504 protections has fewer rights than the child who receives special education services under the IDEA. The child who receives special education services under the IDEA is automatically protected under Section 504.

Access v. Educational Benefit

Change the facts to clarify the differences between these two laws. Assume that your special needs child is in a wheel chair. Under Section 504, your child shall not be discriminated against because of the disability. Your child shall be provided with **access to an education**, to and through the schoolhouse door. Modifications may be made to the building and other accommodations may be made for your child.

Under Section 504 regulations, a free appropriate public education is defined as "the provision of regular or special education and related aids and services that . . . are designed to meet individual educational needs of persons with disabilities **as adequately as the needs of persons without disabilities are met** and . . . are based upon adherence to specified procedures." (34 C.F.R.§ 104.33(b)(1))

Now assume that your child in a wheelchair also has neurological problems that adversely affect the child's ability to learn. Under the IDEA, if your child has a disability that adversely affects educational performance, your child is entitled to an education that is designed to meet the child's unique needs and from which your child receives educational benefit. Section 504 includes no guarantee that your wheelchair-bound child will receive an education from which your child receives educational benefit. Your Section 504 child has access to the same free appropriate public education that is available to children who are not disabled.

Discipline

If the Section 504 child misbehaves and the school decides the child's behavior is not a manifestation of the disability, the child can be expelled from school permanently. The IDEA child has the right to FAPE, even if expelled from school. Section 504 and ADA do not provide these protections.

Procedural Safeguards

Section 504 does not include a clearly established "Prior Written Notice" requirement. In contrast, IDEA includes an elaborate system of procedural safeguards designed to protect the child and parents. These safeguards include written notice before any change of placement and the right to an independent educational evaluation at public expense. Section 504 does not include these protections.

Impartial Hearings

Section 504 and IDEA require school districts to conduct impartial hearings for parents who disagree with identification, evaluation, or placement. Under Section 504, the parent has an opportunity to participate and obtain representation by counsel, but other details are left to the discretion of the school district.

 The complete text of the Rehabilitation Act and regulations are in *Wrightslaw: Special Education Law*, pages 263 to 280.

Section 504, ADA, High Stakes Testing, Statewide Assessments

Parents Engaged in Education Reform (PEER) is a national technical assistance project operated by The Federation for Children with Special Needs (www.fcsn.org) and funded by the U.S. Department of Education, Office of Special Education Programs. PEER seeks to increase the participation of special needs parents and organizations in school reform efforts. PEER prepared an excellent information brief about Section 504, ADA, and statewide and high stakes testing and granted permission for Wrightslaw to reproduce the full text of the document.

PEER Information Brief
Section 504, the Americans with Disabilities Act, and Education Reform (Prepared by the PEER Project)

Introduction

In implementing education reform initiatives, public schools and school systems must abide by Section 504 of the Rehabilitation Act of 1973 (Section 504) and Title II of the Americans with Disabilities Act (ADA) which prohibit discrimination on the basis of disability. Section 504 prohibits recipients of federal funds from discriminating on the basis of disability. Title II of the ADA prohibits discrimination on the basis of disability in state and local government services by state and local governmental entities, whether or not they receive federal funds. This includes public school districts. Virtually all public school systems receive federal funds, and public education is a government service. Both statutes require school districts to provide a free appropriate public education (FAPE) to students with disabilities protected by those laws.

Education reform initiatives, of course, vary from state to state, and sometimes from community to community. There is one kind of initiative, however, that is common nationwide. This approach, known as "standards-based" education reform, has four basic components. First, standards are set for what students should know and be able to do at various grades. Second, curricula are designed, guided by the standards. Third, based on the curricula, teachers design individual courses and instructional strategies, including the materials and methods best suited for their students. Fourth, students are assessed at different points in their school career to determine how well schools are doing at enabling them to meet the standards. The results of these assessments are then used to hold schools accountable for how well they are educating their students.

The theory behind standards-based education reform is that by setting high standards, shaping curriculum and instruction to meet them, and holding schools accountable for how well students meet the standards, educational quality will rise for all students. This PEER Information Brief examines how Section 504 and the ADA should work to ensure that students with disabilities enjoy the benefits of these reforms, and the quality education they aim for. It begins with a discussion of key concepts under Section 504 and the ADA (and the federal regulations implementing these laws), and then applies these concepts to the basic components of standards-based education reform: (1) standards; (2) curriculum; (3) individual courses, instructional strategies, and materials; and (4) assessment for school accountability.

Key Concepts Under Section 504 and the ADA

1. Comparable Benefits and Services

Section 504 and Title II of the ADA are broad civil rights statutes designed to promote equal access to and participation in programs and services. The regulations implementing these laws require that students with disabilities receive benefits and services comparable to those given their nondisabled peers. Specifically, these laws make it illegal for schools to discriminate on the basis of disability by:

- denying a student the opportunity to participate in or benefit from a benefit or service,

- providing an opportunity to participate or benefit that is unequal to that provided others,

- providing a benefit or service that is not as effective as that provided to others,

- providing lower quality benefits, services or programs than those provided others, or

- providing different or separate benefits or services, unless it is necessary to provide benefits or services that are as effective as those provided to others. [1]

For benefits or services provided to be "equally effective," they must afford students with disabilities an equal opportunity to obtain the same result, gain the same benefit, or reach the same level of achievement as other students. [2]

The Section 504 regulations require that school systems receiving federal funds provide a free appropriate public education to children with disabilities in accordance with the Section 504 requirements regarding least restrictive setting, evaluation and placement, and procedural safeguards. FAPE under Section 504 means that the education provided to students with disabilities must meet those students' needs as adequately as the needs of non-disabled students are met. [3]

2. Criteria and Methods of Administration

It is illegal under the Section 504 and ADA regulations for school systems to use policies and practices that, intentionally or not, result in discrimination. [4] The regulations for both Section 504 and ADA use the term "criteria and methods of administration."

"Criteria" are written or formal policies; "methods of administration" are the school system's actual practices and procedures. The ban on discriminatory policies, practices, and procedures includes those that:

- have the effect of discriminating against students with disabilities, or

- have the effect of defeating or impairing accomplishment of the objectives of the education program (or school reform initiative) in regard to students with disabilities.

3. Reasonable Accommodations

In meeting the responsibilities to students with disabilities under Section 504 and Title II of the ADA, school systems must make accommodations and modifications to address the needs of students with disabilities. [5] Making accommodations and modifications means changing the way things are usually done in order to take into account a child's disability-related needs. Examples of accommodations and modifications include modifying rules, policies or practices; removing architectural or communication barriers; or providing aids, services, or assistive technology.

4. Maximum Feasible Integration

Under Section 504, children with disabilities must be educated with their non-disabled peers "to the maximum extent appropriate," and "removal . . . from the regular educational environment" occurs "only when the nature or severity of the disability is such that education in regular classes with the use of supplementary aids and services cannot be achieved satisfactorily." [6] The ADA regulations similarly provide that a public entity, such as a school system, "shall administer services, programs, and activities in the most integrated setting appropriate to the needs of qualified individuals with disabilities." [7] Schools have the burden of demonstrating that any removal from regular education is appropriate. [8]

Key Legal Concepts and Standards-Based Education Reform

Using Standards as a Strategy for Reform

Standards-based education reform aims to attain high quality educational outcomes by identifying desired learning outcomes for students, shaping curricula and instruction accordingly, and holding schools accountable for the results. If a state or school system adopts standards for general education, then students with disabilities have the right to an education based on these same standards. Failure to apply standards to students with disabilities is a failure to provide "comparable benefits and services." Schools **violate** Section 504 and ADA regulations whenever students with disabilities are denied the benefits of education reform standards. [9]

Linking Curriculum, Courses, and Instructional Strategies to the Standards Set for All Students

Standards in standards-based education reform define some of the outcomes of a quality education. The curriculum is then designed to reflect the standards and deliver that quality education. The goal of education reform is to make sure that students learn the curriculum which reflects the standards. Therefore, students with disabilities, like all other children, must be provided with courses and instruction that teach the curriculum. Otherwise, they will be denied comparable benefits and services, in violation of Section 504 and the ADA. For some students, the method of teaching some or all of the curriculum may need to be modified, perhaps as a reasonable accommodation, or as a supplementary aid or service necessary for maximum feasible participation in regular education. For a small number of students who have significant disabilities, it may be necessary to modify, adapt, or expand the curriculum or instruction to provide access to the standards. These decisions must be made on an individual basis, and based upon valid and competent individualized educational evaluations.

Further, it is also discriminatory for school systems to adopt "criteria or methods of administration" (policies and practices) which limit opportunities for students with disabilities to learn the standards. To avoid such discrimination, school systems must identify and examine any policies or practices that may have the effect of limiting students' access to the courses and instruction necessary to learn the curriculum and meet the standards. Depending upon the circumstances, any number of policies and practices might have this effect. Examples include lack of coordination (in terms of both scheduling and content) between pull-out programs, such as resource rooms, and the mainstream academic curriculum; providing a diluted curriculum in separate programs and classes for students with disabilities; and failing to integrate special education supports and related services into regular education classes.

Using Assessment for School Accountability

Assessment is key to ensuring that school reform initiatives actually deliver quality education. The purpose of these assessments, often called "large-scale assessments," is to gather information that shows whether schools are successfully teaching students the standards. This information is then used to identify weaknesses in schools and to make necessary improvements. Assessment is the way that standards-based education reform holds schools accountable for student learning and achievement.

Historically, students with disabilities have been excluded from such assessments in large numbers. As a result, information about the achievement of these students is often missing when the effectiveness of school programs and services is evaluated and decisions about policies and reform initiatives are being made. With exclusion from assessment, schools are not held accountable for the quality of education students with disabilities receive. These students are denied the benefit of this critical aspect of standards-based education reform in violation of the requirement to provide comparable benefits and services under Section 504 and the ADA.

These civil rights laws require not only that students with disabilities take part in these accountability assessments, but that they receive any reasonable accommodations necessary to participate.

For many students, participation in assessment will not require any changes in the way that the assessment is given. Other students will require accommodations such as extra time for the assessment or materials in a different format (e.g., written materials in Braille, or a reader) in order to participate. A small number of students may require a different type of assessment (an "alternate assessment") to demonstrate their knowledge and skills in a nondiscriminatory manner. For example, some students may need a "hands-on" test using models rather than a pencil and paper test to show their understanding of geometry, and some students may require a portfolio assessment.

Endnotes

[1] 34 C.F.R. §104.4(b)(1) (§504 regulation); 28 U.S.C. §35.130(b)(1) (ADA regulation).

[2] 34 C.F.R. §104.4(b)(2); 28 C.F.R. §35.130(b)(iii).

³ 34 C.F.R. §104.33.

⁴ 34 C.F.R. §104.4(b)(4); 28 C.F.R. §35.130(b)(3).

⁵ See 42 U.S.C. 12131(2); 34 C.F.R. 104.4(b); 28 C.F.R. 35.130(b)(7); Alexander v. Choate, 469 U.S. 287, 300-01 (1985); *Thomas v. Davidson Academy*, 846 F. Supp. 611 (M.D. Tenn. 1994).

⁶ 34 C.F.R. §104.34(a).

⁷ 28 C.F.R. §35.130(d). See also 28 C.F.R. §35.130(b)(2) ("[a] public entity may not deny a qualified individual with a disability the opportunity to participate in services, programs, or activities that are not separate or different, despite the existence of permissibly separate or different programs or activities").

⁸ 34 C.F.R. §104.34(a).

⁹ In addition, 1997 amendments to the Individuals with Disabilities Education Act require states to develop "performance goals and indicators" for children with disabilities that are consistent, to the maximum extent appropriate, with the standards set by the state for all students. 20 U.S.C. §1412(a)(16).

The PEER Project gratefully acknowledges the contributions of staff attorneys at the Center for Law and Education in preparation of this Information Brief . The PEER Project drew heavily on their work and legal analysis.

This publication has been reviewed and approved by the U.S. Department of Education, Office of Special Education and Rehabilitative Services (OSERS). Funding for this publication was provided by the Office of Special Education Programs, OSERS, U.S. Department of Education, through grant #H029K50208.

Federation for Children with Special Needs

1135 Tremont Street, Suite 420

Boston, MA 02120

(617) 236-7210

END OF PEER REPRINT

 See Appendix G for legal and advocacy resources.

 As this book goes to press, several cases related to the issues in the "PEER Brief" are pending in the Courts. Visit www.fetaweb.com for updates.

In Summation

    In this chapter, you learned about Section 504 of the Rehabilitation Act and the Americans with Disabilities Act. You learned that these statutes are responsible for accommodations and modifications in testing situations and programs, and improved building accessibility. You also learned that these statutes do not require public schools to provide an educational program that is individualized to meet the needs of a specific child with the goal of enabling the child to become independent and self- sufficient. You have learned that the child with a Section 504 plan does not have the protections available to the child who has an IEP under the IDEA.

20 | Family Educational Rights and Privacy Act

"The great dangers to liberty lurk in insidious encroachment by men of zeal, well meaning but without understanding." — Justice Louis D. Brandeis, Jurist

In this chapter, you will learn about the Family Educational Rights and Privacy Act (FERPA). FERPA deals with privacy and confidentiality, parent access to educational records, parent amendment of records, and destruction of records. The purpose of the FERPA statute is to protect the privacy of parents and students.

FERPA applies to all agencies and institutions that receive federal funds, including elementary and secondary schools, colleges, and universities. The statute is in the United States Code at 20 U.S.C.1232. The regulations are in the Code of Federal Regulations at 34 C.F.R. Part 99.

 Wrightslaw: Special Education Law, pages 283-287, 34 C.F.R. Part 99, pages 289-299.

FERPA

Educational Records

Educational records include "all instructional materials, including teacher's manuals, films, tapes, or other supplementary material which will be used in connection with any survey, analysis, or evaluation as part of any applicable program shall be available for inspection by the parents or guardians of the children."

Schools must disclose test materials, including test protocols and answer sheets. The Office for Civil Rights has determined that the test protocols used by a psychologist to prepare a report are educational records and must be produced to the parents. Destruction of records violates the parents' rights of access.

The transcript of a hearing is an educational record for purposes of Section 504.

Due process decisions are educational records. Tapes of IEP meetings are educational records as are IEPs. Personal notes and memory aids that are used only by the person who made them are not educational records. If notes are shared with or disclosed to another person, the notes are educational records.

Right to Inspect and Review Educational Records

Parents have a right to inspect and review all educational records relating to their child. This right to "inspect and review" includes the right to have copies of records and to receive explanations and interpretations from school officials. Agencies must comply with requests to inspect and review records within forty-five days.

Copies of records must be provided to the parent if failure to do so would prevent the parent from exercising the right to view records. Schools may charge reasonable copying fees unless the fee would "effectively prevent" the parent or student from exercising the right to inspect and review the records. Fees may not be charged for searching and retrieving records.

According to the FERPA regulations "If circumstances effectively prevent the parent or eligible student from exercising the right to inspect and review the student's education records, the educational agency or institution, or SEA or its component, shall (1) Provide the parent or eligible student with a copy of the records requested; or (2) Make other arrangements for the parent or eligible student to inspect and review the requested records."

If the parent believes that the educational record contains inaccurate or misleading information, the parent may ask the agency to amend the record. The parent may also request a hearing to correct or challenge misleading or inaccurate information. You should make these requests in writing.

Disclosures

Schools may release records without consent to "other school officials, including teachers within the educational institution or local educational agency, who have been determined by such agency or institution to have legitimate educational interests."

Records may be released to "officials of other schools or school systems in which the student seeks or intends to enroll, upon condition that the student 's parents be notified of the transfer, receive a copy of the record if desired, and have an opportunity for a hearing to challenge the content of the record."

In health and safety emergencies, schools may make disclosures without consent. Law enforcement agencies and monitoring agencies have access to confidential records. The agency must maintain a log of all disclosures without parental consent. Consent for disclosure must be signed and dated and must include specific information about the recipients of information.

Destruction of Records

Pursuant to the General Educational Provisions Act, schools must retain records for at least five years. The school may not destroy any education records if there is an outstanding request to inspect and review the records under this section.

Test Protocols and Answer Booklets

Completed test instruments or question booklets containing information that identify a particular student, whether or not the name of the student appears on the booklet, constitute "education records" subject to the FERPA requirements. When an answer sheet is related to the student and is separate from the question booklet that is not directly related to a student, the answer sheet is considered an education record under FERPA. If a question booklet includes the questions and the student's responses, the question booklet is an education record subject to FERPA.

An educational agency is required to respond to a reasonable request for an explanation or interpretation of a student's answer sheet. Because answer sheets are usually related to a student, answer sheets fall within the definition of education records that a parent has the right to inspect and review. As a parent, you have a right to access to your child's answer sheet and an explanation or interpretation of that answer sheet.

On October 2, 1997, the Family Policy Compliance Office of the U. S. Department of Education issued this memorandum about a parent's access to test protocols. The full text is reprinted below:

FPCO Policy Letter

Availability of Test Protocols

FROM: LeRoy S. Rooker, Director

Family Policy Compliance Office

DATE: October 2, 1997

SUBJECT: Access to test protocols and test answer sheets

This is in response to your letter dated July 24, 1997, in which you ask several questions regarding a parent's right to have access to test protocols and test answer sheets under the Family Educational Rights and Privacy Act (FERPA). Specifically, you ask, in an effort to protect the integrity of a protocol, for alternative means of providing a parent the opportunity to inspect and review a protocol when he or she does not live within commuting distance of a school. You also ask if a parent of a child in one of the school districts you represent and who will be reviewing a protocol of a test taken by her child is entitled to a copy of the protocol. Finally, you ask if the same parent is entitled to a copy of her child's answer sheet. As you are aware, this Office administers FERPA.

FERPA is a Federal law which affords parents the right to have access to their children's education records, the right to seek to have the records amended, and the right to have some control over the disclosure of information from the records. FERPA requires that a school comply with a parent's request for access to the student's records within 45 days of the receipt of a request. Also, a school would generally be required to provide copies of education records to a parent if a failure to do so would effectively prevent the parent from exercising the right to inspect and review the records. One such case is when the parent does not live within commuting distance of the school.

FERPA generally protects a student's privacy interests in "education records." "Education records" are broadly defined as:

> *those records, files, documents, and other materials, which (i) contain information directly related to a student; and (ii) are maintained by an educational agency or institution or by a person acting for such agency or institution. 20 U.S.C. §1232g(a)(4)(A). See also 34 CFR §99.3.*

Where test "protocols" are meant to refer to test instruments or question booklets that do not identify a student or that do not contain personally identifiable information, such documents are not considered "education records" under FERPA. See 34 CFR §99.3. "Personally identifiable information." In contrast, completed test instruments or question booklets containing information that identify a particular student, whether or not the actual name of the student appears on the booklet, constitute "education records" subject to the FERPA requirements. Therefore, in cases where an answer sheet is directly related to the student and is separate from the question booklet not directly related to a student, only the answer sheet would be considered an education record under FERPA. In cases where a question booklet that includes both the questions and the student's responses, the question booklet is an education record subject to FERPA.

Although under FERPA an educational agency or institution is not required to provide a parent with an opportunity to inspect and review information that is not personally identifiable to his or her child, such as test instruments and question booklets that are not directly related to the student, §99.10(c) of the FERPA regulations provides that an educational institution or agency is required "to respond to reasonable requests for explanations and interpretations of the records." Accordingly, an educational agency or institution would be required to respond to a reasonable request for an explanation or interpretation of a student's answer sheet. This could include reviewing the question booklet with the parent.

Because answer sheets are usually directly related to a student, they generally fall within the definition of education records to which a parent has the right to inspect and review. In response to your questions, therefore, the parent has the right to have access to her child's answer sheet and an explanation or interpretation of that answer sheet which, in some cases, could require access to the question booklet. However, because FERPA requires a parent be given access and not copies, except in specific instances, the school district is not required to provide the parent a copy of the answer sheet or the question booklet (emphasis in original).

There is an alternative to providing copies of records for those parents who do not live within commuting distance of the school [word(s) illegible] (emphasis in original). For example, if a school believes that providing a parent with a copy of a certain education record would violate any copyright laws or jeopardize test security, the school could make arrangements with the local school district in which the parent resides to provide the parent an opportunity to inspect and review the record. Please note that the sending school must ensure that officials at the receiving school do not gain access to the education records while acting on the sending school's behalf.

I trust that the above information is helpful in responding to your concerns. Please do not hesitate to contact us if you have further questions.

Sincerely,

LeRoy S. Rooker

Director

Family Policy Compliance Office

In Summation

In this Section, you learned about the Individuals with Disabilities Education Act, Section 504 of the Rehabilitation Act, the Americans with Disabilities Act, and the Family Educational Rights and Privacy Act. You have learned that interpretations and the application of IDEA, Section 504, ADA, and FERPA often vary widely around the country. These are the basic disability statutes that will affect your child for many years. They are always subject to change by Congress.

Your Notes Here

Section Five

Tactics and Strategies

In this section, you will learn how to use tactics and strategies to anticipate problems, negotiate for services, and avoid crises. If you have a dispute with the school, tactics and strategies will help you influence the outcome.

Chapter 21 is "The Rules of Adverse Assumptions." We describe the assumptions you must make and how preparing for conflict helps you avoid conflict. You will learn about proof and evidence and how to present your case.

In Chapter 22, you learn about documentation. You will learn how to use logs, calendars, and journals to create paper trails. When you train yourself to write things down, you are taking steps to protect your child's interests.

Chapter 23 is about writing letters to the school. We describe the five purposes of letters and strategies you can use to ensure that your letters accomplish their purpose. You will learn editing and presentation techniques to enhance the effectiveness of your letters. This chapter includes frequently asked questions and "nuts and bolts" of business letters.

In Chapter 24, you will learn about writing the "Letter to the Stranger." In this chapter, you will discover the identity of the mysterious Stranger and what you want to accomplish when you write to him or her. You will learn about the blame approach and the story-telling approach, angry letters and the sympathy factor, persuasion, and the importance of making a good impression.

Chapter 25 is "Preparing for Meetings: Taking Control." In this chapter, you will learn how preparing for meetings enables you to control the process. You will learn how to use meeting worksheets and parent agendas to clarify issues, make requests, describe problems, and offer solutions.

Chapter 26 is "Meeting Strategies: Maintaining Control." In this chapter, we teach you how to use a simple problem resolution worksheet to keep track of issues and requests. You will learn how to use 5 Ws + H + E questions to discover hidden agendas, plans, and fears. You will learn to use the post-meeting thank you note to document issues and problems.

Tactics and strategies will help you secure services for your child and resolve problems in other areas of your life. Let's learn about the Rules of Adverse Assumptions.

21 | The Rules of Adverse Assumptions

"It's not the will to win, but the will to prepare to win that makes the difference."
— Bear Bryant, University of Alabama football coach

If you are like most parents, you want the school to provide your child with quality special education services and supports–and you want to avoid a due process hearing. When you think about requesting a due process hearing, you feel anxious so you push these thoughts out of your mind. You will hope for the best.

Assume you ask the school to provide services for your child. The school refuses. You try to resolve your dispute informally and through IEP meetings. Nothing changes. What will you do? Give in? Press on?

Assume you request services for your child. Assume the school responded by requesting a special education due process hearing against you. That is what happened to Lisa:

> *I just had a due process hearing for my son. I do not have a lawyer. I am doing this on my own and I am being killed. The school asked for the due process hearing against me. The school psychologist lied about things I said. The district's attorney trashed me personally. The experience has been awful.*

When the school district requested a due process hearing against Lisa, she was not prepared.

You need to prepare for a "worst case scenario." If you work for a company that recently merged with another company, you may prepare for a layoff. If your spouse becomes distant, begins to stay out all night, you may prepare for a separation.

If you live in earthquake country, you will prepare for an earthquake. If you live in hurricane-prone areas, you should prepare for a hurricane. When you prepare for a disaster, you are more likely to survive a disaster.

If you prepare for a due process hearing, you are more likely to prevail if a hearing is necessary. If you prepare for a due process hearing while maintaining good relationships with school personnel, your child is likely to receive good services and you will probably not have to request a due process hearing.

In this chapter, we will describe the six assumptions you must make to advocate for your child. You will learn about proof and evidence and how to use the school's evidence to prove your case. You will learn why your testimony is not sufficient and how to use letters, documents and independent witnesses to prove your case. You will learn about simple themes and the dangers of presenting a laundry list of complaints against the school.

The Rules of Adverse Assumptions

The Rules of Adverse Assumptions are the keys to your success or failure. If you have a dispute with the school, you must make several negative assumptions.

- Assume that a due process hearing will be held to resolve your dispute.
- Assume you will request the hearing.
- Assume the school personnel on whom you relied for help will testify against you.
- Assume the school personnel that violated your child's rights will not tell the truth.
- Assume the Hearing Officer or Administrative Law Judge is biased against parents of children with disabilities.
- Assume that you cannot testify.

"What?" you ask. "I don't understand."

A due process hearing will be held. All school employees will testify against you. The Judge is biased against you. You cannot testify.

A wave of dizziness hits. Your chest feels tight. Good! Fear is a great motivator. Fear will force you to prepare.

"Wait a minute," you say. "No one would go through a due process hearing if the cards were stacked against them!"

Let's examine these assumptions, one by one.

Assumption 1: There will be a due process hearing.

You must assume that a hearing will be necessary to resolve your dispute. Why? Assume the school draws a line in the sand and refuses to provide your child with the help he or she needs. What will you do? You resolve special education disputes by due process hearings.

Never assume that a hearing will not happen. If you assume that a hearing will not happen, you are assuming that you will back down, or the school district will back down. Never assume that the other side will back down.

If you assume the school district will back down, you will not see the train coming until it is too late. You will get complacent. You will not prepare. In the end, you will lose. This is what happened to Lisa.

In the Wrightslaw model of special education advocacy, you assume a "worst case scenario." You assume you will have a disagreement and that a hearing will be necessary to resolve your dispute. After you take this mental step, you will focus on the steps you must take to enhance your chance of a good outcome. When you change your thinking, you will begin to prepare.

Assumption 2: You will initiate the due process hearing.

"You're crazy," you say. "Why would I request a hearing?"

I ask, "What position do you prefer? Do you want to take the offense and define the issues of the case, or do you want to be on the defense like Lisa?"

From a psychological and a legal perspective, it is better to take the offense. When you take the offense, you gain control of the process.

When you initiate the hearing, you define the theme of the case, the issues to be resolved, when the hearing will be held, and the relief you seek. You set the stage, arrange the props, audition the cast, hold rehearsals, practice, and schedule the play.

Assumption 3: All school personnel will testify against you.

School personnel may empathize with parents, or agree with their concerns and complaints. Perhaps they want you to feel better. Perhaps they agree with you. Does this mean that school staff will be your allies in a legal dispute against their employer?

Will the teacher who said, "The system is damaging your child," testify to this? Is it fair to call this teacher as your witness? Think about it.

The teacher will feel that you betrayed her and are now trying to use her. What happens when people feel betrayed? Betrayed people want revenge!

If the teacher feels you betrayed her, will she be a good witness for you? A witness who feels betrayed and wants revenge will damage your case more than all the other witnesses combined.

Assumption 4: The school personnel you thought could be forced to make damaging admissions will not do so.

By the time your due process hearing rolls around, the school personnel will have reviewed the facts of your case many times. As they review your case, they will become even more convinced that their position and actions were correct. This is how you should expect them to testify:

The regular education teacher will testify:

I did not follow the IEP to the letter because Mom told me she wanted other areas to be given more emphasis. That's what I did.

The special education teacher will testify:

We were just following the parents' wishes when we made changes to the child's program. We've worked so hard to help this child. We certainly didn't think the parents would sue us!

The special education director will testify:

Apparently, Mom and Dad thought they heard me say "resource program." What I said was "remediation program." I was trying to say that a resource program would not be appropriate, but I lost my composure. Please bear with me. Let me explain.

I've worked in this field for more than twenty years and I don't think I've ever been in a more difficult meeting . . . Dad was standing up. You can see that he is a big man. He raised his voice at me . . . well, to be completely honest, he yelled at me. I know they were upset and they want what they think is best for their child.

I was flustered. I may have used the word "resource" by mistake. I cannot remember. I should have written a follow up letter to clarify my statement. But I never dreamed that they would take this statement literally. I am so sorry. This is my fault. I should have known they did not understand what I was saying.

Assumption 5: Your Hearing Officer or Administrative Law Judge is biased against parents of children with disabilities.

Assume that your Hearing Officer views his or her role as the gatekeeper and protector of taxpayer dollars. Assume that your Hearing Officer's spouse works for a neighboring school district.

If the hearing officer is biased against you, how will you present your case? You must prepare your case for the skeptic. Educate the skeptic. Develop a visual picture of the decision-maker in your mind's eye. Persuade the skeptical decision-maker to rule in your favor.

Assumption 6: You cannot testify at your due process hearing.

"What? I can't testify? Why not?"

"Because you are biased in favor of your child," I reply.

Your testimony will have less weight than the testimony of other witnesses. As a parent, you are biased in favor of your child. You have less credibility than public school employees and private sector professionals. Yes, you can testify at your child's hearing. But when you prepare your case, you must assume that you cannot testify.

"If I can't testify, how can I prevail? How can I prevail if the Hearing Officer is biased and all the school witnesses will testify against me," you ask.

To Avoid Conflict, Prepare for Conflict

Change the facts. Assume you were a passenger in a cab. The cab driver ran into a light pole. You were injured. Over the next several months, you had operations and physical therapy. You are partially disabled and cannot return to your job.

The cab driver's insurance company refuses to pay your medical bills. The insurance company claims that you distracted the driver so the accident was not the driver's fault. The insurance company claims you are not disabled and can return to work. What will you do?

You will consult with an attorney who specializes in personal injury cases. The attorney will get your records, including your medical and employee records. The attorney will arrange for you to be evaluated by medical specialists. When you go to court, these specialists will testify about the extent and impact of your injuries and will offer opinions about the scope of your disability.

The insurance company will hire medical specialists who will testify about your injuries and offer their opinions that you can return to work immediately.

You would not go to court without witnesses. You would not assume that your testimony alone would be sufficient to prove your case.

You know that a judge or jury would not rule in your favor based solely on your testimony about the accident, the extent of your injuries, degree of disability, lost income, and long-term prospects. This is normal in civil litigation.

A due process hearing is civil litigation. To prevail in a due process hearing or a personal injury case, you need proof and evidence.

Proof and Evidence

You prepare for a due process hearing because you must have independent evidence to prove your case. Can you testify at your due process hearing? Of course, you can. Your testimony will not be powerful because you are biased in favor of your child. This bias is one reason why you must prepare your case as though you cannot testify at all.

Your Evidence

How will you prove that your child needs a specific service or support? How will you prove that your child needs a different educational program or placement? You cannot testify. The school staff is adverse. Where is the evidence that proves your case?

Your evidence includes the letters you wrote after meetings, notes from meetings, test scores and errors in test scores. Your evidence includes your journal and your contact log of telephone calls. Your evidence includes notes and transcripts of meetings you attended.

Your evidence includes reports, evaluations, IEPs, and observations of your child. Your evidence may include research reports, newspaper articles, school guidelines, handbooks, publications, and audits of your school system.

Your evidence includes new evaluations of your child by independent experts from the private sector–evaluations that you arranged when you realized that your dispute would not be resolved.

Their Evidence

Because you cannot testify, your evidence will come from external sources. Begin with the school district's documents. The best evidence often comes from two surprising sources: the child's school file and reports of conversations and meetings held during the crisis.

Are you still worried that you will not be able to tell your side of the story? If you write polite letters to the school that document your concerns and your efforts to resolve problems, your letters will tell your story.

Your Witnesses

Who will testify for you? You must have independent experts who will testify on your behalf. Your experts will base their testimony on the facts of the case, school evaluations, and their observations and evaluations.

Simple Themes Win Cases

You will make your case to a hearing officer or Administrative Law Judge. The decision-maker will be a stranger who does not know you or your child.

Do not expect the decision-maker to keep an open mind until after all the facts are in. Decision-makers are influenced by first impressions and gather data to support their first impressions. If you make a good impression on the decision-maker, you will make it easier for the decision-maker to rule in your favor.

If you are like most parents, you have a long list of complaints. Do not present a laundry list of complaints and violations. If you present a laundry list of complaints, you will not elicit concern for your child or a desire to help. The decision-maker is likely to view you as whiny, unrealistic, and demanding. They will have difficulty believing that the school committed numerous violations and will minimize your complaints.

Simple themes win cases. Reduce your case to one or two issues. Use a simple theme that is emotionally compelling to bind your issues together in a neat package.

In Summation

In this chapter, you learned about the Rules of Adverse Assumptions. You learned that special education disputes are like other types of civil litigation and that you must have external evidence to prove your case. You learned that documentation and paper trails are good sources of external evidence. We will move on to Chapter 22 where you will learn about documentation and paper trails.

Your Notes Here

22 | Creating Paper Trails

> "If it was not written down, it was not said. If it was not written down, it did not happen."
>
> —Pete Wright

In the last chapter, you learned that if you have a dispute with the school, you must have independent evidence that supports your position. In this chapter, you will learn how to use logs, calendars, and journals to create your paper trail. When you write things down when they happen, you are taking steps to protect your child's interests. In this chapter, you show you how to document problems and handle telephone calls.

Why Document?

Good records are essential to effective advocacy. When you deal with a bureaucracy like the Internal Revenue Service or your state tax office, you understand tht you need to keep detailed records. Many parents do not realize that their school districts are bureaucracies.

Keep a log of your contacts with the school. In addition to meetings, your log should include telephone calls and messages, conversations, and correspondence between you and the school. (You will learn how to write effective letters in Chapter 23).

☑ **Keep copies of all letters, reports, and consent forms.**

Train yourself to write things down! If you have a dispute with the school, your contact log is independent evidence that supports your memory.

Documentation that supports your position is a key to resolving disputes. Your tools are simple:

- Logs
- Calendars
- Journals

Documents Support Testimony

If you have a dispute with the school, assume that you will testify about your recollections. Memories are unreliable and influenced by emotions. If your problem boils down to your word against the word of a school employee, you are not likely to prevail without proper documentation.

However, if your recollections are supported by a journal, contact log, or calendar that describes the problem or event, you will be in a stronger position. To be admissible as evidence, your journal or log must be contemporaneous (i.e., written when the events or incidents occurred). If you can also produce a letter that describes what the school agreed to do or refused to do, your position will be stronger.

☑ **If the school asks you to sign a consent or permission form, get a copy for your records. Your copy establishes what you agreed to.**

Documents Answer Questions

Documents provide answers to "Who, What, Why, When, Where, How and Explain" questions.

- What services or supports did the school agree to provide?
- What services or supports did the school refuse to provide?
- What reasons did the school give for their refusal?
- Who attended the meeting when these decisions were made?
- Why was the parent not advised about this meeting?
- When was this meeting held?
- When did the parent receive the IEP in the mail?
- When did the school inform the parent about this change in program and placement?
- Explain how the new IEP was implemented.

Logs, Journals and Calendars_____

Your Contact Log

Use a log to document all contacts between you and the school. Your log should include telephone calls, messages, meetings, letters, and notes between you and the school staff. (For sample contact log entries, see Table 22-1, Table 22-2, Table 22-3, and Table 22-4.)

You can use a bound notebook as your log. If you use an electronic log, be sure to back up your files on more than one computer. Print the log often.

Table 22-1	Contact Log: Telephone Contact Information
Who	Person's name, title, phone number
When	Date, time, place of contact
What you wanted	A few words about the purpose of the call
What you were told	A short description of what you were told
Notes	Other information that is important or useful

Table 22-2	Contact Log Entry: Telephone call from parent to school
Who	Emily Jones, Guidance counselor. 555-1212
When	5/30/02 at 9:15 am
What you wanted	Information about accommodations Mark will receive when he takes the state achievement test next week.
What you were told	Mrs. Jones will put this information in an envelope. I will pick it up at the school after 4 pm tomorrow.
Notes	

Table 22-3	Contact Log Entry: Telephone call from school to parent
Who	Dr. Matthews, assistant principal. 444-0101
When	4/2/02, 10:15 am.
What person wanted	Left message on my office voicemail to advise that he suspended Chris from school again.
What you were told	Did not speak to him. I called him at school 3 times today (see other entries) but he did not return my calls.
Notes	This is 3rd suspension in 2 weeks

Table 22-4	Contact Log Entry: Meeting with child's teacher
Who	Meeting with Mrs. Smith, social studies teacher, about Joey's grades and need for accommodations.
When	4/12/02, 3:30 pm.
What I wanted	Want teacher to provide the accommodations in Joey's IEP.
What you were told	She is stressed out because has 15 special ed kids and no help. She doesn't believe in accommodations, says they are unfair to other kids. (See my journal for more info)
Notes	Joey failed social studies in last grading period.

Your log is a memory aid and will help you remember what happened and why. Your log is a record of:

- Whom you met or talked with
- When the contact occurred
- What you wanted
- What you were told

Your Journal

Your journal may be important evidence in your child's case. Your journal is like a diary and should be clear and legible.

If you request a due process hearing, your writings, journals, logs, calendars, letters and other items may be subpoenaed by the school district. Assume that school personnel and their attorney will read your papers. Stick to the facts. Do not use the journal to report your feelings and frustrations.

When you write in your journal, write to the Stranger who has the power to fix problems. When the Stranger reads your journal, the Stranger will understand your perspective and want to fix your problems. In the next chapters, you will learn about writing evidence letters and persuasive "Letters to the Stranger."

Your Calendar

Many parents like to record their appointments in a monthly calendar. Calendars can provide good evidence about meeting dates and times. If you document meeting dates and times in a calendar, write a description of what happened at the meeting in your journal or log.

Do not throw your calendar away at the end of the year!

How to Use a Problem Report

If you have chronic problems with the school (i.e., your child is bullied, suspended or expelled), you should document these problems. You can use this Problem Report (Table 22-5) to document most school problems (i.e., frequent suspensions; child is bullied, homework problems).

Table 22-5	*Problem Report*

Date: _____/_____/_____
        Month   Date   Year

Problem: _____

_____

People involved: _____

_____

Facts (5 Ws + H + E)

What happened? _____

When did it happen? _____

Who was involved? _____

Where did it happen? _____

Why did it happen? _____

Who witnessed? _____

What action did school take? _____

What action did you take? _____

Other facts: _____

_____

Handling Telephone Calls

Prepare before you make telephone calls. What do you want? Write your questions before you place the call. When you call, have paper and pencil handy so you can make notes about the answers you receive.

If the person cannot answer your question, ask who can help. Log this information into your contact log. Playing phone tag is frustrating. If you leave a message, include the reason for your call, your phone numbers and email address, and when you can be reached.

If you have good manners and establish rapport with the person with whom you speak, you are more likely to receive the information you want.

☑ **You have a right to a copy of your child's IEP.**

In Summation

In this chapter, you learned why you should document events. We described how to use low-tech tools including logs, journals, and calendars. You learned to think about the powerful decision-making Stranger when you write descriptions of events, concerns and problems. You learned how to use a problem report to document negative events and how to prepare for telephone calls.

In the next chapter, you will learn how to write effective letters to the school.

23 | How to Write Good Evidence Letters

"There are no secrets to success. It is the result of preparation, hard work, and learning from failure."
— Colin Powell, soldier and statesman

In this chapter, you will learn how to write effective letters to the school. You will learn about the five purposes of letters and how to use the letter's purpose to guide you. You will learn strategies you can use to ensure that your letters accomplish their purpose. We provide advice about how to write business letters, letter-writing tips, and sample letters that you can adapt to your circumstances. As you read this chapter, refer to the sample letters in Appendix I.

Why You Write Letters

You write letters to:

- Request information
- Request action
- Provide information or describe an event
- Decline a request
- Express appreciation

You also use letters to build relationships, identify and solve problems, clarify decisions that are made or not made, and motivate people to take action.

When you write a letter, be guided by your purpose. What is your purpose? What do you want your letter to accomplish?

Focus on one issue or two issues at most. Do not use one letter to accomplish several purposes. Long letters about several issues are confusing. If the reader is confused, your letter will not accomplish its purpose. Let's look at the five purposes for writing letters.

To Request Information

You write letters to request information. Most requests for information are straightforward. Read letter #1 in Appendix I. You may:

- Request a copy of your child's confidential and cumulative files
- Request evaluation results before an IEP meeting
- Request test scores as standard scores and percentile ranks

To Request Action

You are likely to write letters to request action. For example, you may write to:

- Request that your child be evaluated for special education
- Request an IEP meeting because you have concerns about your child's educational program or placement
- Request a meeting with a teacher to discuss your child's progress
- Request a re-evaluation of your child's progress

When you write a letter to request action, you may anticipate that your reader will be resistant. If you expect resistance, provide information that supports your request.

Read Letter #2 in Appendix I to learn how to request action and provide information that supports your request.

To Provide Information or Describe an Event

If you have concerns about your child's progress or special education program, you must express these concerns in writing. If you do not express your concerns in writing, then for practical and legal purposes you have never expressed any concerns.

You should also provide the school with important information about your child. For example, you should advise the school about new evaluations of your child, new medical conditions, and changes in medication.

Get into the habit of writing letters after meetings, conversations and events. After meetings, write follow-up letters to document what you requested, the school's response (what the school agreed to provide or refused to provide), and what you were told about these decisions.

You should write letters to document negative incidents and events. For example, if your child is suspended or inappropriately disciplined, you should write a letter to document this event.

Read Letter #3 in Appendix I from the parent who asks the school administrator to reconsider his decision to suspend her child. In this letter, the parent describes the child's educational history and requests a face-to-face meeting with the administrator. Despite her belief that the punishment is inappropriate, she does not discuss feelings in the letter. This letter will elicit sympathy from the Stranger. If the school continues to discipline her child for minor infractions, she can use this letter as evidence.

Problem letters are difficult to write. Your emotions may interfere with your ability to present issues logically. For help writing problem letters, read the sample problem letters in Appendix I. You can adapt these letters to your situation.

To Decline a Request

On occasion, you may have to write a letter to decline a request or convey bad news. When you must decline a request or convey bad news, you should make an effort to maintain a good relationship with the reader. The tone of your letter should be polite not defensive.

Read letter #6 in Appendix I about rescheduling an IEP meeting to see how to decline a request.

To Express Appreciation

Everyone has an invisible sign hanging from his or her neck saying, "Make me feel important." Never forget this when you deal with people.
—Mary Kay, business owner

After meetings, write thank you letters that document what you were told. In letter #6 (Appendix I) the parent graciously thanks the teachers for meeting with her, while she weaves in several important pieces of information.

If a teacher or staff members is especially helpful, write a short note to express your appreciation. When you write thank you letters and offer positive feedback, you are more likely to get help when you ask for it. If you complain and demand, do not be surprised when you run into resistance.

Strategies: Writing Good Letters

When you write a letter, you want someone to read it. If you follow these steps, you increase the odds that someone will read and respond to your letter. Your letter will accomplish your purpose.

Easy Reading

You write letters to communicate. Use clear, everyday language. Avoid vague words, educational jargon, and rambling sentences. Use short sentences (10 to 20 words) and short paragraphs (generally no more than six to eight lines). Short paragraphs are easier to read.

When you use short sentences, short paragraphs, and simple language, your message is easier to understand. You create a favorable first impression.

Getting to the Point

If you are writing to request that your reader take action, get to the point. Tell the reader what you want in the first paragraph. Your readers are busy people. They are unlikely to finish your letter if you do not get to the point and tell them what you want them to do.

Think about your reaction to letters. If you begin to read a letter and do not know what the letter wants you to do within the first few sentences, you are likely to put the letter down.

Should you always get to the point immediately?

There are two exceptions to this rule: when you are writing to convey bad news or to persuade the reader to take action that he or she may not want to take. If you anticipate that getting to the point immediately may upset, anger, or alienate your reader, follow the advice in "To Decline a Request (above). You will learn how to write persuasive letters in the next chapter.

Speaking to the Recipient

You write letters to communicate. What do you want your reader to get from this letter? Consider your reader's perspective. You can add empathy to your letters by using the words "you," "we," and "our."

Being Courteous

When you write a letter to request information, request action, or provide information, treat your reader with courtesy and kindness.

Do not demand that the reader take action. If you make demands, you ensure that your reader will try not to comply with your request. (You will learn about demanding letters in Chapter 24.). If you need to provide the reader with suggestions or guidance, direct the reader with courtesy. Be sure to say "please" and "thank you."

Making It Easy to Follow

Each paragraph of a letter should convey one idea that is expressed within the first sentence or two. Supporting information should follow the main idea. Do not make your reader slog through the paragraph to discover the main idea.

Prompting the Reader to Act

At the beginning of a letter, explain why you are writing and what you want the reader to do. Your reader is more likely to remember the first and last thing he or she reads. In the last line of your letter, restate the action you want the reader to take.

Ending with Courtesy

Your reader will remember the final impression of your letter. Make sure you end your letter with courtesy. The decision to help is in the reader's hands. Convey your request as a request, not as a demand.

For example, you should write: " I would appreciate a prompt response" not, "I demand a response within ten days."

You should write: "Please let me know when I can pick up this information" not, "I expect you to comply with my request immediately."

Giving Contact Information

Make it easy for the reader to respond to your letter. Include a telephone number, fax number, or email address at the end of your letters. If the reader has questions, you make it easy to contact you immediately for answers.

You may write, "If you have questions about my request for a meeting, please call me at work (877-555-1212) or at home (877-555-1313) weekdays after 6 p.m."

☑ **Try to end the letter with a benefit for the reader. For example:**

To save us both time during this hectic season, please send the evaluation results to me at least five days before the IEP meeting scheduled for May 25. Please advise by phone if you would prefer that I come by the school on May 18 to pick up this information.

Letter Writing Pitfalls

If you are like most parents, you are more likely to write a letter if you have a problem. Perhaps you want to protect your child or right a wrong. Perhaps you experienced a series of negative incidents with the school. Do not send that angry letter! Before you send an angry letter, think about these statements.

- **After you send a letter, you cannot change it**. Your letter will live on, forever.

- **Strangers will read your letter**. School administrators are Strangers who have power and will not feel intimidated by you. Strangers who do not know you, your child, or the history behind your letter may have the power to resolve your problem.

- **People do not read long letters.** You must capture the reader's interest and attention within the first few sentences. If you do not get the reader's interest quickly, the reader will skim the first paragraph or two and then put your letter aside.

- **People do not like angry letter-writers.** Your letter is a personal statement about you and your situation. If you write an angry, threatening, or demanding letter, what are impression will you make? What are you saying about yourself? Decision-making Strangers do not know or care about your pain, suffering, or frustration.

Think about the impression you want to make. Your letters are opportunities to make a good impression and tell your side of the story.

Think about the Stranger who has the power to fix the problem. Do you want the Stranger to view you as an angry hothead? Do you want the Stranger to conclude that you are a complainer? Do you want the Stranger to understand that you are a thoughtful person who expresses concerns calmly and rationally?

 Read *Letter Writing Tips* (Table 23-1).

Before you write a letter, think about your purpose. Jot down your thoughts. Do not worry about sentence structure or prioritizing. Get your thoughts on paper. In a few minutes, you will have the important issues written down. You should be able to answer these questions:

- Why are you writing this letter?
- What is your purpose?
- What are you trying to accomplish?
- What do you want?

Using Strategies in Letters

If you are writing a letter to describe a problem or negative event, you need to use tactics and strategies.

Remember the Rules of Adverse Assumptions

Assume your problem will not be resolved. Your problem will escalate into a serious dispute. Do you remember the Rules of Adverse Assumptions? You must assume that a due process hearing will be held and that you will not be able to testify.

These assumptions are the keys to successful letter writing. Assume that the problem will get worse. Assume that a successful outcome depends on how well you describe the events that caused you to write this letter.

The letter you write today will be placed in your child's file. If a problem occurs later, your well-written letters are powerful evidence in your favor. Similarly, angry, irrational letters will work against you. If you are still tempted to write an angry letter, read about the "Sympathy Factor" in the next chapter.

Table 23-1 | *Letter Writing Tips*

Image & Presentation
- First impressions are lasting impressions
- Use businesslike letters to create a good impression.
- Type letters or print from your computer.
- Use quality paper. Do not use cute stationery with flowers or little animals.
- Include contact information – phone number, fax number, and/or email.

Set the Right Tone
- Do not demand. Do not apologize. Do not threaten to sue.
- End your letter with courtesy.

Write to the Right Person
- Who can resolve your problem? Write your letter to this person.
- Address your letter to a real person. Use the person's name and job title. No one likes to receive letters addressed "To Whom It May Concern."

Delivery Options
- Deliver important letters by hand. Log in the time and date, identity of the person who received the letter, what the person told you, what they were wearing, what was happening at the time.
- Do not send certified or registered letters to the school.
- Do not mark letters "personal" or "confidential."

How Long?
- In general, keep your letters short, no more than one page.
- Get to the point in the first paragraph.

What To Include
- Tell the reader why you are writing the letter and what you want the reader to do.
- Cite facts that support your position or request. Be sure your facts are correct.

Deadlines
- Set a time limit for a reply. Two weeks is fair. (Do not make demands!)
- Write, call, write. Write a letter. Wait ten days, then call.

What to Do If They Do Not Respond
- If you do not receive a response, write a second letter, and include a copy of your first letter.
- If you get no response, set a short deadline before going higher. Ten days is reasonable.
- If you receive no response to the second letter, go higher in the chain of command.

Visualize the Stranger

When you write a letter about problems or concerns, you are writing a "Letter to the Stranger" Assume that someone outside of the school district will decide the issue. This decision-making Stranger has no personal interest in you or your child. The Stranger does not care that your child is enrolled in a One-Size-Fits-All (OSFA) program. If you go to court, the Stranger who controls outcome may be the Judge's young law clerk.

Assume that before you mail your letter, your letter slips out of your notebook and falls into the street. Later, a Stranger sees your letter and picks it up. The Stranger puts the letter in his pocket and takes it home to read. What impression will your letter make on the Stranger?

Who is the Stranger? How does he think? Visualize the Stranger in your mind's eye. The Stranger is an older person who is conservative, fair, and open-minded. He dresses casually. When he sits down to read your letter, he sips a cup of tea and lights a pipe.

Read the original "Letter to the Stranger" at the Wrightslaw site: www.wrightslaw.com

The Stranger does not know you, your child, or your situation. Your letter is your opportunity to sell the Stranger on the justice of your cause. Describe your problem. Tell the Stranger what should be done to make things right. Judges are Strangers. Most judges do not know about children with disabilities or special education. When you write letters, you want to educate and inform the Stranger.

☑ **When you write letters, do not use acronyms. Do not expect a Stranger to understand the alphabet soup of special education acronyms. Write out the full names of programs and teams.**

Make Your Problem Unique

Once dispelled, ignorance is difficult to re-establish. —Laurence J. Peter

Assume you are writing about a problem. Try to make your problem unique. You want the reader to believe your problem is different and think, " We've never had this problem before!"

You want to avoid these responses:

- We always handle this situation this way
- We have always handled this situation this way
- We will always handle this situation this way
- We never make exceptions
- We cannot make an exception for you

Schools are bureaucracies. Bureaucracies run by rules. If you can make your problem unique, your problem is less likely to be listed in the ***Bureaucrat's Big Book of Rules and Procedures.*** If your situation is unique, people who work in the system may view your situation differently. If they see things differently, they may handle your situation differently.

Edit and Revise

The first letter you write is always a draft. After you write the first draft, put your letter away. Allow yourself a cooling-off period of at least 24 to 48 hours before you edit the letter.

After the cooling-off period, you will be able to view your letter more objectively. When you edit a letter, you want to clarify, condense and strengthen your message.

Ask at least one cool-headed person to edit your letter. Choose a person who will tell you the truth and respect your confidentiality. Ask your editor to answer these questions:

- What is the purpose of my letter?
- What is my point?
- What do I want?
- Should I shorten the letter?
- Should I tone the letter down?

If your reader cannot answer the first three questions easily and quickly without more explanations or prompting from you, your letter is not clear. You need to do more editing.

☑ **When you edit, read your letter aloud. When you proofread and edit, read your letter backwards. These strategies will help you spot spelling and grammar errors.**

Make a Good First Impression

Write your letter on a computer. After your write the first draft, double-space the letter and change your font to Courier 14 points. When you print your letter, typographical errors, poor sentence structure, and rambling sentences will be easier to spot. Edit the letter again. **Remove every unnecessary word.** Read aloud to find spelling errors.

If you have access to a computer, you can use the spell check and grammar check programs to flag some spelling errors. If you use a spell check program, be careful! Spell check programs do not catch many spelling errors (e.g., if you write "it" instead of "if")

For more advice about letters, read ***Nuts and Bolts of Letter Writing*** (Table 23-2) and ***Frequently Asked Questions about Letters*** (Table 23-3) at the end of this chapter.

Table 23-2	*Nuts and Bolts of Letter Writing*

Your letters to the school are business letters. The parts of business letters are standard.

Parts of a Letter

Heading or Letterhead. Your heading or letterhead will include your name, address, and telephone number.

Date. The month, day and year you write the letter.

Inside address. The recipient's full name, title, school, and address.

Reference line. Your child's full name, grade and school.

Salutation. Greeting that begins with the word "Dear." Examples: Dear Mr. Clark, Dear Dr. Jones.

Body of the Letter. The body of your letter should be single-spaced with two spaces between paragraphs. The first line of each paragraph may or may not be indented. Be consistent.

Closing. Appropriate closings include:

- Sincerely
- Sincerely Yours
- Respectfully
- Regards

Signature. You should sign all letters. Type your full name beneath your signature.

Additional Notations. Use notations at the end of your letter to indicate that:

- something is enclosed with the letter
- something is attached to the letter
- something else has been sent
- other individuals will receive copies of the letter

Table 23-3 | *Frequently Asked Questions About Business Letters*

Question: Should I type letters?

Answer: Letters carry more weight if they are typed, especially if the topic is serious. If you are writing a note to your child's teacher about a routine matter, you may write your letter by hand. If the topic of your letter is important, you should type the letter, sign it, and keep a signed copy for your records. Use Times New Roman font. Never use a script or cursive type font.

Question: What kind of paper should I use?

Answer: Your letters to the school are business letters and should be written on 8½ x 11-inch paper. Paper can be white, off-white, ivory, or pale gray.

Question: How should I format the second page of a letter?

Answer: If your letter goes to a second page, try to condense it into one page. Many people will set two-page letters aside, believing they will get to them later.

If you cannot avoid a second page, follow these guidelines:

- Keep your page margins the same as page one
- Do not write "Continued," or "over" on page one
- Write the recipient's name as it appeared on the inside address, the date, and page number on the top of page two.

The left margin of your second page should look like this.

Louise Jones
January 21, 2002
Page 2

Question: How wide should my margins be?

Answer: Consistent symmetrical margins will make your letter easy to read. In a short letter, use wider margins. In a long letter, use narrower margins (but no less than one inch). The text should appear centered or slightly higher on the page.

Question: How should I address the envelope?

Answer: Send letters in # 10 envelopes (4 ½ x 9 ½ inches). Type the address with no punctuation. Use two letter state abbreviations and zip codes. Include the additional four digits if you can.

Speak to the Reader

You are writing to a person who has the power to resolve the problem. You are not writing to the person at a meeting who blamed you for your child's problems. Imagine you are talking to the Stranger about your problem. Use words like "you," "we," and "our" to make your letter more personal. When people read your letter, they will feel that your message is directed at them.

In Summation

In this chapter, you learned that you write letters to request information, request action, provide information, describe a problem or event, decline a request, and express appreciation. You learned about the qualities of good letters that will accomplish their purpose.

You learned strategies that will help you make a good impression. In the next chapter, you will learn about persuasive letters and how to write a "Letter to the Stranger."

24 | Writing the "Letter to the Stranger"

"If you would persuade, you must appeal to interest rather than intellect."
— Benjamin Franklin, inventor

In this chapter, you will learn about two approaches to letter writing – the Blame Approach and the Story-Telling Approach. You will learn about the Sympathy Factor and why you must not write angry letters to the school. Your goal is to use the Story-Telling Approach to write persuasive letters.

The Blame Approach

A father wrote this letter after an IEP meeting. This father is a businessman who writes letters in his work. This letter was a trial exhibit and an issue in his child's case. When you read his letter, pay attention to your reactions.

Dear Dr. Smith:

You asked that I advise you about my objections to the IEP that your staff of "professional educators" wrote for my daughter. Despite my own lack of training, I can say that the IEP developed by your staff was preposterous. Let me share a few observations with you.

Your staff FAILED to include anyone on the IEP team who thoroughly understands my daughter's background.

Your staff FAILED to perform an observation on my daughter before they developed the IEP.

Your staff FAILED to include information from the most recent testing by the private evaluator and relied on out-dated testing that is nearly two years old.

Your staff FAILED to target her specific needs and unique abilities.

Your staff FAILED to include any objective criteria to measure her progress or lack of progress.

Your staff FAILED to include any evaluation procedures to measure progress, as related to annual goals and objectives.

(This list continued for two pages . . .)

Given their years of training and experience I would expect your staff to be capable of writing a simple IEP. Although I have no training in IEPs or special education, I can see how inadequate this document is.

I must conclude that your staff is incompetent and inept. This IEP is evidence that your staff is incapable of teaching my daughter, who is smarter than your entire team.

Sincerely,

Bob Bombastic

What is your reaction to this letter? Do you understand why Bob wrote the letter? Do you know what Bob wants from the school? What solution did he suggest? Do you understand his position? Do you agree with him? Alternatively, did you have a different response?

A few weeks before Bob wrote this letter, the special education director accused him of not advising the school about his objections to their IEP. Bob was not going to let this happen again! He included a laundry list of complaints in his letter. Bob believed he had to give detailed notice about his objections to the proposed IEP. He felt angry and defensive.

Impact of Angry Letters

Unfortunately, when the decision-making Stranger read Bob's letter, he did not know the history behind the letter because Bob neglected to include this information. Bob's letter is worded so strongly that it created sympathy for the people who received it.

Have you seen couples arguing or parents disciplining their children in public? What was your reaction?

If you are like most people, you felt uncomfortable. Perhaps you had a stronger emotional reaction. You did not like it! You felt sympathy for the person who was being humiliated. People have the same reaction when they read angry letters.

If you are tempted to write an angry and demanding letter, think about Bob.

The Story-Telling Approach

Let's look at another letter written by a father after an IEP meeting. This father's letter was a trial exhibit in a case too.

Dear Dr. Smith;

First, let me thank you for allowing me to participate in the developme[n]t [of] Carrie's IEP. I appreciate your willingness to meet with me.

As you know, Carrie has received special education services for two yea[rs] [you] may remember that Dr. Smith completed a comprehensive evaluation on her on [date]. I provided you with a copy of this evaluation and expressed concerns that Carrie has made no progress in the two years she has received special education services.

At last week's IEP meeting, your staff kindly answered my questions. I appreciated their kindness since I had not met most of the people at the IEP meeting before. I was sorry that neither of Carrie's teachers could attend the meeting. I understand that one teacher was on a field trip and the other teacher had a doctor's appointment.

Unfortunately, we did not have enough time to develop an IEP for Carrie. Although the team allotted twenty-five minutes for the meeting, the meeting began late. I understand that several IEP meetings ran late that day. I know that things are very rushed at the end of the school year.

We did not have time to discuss the new evaluation results. The psychologist thought the new evaluation might have been misfiled. Perhaps this is why the team leader gave me an IEP to sign that placed Carrie in the same program. You will recall that I expressed reservations about last year's IEP because it did not include current test results in the present levels of educational performance. I also expressed concerns about the vague goals, objectives, and evaluation procedures.

I am sure you understand why I could not sign the IEP presented to me. Given the confusion and rushed atmosphere, I thought we should schedule another meeting later, when we have enough time to discuss these issues.

I asked the IEP team to review the new evaluation results before we get together to write the IEP. I am including another copy of the new [date] evaluation with this letter.

Please check with your staff and send me times that are convenient for them. I look forward to a productive meeting. If you have any questions, please call me at work (888-555-1212) or at home (888-444-1110). You can also contact me by email at mike@mikemanners.com.

Sincerely,

Mike Manners

What is your reaction to Mike Manners' letter? Do you know why Mike wrote this letter? Do you know what he wants? Do you understand his position? When you read Mike's letter did you realize what he was dealing with the same factual issues as Bob? Read Bob's letter again.

Both letters describe an IEP meeting for a child. Each letter refers to procedural violations by the school in developing the child's IEP. In each case, the parent was presented with an IEP that pre-determined the child's program and placement. Neither parent had any input into the child's IEP. The IEP teams did not include the results of new testing in the children's IEPs. The teachers did not attend the IEP meetings.

Using Persuasive Strategies in Letters

You want to write persuasive "Mike Manners" letters. List your concerns in a pleasant business-like way. How you lay out the facts in a letter is important. Mike lays out his facts without blaming or name-calling. If Mike needs to go to a mediator, hearing officer, or judge, his letters will make a good impression.

When Bob took his case to a decision maker, he was in trouble. Bob's letters included angry blaming statements. He did not include information that would help the Stranger understand the background of his case. The tone of his letters was harsh. His angry letters alienated neutral decision-makers.

Avoiding the "Sympathy Factor"

If you write an angry demanding letter, you may trigger the "Sympathy Factor." This sympathy will not be for you or for your child. When people read angry, demanding letters, they feel sympathy is for the person who received the letter. This is what happened in Bob's case.

At some point in our lives, most people have received angry letters. You may have received angry letters from a jilted lover, jealous ex-spouse, angry relative, or a demanding creditor. When you read your angry letter, you felt threatened, guilty, ashamed, or angry. You filed these reactions in your emotional memory bank.

When you read an angry letter, the letter may evoke sympathy for the recipient. Based on your personal experiences, you may decide that the recipient did not deserve the attack. You may think, "Maybe the person did make a mistake. Everyone makes mistakes. No one is perfect." From the Stranger's perspective, the fact that a person makes a mistake does not give you an excuse to attack.

Making a Good Impression

When you write letters to the school, expect that people who do not know you will read your letters. In many cases, teachers, guidance counselors, and assistant principals do not have the authority to make important decisions. If you write a letter to the school, you should assume you are writing to a Stranger who has the power to make decisions.

In your letter, you introduce yourself to the decision-making Stranger. While reading your letter, the Stranger will form an impression of you. First impressions are powerful. If you make a negative first impression, the Stranger will have difficulty accepting positive information about you. This happened to Bob.

After Bob fired off his letter, the school went into the defensive mode. From their perspective, if they gave Bob anything he wanted, they would admit that he was right and that they FAILED to educate his child. Of course, the school had a different perspective. They disagreed with Bob. They did not believe they failed to provide his daughter with an appropriate education. What happened next?

The school responded with a pleasant non-committal letter to Bob. They explained that they disagreed with him but were willing to meet with him to resolve their differences. They offered several meeting times. The tone of their letter was pleasant. Bob did not respond. He believed he made his point and provided them with the "Notice." The school filed his letter away. Nothing changed.

A few months later, Bob requested a due process hearing. The school board attorney submitted this letter and other similar letters from him as exhibits in their case.

The school wanted the hearing officer to see Bob from their perspective and conclude that he was a jerk. They wanted the hearing officer to understand that, while Bob was a "difficult parent," they were prepared to meet with him. Although Bob was difficult, the school could provide his unfortunate daughter with an excellent education.

What are the lessons you can learn from this story? If you create a negative first impression, you increase the odds that you will lose the battle and the war. Strangers who read your negative letters will write you off as a loose cannon and may feel sorry for your child.

That poor kid. No wonder he has so many problems. Can you imagine what it must be like to live with such an irrational self-centered parent?

You do not want this reaction!

Writing "Letters to the Stranger"

In the last chapter, you learned that one purpose of letters is to persuade someone to take action. If you want to persuade the school to take an action or provide a service and you expect them to resist, write your letter to the decision-making Stranger.

Judges are Strangers. Most judges are not knowledgeable about special education or children with disabilities. When you write your letter, your goals are to educate, inform, and persuade the Stranger.

To Negotiate

As a parent, you negotiate with the school district for special education services. Whether you negotiate with the school about services or you negotiate with a salesman about a new car, the principles are the same.

You do not begin negotiations by telling the other side your bottom line. Many parents assume they must share everything with the school immediately. They hope the school will reward them by providing the help their child needs. In most cases, this does not happen.

You should share the results of an evaluation or other information about your child when you receive it. However, when you negotiate, you do not share your wish list or your bottom line. You will learn more about negotiating in Chapters 25 and 26 about meetings.

To Persuade

When you write a persuasive Letter to the Stranger, you will present your case. The Stranger will not understand the background or history of your problem unless you include this information in your letter. You can provide background naturally and easily by going back to the beginning and telling your story chronologically.

For example: "On September 1, our son entered your special education program because . . . "

You can move the clock back: "We realized that our daughter's problems were serious when she was not talking by her third birthday."

Where should you begin? Begin where you want to begin. In your mind, you know when things began. Continue with your story: "When she entered school . . .

Use facts to tell your story. Select your facts carefully. Keep your opinions to a minimum. When you tell your story, you want to plant seeds in the mind of the Stranger who will read your letter. Let the Stranger's imagination water the seeds.

Write your letter chronologically. If you jump from one issue to another, the Stranger will get confused, then frustrated. If the Stranger is frustrated, he will quit reading and will blame you for this frustration. You will create a negative first impression. You do not want this to happen!

When you write a persuasive letter, speak directly to the reader. Use the same words and figures of speech you use in normal conversation. Visualize the Stranger. Imagine that you are talking to him about your problems. Re-read the advice about editing in Chapter 23. Revise your letter so it makes a good impression and persuades the Stranger.

Do Not Send Certified Letters

If you are like many parents, you think you should send important letters by certified mail. If you send a letter to the school by certified mail, you put the recipient on notice that you want proof of delivery, probably for legal and evidence purposes. The recipient will feel defensive and mistrustful. If you send a certified letter, this will have a negative impact on your relationship with school personnel.

When you deal with the school, your goal is to secure a good educational program for your child. If you take actions that cause school personnel to feel defensive, you are less likely to accomplish your goal.

How can you establish that the school received your letter? Hand-deliver your letter to the recipient.

Strategies: Hand-Deliver Letters

When you go to the school, take your original letter and one signed copy. When you enter the office, note the time. Observe the office layout. Do you recognize anyone? When you hand your letter to the secretary or office manager, pay attention to the person. Note the person's age, dress, hair color and style, and other distinctive characteristics. Ask the person to give your letter to Dr. Kate Gardner, principal. Do not ask the person to sign a receipt.

If you do not know the person's name, you can get the person's name by introducing yourself, "Hi. I'm Gillian Harrison's mom. I have a letter for Dr. Gardner. Would you mind giving it to her? I don't think we've met before. Your name is . . . "

After you get to your car, write the date, time, name, and description of the person who received your letter on the back of your copy of the letter. Write what you said and what you were told.

If a week passes and you do not receive a response, write a short follow-up letter. Attach a copy of your original letter to the follow-up letter. (See sample letters in Appendix I.)

When you go to the office, you may have a chance to refresh the secretary's memory, "Hi, I'm Gillian Harrison's mom. We met last week. You are Karen Brannen, Dr. Gardner's assistant. You may remember that I gave you a letter for Dr. Gardner last week. I have not heard from her yet. Do you know if she got the letter? I wrote another letter, in case the other one got lost. Here it is."

The secretary will probably say, "Oh, I remember. Yes, she got it. I gave it to her right away. I don't know what happened. She has been very busy. I'll check on it." Thank the secretary and leave. Because you remembered her name, she will not forget you. She will not deny that you delivered the letters to her. When you leave, write the details of what happened on the back of your follow-up letter.

You have proof of receipt. Your proof includes your testimony and your contemporaneous notes that you wrote when you delivered the letters. You did not create hostility and mistrust. You did not polarize the relationship with the school. You may have made a new friend in Karen.

In Summation_____

In this chapter, you learned about persuasive letters. You learned about the Blame Approach and the Story-Telling Approach, first impressions, and why you must not write angry letters to the school. You learned strategies that allow you to prove that the school received your letter without polarizing your relationships with school staff.

In the next chapter, you will learn how to prepare for meetings. You will learn how preparation and presentation can help you control meeting outcomes.

25 | Preparing for Meetings: Taking Control

> "If you're sure you can't, you won't. If you think you can, you might. If you know you can, you will."   — Fable

If you are like most parents, you feel confused, frustrated and intimidated at school meetings. How can you get the school to answer your questions? How can you get the school to respond to your requests? How can you get the school to provide the services and supports your child needs? What is your role?

As a parent, you negotiate with the school for services on your child's behalf. In this chapter, you will learn about negotiating and problem solving. You will learn about organizing the file, knowing what you want, anticipating obstacles, and presenting your requests.

The pre-meeting worksheet will help you clarify concerns, make requests, and anticipate problems. You will learn how to use a parent agenda to express concerns, describe problems, and make requests. If your relationship with the school is strained or damaged, these steps will help you mend fences and build healthy working relationships with school personnel.

You are a Negotiator

If you are like many parents, you did not realize that you negotiate with the school for special education services and supports. When you attend meetings about your child's special education program, you are representing your child's interests.

When you understand that you are negotiating, the process begins to make sense. Think about other situations where you negotiate. You may have more experience as a negotiator than you realize.

You negotiate with co-workers about work schedules. You negotiate with your employer about your salary. You negotiate with family members about housework and the budget. When you purchase a car or house, you negotiate with strangers. When you negotiate with the school, you have an advantage–you can prepare.

Here are five rules for successful problem solving . Keep these rules in mind when you prepare for meetings.

Five Rules for Successful Problem Solving————————

"If we or our argument is perceived as a threat, we will never be heard."

— Gerry Spence, trial lawyer and writer

Rule 1: Know what you want.

"When I told the team that I was dissatisfied with Jeremy's progress, the chairman said, 'What do you want us to do?' Several people laughed. I was so embarrassed! Don't they know what to do? They were trying to make me feel stupid." Marie at a parent training session.

Did the team intend to make Marie feel stupid? We do not know. Was the school's request unreasonable? No.

If you have a problem, you need to think about possible solutions to the problem. Prepare solutions that may resolve the problem. If the school ignores or belittles your solutions, you should document this in your polite follow-up letter.

If you are like many parents, you think you must use educational jargon to make requests and express concerns. Not so! You will not gain credibility with educators by speaking their jargon. Make your requests in clear simple language. You want the decision-making Stranger to understand the problem and your proposed solutions. Prepare to answer these questions:

- What do you want?
- What action do you want the school to take?
- What facts support your request?

Rule 2. Do not blame or criticize.

When you report problems or express concerns to a school team, stick to the facts. Do not blame or criticize. If a team member reacts defensively, be careful!

Assume you take off work to attend an IEP meeting. The special education supervisor does not show up. After 30 minutes, the team cancels the meeting. When you leave the building and walk toward your car, you pass the supervisor in the parking lot. You say, "I have to go back to work."

The supervisor says, "I have five hundred kids." What happened? Because the supervisor felt defensive about missing the meeting, she reacted to your statement as personal criticism.

Look at your statement again. You made a simple statement, not a criticism. Because she assumed your comment was criticism, she feels angry and overwhelmed.

You may be able to use this information to create a different relationship with the supervisor – and gain services for your child. When you meet again, she expects you to criticize her. This expectation will keep her guilt feelings alive. The next time you see her, make a friendly comment about her workload. Express your understanding that she cannot be in two places at one time. Do not mention any problems caused by her failure to show up.

What do you think will happen? It is likely that her defensiveness toward you will dissipate. She may feel grateful that you did not criticize her. By taking this approach, you may increase the odds that she will give you what your child needs.

When you negotiate, you are dealing with people. When people feel defensive, anxious or angry, their ability to solve problems drops. If you stick to facts, you make it more likely that the team will develop creative solutions to problems.

Rule 3. Protect the parent-school relationship.

In parent-school negotiations, personal relations are entangled with problems. Separate your relationships with people from the problems. If you view the people and the problem as the same, you will feel angry, bitter, and mistrustful.

When you negotiate, you have two interests:

- To solve problems
- To protect relationships

You will negotiate again!

Rule 4. Seek win-win solutions to problems.

When you use traditional win-lose bargaining, you are playing hardball. People who play hardball believe that if they give in, they lose. When parents and school play hardball, the relationship and the issue are at risk.

Do not play hardball to resolve parent-school problems. When teams develop win-win solutions to problems, the members are committed to the success of their solutions. If the school loses, expect them to undermine and sabotage the solution.

Rule 5. Understand the school district's position.

You need to be able to walk in the shoes of the other side. You need to be able to answer questions like these:

- What are their perceptions? How does the school see the problem?
- What are their interests? What does the school want?
- What are their fears? What are they afraid will happen if they give you what you want?

When you answer these questions, it will be easier to develop solutions that allow you and the school district to get your needs and wants met.

Discovering the School's Position

How do you find out what the school wants and what they fear? Do not expect them to tell you. It is possible that they do not know what they want and fear. You will discover the answers to these questions by asking 5 Ws + H + E questions and listening carefully to the answers.

Perceptions

How does your school district perceive parents? How does the school perceive parents of children with disabilities? How does your child's school perceive you? Does the school think you are demanding? Are you a complainer? Do they believe you are passive and uninvolved?

Interests

What is important to your school district? What do they want? What is their mission?

Fears

What does your school district fear? If the school gives you what you want, have they failed? Will school personnel have to admit that they were wrong? Will school personnel have to do things they do not want to do?

If the district gives you what you want, are they afraid the floodgates will open? Is the district afraid they will lose power? Will the district lose face?

Preparing for School Meetings

The keys to successful IEP meetings are organizing, preparing, and knowing how to present your requests. When you learn that a meeting is scheduled, follow this process to prepare.

Use the Pre-Meeting Worksheet

Make several copies of the pre-meeting worksheet (Table 25-1). Fill in the information about the meeting time and date, location, purpose, and who requested the meeting. As you prepare, you will be able to answer more of the questions in the pre-meeting worksheet.

Organize and Review the File

Review your child's file. File loose documents. Do you have all recent test data?

If your child has an IEP, review the IEP goals, objectives and benchmarks. Com-

| **Table 25-1** | *Pre-Meeting Worksheet* |

Location:_____

Date:_____

What is purpose of the meeting?_____

Who requested the meeting?_____

Who will attend the meeting (e.g., teachers, administrators, parent, child)?

_____

_____

What do you want? _____

_____

What do they want? _____

_____

What action do you want them to take? _____

_____

How motivated are they to give you what you want?_____

_____

What will prevent them from giving you want you want?_____

_____

How can you alleviate their concerns?_____

_____

pare the current test data to the earlier test data. Is your child making progress? Is your child's progress acceptable? Do you have concerns about your child's program or progress?

Review your notes from prior meetings. Review your contact log. What issues are unresolved? Are there problems you want to bring up at the meeting?

Brainstorm

When you review your child's file, your contact logs, and your notes, think about issues you want the team to address. Open your notebook and write 5 Ws + H + E at the top of the page. List your questions and concerns.

How do you view your child's problems? How does the school view your child's problems? How is the school likely to respond to your concerns? Your success in devising solutions to problems will depend on knowing what they want. If you know the perceptions of your school district, it will easier to answer these questions.

Write the answers to these questions in the pre-meeting worksheet:

- What do you want?
- What does the school want?
- What action do you want the school to take?
- How motivated are they to give you what you want?
- What will prevent them from giving you what you want?
- How can you address their concerns and fears?

Use a Parent Agenda

The parent agenda is a valuable tool. You can use a parent agenda to:

- Prepare for meetings
- Identify concerns and list problems
- Propose solutions to problems
- Identify issues and problems that are not resolved
- Improve parent-school relationships

To learn how to use a parent agenda, read the agenda written by AJ's parents (Table 25-2). AJ is in middle school. He is failing several subjects. He is embarrassed about having to go to the nurse's office to get his medication. His disability makes it difficult for him to produce written work. His teacher makes negative comments about AJ to other students and their parents.

This parent agenda begins with "Good News." Because the agenda does not begin with complaints, you continue to read. Good News is followed by "Our Frustrations (parents and teachers)." By framing AJ's problems as "Our Frustrations," his parents emphasize their belief that parents and educators share responsibility for developing solutions to AJ's problems.

Table 25-2	*Sample Parent Agenda*

The Good News

AJ is a bright, energetic, sensitive, thoughtful child. He grasps complex concepts easily. He has good memory for facts and details. He loves to read. He is patient with his six-year-old sister Suzy who has Down's Syndrome.

Our Frustrations (Parents and Teachers)

AJ is easily distracted and has difficulty focusing on tasks. His organizational skills are immature. He is "consistently inconsistent."

AJ is sometimes driven to tears over his inability to get organized, find homework assignments, notes, and papers. He completes assignments, misplaces them, completes them again, and forgets to turn them in. AJ is described by teachers as "lazy, careless, uncooperative, and choosing not to complete assignments."

AJ's Frustrations

I DON'T WANT to have ADD. I want to be normal. I don't want to take medication that changes my appetite and emotions. It is embarrassing to go to the nurse's office for medication. It is obvious that I'm not normal. I've been on different medications and I've been failing school since the 4th grade.

I have three or four hours of homework a night. I don't think the teachers talk to each other because they all give long projects on the same day. When I don't understand an assignment, they get mad at me.

What AJ Needs

1. **Please understand that ADD is a MEDICAL condition**.
2. **A drastic reduction in written work and homework**. An average child may spend 20 minutes on an assignment that takes AJ several hours to complete. Homework is a nightmare. Teachers add to the stress by sending class work home. If AJ cannot complete the work during the school day, it is unlikely that he will complete it in the evening.
3. **Prioritize and modify AJ's assignments**. These homework problems are preventing AJ from being a child. We arranged for him to take Aikido because it is a healthy outlet and good therapy. He must miss Aikido to do homework.
4. **Avoid ridicule.** AJ's self-esteem is fragile. He perceives himself as a failure. Negative comments sent home or made to parents in front of him are inappropriate and ineffective. We have received one positive note and dozens of negative notes from the school. Would you want to be AJ?
5. **Teach AJ organizational skills.** AJ needs your help to keep track of homework and assignments.
6. **AJ is distractible**. He needs to sit in front of the class.
7. **Value AJ's strengths**. Provide him with chances to do well in front of his peers. Catch him doing something right. *"AJ, I'm very proud of your perfect attendance. Even when school is frustrating, you don't give up. Good for you!"*
8. **Believe in him**. Don't give up when Plans A and B fail. Try Plans C and D.
9. **Accept our support**. We understand and appreciate your efforts. We are here to help you in any way we can.

When the parents use AJ's words to describe his perception of school, you step into his shoes. As a Stranger, you feel sympathy for him. After you read his frustrations, the parents express their concerns and make their requests.

AJ's parents used this parent agenda to identify problems and offer solutions without blaming school personnel or making them feel defensive. The parents understood the importance of presentation.

In the final section of the agenda, "What AJ Needs," the parents describe problems and offer solutions. The parents use facts to support each request. You learn that AJ has Attention Deficit Disorder (ADD) and that ADD is a medical condition.

When AJ's parents ask the teachers to reduce homework, they support their request by describing the toll homework is taking on AJ. As the Stranger, you find yourself agreeing that several hours of homework are unreasonable.

The parents bring up more difficult issues when they ask the teacher to avoid ridicule, value AJ's strengths, and "believe in him."

This agenda ends with the parents' offer of support and appreciation for efforts made on behalf of their son. Wisely, the parents placed these statements at the end. They know that what is read last is most likely to be remembered.

Writing a parent agenda is hard work. As these parents told their son's story, you stepped into AJ's shoes and saw the world through his eyes. The parents did not overtly blame or criticize the school.

AJ's parents were surprised at the success of this strategy. The special education director and school psychologist recommended that AJ be transferred to a new school with a low student-teacher ratio.

Instead of failing grades, AJ is getting A's. His medication has been reduced. His attitude has turned around. He is so bright and capable. A few months ago, we thought he was lost.

Handouts and Charts

If you plan to use handouts, visual aids or graphs, prepare them ahead of time. If you use handouts, bring several extra copies to the meeting. If you are concerned about your child's lack of progress, use test data to support your position.

If you use a parent agenda, you may want to send your agenda to team members before the meeting. Do not assume that the team members will read your agenda ahead of time. Most people will not read the agenda until they get into the meeting. Bring extra copies for people who misplaced or lost their copies.

Practice!

When you make requests, practice. When you practice, you prepare. Practice will reduce your anxiety. You need to state your problems or concerns clearly and offer suggestions about how you want the problem to be resolved.

If you belong to a support group, role-play or rehearse what you plan to say before your group. Ask the group for help in polishing your presentation.

Image and Presentation

Your goal is to develop a good working relationship with school personnel. When you dress neatly and conservatively for school meetings, you convey a businesslike image. When you organize your child's file and bring the file to meetings, you send a message that you expect to work with the school as a partner.

Arrive early. When you arrive early, you will have time to relax and focus on what you want to accomplish. You may also discover who attended the "pre-meeting" that was held before the real meeting with you.

A Secret Weapon: Food

Most parent-school communication is by letters, telephone calls, and face-to-face meetings. If you have a problem, it is likely to be resolved in a meeting.

If you anticipate a long meeting, bring food. For an early morning meeting, bring donuts or sweet rolls. If you have a lunch meeting, bring a sandwich tray. For a late afternoon meeting, bring energy food (i.e., fruit, cookies, brownies). Always bring more food than the group will consume. Never take leftovers when you leave.

Sharing food and drink helps to build productive working relationships. This is especially true if the parties have been polarized and mistrustful. When school personnel consume food you bring to a meeting, it is difficult for them to feel angry or antagonistic toward you.

After you leave, other school personnel will share your offerings. A positive buzz will begin in the teacher's lounge. "Mrs. Harrison, you know, Gillian's mom. She is a character. She has an iron fist in a velvet glove. She knows her stuff. We have some battles with her but she's a great Mom!"

In Summation

In this chapter, you learned that you negotiate with the school for services. The keys to successful meetings are preparing, organizing information, and knowing how to present your requests.

You learned how to use the pre-meeting worksheet to prepare for meetings and the parent agenda to describe problems, offer solutions, and make requests. You discovered that you have a secret weapon – food!

Let's move on to the next chapter and learn about strategies for successful meetings.

Your Notes Here

26 | Meeting Strategies: Maintaining Control

> "Winning is getting what we want, which also means helping others get what they want."
> — Gerry Spence, Trial Lawyer and Author

You have learned that preparation and planning are the keys to successful advocacy. In the last chapter, you learned how to use the pre-meeting worksheet to clarify issues and identify problems and the parent agenda to present problems, offer solutions and make requests. In this chapter, you will learn strategies to control the outcome of meetings, including the problem resolution worksheet and the post-meeting thank you note.

School Meeting Anxiety

This is how one father, a successful salesman, describes school meetings:

I always feel anxious when I go to the school for a meeting. I start to feel anxious before I get there. By the time I drive into the parking lot, my stomach is in knots. I feel intimidated. When they ask me what I think, I do not know what to say.

If you have a child in special education, you know about school meeting anxiety. Many factors contribute to school meeting anxiety, including your life experiences, fears about your child, uncertainty about your role, and your interpersonal style.

Your personal experiences will affect your feelings about school meetings. When you walk into your child's school, you are transported back to your own earlier years in school. For many parents, memories of school are painful and unpleasant. If you had school problems, school meetings may bring back old feelings of guilt, shame, and anxiety.

Your reaction to school meetings is also influenced by your interpersonal style. If you are a conflict-avoider, your motto is "peace at any price." You may keep your concerns about your child's education to yourself until you cannot avoid conflict any longer. If you are eager to please, your desire to be liked may cause you to agree to anything the school proposes. If you are a controller, you may feel out of control at school meetings.

Meeting Strategies

The right word may be effective, but no word was ever as effective as a rightly timed pause. —Mark Twain

Both Parents Attend Meetings

If possible, both parents should attend school meetings. When parents go to meetings together, they present a strong, unified front. If one parent has more business experience, that parent may be more comfortable in the role of negotiator.

Fathers should take an active role in educational decisions and planning. **Mothers who attend meetings alone do not operate from a position of strength.** School personnel tend to view mothers as more emotional and less objective about their children.

Discuss what you want to accomplish ahead of time. Decide what your child needs. Do not air your personal problems during school meetings.

Do Not Go Alone

If the other parent cannot attend, ask a friend or family member to accompany you. If you go alone, you are more likely to feel intimidated and to make decisions that you will regret later. When you have a friend or family member with you, you will feel less vulnerable. This person can provide support and help you analyze the meeting afterwards.

Tape Recording Meetings

If you have problems or you anticipate a dispute about your child's IEP, it is a good idea to tape record IEP meetings. Some parents routinely record all meetings, even when parent-school relationships are good. There are several advantages to recording meetings.

If you are like most parents, IEP meetings are confusing and overwhelming. You want to take an active role in the IEP process but you cannot ask questions, discuss issues, make decisions, and take notes at the same time. When you tape record meetings, you can ask questions, express concerns, offer solutions, and make decisions without also having to take notes.

Perhaps you asked an important question. After the meeting, you cannot remember how or if your question was answered. If you recorded the meeting, you can listen to the tape and find the answer to your question.

After the tapes are transcribed, you have a transcript of what was proposed,

Table 26-1	*Tips for Recording Meetings*

▷ Practice using the recorder several times before the meeting.
▷ Put fresh batteries in the recorder before the meeting
▷ Mark tapes as #1, #2, and #3 before the meeting.
▷ Bring several blank tapes to the meeting.
▷ For a clear recording, place the recorder on a book on the table.
▷ Use an external, battery-powered microphone like those used by newscasters.
▷ To make the microphone omni-directional, clip the microphone to an object a few feet away from the recorder.
▷ Make sure the microphone battery is turned on.

considered, and rejected during the meeting. If you request a hearing to resolve a dispute, transcripts of meetings may be evidence that supports your position.

Assume that you successfully recorded a meeting. The meeting is ending. Do not turn off your recorder until after you leave the room. School personnel often make important statements when your hand is on the doorknob.

Within a day or two, listen to the tapes. When you listen to the tapes, you may hear questions that were not answered. You may discover issues that you thought were resolved are still on the table.

At school meetings where several people talk at once, there is often confusion about who agreed to deal with an issue. You may believe that Ms. Jones agreed to examine the issue, while Ms. Jones believes that Mr. Smith agreed to look into the issue. When meetings are recorded, these problems are easier to resolve.

Tape-recording: What Does the Law Say?

The IDEA statute does not mention tape-recording meetings. Many states have language in their special education regulations about their policy on audio- and video-taping. Read your state's regulation about recording before you broach the subject to the school.

The federal statutes do not authorize or prohibit parents or school officials from recording IEP meetings. According to *Appendix A* to the Code of Federal Regulations:

. . . an SEA or public agency has the option to require, prohibit, limit, or otherwise regulate the use of recording devices at IEP meetings . . . If a public agency has a policy that prohibits or limits the use of recording devices at IEP meetings, that policy must provide for exceptions if they are necessary to ensure that the parent understands the IEP or the IEP process or to implement other parental rights guaranteed . . . (*Appendix A*, Question 21)

☑ Appendix A to the special education regulations is Appendix A to this book.

If your school district adopts a rule about taping, the school must apply this rule uniformly. Schools cannot record meetings while prohibiting parents from recording. If the school records a meeting, the tapes become part of your child's educational record. You are entitled to copies of your child's educational records, including tapes of meetings.

If the school claims they have a policy that prohibits parents from taping, write a polite letter to request a copy of this policy. Ask if the taping policy was adopted by the school administration, school board, or other entity. If the school district has a policy that prohibits taping, the district must make exceptions if this policy interferes with your ability to participate in the IEP process.

- If the policy prevents you from participating in an IEP meeting
- If your spouse is unable to attend the meeting
- Other factors that interfere with your parental rights

More Meeting Strategies

Taping Issues

Put the recorder on a book in the middle of the table, turn it on, and identify the meeting. If a school employee says you cannot record, pick up the microphone and ask the person to state his or her name and that, the school district is forbidding you to record the meeting. In most cases, the person will back down. If the person does not back down, you have this on tape.

Meeting Dynamics

When you enter the meeting room, make a pleasant comment to break the ice. Shake hands. Make eye contact with each team member.

Pay attention to non-verbal behavior. Watch body language. Who sits at the head of the table? Who takes notes? Who is the most powerful person in the room?

☑ **If you sit next to the most powerful person, you make it more difficult for this person to minimize you and your concerns.**

Common Meeting Problems

"We Can't Do That"

School personnel often tell parents that "the law" does not allow the school to provide a service. Do not accept legal advice from your child's special education team.

Read the law and regulations for yourself. You may need to consult with a qualified special education attorney so you have a clear sense of what the law says.

Ask questions. When you ask 5 Ws + H + E questions, frame your sentences so they begin with one of these words: What, Why, When, Who, Where, How, and Explain.

"Where does it say you can't provide one-on-one speech therapy?" "Where does it say that my child's IEP cannot have more than four goals?"

You will not change minds by arguing with people. When you ask questions, you often raise questions. When you ask questions, you will learn how the school views your child's problem and what the school plans to do to help your child. This information will help you anticipate problems and develop solutions that may resolve the problem and allow both sides to win. You will discover the answers to questions like these:

- How does the school view my child's problems?
- What does the school think my child needs?
- What does the school think they should do about my child's problem?
- Does the school have a plan to educate my child?
- What are the components of this plan?
- What does the school propose to do now?
- How will I know if the plan is working?
- What does the school propose to do if their plan does not work?

☑ **When you go to meetings at the school, bring your state special education regulations and *Wrightslaw: Special Education Law*.**

"The Law Does Not Allow Us to Do That"

If the school says, "The law does not allow us to do that," take out your copy of *Wrightslaw: Special Education Law* and ask the team to help you find this in the law. Ask for help. You must be sincere. "When I read the law, I did not find this."

If you cannot find the issue, the usual fallback position is, "It's in the regulations." If the team cannot find the answer, you can say, "I haven't found this in the state regulations either." Make sure you have done your legal research and are on firm ground!

If you cannot find an answer to the question in the regulations, the school may claim that the issue is in their school district policies and guidelines. Ask for these documents. Be polite. In most cases, the school policies and guidelines will not deal with the issue.

Dealing with the "Draft IEP"

Many parents complain that when they go to an IEP meeting, they are handed a completed IEP to sign. If this happens to you, do not panic and do not get mad.

You have a right to participate in the development of your child's IEP. The fact that the school presents you with a draft IEP does not mean that you must accept the IEP. View the draft IEP as a "draft" and as information about what the school wants to provide. The draft IEP gives you information about the resources the school is willing to commit. The draft IEP is their first offer in the negotiation process.

You can say, "Thank you for drafting your ideas as a starting point for our discussion." Then pass out copies of your parent agenda or problem resolution worksheet!

When the Meeting Ends Without Resolution

Do not be surprised if the meeting ends before you finish the IEP. Do not be surprised if the school asks you to sign the incomplete IEP. Do not sign! Write that you attended the meeting but have not agreed to the services or program.

If you are being rushed to sign the IEP, you can say:

"This is an important document. I have not read it or had time to go over it so I cannot sign it. I would like to take a copy home with me. After I have reviewed it, I will send you a written consent or I will contact you to discuss any problems that I have with it."

☑ **When you sign an IEP, get a copy for your records. If you are advised that the IEP will be cleaned up and typed, get a "dirty" copy before you leave. Your copy establishes what the team agreed to.**

Strategies to Use in Disputes

If you have a dispute or disagreement, expect the school to put their defenses in place. They are preparing for battle. Will you request a due process hearing? The fear of the unknown will make everyone anxious.

Try to discover the basis of their refusal. How can you get school personnel to tell you their perceptions, interests and fears when they feel defensive and anxious?

Ask 5 Ws + H + E questions. Listen to the answers. Do not argue. You may be surprised at the useful information you discover!

Use the Problem-Resolution Worksheet

In the last chapter, you learned how to use the pre-meeting worksheet to prepare for meetings. You learned how to use a parent agenda to describe problems and propose solutions.

If you anticipate problems, fill out the problem resolution worksheet before you go to the meeting (Table 26-2). The problem resolution worksheet is a simple strategy that will help you keep track of the issues you want to resolve.

Table 26-2	Problem Resolution Worksheet

Child's Name:

Date:

School:

Child's Need/ Parent Request	School's Response	Resolved	Start Date	Responsible Person

Table 26-3	Problem Resolution Worksheet with Parent's Requests

Name: Joseph Doe

Date: December 2, 2001, 3:30 pm

School: Park Valley Middle School

Child's Need/ Parent Request	School's Response	Resolved	Start Date	Responsible Person
1. Reading skills 2 years behind. Needs 1:1 remediation.				
2. Teacher trained in Wilson Reading Method.				
3. Reduced homework (no more than 1 hour a night)				
4. Preferential Seating (front row, close to teacher)				

Make a table with five columns. Write "Child's need/ Parent's request" above the first column, "School's response" above the second column, "Resolved?" above the third column, "Start Date" above the fourth column, and "Responsible Person" above the fifth column. (See the problem resolution worksheet in Table 26-2)

In the first column, list the services and supports you think your child needs. For example, "My child needs one-on-one reading help" or "My child needs an aide." See Table 26-3 for the problem resolution worksheet that has the parent's requests filled in.

At the beginning of the meeting, provide the team members with your problem resolution worksheet. Advise the team that these are the issues you want to resolve. This strategy will help the team focus on important issues.

If the team does not respond to a request or question, you can say, "Shall I write that one down as 'no response'?"

Do not argue. Ask questions and take notes. Before the meeting ends, tell the team that you want to review your notes. Read what you have written. If the team does not agree with your notes, ask them to tell you what they do not agree with. Note this on your worksheet.

At the end of the meeting, you have a document that is a concise list of your requests, the school's response to your requests, and a list of the issues that were resolved

Table 26-4	*Problem Resolution Worksheet at End of Meeting*

Problem Resolution Worksheet (includes your notes)

Name: Joseph Doe

Date: December 2, 2001, 3:30 pm

School: Park Valley Middle School

Child's Need/ Parent Request	School's Response	Resolved	Start Date	Responsible Person
1. Reading skills 2 years behind. Needs 1:1 remediation.	We don't do that	No		
2. Teacher trained in Wilson Reading Method.	We have never done that	No		
3. Reduced homework (no more than 1 hour a night)	We can't write that into the IEP, it's up to the teachers	No		
4. Preferential Seating (front row, close to teacher)	We will try it in Ms. Jones' class	Yes	12/2/01	Mrs. Jones

and not resolved. Your worksheet is a written record created during the meeting. If you need to request a hearing later, this document is powerful evidence. To see how the problem resolution worksheet may look at the end of the meeting, see Table 26-4.

Post-meeting Strategies

Your most important post-meeting strategies are your written recollections and your thank-you letter.

Your Recollections

After the meeting, write or dictate your recollections about what happened. Do this immediately. Do not wait. Memories fade. What issues were resolved? What issues are still on the table? We recommend that you use a small tape recorder to dictate your recollections.

When you write or dictate your recollections, you may realize that the meeting was more successful than you thought. Perhaps you resolved some of your problems. Perhaps the school agreed to provide some of the services you requested. What do you think? Did you make some progress?

Your Thank-You Letter

After the meeting, write a thank-you letter. In this letter, describe the meeting, your understanding of what the school agreed to, and the issues that are still on the table. Your letter should be polite. Frame issues and problems as "ours." Offer to meet again to resolve the remaining issues.

 Review Chapter 23 about writing letters to the school.

Make a copy of your problem resolution worksheet or parent agenda and attach this document to your thank-you letter. Send your thank-you letter and supporting documents to the IEP team leader.

Keep a copy of your signed letter and documents for your records.

When you use these strategies, you will resolve many problems with the school. You created contemporaneous documentation during the meeting. After the meeting, you documented what you requested, what you were told, what was agreed to, and what was not resolved.

In Summation

In this chapter, you learned strategies for successful school meetings. You learned about common meeting problems and strategies you can use to deal with these problems. You learned how to use the problem resolution worksheet and the post-meeting thank-you letter to create a contemporaneous record of meetings.

When you prepare for meetings, write agendas, use problem resolution worksheets, and write polite thank-you letters that document what happened during meetings, you can prevent problems and get the services your child needs. Now, it's time to take stock of what you have learned. If you turn the page, we will offer our thoughts and ideas.

27 | In Summation

"Revenge is the bastard child of justice.
If we or our argument are perceived as a threat, we will never be heard."
— Gerry Spence, trial lawyer and writer

In this final chapter of *From Emotions to Advocacy*, we will offer advice and issue a warning about pitfalls to avoid. First, we will summarize the components of effective advocacy.

Learn about your child's unique needs. Think about the skills your child must acquire to be an independent, self-sufficient member of society: communication skills, social skills, and reading skills. Ensure that your child acquires these skills.

Learn about researched-based educational methods and "proven methods of teaching and learning for children with disabilities." (20 U.S.C. 1400(c)(4)). Learn about assistive technology and how technology can help your child master essential skills.

Learn the law so you can find answers to your questions in the statutes, regulations or legal decisions. Do not learn the law so you can threaten or browbeat school personnel.

Get your state special education regulations and *Wrightslaw: Special Education Law*. When you cross-reference these publications, you will understand the relationships between the rules of procedure (as discussed in Section 1415) and substantive issues (as discussed in Sections 1412 and 1414). Because you are familiar with the statute, you will know that the statutes about evaluations are in Section 1414 and that the statutes about IEPs are in Section 1414(d).

But learning the law is less important than learning about evaluations and test results. You cannot be an effective advocate until you understand how to use test scores to measure learning. You learned about standard scores, percentile ranks, standard deviations, and subtest scores. When you look at your child's test results, you should know if your child is acquiring skills or is falling further behind.

The IEP drives your child's educational program. You have learned about SMART IEPs that are **S**pecific, **M**easurable, use **A**ction words, are **R**ealistic and **T**ime Specific. Work with school personnel to develop SMART IEPs that relate to the purposes of the IDEA.

Your child's IEPs should be designed to meet the child's unique needs and prepare the child for employment and independent living. This is your mission. Do not allow yourself to be distracted from this long-term goal: to prepare your child for employment and independent living.

Learn about evidence and presentation. Organize your child's file. Secure private evaluations. Apply the Rules of Adverse Assumptions. Use 5 Ws + H + E questions to discover hidden agendas. Document events. Use negotiation skills. Write persuasive letters. These are the keys to successful advocacy.

How can you master these skills if you are feeling frustrated, angry, and frightened about the future? Accept your emotions as normal. Understand that if you do not control your emotions, you may damage or destroy your child. Use your emotions to motivate you to learn new information and skills. Remember – your journey is from emotions to advocacy.

From Emotions to Advocacy

Do not blame or find fault. If you want to force your district to admit that they are wrong, you will lose the battle and the war. If you want your district to change their policies and practices, you need to educate and persuade the decision-makers.

Prepare. Prepare. Prepare. And win.   –Gerry Spence

This chapter opened with statements by Gerry Spence, famous trial attorney and writer. Pete's style of litigation is similar that of Gerry Spence, and relies on tactics and strategies. Read *How to Argue and Win Every Time* by Gerry Spence (see bibliography). *How to Argue* will teach you about persuasion. If you can see issues through their eyes, you can help others see through your eyes. They are more likely to use their power to give you what you want.

The strategies in this book are not unique to special education advocacy. You can use these strategies to resolve problems and disputes in other areas of your life. If you have a dispute with an insurance company, a government bureaucrat, your boss, or your neighbor, think about the Rules of Adverse Assumptions, documentation, paper trails, and writing persuasive Letters to the Stranger.

As your child's advocate, your goal is not to litigate. Your goal is to use tactics and strategies to secure quality services for your child. When you negotiate with school personnel, you market win-win solutions to problems. In the end, you and school personnel should be able to sit down together and break bread. When you do this, you have successfully completed your journey from emotions to advocacy.

I am only one.
But still I am one.
I cannot do everything.
And because I cannot do everything,
I will not refuse to do the something that I can do.

   –Helen Keller, advocate for people with disabilities

APPENDIX A

Appendix A to 34 C.F.R. Part 300

Notice of Interpretation

Authority: Part B of the Individuals with Disabilities Education Act (20 U.S.C. 1401, et seq.), unless otherwise noted.

Individualized Education Programs (IEPS) and Other Selected Implementation Issues

Introduction

The IEP requirements under Part B of the IDEA emphasize the importance of three core concepts:

(1) the involvement and progress of each child with a disability in the general curriculum including addressing the unique needs that arise out of the child's disability;

(2) the involvement of parents and students, together with regular and special education personnel, in making individual decisions to support each student's (child's) educational success, and

(3) the preparation of students with disabilities for employment and other post-school activities.

The first three sections of this Appendix (I-III) provide guidance regarding the IEP requirements as they relate to the three core concepts described above. Section IV addresses other questions regarding the development and content of IEPs, including questions about the timelines and responsibility for developing and implementing IEPs, participation in IEP meetings, and IEP content. Section IV also addresses questions on other selected requirements under IDEA.

I. Involvement and Progress of Each Child With a Disability in the General Curriculum

In enacting the IDEA Amendments of 1997, the Congress found that research, demonstration, and practice over the past 20 years in special education and related disciplines have demonstrated that an effective educational system now and in the future must maintain high academic standards and clear performance goals for children with disabilities, consistent with the standards and expectations for all students in the educational system, and provide for appropriate and effective strategies and methods to ensure that students who are children with disabilities have maximum opportunities to achieve those standards and goals. [Section 651(a)(6)(A) of the Act.]

Accordingly, the evaluation and IEP provisions of Part B place great emphasis on the involvement and progress of children with disabilities in the general curriculum. (The term "general curriculum," as used in these regulations, including this Appendix, refers to the curriculum that is used with nondisabled children.)

While the Act and regulations recognize that IEP teams must make individualized decisions about the special education and related services, and supplementary aids and services, provided to each child with a disability, they are driven by IDEA's strong preference that, to the maximum extent appropriate, children with disabilities be educated in regular classes with their nondisabled peers with appropriate supplementary aids and services.

In many cases, children with disabilities will need appropriate supports in order to successfully progress in the general curriculum, participate in State and district-wide assessment programs, achieve the measurable goals in their IEPs, and be educated together with their nondisabled peers. Accordingly, the Act requires the IEP team to determine, and the public agency to provide, the accommodations, modifications, supports, and supplementary aids and services, needed by each child with a disability to successfully be involved in and progress in the general curriculum achieve the goals of the IEP, and successfully demonstrate his or her competencies in State and district-wide assessments.

1. What are the major Part B IEP requirements that govern the involvement and progress of children with disabilities in the general curriculum?

Present Levels of Educational Performance

Section 300.347(a)(1) requires that the IEP for each child with a disability include

"* * * a statement of the child's present levels of educational performance, including—(i) how the child's disability affects the child's involvement and progress in the general curriculum;

or

(ii) for preschool children, as appropriate, how the child's disability affects the child's participation in appropriate activities * * *" ("Appropriate activities" in this context refers to age-relevant developmental abilities or milestones that typically developing children of the same age would be performing or would have achieved.)

The IEP team's determination of how each child's disability affects the child's involvement and progress in the general curriculum is a primary consideration in the development of the child's IEP. In assessing children with disabilities, school districts may use a variety of assessment techniques to determine the extent to which these children can be involved and progress in the general curriculum, such as criterion-referenced tests, standard achievement tests, diagnostic tests, other tests, or any combination of the above.

The purpose of using these assessments is to determine the child's present levels of educational performance and areas of need arising from the child's disability so that approaches for ensuring the child's involvement and progress in the general curriculum and any needed adaptations or modifications to that curriculum can be identified.

Measurable Annual Goals, including Benchmarks or Short-term objectives

Measurable annual goals, including benchmarks or short-term objectives, are critical to the strategic planning process used to develop and implement the IEP for each child with a disability. Once the IEP team has developed measurable annual goals for a child, the team (1) can develop strategies that will be most effective in realizing those goals and (2) must develop either measurable, intermediate steps (short-term objectives) or major milestones (benchmarks) that will enable parents, students, and educators to monitor progress during the year, and, if appropriate, to revise the IEP consistent with the student's instructional needs.

The strong emphasis in Part B on linking the educational program of children with disabilities to the general curriculum is reflected in § 300.347(a)(2), which requires that the IEP include:

a statement of measurable annual goals, including benchmarks or short-term objectives, related to—(i) meeting the child's needs that result from the child's disability to enable the child to be involved in and progress in the general curriculum; and (ii) meeting each of the child's other educational needs that result from the child's disability.

As noted above, each annual goal must include either short-term objectives or benchmarks. The purpose of both is to enable a child's teacher(s), parents, and others involved in developing and implementing the child's IEP, to gauge, at intermediate times during the year, how well the child is progressing toward achievement of the annual goal. IEP teams may continue to develop short-term instructional objectives that generally break the skills described in the annual goal down into discrete components. The revised statute and regulations also provide that, as an alternative, IEP teams may develop benchmarks, which can be thought of as describing the amount of progress the child is expected to make within specified segments of the year. Generally, benchmarks establish expected performance levels that allow for regular checks of progress that coincide with the reporting periods for informing parents of their child's progress toward achieving the annual goals. An IEP team may use either short-term objectives or benchmarks or a combination of the two depending on the nature of the annual goals and the needs of the child.

Special Education and Related Services and Supplementary Aids and Services

The requirements regarding services provided to address a child's present levels of educational performance and to make progress toward the identified goals reinforce the emphasis on progress in the general curriculum, as well as maximizing the extent to which children with disabilities are educated with nondisabled children. Section 300.347(a)(3) requires that the IEP include:

a statement of the special education and related services and supplementary aids and services to be provided to the child, or on behalf of the child, and a statement of the program modifications or supports for school personnel that will be provided for the child— (i) to advance appropriately toward attaining the annual goals; (ii) to be involved and progress in the general curriculum * * * and to participate in extracurricular and other nonacademic activities; and (iii) to be educated and participate with other children with disabilities and nondisabled children in [extracurricular and other nonacademic activities] * * *

Extent to Which Child Will Participate With Nondisabled Children

Section 300.347(a)(4) requires that each child's IEP include "An explanation of the extent, if any, to which the child will not participate with nondisabled children in the regular class and in [extracurricular and other nonacademic] activities * * *" This is consistent with the least restrictive environment (LRE) provisions at Secs. 300.550-300.553, which include requirements that:

(1) each child with a disability be educated with nondisabled children to the maximum extent appropriate (§ 300.550(b)(1));

(2) each child with a disability be removed from the regular educational environment only when the nature or severity of the child's disability is such that education in regular classes with the use of supplementary aids and services cannot be achieved satisfactorily (§ 300.550(b)(1)); and

(3) to the maximum extent appropriate to the child's needs, each child with a disability participates with nondisabled children in nonacademic and extracurricular services and activities (§ 300.553).

All services and educational placements under Part B must be individually determined in light of each child's unique abilities and needs, to reasonably promote the child's educational success. Placing children with disabilities in this manner should enable each disabled child to meet high expectations in the future.

Although Part B requires that a child with a disability not be removed from the regular educational environment if the child's education can be achieved satisfactorily in regular classes with the use of supplementary aids and services, Part B's LRE principle is intended to ensure that a child with a disability is served in a setting where the child can be educated successfully. Even though IDEA does not mandate regular class placement for every disabled student, IDEA presumes that the first placement option considered for each disabled student by the student's placement team, which must include the parent, is the school the child would attend if not disabled, with appropriate supplementary aids and services to facilitate such placement. Thus, before a disabled child can be placed outside of the regular educational environment, the full range of supplementary aids and services that if provided would facilitate the student's placement in the regular classroom setting must be considered. Following that consideration, if a determination is made that particular disabled student cannot be educated satisfactorily in the regular educational environment, even with the provision of appropriate supplementary aids and services, that student then could be placed in a setting other than the regular classroom. Later, if it becomes apparent that the child's IEP can be carried out in a less restrictive setting, with the provision of appropriate supplementary aids and services, if needed, Part B would require that the child's placement be changed from the more restrictive setting to a less restrictive setting. In all cases, placement decisions must be individually determined on the basis of each child's abilities and needs, and not solely on factors such as category of disability, significance of disability, availability of special education and related services, configuration of the service delivery system, availability of space, or administrative convenience. Rather, each student's IEP forms the basis for the placement decision.

Further, a student need not fail in the regular classroom before another placement can be considered. Conversely, IDEA does not require that a student demonstrate achievement of a specific performance level as a prerequisite for placement into a regular classroom.

Participation in State or District-Wide Assessments of Student Achievement

Consistent with § 300.138(a), which sets forth a presumption that children with disabilities will be included in general State and district-wide assessment programs, and provided with appropriate accommodations if necessary, § 300.347(a)(5) requires that the IEP for each student with a disability include:

"(i) a statement of any individual modifications in the administration of State or district-wide assessments of student achievement that are needed in order for the child to participate in the assessment; and (ii) if the IEP team determines that the child will not participate in a particular State or district-wide assessment of student achievement (or part of an assessment of student achievement), a statement of— (A) Why that assessment is not appropriate for the child; and (B) How the child will be assessed."

Regular Education Teacher Participation in the Development, Review, and Revision of IEPs

Very often, regular education teachers play a central role in the education of children with disabilities (H. Rep. No. 105-95, p. 103 (1997); S. Rep. No. 105-17, p. 23 (1997)) and have important expertise regarding the general curriculum and the general education environment. Further, with the emphasis on involvement and progress in the general curriculum added by the IDEA Amendments of 1997, regular education teachers have an increasingly critical role (together with special education and related services personnel) in implementing the program of FAPE for most children with disabilities, as described in their IEPs.

Accordingly, the IDEA Amendments of 1997 added a requirement that each child's IEP team must include at least one regular education teacher of the child, if the child is, or may be, participating in the regular education environment (see § 300.344(a)(2)). (See also Secs. 300.346(d) on the role of a regular education teacher in the development, review and revision of IEPs.)

2. Must a child's IEP address his or her involvement in the general curriculum, regardless of the nature and severity of the child's disability and the setting in which the child is educated?

Yes. The IEP for each child with a disability (including children who are educated in separate classrooms or schools) must address how the child will be involved and progress in the general curriculum. However, the Part B regulations recognize that some children have other educational needs resulting from their disability that also must be met, even though those needs are not directly linked to participation in the general curriculum.

Accordingly, § 300.347(a)(1)(2) requires that each child's IEP include:

A statement of measurable annual goals, including benchmarks or short-term objectives related to–(i) Meeting the child's needs that result from the child's disability to enable the child to be involved in and progress in the general curriculum; and (ii) meeting each of the child's other educational needs that result from the child's disability.

Thus, the IEP team for each child with a disability must make an individualized determination regarding (1) how the child will be involved and progress in the general curriculum and what needs that result from the child's disability must be met to facilitate that participation; (2) whether the child has any other educational needs resulting from his or her disability that also must be met; and (3) what special education and other services and supports must be described in the child's IEP to address both sets of needs (consistent with § 300.347(a)). For example, if the IEP team determines that in order for a child who is deaf to participate in the general curriculum he or she needs sign language and materials which reflect his or her language development, those needs (relating to the child's participation in the general curriculum) must be addressed in the child's IEP. In addition, if the team determines that the child also needs to expand his or her vocabulary in sign language that service must also be addressed in the applicable components of the child's IEP. The IEP team may also wish to consider whether there is a need for members of the child's family to receive training in sign language in order for the child to receive FAPE.

3. What must public agencies do to meet the requirements at Secs. 300.344(a)(2) and 300.346(d) regarding the participation of a "regular education teacher" in the development, review, and revision of IEPs, for children aged 3 through 5 who are receiving preschool special education services?

If a public agency provides "regular education" preschool services to non-disabled children, then the requirements of Secs. 300.344(a)(2) and 300.346(d) apply as they do in the case of older children with disabilities. If a public agency makes kindergarten available to nondisabled children, then a regular education kindergarten teacher could appropriately be the regular education teacher who would be a member of the IEP team, and, as appropriate, participate in IEP meetings, for a kindergarten-aged child who is, or may be, participating in the regular education environment.

If a public agency does not provide regular preschool education services to nondisabled children, the agency could designate an individual who, under State standards, is qualified to serve nondisabled children of the same age.

4. Must the measurable annual goals in a child's IEP address all areas of the general curriculum, or only those areas in which the child's involvement and progress are affected by the child's disability?

Section 300.347(a)(2) requires that each child's IEP include "A statement of measurable annual goals, including benchmarks or short- term objectives, related to–(i) meeting the child's needs that result from the child's disability to enable the child to be involved in and progress in the general curriculum * * *; and (ii) meeting each of the child's other educational needs that result from the child's disability . . . "

Thus, a public agency is not required to include in an IEP annual goals that relate to areas of the general curriculum in which the child's disability does not affect the child's ability to be involved in and progress in the general curriculum. If a child with a disability needs only modifications or accommodations in order to progress in an area of the general curriculum, the IEP does not need to include a goal for that area; however, the IEP would need to specify those modifications or accommodations.

Public agencies often require all children, including children with disabilities, to demonstrate mastery in a given area of the general curriculum before allowing them to progress to the next level or grade in that area. Thus, in order to ensure that each child with a disability can effectively demonstrate competencies in an applicable area of the general curriculum, it is important for the IEP team to consider the accommodations and modifications that the child needs to assist him or her in demonstrating progress in that area.

II. Involvement of Parents and Students

The Congressional Committee Reports on the IDEA Amendments of 1997 express the view that the Amendments provide an opportunity for strengthening the role of parents, and emphasize that one of the purposes of the Amendments is to expand opportunities for parents and key public agency staff (e.g., special education, related services, regular education, and early intervention service providers, and other personnel) to work in new partnerships at both the State and local levels (H. Rep. 105-95, p. 82 (1997); S. Rep. No. 105-17, p. 4 and 5 (1997)). Accordingly, the IDEA Amendments of 1997 require that parents have an opportunity to participate in meetings with respect to the identification, evaluation, and educational placement of the child, and the provision of FAPE to the child. (§ 300.501(a)(2)). Thus, parents must now be part of:

(1) the group that determines what additional data are needed as part of an evaluation of their child (§ 300.533(a)(1));

(2) the team that determines their child's eligibility (§ 300.534(a)(1)); and (3) the group that makes decisions on the educational placement of their child (§ 300.501(c)).

In addition, the concerns of parents and the information that they provide regarding their children must be considered in developing and reviewing their children's IEPs (Secs. 300.343(c)(iii) and 300.346(a)(1)(i) and (b)); and the requirements for keeping parents informed about the educational progress of their children, particularly as it relates to their progress in the general curriculum, have been strengthened (§ 300.347(a)(7)).

The IDEA Amendments of 1997 also contain provisions that greatly strengthen the involvement of students with disabilities in decisions regarding their own futures, to facilitate movement from school to post-school activities. For example, those amendments (1) retained, essentially verbatim, the "transition services" requirements from the IDEA Amendments of 1990 (which provide that a statement of needed transition services must be in the IEP of each student with a disability, beginning no later than age 16); and (2) significantly expanded those provisions by adding a new annual requirement for the IEP to include "transition planning" activities for students beginning at age 14. (See section IV of this appendix for a description of the transition services requirements and definition.)

With respect to student involvement in decisions regarding transition services, § 300.344(b) provides that (1) "the public agency shall invite a student with a disability of any age to attend his or her IEP meeting if a purpose of the meeting will be the consideration of—(i) The student's transition services needs under § 300.347(b)(1); or (ii) The needed transition services for the student under § 300.347(b)(2); or (iii) Both;" and (2) "If the student does not attend the IEP meeting, the public agency shall take other steps to ensure that the student's preferences and interests are considered." (§ 300.344(b)(2)).

The IDEA Amendments of 1997 also give States the authority to elect to transfer the rights accorded to parents under Part B to each student with a disability upon reaching the age of majority under State law (if the student has not been determined incompetent under State law) (§ 300.517). (Part B requires that if the rights transfer to the student, the public agency must provide any notice required under Part B to both the student and the parents.) If the State elects to provide for the transfer of rights from the parents to the student at the age of majority, the IEP must, beginning at least one year before a student reaches the age of majority under State law, include a statement that the student has been informed of any rights that will transfer to him or her upon reaching the age of majority. (§ 300.347(c)).

The IDEA Amendments of 1997 also permit, but do not require, States to establish a procedure for appointing the parent, or another appropriate individual if the parent is not available, to represent the educational interests of a student with a disability who has reached the age of majority under State law and has not been determined to be incompetent, but who is determined not to have the ability to provide informed consent with respect to his or her educational program.

5. What is the role of the parents, including surrogate parents, in decisions regarding the educational program of their children?

The parents of a child with a disability are expected to be equal participants along with school personnel, in developing, reviewing, and revising the IEP for their child. This is an active role in which the parents (1) provide critical information regarding the strengths of their child and express their concerns for enhancing the education of their child; (2) participate in discussions about the child's need for special education and related services and supplementary aids and services; and (3) join with the other participants in deciding how the child will be involved and progress in the general curriculum and participate in State and district-wide assessments, and what services the agency will provide to the child and in what setting.

As previously noted in the introduction to section II of this Appendix, Part B specifically provides that parents of children with disabilities–

Have an opportunity to participate in meetings with respect to the identification, evaluation, and educational placement of their child, and the provision of FAPE to the child (including IEP meetings) (Secs. 300.501(b), 300.344(a)(1), and 300.517;

Be part of the groups that determine what additional data are needed as part of an evaluation of their child (§ 300.533(a)(1)), and determine their child's eligibility (§ 300.534(a)(1)) and educational placement (§ 300.501(c));

Have their concerns and the information that they provide regarding their child considered in developing and reviewing their child's IEPs (Secs. 300.343(c)(iii) and 300.346(a)(1)(i) and (b)); and

Be regularly informed (by such means as periodic report cards), as specified in their child's IEP, at least as often as parents are informed of their nondisabled children's progress, of their child's progress toward the annual goals in the IEP and the extent to which that progress is sufficient to enable the child to achieve the goals by the end of the year (§ 300.347(a)(7)).

A surrogate parent is a person appointed to represent the interests of a child with a disability in the educational decision- making process when no parent (as defined at § 300.20) is known, the agency, after reasonable efforts, cannot locate the child's parents, or the child is a ward of the State under the laws of the State. A surrogate parent has all of the rights and responsibilities of a parent under Part B (§ 300.515.)

6. What are the Part B requirements regarding the participation of a student (child) with a disability in an IEP meeting?

If a purpose of an IEP meeting for a student with a disability will be the consideration of the student's transition services needs or needed transition services under § 300.347(b)(1) or (2), or both, the public agency must invite the student and, as part of the notification to the parents of the IEP meeting, inform the parents that the agency will invite the student to the IEP meeting.

If the student does not attend, the public agency must take other steps to ensure that the student's preferences and interests are considered. (See § 300.344(b)).

Section § 300.517 permits, but does not require, States to transfer procedural rights under Part B from the parents to students with disabilities who reach the age of majority under State law, if they have not been determined to be incompetent under State law. If those rights are to be transferred from the parents to the student, the public agency would be required to ensure that the student has the right to participate in IEP meetings set forth for parents in § 300.345. However, at the discretion of the student or the public agency, the parents also could attend IEP meetings as "* * * individuals who have knowledge or special expertise regarding the child * * *" (see § 300.344(a)(6).

In other circumstances, a child with a disability may attend "if appropriate." (§ 300.344(a)(7)). Generally, a child with a disability should attend the IEP meeting if the parent decides that it is appropriate for the child to do so. If possible, the agency and parents should discuss the appropriateness of the child's participation before a decision is made, in order to help the parents determine whether or not the child's attendance would be (1) helpful in developing the IEP or (2) directly beneficial to the child or both. The agency should inform the parents before each IEP meeting—as part of notification under § 300.345(a)(1)—that they may invite their child to participate.

7. Must the public agency inform the parents of who will be at the IEP meeting?

Yes. In notifying parents about the meeting, the agency "must indicate the purpose, time, and location of the meeting, and who will be in attendance." (§ 300.345(b) In addition, if a purpose of the IEP meeting will be the consideration of a student's transition services needs or needed transition services under § 300.347(b)(1) or (2) or both, the notice must also inform the parents that the agency is inviting the student, and identify any other agency that will be invited to send a representative.

The public agency also must inform the parents of the right of the parents and the agency to invite other individuals who have knowledge or special expertise regarding the child, including related services personnel as appropriate to be members of the IEP team. (§ 300.345(b)(1)(ii).)

It also may be appropriate for the agency to ask the parents to inform the agency of any individuals the parents will be bringing to the meeting. Parents are encouraged to let the agency know whom they intend to bring. Such cooperation can facilitate arrangements for the meeting, and help ensure a productive, child-centered meeting.

8. Do parents have the right to a copy of their child's IEP?

Yes. Section 300.345(f) states that the public agency shall give the parent a copy of the IEP at no cost to the parent.

9. What is a public agency's responsibility if it is not possible to reach consensus on what services should be included in a child's IEP?

The IEP meeting serves as a communication vehicle between parents and school personnel, and enables them, as equal participants, to make joint, informed decisions regarding the (1) child's needs and appropriate goals; (2) extent to which the child will be involved in the general curriculum and participate in the regular education environment and State and district-wide assessments; and (3) services needed to support that involvement and participation and to achieve agreed-upon goals. Parents are considered equal partners with school personnel in making these decisions, and the IEP team must consider the parents' concerns and the information that they provide regarding their child in developing, reviewing, and revising IEPs (Secs. 300.343(c)(iii) and 300.346(a)(1) and (b)).

The IEP team should work toward consensus, but the public agency has ultimate responsibility to ensure that the IEP includes the services that the child needs in order to receive FAPE. It is not appropriate to make IEP decisions based upon a majority "vote." If the team cannot reach consensus, the public agency must provide the parents with prior written notice of the agency's proposals or refusals, or both, regarding the child's educational program, and the parents have the right to seek resolution of any disagreements by initiating an impartial due process hearing.

Every effort should be made to resolve differences between parents and school staff through voluntary mediation or some other informal step, without resort to a due process hearing. However, mediation or other informal procedures may not be used to deny or delay a parent's right to a due process hearing, or to deny any other rights afforded under Part B.

10. Does Part B require that public agencies inform parents regarding the educational progress of their children with disabilities?

Yes. The Part B statute and regulations include a number of provisions to help ensure that parents are involved in decisions regarding, and are informed about, their child's educational progress, including the child's progress in the general curriculum. First, the parents will be informed regarding their child's present levels of educational performance through the development of the IEP. Section 300.347(a)(1) requires that each IEP include:

* * * A statement of the child's present levels of educational performance, including—(i) how the child's disability affects the child's involvement and progress in the general curriculum; or (ii) for preschool children, as appropriate, how the disability affects the child's participation in appropriate activities * * *

Further, § 300.347(a)(7) sets forth new requirements for regularly informing parents about their child's educational progress, as regularly as parents of nondisabled children are informed of their child's progress. That section requires that the IEP include:

A statement of—(i) How the child's progress toward the annual goals * * * will be measured; and (ii) how the child's parents will be regularly informed (by such means as periodic report cards), at least as often as parents are informed of their nondisabled children's progress, of—(A) their child's progress toward the annual goals; and (B) the extent to which that progress is sufficient to enable the child to achieve the goals by the end of the year.

One method that public agencies could use in meeting this requirement would be to provide periodic report cards to the parents of students with disabilities that include both (1) the grading information provided for all children in the agency at the same intervals; and (2) the specific information required by § 300.347(a)(7)(ii)(A) and (B).

Finally, the parents, as part of the IEP team, will participate at least once every 12 months in a review of their child's educational progress. Section 300.343(c) requires that a public agency initiate and conduct a meeting, at which the IEP team:

* * * (1) Reviews the child's IEP periodically, but not less than annually to determine whether the annual goals for the child are being achieved; and (2) revises the IEP as appropriate to address— (i) any lack of expected progress toward the annual goals * * * and in the general curriculum, if appropriate; (ii) The results of any reevaluation * * *; (iii) Information about the child provided to, or by, the parents * * *; (iv) The child's anticipated needs; or (v) Other matters.

III. Preparing Students With Disabilities for Employment and Other Post-School Experiences

One of the primary purposes of the IDEA is to "* * * ensure that all children with disabilities have available to them a free appropriate public education that emphasizes special education and related services designed to meet their unique needs and prepare them for employment and independent living * * *" (§ 300.1(a)). Section 701 of the Rehabilitation Act of 1973 describes the philosophy of independent living as including a philosophy of consumer control, peer support, self-help, self-determination, equal access, and individual and system advocacy, in order to maximize the leadership, empowerment, independence, and productivity of individuals with disabilities, and the integration and full inclusion of individuals with disabilities into the mainstream of American society. Because many students receiving services under IDEA will also receive services under the Rehabilitation Act, it is important, in planning for their future, to consider the impact of both statutes.

Similarly, one of the key purposes of the IDEA Amendments of 1997 was to "promote improved educational results for children with disabilities through early intervention, preschool, and educational experiences that prepare them for later educational challenges and employment." (H. Rep. No. 105-95, p. 82 (1997); S. Rep. No. 105-17, p. 4 (1997)).

Thus, throughout their preschool, elementary, and secondary education, the IEPs for children with disabilities must, to the extent appropriate for each individual child, focus on providing instruction and experiences that enable the child to prepare himself or herself for later educational experiences and for post-school activities, including formal education, if appropriate, employment, and independent living. Many students with disabilities will obtain services through State vocational rehabilitation programs to ensure that their educational goals are effectively implemented in post- school activities. Services available through rehabilitation programs are consistent with the underlying purpose of IDEA.

Although preparation for adult life is a key component of FAPE throughout the educational experiences of students with disabilities, Part B sets forth specific requirements related to transition planning and transition services that must be implemented no later than ages 14 and 16, respectively, and which require an intensified focus on that preparation as these students begin and prepare to complete their secondary education.

11. What must the IEP team do to meet the requirements that the IEP include "a statement of * * * transition service needs" beginning at age 14 (§ 300.347(b)(1)(i))," and a statement of needed transition services" no later than age 16 (§ 300.347(b)(2)?

Section 300.347(b)(1) requires that, beginning no later than age 14, each student's IEP include specific transition-related content, and, beginning no later than age 16, a statement of needed transition services:

Beginning at age 14 and younger if appropriate, and updated annually, each student's IEP must include:

"* * * a statement of the transition service needs of the student under the applicable components of the student's IEP that focuses on the student's courses of study (such as participation in advanced-placement courses or a vocational education program)" (§ 300.347(b)(1)(i)).

Beginning at age 16 (or younger, if determined appropriate by the IEP team), each student's IEP must include:

"* * * a statement of needed transition services for the student, including, if appropriate, a statement of the interagency responsibilities or any needed linkages." (§ 300.347(b)(2)).

The Committee Reports on the IDEA Amendments of 1997 make clear that the requirement added to the statute in 1997 that beginning at age 14, and updated annually, the IEP include "a statement of the transition service needs" is "* * * designed to augment, and not replace," the separate, preexisting requirement that the IEP include, "* * * beginning at age 16 (or younger, if determined appropriate by the IEP team), a statement of needed transition services * * *" (H. Rep. No. 105-95, p. 102 (1997); S. Rep. No. 105-17, p. 22 (1997)). As clarified by the Reports, "The purpose of [the requirement in § 300.347(b)(1)(i)] is to focus attention on how the child's educational program can be planned to help the child make a successful transition to his or her goals for life after secondary school." (H. Rep. No. 105-95, pp. 101-102 (1997); S. Rep. No. 105-17, p. 22 (1997)). The Reports further explain that "[F]or example, for a child whose transition goal is a job, a transition service could be teaching the child how to get to the job site on public transportation." (H. Rep. No. 105-95, p. 102 (1997); S. Rep. No. 105-17, p. 22 (1997)).

Thus, beginning at age 14, the IEP team, in determining appropriate measurable annual goals (including benchmarks or short- term objectives) and services for a student, must determine what instruction and educational experiences will assist the student to prepare for transition from secondary education to post-secondary life.

The statement of transition service needs should relate directly to the student's goals beyond secondary education, and show how planned studies are linked to these goals. For example, a student interested in exploring a career in computer science may have a statement of transition services needs connected to technology course work, while another student's statement of transition services needs could describe why public bus transportation training is important for future independence in the community.

Although the focus of the transition planning process may shift as the student approaches graduation, the IEP team must discuss specific areas beginning at least at the age of 14 years and review these areas annually. As noted in the Committee Reports, a disproportionate number of students with disabilities drop out of school before they complete their secondary education:

"Too many students with disabilities are failing courses and dropping out of school. Almost twice as many students with disabilities drop out as compared to students without disabilities." (H. Rep. No. 105-95, p. 85 (1997), S. Rep. No. 105-17, p. 5 (1997).)

To help reduce the number of students with disabilities that drop out, it is important that the IEP team work with each student with a disability and the student's family to select courses of study that will be meaningful to the student's future and motivate the student to complete his or her education.

This requirement is distinct from the requirement, at § 300.347(b)(2), that the IEP include:

* * * beginning at age 16 (or younger, if determined appropriate by the IEP team), a statement of needed transition services for the child, including, if appropriate, a statement of the interagency responsibilities or any needed linkages.

The term "transition services" is defined at § 300.29 to mean:

* * * a coordinated set of activities for a student with a disability that–(1) Is designed within an outcome-oriented process, that promotes movement from school to post-school activities, including postsecondary education, vocational training, integrated employment (including supported employment), continuing and adult education, adult services, independent living, or community participation; (2) Is based on the individual student's needs, taking into account the student's preferences and interests; and (3) Includes--i) Instruction; (ii) Related services; (iii) Community experiences; (iv) The development of employment and other post- school adult living objectives; and (v) If appropriate, acquisition of daily living skills and functional vocational evaluation.

Thus, while § 300.347(b)(1) requires that the IEP team begin by age 14 to address the student's need for instruction that will assist the student to prepare for transition, the IEP must include by age 16 a statement of needed transition services under § 300.347(b)(2) that includes a "coordinated set of activities * * *, designed within an outcome-oriented process, that promotes movement from school to post-school activities * * *." (§ 300.29) Section 300.344(b)(3) further requires that, in implementing § 300.347(b)(1), public agencies (in addition to required participants for all IEP meetings), must also invite a representative of any other agency that is likely to be responsible for providing or paying for transition services. Thus, § 300.347(b)(2) requires a broader focus on coordination of services across, and linkages between, agencies beyond the SEA and LEA.

12. Must the IEP for each student with a disability, beginning no later than age 16, include all "needed transition services," as identified by the IEP team and consistent with the definition at § 300.29, even if an agency other than the public agency will provide those services? What is the public agency's responsibility if another agency fails to provide agreed-upon transition services?

Section 300.347(b)(2) requires that the IEP for each child with a disability, beginning no later than age 16, or younger if determined appropriate by the IEP team, include all "needed transition services," as identified by the IEP team and consistent with the definition at § 300.29, regardless of whether the public agency or some other agency will provide those services. Section 300.347(b)(2) specifically requires that the statement of needed transition services include, "* * * if appropriate, a statement of the interagency responsibilities or any needed linkages."

Further, the IDEA Amendments of 1997 also permit an LEA to use up to five percent of the Part B funds it receives in any fiscal year in combination with other amounts, which must include amounts other than education funds, to develop and implement a coordinated services system. These funds may be used for activities such as:

(1) linking IEPs under Part B and Individualized Family Service Plans (IFSPs) under Part C, with Individualized Service Plans developed under multiple Federal and State programs, such as Title I of the Rehabilitation Act; and (2) developing and implementing interagency financing strategies for the provision of services, including transition services under Part B.

The need to include, as part of a student's IEP, transition services to be provided by agencies other than the public agency is contemplated by § 300.348(a), which specifies what the public agency must do if another agency participating in the development of the statement of needed transition services fails to provide a needed transition service that it had agreed to provide.

If an agreed-upon service by another agency is not provided, the public agency responsible for the student's education must implement alternative strategies to meet the student's needs. This requires that the public agency provide the services, or convene an IEP meeting as soon as possible to identify alternative strategies to meet the transition services objectives, and to revise the IEP accordingly.

Alternative strategies might include the identification of another funding source, referral to another agency, the public agency's identification of other district-wide or community resources that it can use to meet the student's identified needs appropriately, or a combination of these strategies. As emphasized by § 300.348(b), however:

Nothing in [Part B] relieves any participating agency, including a State vocational rehabilitation agency, of the responsibility to provide or pay for any transition service that the agency would otherwise provide to students with disabilities who meet the eligibility criteria of that agency.

However, the fact that an agency other than the public agency does not fulfill its responsibility does not relieve the public agency of its responsibility to ensure that FAPE is available to each student with a disability. (Section 300.142(b)(2) specifically requires that if an agency other than the LEA fails to provide or pay for a special education or related service (which could include a transition service), the LEA must, without delay, provide or pay for the service, and may then claim reimbursement from the agency that failed to provide or pay for the service.)

13. Under what circumstances must a public agency invite representatives from other agencies to an IEP meeting at which a child's need for transition services will be considered?

Section 300.344 requires that, "In implementing the requirements of [§ 300.347(b)(1)(ii) requiring a statement of needed transition services], the public agency shall also invite a representative of any other agency that is likely to be responsible for providing or paying for transition services." To meet this requirement, the public agency must identify all agencies that are "likely to be responsible for providing or paying for transition services" for each student addressed by § 300.347(b)(1), and must invite each of those agencies to the IEP meeting; and if an agency invited to send a representative to a meeting does not do so, the public agency must take other steps to obtain the participation of that agency in the planning of any transition services.

If, during the course of an IEP meeting, the team identifies additional agencies that are "likely to be responsible for providing or paying for transition services" for the student, the public agency must determine how it will meet the requirements of § 300.344.

IV. Other Questions Regarding the Development and Content of IEPs

14. For a child with a disability receiving special education for the first time, when must an IEP be developed—before or after the child begins to receive special education and related services?

Section 300.342(b)(1) requires that an IEP be "in effect before special education and related services are provided to an eligible child * * *"

The appropriate placement for a particular child with a disability cannot be determined until after decisions have been made about the child's needs and the services that the public agency will provide to meet those needs. These decisions must be made at the IEP meeting, and it would not be permissible first to place the child and then develop the IEP. Therefore, the IEP must be developed before placement. (Further, the child's placement must be based, among other factors, on the child's IEP.)

This requirement does not preclude temporarily placing an eligible child with a disability in a program as part of the evaluation process–before the IEP is finalized—to assist a public agency in determining the appropriate placement for the child. However, it is essential that the temporary placement not become the final placement before the IEP is finalized. In order to ensure that this does not happen, the State might consider requiring LEAs to take the following actions:

a. Develop an interim IEP for the child that sets out the specific conditions and timelines for the trial placement. (See paragraph c, following.)

b. Ensure that the parents agree to the interim placement before it is carried out, and that they are involved throughout the process of developing, reviewing, and revising the child's IEP.

c. Set a specific timeline (e.g., 30 days) for completing the evaluation, finalizing the IEP, and determining the appropriate placement for the child.

d. Conduct an IEP meeting at the end of the trial period in order to finalize the child's IEP.

15. Who is responsible for ensuring the development of IEPs for children with disabilities served by a public agency other than an LEA?

The answer as to which public agency has direct responsibility for ensuring the development of IEPs for children with disabilities served by a public agency other than an LEA will vary from

State to State, depending upon State law, policy, or practice. The SEA is ultimately responsible for ensuring that all Part B requirements, including the IEP requirements, are met for eligible children within the State, including those children served by a public agency other than an LEA. Thus, the SEA must ensure that every eligible child with a disability in the State has FAPE available, regardless of which State or local agency is responsible for educating the child. (The only exception to this responsibility is that the SEA is not responsible for ensuring that FAPE is made available to children with disabilities who are convicted as adults under State law and incarcerated in adult prisons, if the State has assigned that responsibility to a public agency other than the SEA. (See § 300.600(d)).

Although the SEA has flexibility in deciding the best means to meet this obligation (e.g., through interagency agreements), the SEA must ensure that no eligible child with a disability is denied FAPE due to jurisdictional disputes among agencies.

When an LEA is responsible for the education of a child with a disability, the LEA remains responsible for developing the child's IEP, regardless of the public or private school setting into which it places the child.

16. For a child placed out of State by an educational or non- educational State or local agency, is the placing or receiving State responsible for the child's IEP?

Regardless of the reason for the placement, the "placing" State is responsible for ensuring that the child's IEP is developed and that it is implemented. The determination of the specific agency in the placing State that is responsible for the child's IEP would be based on State law, policy, or practice. However, the SEA in the placing State is ultimately responsible for ensuring that the child has FAPE available.

17. If a disabled child has been receiving special education from one public agency and transfers to another public agency in the same State, must the new public agency develop an IEP before the child can be placed in a special education program?

If a child with a disability moves from one public agency to another in the same State, the State and its public agencies have an ongoing responsibility to ensure that FAPE is made available to that child. This means that if a child moves to another public agency the new agency is responsible for ensuring that the child has available special education and related services in conformity with an IEP.

The new public agency must ensure that the child has an IEP in effect before the agency can provide special education and related services. The new public agency may meet this responsibility by either adopting the IEP the former public agency developed for the child or by developing a new IEP for the child. (The new public agency is strongly encouraged to continue implementing the IEP developed by the former public agency, if appropriate, especially if the parents believe their child was progressing appropriately under that IEP.)

Before the child's IEP is finalized, the new public agency may provide interim services agreed to by both the parents and the new public agency. If the parents and the new public agency are unable to agree on an interim IEP and placement, the new public agency must implement the old IEP to the extent possible until a new IEP is developed and implemented.

In general, while the new public agency must conduct an IEP meeting, it would not be necessary if:

(1) A copy of the child's current IEP is available; (2) the parents indicate that they are satisfied with the current IEP; and (3) the new public agency determines that the current IEP is appropriate and can be implemented as written.

If the child's current IEP is not available, or if either the new public agency or the parent believes that it is not appropriate, the new public agency must develop a new IEP through appropriate procedures within a short time after the child enrolls in the new public agency (normally, within one week).

18. What timelines apply to the development and implementation of an initial IEP for a child with a disability?

Section 300.343(b) requires each public agency to ensure that within a reasonable period of time following the agency's receipt of parent consent to an initial evaluation of a child, the child is evaluated and, if determined eligible, special education and related services are made available to the child in accordance with an IEP. The section further requires the agency to conduct a meeting to develop an IEP for the child **within 30 days** of determining that the child needs special education and related services.

Section 300.342(b)(2) provides that an IEP must be implemented as soon as possible following the meeting in which the IEP is developed.

19. Must a public agency hold separate meetings to determine a child's eligibility for special education and related services, develop the child's IEP, and determine the child's placement, or may the agency meet all of these requirements in a single meeting?

A public agency may, after a child is determined by "a group of qualified professionals and the parent" (see § 300.534(a)(1)) to be a child with a disability, continue in the same meeting to develop an IEP for the child and then to determine the child's placement. However, the public agency must ensure that it meets:

(1) the requirements of § 300.535 regarding eligibility decisions; (2) all of the Part B requirements regarding meetings to develop IEPs (including providing appropriate notification to the parents, consistent with the requirements of Secs. 300.345, 300.503, and 300.504, and ensuring that all the required team members participate in the development of the IEP, consistent with the requirements of § 300.344;) and (3) ensuring that the placement is made by the required individuals, including the parent, as required by Secs. 300.552 and 300.501(c).

20. How frequently must a public agency conduct meetings to review, and, if appropriate, revise the IEP for each child with a disability?

A public agency must initiate and conduct meetings periodically, but at least once every twelve months, to review each child's IEP, in order to determine whether the annual goals for the child are being achieved, and to revise the IEP, as appropriate, to address:

(a) Any lack of expected progress toward the annual goals and in the general curriculum, if appropriate;

(b) the results of any reevaluation;

(c) information about the child provided to, or by, the parents;

(d) the child's anticipated needs; or (e) other matters (§ 300.343(c)).

A public agency also must ensure that an IEP is in effect for each child at the beginning of each school year (§ 300.342(a)). It may conduct IEP meetings at any time during the year. However, if the agency conducts the IEP meeting prior to the beginning of the next school year, it must ensure that the IEP contains the necessary special education and related services and supplementary aids and services to ensure that the student's IEP can be appropriately implemented during the next school year. Otherwise, it would be necessary for the public agency to conduct another IEP meeting.

Although the public agency is responsible for determining when it is necessary to conduct an IEP meeting, the parents of a child with a disability have the right to request an IEP meeting at any time. For example, if the parents believe that the child is not progressing satisfactorily or that there is a problem with the child's current IEP, it would be appropriate for the parents to request an IEP meeting.

If a child's teacher feels that the child's IEP or placement is not appropriate for the child, the teacher should follow agency procedures with respect to:

(1) calling or meeting with the parents or (2) requesting the agency to hold another IEP meeting to review the child's IEP.

The legislative history of Public Law 94-142 makes it clear that there should be as many meetings a year as any one child may need (121 Cong. Rec. S20428-29 (Nov. 19, 1975) (remarks of Senator Stafford)). Public agencies should grant any reasonable parent request for an IEP meeting. For example, if the parents question the adequacy of services that are provided while their child is suspended for short periods of time, it would be appropriate to convene an IEP meeting.

In general, if either a parent or a public agency believes that a required component of the student's IEP should be changed, the public agency must conduct an IEP meeting if it believes that a change in the IEP may be necessary to ensure the provision of FAPE.

If a parent requests an IEP meeting because the parent believes that a change is needed in the provision of FAPE to the child or the educational placement of the child, and the agency refuses to convene an IEP meeting to determine whether such a change is needed, the agency must provide written notice to the parents of the refusal, including an explanation of why the agency has determined that conducting the meeting is not necessary to ensure the provision of FAPE to the student.

Under § 300.507(a), the parents or agency may initiate a due process hearing at any time regarding any proposal or refusal regarding the identification, evaluation, or educational placement of the child, or the provision of FAPE to the child, and the public agency must inform parents about the availability of mediation.

21. May IEP meetings be audio- or video-tape-recorded?

Part B does not address the use of audio or video recording devices at IEP meetings, and no other

Federal statute either authorizes or prohibits the recording of an IEP meeting by either a parent or a school official. Therefore, an SEA or public agency has the option to require, prohibit, limit, or otherwise regulate the use of recording devices at IEP meetings.

If a public agency has a policy that prohibits or limits the use of recording devices at IEP meetings, that policy must provide for exceptions if they are necessary to ensure that the parent understands the IEP or the IEP process or to implement other parental rights guaranteed under Part B. An SEA or school district that adopts a rule regulating the tape recording of IEP meetings also should ensure that it is uniformly applied.

Any recording of an IEP meeting that is maintained by the public agency is an "education record," within the meaning of the Family Educational Rights and Privacy Act ("FERPA"; 20 U.S.C. 1232g), and would, therefore, be subject to the confidentiality requirements of the regulations under both FERPA (34 CFR part 99) and part B (Secs. 300.560-300.575).

Parents wishing to use audio or video recording devices at IEP meetings should consult State or local policies for further guidance.

22. Who can serve as the representative of the public agency at an IEP meeting?

The IEP team must include a representative of the public agency who:

(a) Is qualified to provide, or supervise the provision of, specially designed instruction to meet the unique needs of children with disabilities; (b) is knowledgeable about the general curriculum; and (c) is knowledgeable about the availability of resources of the public agency (§ 300.344(a)(4)).

Each public agency may determine which specific staff member will serve as the agency representative in a particular IEP meeting, so long as the individual meets these requirements. It is important, however, that the agency representative have the authority to commit agency resources and be able to ensure that whatever services are set out in the IEP will actually be provided.

A public agency may designate another public agency member of the IEP team to also serve as the agency representative, so long as that individual meets the requirements of § 300.344(a)(4).

23. For a child with a disability being considered for initial provision of special education and related services, which teacher or teachers should attend the IEP meeting?

A child's IEP team must include at least one of the child's regular education teachers (if the child is, or may be participating in the regular education environment) and at least one of the child's special education teachers, or, if appropriate, at least one of the child's special education providers (§ 300.344(a)(2) and (3)).

Each IEP must include a statement of the present levels of educational performance, including a statement of how the child's disability affects the child's involvement and progress in the general curriculum (§ 300.347(a)(1)). At least one regular education teacher is a required member of the IEP team of a child who is, or may be, participating in the regular educational environment, regardless of the extent of that participation.

The requirements of § 300.344(a)(3) can be met by either:

(1) a special education teacher of the child; or (2) another special education provider of the child,

such as a speech pathologist, physical or occupational therapist, etc., if the related service consists of specially designed instruction and is considered special education under applicable State standards.

Sometimes more than one meeting is necessary in order to finalize a child's IEP. In this process, if the special education teacher or special education provider who will be working with the child is identified, it would be useful to have that teacher or provider participate in the meeting with the parents and other members of the IEP team in finalizing the IEP. If this is not possible, the public agency must ensure that the teacher or provider has access to the child's IEP as soon as possible after it is finalized and before beginning to work with the child.

Further, (consistent with § 300.342(b)), the public agency must ensure that each regular education teacher, special education teacher, related services provider and other service provider of an eligible child under this part (1) has access to the child's IEP, and (2) is informed of his or her specific responsibilities related to implementing the IEP, and of the specific accommodations, modifications, and supports that must be provided to the child in accordance with the IEP. This requirement is crucial to ensuring that each child receives FAPE in accordance with his or her IEP, and that the IEP is appropriately and effectively implemented.

24. What is the role of a regular education teacher in the development, review and revision of the IEP for a child who is, or may be, participating in the regular education environment?

As required by § 300.344(a)(2), the IEP team for a child with a disability must include at least one regular education teacher of the child if the child is, or may be, participating in the regular education environment. Section 300.346(d) further specifies that the regular education teacher of a child with a disability, as a member of the IEP team, must, to the extent appropriate, participate in the development, review, and revision of the child's IEP, including assisting in—(1) the determination of appropriate positive behavioral interventions and strategies for the child; and (2) the determination of supplementary aids and services, program modifications, and supports for school personnel that will be provided for the child, consistent with 300.347(a)(3) (§ 300.344(d)).

Thus, while a regular education teacher must be a member of the IEP team if the child is, or may be, participating in the regular education environment, the teacher need not (depending upon the child's needs and the purpose of the specific IEP team meeting) be required to participate in all decisions made as part of the meeting or to be present throughout the entire meeting or attend every meeting. For example, the regular education teacher who is a member of the IEP team must participate in discussions and decisions about how to modify the general curriculum in the regular classroom to ensure the child's involvement and progress in the general curriculum and participation in the regular education environment.

Depending upon the specific circumstances, however, it may not be necessary for the regular education teacher to participate in discussions and decisions regarding, for example, the physical therapy needs of the child, if the teacher is not responsible for implementing that portion of the child's IEP.

In determining the extent of the regular education teacher's participation at IEP meetings, public agencies and parents should discuss and try to reach agreement on whether the child's regular education teacher that is a member of the IEP team should be present at a particular IEP meeting and, if so, for what period of time. The extent to which it would be appropriate for the regular education teacher member of the IEP team to participate in IEP meetings must be decided on a case-by-case basis.

25. If a child with a disability attends several regular classes, must all of the child's regular education teachers be members of the child's IEP team?

No. The IEP team need not include more than one regular education teacher of the child. If the participation of more than one regular education teacher would be beneficial to the child's success in school (e.g., in terms of enhancing the child's participation in the general curriculum), it would be appropriate for them to attend the meeting.

26. How should a public agency determine which regular education teacher and special education teacher will be members of the IEP team for a particular child with a disability?

The regular education teacher who serves as a member of a child's IEP team should be a teacher who is, or may be, responsible for implementing a portion of the IEP, so that the teacher can participate in discussions about how best to teach the child.

If the child has more than one regular education teacher responsible for carrying out a portion of the IEP, the LEA may designate which teacher or teachers will serve as IEP team member(s), taking into account the best interest of the child.

In a situation in which not all of the child's regular education teachers are members of the child's IEP team, the LEA is strongly encouraged to seek input from the teachers who will not be attending. In addition, (consistent with § 300.342(b)), the LEA must ensure that each regular education teacher (as well as each special education teacher, related services provider, and other service provider) of an eligible child under this part (1) has access to the child's IEP, and (2) is informed of his or her specific responsibilities related to implementing the IEP, and of the specific accommodations, modifications and supports that must be provided to the child in accordance with the IEP.

In the case of a child whose behavior impedes the learning of the child or others, the LEA is encouraged to have a regular education teacher or other person knowledgeable about positive behavior strategies at the IEP meeting. This is especially important if the regular education teacher is expected to carry out portions of the IEP.

Similarly, the special education teacher or provider of the child who is a member of the child's IEP team should be the person who is, or will be, responsible for implementing the IEP. If, for example, the child's disability is a speech impairment, the special education teacher on the IEP team could be the speech-language pathologist.

27. For a child whose primary disability is a speech impairment, may a public agency meet its responsibility under § 300.344(a)(3) to ensure that the IEP team includes "at least one special education teacher, or, if appropriate, at least one special education provider of the child" by including a speech-language pathologist on the IEP team?

Yes, if speech is considered special education under State standards. As with other children with disabilities, the IEP team must also include at least one of the child's regular education teachers if the child is, or may be, participating in the regular education environment.

28. Do parents and public agencies have the option of inviting any individual of their choice be participants on their child's IEP team?

The IEP team may, at the discretion of the parent or the agency, include "other individuals who have knowledge or special expertise regarding the child * * *" (§ 300.344(a)(6) Under § 300.344(a)(6), these individuals are members of the IEP team. This is a change from prior law, which provided, without qualification, that parents or agencies could have other individuals as members of the IEP team at the discretion of the parents or agency.

Under § 300.344(c), the determination as to whether an individual has knowledge or special expertise, within the meaning of § 300.344(a)(6), shall be made by the parent or public agency who has invited the individual to be a member of the IEP team.

Part B does not provide for including individuals such as representatives of teacher organizations as part of an IEP team, unless they are included because of knowledge or special expertise regarding the child. (Because a representative of a teacher organization would generally be concerned with the interests of the teacher rather than the interests of the child, and generally would not possess knowledge or expertise regarding the child, it generally would be inappropriate for such an official to be a member of the IEP team or to otherwise participate in an IEP meeting.)

29. Can parents or public agencies bring their attorneys to IEP meetings, and, if so under what circumstances? Are attorney's fees available for parents' attorneys if the parents are prevailing parties in actions or proceedings brought under Part B?

Section 300.344(a)(6) authorizes the addition to the IEP team of other individuals at the discretion of the parent or the public agency only if those other individuals have knowledge or special expertise regarding the child. The determination of whether an attorney possesses knowledge or special expertise regarding the child would have to be made on a case-by-case basis by the parent or public agency inviting the attorney to be a member of the team.

The presence of the agency's attorney could contribute to a potentially adversarial atmosphere at the meeting. The same is true with regard to the presence of an attorney accompanying the parents at the IEP meeting. Even if the attorney possessed knowledge or special expertise regarding the child (§ 300.344(a)(6)), an attorney's presence would have the potential for creating an adversarial atmosphere that would not necessarily be in the best interests of the child.

Therefore, the attendance of attorneys at IEP meetings should be strongly discouraged. Further, as specified in Section 615(i)(3)(D)(ii) of the Act and § 300.513(c)(2)(ii), Attorneys' fees may not be awarded relating to any meeting of the IEP team unless the meeting is convened as a result of an administrative proceeding or judicial action, or, at the discretion of the State, for a mediation conducted prior to the request for a due process hearing.

30. Must related services personnel attend IEP meetings?

Although Part B does not expressly require that the IEP team include related services personnel as part of the IEP team (§ 300.344(a)), it is appropriate for those persons to be included if a particular related service is to be discussed as part of the IEP meeting. Section 300.344(a)(6) provides that the IEP team also includes "at the discretion of the parent or the agency, other individuals who have knowledge or special expertise regarding the child, including related services personnel as appropriate. * * *"

Further, § 300.344(a)(3) requires that the IEP team for each child with a disability include "at least one special education teacher, or, if appropriate, at least one special education provider of the child * * *" This requirement can be met by the participation of either (1) a special education teacher of the child, or (2) another special education provider such as a speech- language pathologist, physical or occupational therapist, etc., if the related service consists of specially designed instruction and is considered special education under the applicable State standard.

If a child with a disability has an identified need for related services, it would be appropriate for the related services personnel to attend the meeting or otherwise be involved in developing the IEP. As explained in the Committee Reports on the IDEA Amendments of 1997, "Related services personnel should be included on the team when a particular related service will be discussed at the request of the child's parents or the school." (H. Rep. No. 105-95, p. 103 (1997); S. Rep. No. 105-17, p. 23 (1997)). For example, if the child's evaluation indicates the need for a specific related service (e.g., physical therapy, occupational therapy, special transportation services, school social work services, school health services, or counseling), the agency should ensure that a qualified provider of that service either (1) attends the IEP meeting, or (2) provides a written recommendation concerning the nature, frequency, and amount of service to be provided to the child. This written recommendation could be a part of the evaluation report.

A public agency must ensure that all individuals who are necessary to develop an IEP that will meet the child's unique needs, and ensure the provision of FAPE to the child, participate in the child's IEP meeting.

31. Must the public agency ensure that all services specified in a child's IEP are provided?

Yes. The public agency must ensure that all services set forth in the child's IEP are provided, consistent with the child's needs as identified in the IEP. The agency may provide each of those services directly, through its own staff resources; indirectly, by contracting with another public or private agency; or through other arrangements. In providing the services, the agency may use whatever State, local, Federal, and private sources of support are available for those purposes (see § 300.301(a)); but the services must be at no cost to the parents, and the public agency remains responsible for ensuring that the IEP services are provided in a manner that appropriately meets the student's needs as specified in the IEP. The SEA and responsible public agency may not allow the failure of another agency to provide service(s) described in the child's IEP to deny or delay the provision of FAPE to the child. (See § 300.142, Methods of ensuring services.)

32. Is it permissible for an agency to have the IEP completed before the IEP meeting begins?

No. Agency staff may come to an IEP meeting prepared with evaluation findings and proposed recommendations regarding IEP content, but the agency must make it clear to the parents at the outset of the meeting that the services proposed by the agency are only recommendations for review and discussion with the parents. Parents have the right to bring questions, concerns, and recommendations to an IEP meeting as part of a full discussion, of the child's needs and the services to be provided to meet those needs before the IEP is finalized.

Public agencies must ensure that, if agency personnel bring drafts of some or all of the IEP content to the IEP meeting, there is a full discussion with the child's parents, before the child's IEP is finalized, regarding drafted content and the child's needs and the services to be provided to meet those needs.

33. Must a public agency include transportation in a child's IEP as a related service?

As with other related services, a public agency must provide transportation as a related service if it is required to assist the disabled child to benefit from special education. (This includes transporting a preschool-aged child to the site at which the public agency provides special education and related services to the child, if that site is different from the site at which the child receives other preschool or day care services.)

In determining whether to include transportation in a child's IEP, and whether the child needs to receive transportation as a related service, it would be appropriate to have at the IEP meeting a person with expertise in that area. In making this determination, the IEP team must consider how the child's disability affects the child's need for transportation, including determining whether the child's disability prevents the child from using the same transportation provided to nondisabled children, or from getting to school in the same manner as nondisabled children.

The public agency must ensure that any transportation service included in a child's IEP as a related service is provided at public expense and at no cost to the parents, and that the child's IEP describes the transportation arrangement.

Even if a child's IEP team determines that the child does not require transportation as a related service, Section 504 of the Rehabilitation Act of 1973, as amended, requires that the child receive the same transportation provided to nondisabled children. If a public agency transports nondisabled children, it must transport disabled children under the same terms and conditions. However, if a child's IEP team determines that the child does not need transportation as a related service, and the public agency transports only those children whose IEPs specify transportation as a related service, and does not transport nondisabled children, the public agency would not be required to provide transportation to a disabled child.

It should be assumed that most children with disabilities receive the same transportation services as nondisabled children. For some children with disabilities, integrated transportation may be achieved by providing needed accommodations such as lifts and other equipment adaptations on regular school transportation vehicles.

34. Must a public agency provide related services that are required to assist a child with a disability to benefit from special education, whether or not those services are included in the list of related services in § 300.24?

The list of related services is not exhaustive and may include other developmental, corrective, or supportive services if they are required to assist a child with a disability to benefit from special education. This could, depending upon the unique needs of a child, include such services as nutritional services or service coordination.

These determinations must be made on an individual basis by each child's IEP team.

35. Must the IEP specify the amount of services or may it simply list the services to be provided?

The amount of services to be provided must be stated in the IEP, so that the level of the agency's commitment of resources will be clear to parents and other IEP team members (§ 300.347(a)(6)). The amount of time to be committed to each of the various services to be provided must be (1) appropriate to the specific service, and (2) stated in the IEP in a manner that is clear to all who are involved in both the development and implementation of the IEP.

The amount of a special education or related service to be provided to a child may be stated in the IEP as a range (e.g., speech therapy to be provided three times per week for 30-45 minutes per session) only if the IEP team determines that stating the amount of services as a range is necessary to meet the unique needs of the child. For example, it would be appropriate for the IEP to specify, based upon the IEP team's determination of the student's unique needs, that particular services are needed only under specific circumstances, such as the occurrence of a seizure or of a particular behavior. A range may not be used because of personnel shortages or uncertainty regarding the availability of staff.

36. Under what circumstances is a public agency required to permit a child with a disability to use a school-purchased assistive technology device in the child's home or in another setting?

Each child's IEP team must consider the child's need for assistive technology (AT) in the development of the child's IEP (§ 300.346(a)(2)(v)); and the nature and extent of the AT devices and services to be provided to the child must be reflected in the child's IEP (§ 300.346(c)).

A public agency must permit a child to use school-purchased assistive technology devices at home or in other settings, if the IEP team determines that the child needs access to those devices in nonschool settings in order to receive FAPE (to complete homework, for example).

Any assistive technology devices that are necessary to ensure FAPE must be provided at no cost to the parents, and the parents cannot be charged for normal use, wear and tear. However, while ownership of the devices in these circumstances would remain with the public agency, State law, rather than Part B, generally would govern whether parents are liable for loss, theft, or damage due to negligence or misuse of publicly owned equipment used at home or in other settings in accordance with a child's IEP.

37. Can the IEP team also function as the group making the placement decision for a child with a disability?

Yes, a public agency may use the IEP team to make the placement decision for a child, so long as the group making the placement decision meets the requirements of Secs. 300.552 and 300.501(c), which requires that the placement decision be made by a group of persons, including the parents, and other persons knowledgeable about the child, the meaning of the evaluation data, and the placement options.

38. If a child's IEP includes behavioral strategies to address a particular behavior, can a child ever be suspended for engaging in that behavior?

If a child's behavior impedes his or her learning or that of others, the IEP team, in developing the child's IEP, must consider, if appropriate, development of strategies, including positive behavioral interventions, strategies and supports to address that behavior, consistent with § 300.346(a)(2)(i). This means that in most cases in which a child's behavior that impedes his or her learning or that of others is, or can be readily anticipated to be, repetitive, proper development of the child's IEP will include the development of strategies, including positive behavioral interventions, strategies and supports to address that behavior. See § 300.346(c). This includes behavior that could violate a school code of conduct. A failure to, if appropriate, consider and address these behaviors in developing and implementing the child's IEP would constitute a denial of FAPE to the child. Of course, in appropriate circumstances, the IEP team, which includes the child's parents, might determine that the child's behavioral intervention plan includes specific regular or alternative disciplinary measures, such as denial of certain privileges or short suspensions, that would result from particular infractions of school rules, along with positive behavior intervention strategies and supports, as a part of a comprehensive plan to address the child's behavior. Of course, if short suspensions that are included in a child's IEP are being implemented in a manner that denies the child access to the ability to progress in the educational program, the child would be denied FAPE.

Whether other disciplinary measures, including suspension, are ever appropriate for behavior that is addressed in a child's IEP will have to be determined on a case by case basis in light of the particular circumstances of that incident. However, school personnel may not use their ability to suspend a child for 10 days or less at a time on multiple occasions in a school year as a means of avoiding appropriately considering and addressing the child's behavior as a part of providing FAPE to the child.

39. If a child's behavior in the regular classroom, even with appropriate interventions, would significantly impair the learning of others, can the group that makes the placement decision determine that placement in the regular classroom is inappropriate for that child?

The IEP team, in developing the IEP, is required to consider, when appropriate, strategies, including positive behavioral interventions, strategies and supports to address the behavior of a child with a disability whose behavior impedes his or her learning or that of others. If the IEP team determines that such supports, strategies or interventions are necessary to address the behavior of the child, those services must be included in the child's IEP. These provisions are designed to foster increased participation of children with disabilities in regular education environments or other less restrictive environments, not to serve as a basis for placing children with disabilities in more restrictive settings.

The determination of appropriate placement for a child whose behavior is interfering with the education of others requires careful consideration of whether the child can appropriately function in the regular classroom if provided appropriate behavioral supports, strategies and interventions. If the child can appropriately function in the regular classroom with appropriate behavioral supports, strategies or interventions, placement in a more restrictive environment would be inconsistent with the least restrictive environment provisions of the IDEA. If the child's behavior in the regular classroom, even with the provision of appropriate behavioral supports, strategies or interventions, would significantly impair the learning of others, that placement would not meet his or her needs and would not be appropriate for that child.

40. May school personnel during a school year implement more than one short-term removal of a child with disabilities from his or her classroom or school for misconduct?

Yes. Under § 300.520(a)(1), school personnel may order removal of a child with a disability from the child's current placement for not more than 10 consecutive school days for any violation of school rules, and additional removals of not more than 10 consecutive school days in that same school year for separate incidents of misconduct, as long as these removals do not constitute a change of placement under § 300.519(b). However, these removals are permitted only to the extent they are consistent with discipline that is applied to children without disabilities. Also, school personnel should be aware of constitutional due process protections that apply to suspensions of all children. *Goss v. Lopez*, 419 U.S. 565 (1975). Section 300.121(d) addresses the extent of the obligation to provide services after a child with a disability has been removed from his or her current placement for more than 10 school days in the same school year.

[**Author's note:** Appendix A refers to federal regulations that are contained in our companion book, *Wrightslaw: Special Education Law.*]

END OF Appendix A

Your Notes Here

APPENDIX B

Your Rights and Responsibilites Under IDEA

[Author's note: This article is an excellent overview of your rights and responsibilities that was adapted from *A Parent's Guide to Special Education and Related Services: Communicating through Letterwriting* by Susan Ferguson and Suzanne Ripley, #PA9, September, 1991 and published by NICHCY.]

Right to a Free and Appropriate Public Education

Your rights begin with your child's right to a Free and Appropriate Public Education. This is often referred to as FAPE.

Free means that your child's education is at public expense, at no cost to you. **Appropriate** means that the educational program for your child will be tailored to his or her individual needs. Any change in the provision of FAPE to your child should be in writing.

Your Rights.

You, as a parent, have the right to be fully informed by the school of all rights that are guaranteed to you under the law. Each state, county, and school system has written policies and guidelines that are available to you. Ask your child's school to send you copies.

Your rights include:

1. The right to be notified, whenever the school wants to evaluate your child, either to identify a possible disability or to measure changes in your child's needs; the school wants to change your child's educational placement; or the school refuses your request for an evaluation or a change of placement. The school must notify you in writing for all of the above.

2. The right to request an evaluation of your child if you think your child may need special education and/or related services. You should put this request in writing.

3. The right to informed consent.

For example, if the school is suggesting that your child be evaluated for a possible disability, then this means that you sign a form that says you understand and agree with the proposed plan to evaluate your child. There are other occasions when a family's written consent will be required.

4. The right to an independent evaluation from professionals outside the school system.

The results of these evaluations must be considered in any educational decisions made for your child. You also have the right to request that the school system pay for an independent evaluation if you believe the school's evaluation was not appropriate.

5. The right to a re-evaluation to determine if your child's educational needs have changed.

Depending on the results of this re-evaluation, a new Individualized Education Program (IEP) may be developed and a change in placement may be recommended.

6. The right to have your child tested in the language he or she knows best.

For example, if your child's primary language is Spanish, and he or she is not fluent in English, then you have the right to request that your child be tested in Spanish. If your child is deaf, he or she has the right to an interpreter during testing.

7. The right to review all your child's records.

You may also obtain copies of these records, although the school may charge you a reasonable fee for making copies. If you feel that any of the information contained in your child's records is inaccurate or misleading or violates the privacy or other rights of your child, you may request that the information be changed. If the school refuses your request, you have the right to request a hearing to question the school's refusal.

8. The right to participate in the development of your child's IEP.

The school must make every effort to notify you of the IEP meeting and to arrange it at a time and place that is convenient for everyone who will attend.

9. The right to have your child educated in the least restrictive educational environment.

Whenever possible, students should be educated in their neighborhood school with other children their age. The specifics of how this will be accomplished is part of the IEP.

10. The right to have your child's IEP reviewed and revised.

The school must review your child's IEP at least once a year and must re-evaluate your child at least once every three years. But you, as parents, can request an IEP review at any time you feel that your child's needs have changed.

11. The right to mediation; a due process hearing.

If the school and family cannot come to an agreement on the needs, placement, or program of a student, both parties have the right to request a due process hearing to resolve their differences.

Your Responsibilities

The special education team includes education specialists, therapists, medical personnel, the parent(s) or person(s) who have custody of the child, and the child when appropriate. As a full member of this team, the parent has responsibilities. These may not be as clearly defined as your rights, but they are just as important. Your most basic responsibility is to be an active team member, to establish effective communication between home and school, and to share information about your child's education and development with other members of the team.

Your responsibilities include:

1. After finding that your child is eligible for special education and after an IEP has been written, but before placement is determined, try to visit the proposed classes/ schools and any alternatives that are being considered for your child. This will help you become familiar with the programs under consideration. Talking to other parents is very useful, but seeing programs for yourself is also important.

2. Before going to visit a school to look at a program, call ahead and ask the principal to schedule a time for you to visit. This is not only polite, but will assure that your visit comes during a regularly scheduled activity. If you also want to talk to the teacher, let the people arranging the observation time know, so that they can schedule a meeting.

3. Once your child is settled in his or her school class, find time to visit at least once or twice a year to see how your child is doing. Often volunteering to help with school or classroom activities is an effective way to get involved. Teachers appreciate the help, and it gives you the opportunity to see your child in a school situation.

4. Notify your child's school, teacher, therapist(s), or nurse of any changes that would affect your child's participation in school. Examples include: changes in your child's medical condition or medication; extreme difficulty with homework; boredom with school work; social difficulties; or any other related difficulties the school personnel should be aware of.

5. Provide the school staff with any relevant information from outside evaluations. Have copies of these reports sent to your child's school.

6. If problems arise, you should communicate your concerns about your child's special education program to the school. Talk to the principal, teachers, therapist(s) etc. to allow everyone involved in your child's schooling to informally observe the situation and make adjustments before minor problems become major difficulties.

7. Let school staff know when you observe signs that your child's current program

may need to be changed. The more time the school has to arrange for re-evaluations, the better.

8. If your child needs any special arrangements for testing, such as assistive technology, an interpreter, or foreign language tester, let the school know right away. Even if your child's teacher knows about his or her unique needs, the evaluation staff may not be aware of them and will need time to make the proper arrangements.

9. If you would like to review and/or obtain copies of your child's records, make this request, in writing, several weeks before you need to have these records. School secretarial staff may be quite busy, especially at certain times of the year. Also, records from previous years may be kept somewhere other than in the school building, making access more complicated than just opening a file drawer.

10. It is very important that you attend IEP meetings. These meetings generally occur only once a year and are usually held during the day.

If you have a job, talk to your employer or make any necessary child care arrangements so that you will be able to attend during the work day. If you have difficulties getting away during these hours, inform your child's teacher and ask if the school can be of assistance. Sometimes the school can work out child care needs or talk to an employer to help you find the time to attend the IEP meeting.

11. Any time you have scheduling difficulties with school meetings, tell the school people involved in that meeting. They will want to know that you are interested in your child's schooling and that you want to be actively involved. There are always situations in which people cannot coordinate their schedules; the more information the school has about your schedule, the more they can work to arrange meetings and school functions at more convenient times for you. All too often, educators interpret poor attendance as lack of interest.

12. If you are in disagreement with the school on any aspect of your child's program, try to work out the disagreement before resorting to a due process hearing.

Many schools now have formalized methods for mediation or can make such arrangements. Mediation can often bring solutions to light and is less negative than more formal or legal action. In any discussion of rights and responsibilities, it is important to remember the spirit of the law. The goal should always be the same: to provide the best opportunities for success for all children, including those who have differing needs and abilities. To achieve this goal it is important that all people involved in special education planning work together. It's even part of the law. As team members you will each need to communicate your opinions and concerns constructively. It is not always clear what opportunities are needed for a student with special needs and which will be best. Thus, arriving at a solution to disagreements may require some trial and error and some compromising.

END OF APPENDIX B. Your Rights and Responsibilities Under IDEA

[This document was originally developed in 1991 by Interstate Research Associates, Inc., pursuant to Cooperative Agreement #H030A00002 with the Office of Special Education Programs of the United States Department of Education. It was made available via the Internet through Cooperative Agreement #H030A30003 between the Academy for Educational Development and the Office of Special Education Programs of the U.S. Department of Education.]

APPENDIX C

Frequently Asked Questions About Special Education by NICHCY

[Author's note: **Questions Often Asked by Parents about Special Education Services** is also known as the NICHCY Briefing Paper, LG1 (4th Edition), September 1999. It is divided into five parts.

Part I: Your Child's Evaluation
Part II: Your Child's Eligibility
Part III: Writing an IEP
Part IV: Reevaluation
Part V: Other Special Education Issues

Questions Often Asked by Parents about Special Education Services

I think my child may need special help in school. What do I do?

Begin by finding out more about special services and programs for students in your school system. Also find out more about the Individuals with Disabilities Education Act (IDEA). This law gives eligible children with disabilities the right to receive special services and assistance in school. These services are known as special education and related services. They can be important in helping your child at school.

To learn more about special education, keep reading. This Briefing Paper will also help you learn how you and the school can work together to help your child.

What is special education?

Special education is instruction that is specially designed to meet the unique needs of children who have disabilities. This is done at no cost to the parents. Special education can include special instruction in the classroom, at home, in hospitals or institutions, or in other settings.

Over 5 million children ages 6 through 21 receive special education and related services each year in the United States. Each of these children receives instruction that is specially designed:

a. to meet the child's unique needs (that result from having a disability); and

b. to help the child learn the information and skills that other children are learning.

This definition of special education comes from the Individuals with Disabilities Education Act (IDEA), Public Law 105-17.

Who is eligible for special education?

Certain children with disabilities are eligible for special education and related services. The IDEA provides a definition of a "child with a disability." This law lists 13 different disability categories under which a child may be found eligible for special education and related services. These categories are listed in the box below.

According to the IDEA, the disability must affect the child's educational performance. The question of eligibility, then, comes down to a question of whether the child has a disability that fits in one of IDEA's 13 categories and whether that disability affects how the child does in school. That is, the disability must cause the child to need special education and related services.

Part I: Your Child's Evaluation

How do I find out if my child is eligible for special education?

The first step is to find out if your child has a disability. To do this, ask the school to evaluate your child. Call or write the Director of Special Education or the principal of your child's school. Say that you think your child has a disability and needs special education help. Ask the school to evaluate your child as soon as possible.

The public school may also think your child needs special help, because he or she may have a disability. If so, then the school must evaluate your child at no cost to you.

However, the school does not have to evaluate your child just because you have asked. The school may not think your child has a disability or needs special education. In this case, the school may refuse to evaluate your child. It must let you know this decision in writing, as well as why it has refused.

If the school refuses to evaluate your child, there are two things you can do immediately:

a. Ask the school system for information about its special education policies, as well as parent rights to disagree with decisions made by the school system. These materials should describe the steps parents can take to challenge a school system's decision.

b. Get in touch with your state's Parent Training and Information (PTI) center. The PTI is an excellent resource for parents to learn more about special education, their rights and responsibilities, and the law. The PTI can tell you what steps to take next to find help for your child. Call NICHCY to find out how to get in touch with your PTI, or see our State Resource Sheet for your state. The PTI is listed there.

Services to Very Young Children

Infants and toddlers can have disabilities, too. Services to these very young children are also part of the IDEA. These services are called early intervention services (for children birth through two years) and preschool services (for children ages 3-5). These services can be very important in helping the young child develop and learn.

For more information about early intervention and preschool programs, contact NICHCY. Ask for *A Parent's Guide: Accessing Programs for Infants, Toddlers, and Preschoolers with Disabilities.*

What happens during an evaluation?

Evaluating your child means more than the school just giving your child a test or two. The school must evaluate your child in all the areas where your child may be affected by the possible disability. This may include looking at your child's health, vision, hearing, social and emotional well-being, general intelligence, performance in school, and how well your child communicates with others and uses his or her body. The evaluation must be complete enough (full and individual) to identify all of your child's needs for special education and related services.

Evaluating your child appropriately will give you and the school a lot of information about your child. This information will help you and the school:

    a. decide if your child has a disability; and

    b. design instruction for your child.

The evaluation process involves several steps. These are listed below.

Reviewing existing information.

A group of people, including you, begins by looking at the information the school already has about your child. You may have information about your child you wish to share as well. The group will look at information such as:

    a. your child's scores on tests given in the classroom or to all students in your child's grade;

    b. the opinions and observations of your child's teachers and other school staff who know your child; and

c. your feelings, concerns, and ideas about how your child is doing in school.

Deciding if more information is still needed.

The information collected above will help the group decide:

    a. if your son or daughter has a particular type of disability;

    b. how your child is currently doing in school;

    c. whether your child needs special education and related services; and

    d. what your child's educational needs are.

Group members will look at the information they collected above and see if they have enough information to make these decisions. If the group needs more information to make these decisions, the school must collect it.

Collecting more information about your child.

If more information about your child is needed, the school will give your child tests or collect the information in other ways. Your informed written permission is required before the school may collect this information. The evaluation group will then have the information it needs to make the types of decisions listed above.

So the school needs my permission to collect this extra information?

Yes. Before the school can conduct additional assessments of your child to see if he or she has a disability, the school must ask for your informed written permission. It must also describe how it will conduct this evaluation. This includes describing the tests that will be used and the other ways the school will collect information about your child. After you give your informed written permission, the school may evaluate your child.

How does the school collect this information?

The school collects information about your child from many different people and in many different ways. Tests are an important part of an evaluation, but they are only a part. The evaluation should also include:

a. the observations and opinions of professionals who have worked with your child;

b. your child's medical history, when it relates to his or her performance in school; and

c. your ideas about your child's school experiences, abilities, needs, and behavior outside of school, and his or her feelings about school.

The following people will be part of the group evaluating your child:

a. you, as parents;

b. at least one regular education teacher, if your child is or may be participating in the regular education environment;

c. at least one of your child's special education teachers or service providers;

d. a school administrator who knows about policies for special education, about children with disabilities, about the general curriculum (the curriculum used by nondisabled students), and about available resources;

e. someone who can interpret the evaluation results and talk about what instruction may be necessary for your child;

f. individuals (invited by you or the school) who have knowledge or special expertise about your child;

g. your child, if appropriate;

h. representatives from any other agencies that may be responsible for paying for or providing transition services (if your child is 16 years or, if appropriate, younger and will be planning for life after high school); and

i. other qualified professionals.

These other qualified professionals may be responsible for collecting specific kinds of information about your child. They may include:

a. a school psychologist;

b. an occupational therapist;

c. a speech and language pathologist (sometimes called a speech therapist);

d. a physical therapist and/or adaptive physical education therapist or teacher;

e. a medical specialist; and

f. others.

Professionals will observe your child. They may give your child written tests or talk personally with your child. They are trying to get a picture of the "whole child." For example, they want to understand:

a. how well your child speaks and understands language;

b. how your child thinks and behaves;

c. how well your child adapts to changes in his or her environment;

d. how well your child has done academically;

e. what your child's potential or aptitude (intelligence) is;

f. how well your child functions in a number of areas, such as moving, thinking, learning, seeing, hearing; and

g. what job-related and other post-school interests and abilities your child has.

The IDEA gives clear directions about how schools must conduct evaluations. For example, tests and interviews must be given in your child's native language (for example, Spanish) or in the way he or she typically communicates (for example, sign language). The tests must also be given in a way that does not discriminate against your child, because he or she has a disability or is from a different racial or cultural background.

The IDEA states that schools may not place children into special education programs based on the results of only one procedure such as a test. More than one procedure is needed to see where your child may be having difficulty and to identify his or her strengths.

In some cases, schools will be able to conduct a child's entire evaluation within the school. In other cases, schools may not have the staff to do all of the evaluation needed. These schools will have to hire outside people or agencies to do some or all of the evaluation. If your child is evaluated outside of the school, the school must make the arrangements. The school will say in writing exactly what type of testing is to be done. All of these evaluation procedures are done at no cost to parents.

In some cases, once the evaluation has begun, the outside specialist may want to do more testing. If the specialist asks you if it is okay to do more testing, make sure you tell the specialist to contact the school. If the testing is going beyond what the school originally asked for, the school needs to agree to pay for the extra testing.

Part II: Your Child's Eligibility

What does the school do with these evaluation results?

The information gathered from the evaluation will be used to make important decisions about your child's education. All of the information about your child will be used:

a. to decide if your child is eligible for special education and related services; and

b. to help you and the school decide what your child needs educationally.

How is a decision made about my child's eligibility for special education?

As was said earlier, the decision about your child's eligibility for services is based on whether your son or daughter has a disability that fits into one of the IDEA's 13 disability categories (see the list between the dashed lines below) and whether that disability affects how your child does in school. This decision will be made when the evaluation has been completed, and the results are in.

In the past, parents were not involved under IDEA in making the decision about their child's eligibility for special education and related services. Now, under the newest changes to IDEA (passed in 1997), parents are included in the group that decides a child's eligibility for special education services. This group will look at all of the information gathered during the evaluation and decide if your child meets the definition of a "child with a disability." (This definition will come from the IDEA and from the policies your state or district uses.) If so, your child will be eligible for special education and related services.

Under the IDEA, a child may not be found eligible for services if the determining reason for thinking the child is eligible is that:

a. the child has limited English proficiency, or

b. the child has a lack of instruction in math or reading.

If your child is found eligible, you and the school will work together to design an educational program for your child. This process is described in detail in Part III of this Briefing Paper.

As parents, you have the right to receive a copy of the evaluation report on your child and the paperwork about your child's eligibility for special education and related services.

IDEA's Categories of Disability

a. Autism

b. Deafness

c. Deaf-blindness

d. Hearing impairment

e. Mental retardation

f. Multiple disabilities

g. Orthopedic impairment

h. Other health impairment

i. Serious emotional disturbance

j. Specific learning disability

k. Speech or language impairment

l. Traumatic brain injury

m. Visual impairment, including blindness

To find out more about these disabilities and how IDEA defines them, contact NICHCY and ask for "General Information about Disabilities."

What happens if my child is not eligible for services?

If the group decides that your child is not eligible for special education services, the school system must tell you this in writing and explain why your child has been found "not eligible." Under the IDEA, you must also be given information about what you can do if you disagree with this decision.

Read the information the school system gives you. Make sure it includes information about how to challenge the school system's decision. If that information is not in the materials the school gives you, ask the school for it.

Also get in touch with your state's Parent Training and Information (PTI) center. The PTI can tell you what steps to take next. Your PTI is listed on NICHCY's State Resource Sheet for your state.

Part III. Writing an IEP

So my child has been found eligible for special education. What next?

The next step is to write what is known as an Individualized Education Program—usually called an IEP. After a child is found eligible, a meeting must be held within 30 days to develop to the IEP.

What is an Individualized Education Program?

An Individualized Education Program (IEP) is a written statement of the educational program designed to meet a child's individual needs. Every child who receives special education services must have an IEP.

The IEP has two general purposes:

(1) to set reasonable learning goals for your child; and

(2) to state the services that the school district will provide for your child.

What type of information is included in an IEP?

According to the IDEA, your child's IEP must include specific statements about your child. These are listed below. Take a moment to read over this list. This will be the information included in your child's IEP.

Your child's IEP will contain the following statements:

a. Present levels of educational performance.

This statement describes how your child is currently doing in school. This includes how your child's disability affects his or her involvement and progress in the general curriculum.

b. Annual goals.

The IEP must state annual goals for your child, meaning what you and the school team think he or she can reasonably accomplish in a year. This statement of annual goals includes individual steps that make up the goals (often called short-term objectives) or major milestones (often called benchmarks). The goals must relate to meeting the needs that result from your child's disability. They must also help your son or daughter be involved in and progress in the general curriculum.

c. Special education and related services to be provided.

The IEP must list the special education and related services to be provided to your child. This includes supplementary aids and services (such as a communication device). It also includes changes to the program or supports for school personnel that will be provided for your child.

d. Participation with nondisabled children.

How much of the school day will your child be educated separately from nondisabled children or not participate in extracurricular or other nonacademic activities such as lunch or clubs? The IEP must include an explanation that answers this question.

e. Participation in state and district-wide assessments.

Your state and district probably give tests of student achievement to children in certain grades or age groups. In order to participate in these tests, your child may need individual modifications or changes in how the tests are administered. The IEP team must decide what modifications your child needs and list them in the IEP. If your child will not be taking these tests, the IEP must include a statement as to why the tests are not appropriate for your child and how your child will be tested instead.

f. Dates and location.

The IEP must state

(a) when services and modifications will begin;

(b) how often they will be provided;

(c) where they will be provided; and

(d) how long they will last.

g. Transition service needs.

If your child is age 14 (or younger, if the IEP team determines it appropriate), the IEP must include a statement of his or her transition service needs. Transition planning will help your child move through school from grade to grade.

h. Transition services.

If your child is age 16 (or younger, if determined appropriate by the IEP team), the IEP must include a statement of needed transition services and, if appropriate, a statement of the interagency responsibilities or any needed linkages.

i. Measuring progress.

The IEP must state how school personnel will measure your child's progress toward the annual goals. It must also state how you, as parents, will be informed regularly of your child's progress and whether that progress is enough to enable your child to achieve his or her goals by the end of the year.

It is very important that children with disabilities participate in the general curriculum as much as possible. That is, they should learn the same curriculum as nondisabled children, for example, reading, math, science, social studies, and physical education, just as nondisabled children do. In some cases, this curriculum may need to be adapted for your child to learn, but it should not be omitted altogether. Participation in extracurricular activities and other nonacademic activities is also important. Your child's IEP needs to be written with this in mind.

For example, what special education services will help your child participate in the general curriculum—in other words, to study what other students are studying? What special education services or supports will help your child take part in extracurricular activities such as school clubs or sports? When your child's IEP is developed, an important part of the discussion will be how to help your child take part in regular classes and activities in the school.

Who develops my child's IEP?

Many people come together to develop your child's IEP. This group is called the IEP team and includes most of the same types of individuals who were involved in your child's evaluation. Team members will include:

a. you, the parents;

b. at least one regular education teacher, if your child is (or may be) participating in the regular education environment;

c. at least one of your child's special education teachers or special education providers;

d. a representative of the public agency (school system) who (a) is qualified to provide or supervise the provision of special education, (b) knows about the general curriculum; and (c) knows about the resources the school system has available;

e. an individual who can interpret the evaluation results and talk about what instruction may be necessary for your child;

f. your child, when appropriate;

g. representatives from any other agencies that may be responsible for paying for or providing transition services (if your child is 16 years or, if appropriate, younger); and

h. other individuals (invited by you or the school) who have knowledge or special expertise about your child. For example, you may wish to invite a relative who is close to the child or a child care provider.

Together, these people will work as a team to develop your child's IEP.

So I can help develop my child's IEP?

Yes, absolutely. The law is very clear that parents have the right to participate in developing their child's IEP. In fact, your input is invaluable. You know your child so very well, and the school needs to know your insights and concerns.

The school staff will try to schedule the IEP meeting at a time that is convenient for all team members to attend. If the school suggests a time that is impossible for you, explain your schedule and needs. It's important that you attend this meeting and share your ideas about your child's needs and strengths. Often, another time or date can be arranged. However, if you cannot agree on a time or date, the school may hold the IEP meeting without you. In this event, the school must keep you informed, for example, by phone or mail.

What should I do before the IEP meeting?

The purpose of the IEP meeting is to develop your child's Individualized Education Program. You can prepare for this meeting by:

   a. making a list of your child's strengths and weaknesses,

   b. talking to teachers and/or therapists and getting their thoughts about your child,

   c. visiting your child's class and perhaps other classes that may be helpful to him or her, and

   d. talking to your child about his or her feelings toward school.

It is a good idea to write down what you think your child can accomplish during the school year. It also helps to make notes about what you would like to say during the meeting.

What happens during an IEP meeting?

During the IEP meeting, the different members of the IEP team share their thoughts and suggestions. If this is the first IEP meeting after your child's evaluation, the team may go over the evaluation results, so your child's strengths and needs will be clear. These results will help the team decide what special help your child needs in school.

Remember that you are a very important part of the IEP team. You know your child better than anyone. Don't be shy about speaking up, even though there may be a lot of other people at the meeting. Share what you know about your child and what you wish others to know.

After the various team members (including you, the parent) have shared their thoughts and concerns about your child, the group will have a better idea of your child's strengths and needs. This will allow the team to discuss and decide on:

   a. the educational and other goals that are appropriate for your child; and

   b. the type of special education services your child needs.

The IEP team will also talk about the related services your child may need to benefit from his or her special education. The IDEA lists many related services that schools must provide if eligible children need them. The related services listed in IDEA are presented between the dashed lines below. Examples of related services include:

a. occupational therapy, which can help a child develop or regain movement that he or she may have lost due to injury or illness; and

b. speech therapy (called speech-language pathology), which can help children who have trouble speaking.

Related Services, as listed in IDEA

a. Transportation

b. Speech-language pathology

c. Audiology services

d. Psychological services

e. Physical therapy

f. Occupational therapy

g. Recreation (including therapeutic recreation)

h. Early identification and assessment of disabilities in children

i. Counseling services (including rehabilitation counseling)

j. Orientation & mobility services

k. Medical services for diagnostic or evaluation purposes

l. School health services

m. Social work services in schools

n. Parent counseling & training

This list does not include every related service a child might need or that a school system may offer. To learn more about these related services and how IDEA defines them, contact NICHCY and ask for our News Digest on Related Services.

Depending on the needs of your child, the IEP team may also discuss the special factors listed below:

a. If your child's behavior's interferes with his or her learning or the learning of others: The IEP team will talk about strategies and supports to address your child's behavior.

b. If your child has limited proficiency in English: The IEP team will talk about your child's language needs as these needs relate to his or her IEP.

c. If your child is blind or visually impaired: The IEP team must provide for instruction in Braille or the use of Braille, unless it determines after an appropriate evaluation that your child does not need this instruction.

d. If your child has communication needs: The IEP team must consider those needs.

e. If your child is deaf or hard of hearing: The IEP team will consider your child's language and communication needs. This includes your child's opportunities to communicate directly with classmates and school staff in his or her usual method of communication (for example, sign language).

The IEP team will also talk about whether your child needs any assistive technology devices or services. Assistive technology devices can help many children do certain activities or tasks. Examples of these devices are:

a. devices that make the words bigger on the computer screen or that "read" the typed words aloud—which can help children who do not see well;

b. electronic talking boards—which can help students who have trouble speaking; and

c. computers and special programs for the computer—which can help students with all kinds of disabilities learn more easily.

Assistive technology services include evaluating your child to see if he or she could benefit from using an assistive device. These services also include providing the devices and training your child (or your family or the professionals who work with your child) to use the device.

As you can see, there are a lot of important matters to talk about in an IEP meeting. You may feel very emotional during the meeting, as everyone talks about your child's needs. Try to keep in mind that the other team members are all there to help your child. If you hear something about your child which surprises you, or which is different from the way you see your child, bring this to the attention of the other members of the team. In order to design a good program for your child, it is important to work closely with the other team members and share your feelings about your child's educational needs. Feel free to ask questions and offer opinions and suggestions.

Based on the above discussions, the IEP team will then write your child's IEP. This includes the services and supports the school will provide for your child. It will also include the location where particular services will be provided.

Your child's placement (where the IEP will be carried out) will be determined every year, must be based on your child's IEP, and must be as close as possible to your child's home. The placement decision is made by a group of persons, including you the parent, and others knowledgeable about your child, the meaning of the evaluation data, and the placement options. In some states, the IEP team makes the placement decision. In other states, the placement decision is made by another group of people. In all cases, you as parents have the right to be members of the group that makes decisions on the educational placement of your child.

Depending on the needs of your child and the services to be provided, your child's IEP could be carried out:

a. in regular classes,

b. in special classes (where all the students are receiving special education services),

c. in special schools,

d. at home,

e. in hospitals and institutions, and

f. in other settings.

Which of these placements is best suited for your child?

Can he or she be educated in the regular classroom, with supplementary aids and services? (The IDEA prefers this placement.) If not, then the placement group will look at other placements for your child. Before the school system can provide your child with special education for the first time, you, as parents, must give your written consent.

Can my child's IEP be changed?

Yes. At least once a year a meeting must be scheduled with you to review your child's progress and develop your child's next IEP. The meeting will be similar to the IEP meeting described above. The team will talk about:

a. your child's progress toward the goals in the current IEP,

b. what new goals should be added, and

c. whether any changes need to be made to the special education and related services your child receives.

This annual IEP meeting allows you and the school to review your child's educational program and change it as necessary. But you don't have to wait for this annual review. You (or any other team member) may ask to have your child's IEP reviewed or revised at any time.

For example, you may feel that your child is not making good progress toward his or her annual goals. Or you may want to write new goals, because your son or daughter has made such great progress! Call the principal of the school, or the special education director or your child's teacher, and express your concerns. If necessary, they will call the IEP team together to talk about changing your child's IEP.

Part IV. Reevaluation

Will my child be re-evaluated?

Yes. Under the IDEA, your child must be re-evaluated at least every three years. The purpose of this re-evaluation is to find out:

a. if your child continues to be a "child with a disability," as defined within the law, and

b. your child's educational needs.

The re-evaluation is similar to the initial evaluation. It begins by looking at the information already available about your child. More information is collected only if it's needed. If the group decides that additional assessments are needed, you must give your informed written permission before the school system may collect that information. The school system may only go ahead without your informed written permission if they have tried to get your permission and you did not respond.

Although the law requires that children with disabilities be re-evaluated at least every three years, your child may be re-evaluated more often if you or your child's teacher(s) request it.

Part V. Other Special Education Issues

Is the school responsible for ensuring that my child reaches the goals in his or her IEP?

No. The IEP sets out the individualized instruction to be provided to your child, but it is not a contract. The school is responsible for providing the instructional services listed in an IEP. School officials must make a good-faith effort to help your child meet his or her goals. However, the school is not responsible if your child does not reach the goals listed in the IEP. If you feel that your child is not making progress toward his or her goals, then you may wish to contact the school and express your concerns. The IEP team may need to meet and revise your child's IEP.

What if I disagree with the school about what is right for my child?

You have the right to disagree with the school's decisions concerning your child. This includes decisions about:

    a. your child's identification as a "child with a disability,"

    b. his or her evaluation,

    c. his or her educational placement, and

    d. the special education and related services that the school provides to your child.

In all cases where the family and school disagree, it is important for both sides to first discuss their concerns and try to compromise. The compromise can be temporary. For example, you might agree to try out a particular plan of instruction or classroom placement for a certain period of time. At the end of that period, the school can check your child's progress. You and other members of your child's IEP team can then meet again, talk about how your child is doing, and decide what to do next. The trial period may help you and the school come to a comfortable agreement on how to help your child.

If you still cannot agree with the school, it's useful to know more about the IDEA's protections for parents and children. The law and regulations include ways for parents and schools to resolve disagreements. These include:

    a. mediation, where you and school personnel sit down with an impartial third person (called a mediator), talk openly about the areas where you disagree, and try to reach agreement;

    b. due process, where you and the school present evidence before an impartial third person (called a hearing officer), and he or she decides how to resolve the problem; and

    c. filing a complaint with the State Education Agency (SEA), where you write directly to the SEA and describe what requirement of IDEA the school has violated. The SEA must either resolve your complaint itself, or it can have a system where complaints are filed with the school district and parents can have the district's decision reviewed by the SEA. In most cases, the SEA must resolve your complaint within 60 calendar days.

Your state will have specific ways for parents and schools to resolve their differences. You will need to find out what your state's policies are. Your local department of special education will probably have these guidelines. If not, contact the state department of education and ask for a copy of their special education policies. The telephone number and address of the state department of education are listed on NICHCY's State Resource Sheet for your state.

You may also wish to call the Parent Training and Information (PTI) center in your state. We've mentioned the PTI several times in this Briefing Paper. They are an excellent resource for parents to learn more about special education. Your PTI is listed on NICHCY's State Resource Sheet for your state. (NOTE: Your PTI is listed in Appendix E of this book)

Talking with other parents helps!

You can learn a lot from talking to parents of children who are already receiving special education services. There are many different local parent groups. Find one, and go to a meeting. If there aren't any groups in your area, contact the nearest group and ask for its newsletter. These can be full of information, too!

How do you find parent groups? NICHCY has a State Resource Sheet for your state. This sheet is a good source of information about parent groups or disability groups in your state. These state groups can tell you about groups in your area. If you do not already have a State Resource Sheet, call NICHCY and ask for one. It's free and can be very useful.

How can I get more services for my child?

Suppose your child gets speech therapy two times a week, and you think he or she needs therapy three times a week. What do you do?

First, you can talk with your child's teacher or speech-language pathologist (sometimes called a speech therapist). Ask to see the evaluation of his or her progress. If you are not satisfied with your child's progress, then request an IEP meeting to review your child's progress and increase speech therapy. Discuss your child's needs with the IEP team and talk about changing the IEP. The other team members will either agree with you and change the IEP, or they will disagree with you.

If the rest of the IEP team does not agree that your child needs more services, try to work out a compromise. If you cannot, then parents can take the problem beyond the IEP team. As was mentioned above, mediation, due process, and filing a complaint are ways to resolve disagreements. But always remember that you and the school will be making decisions together about your child's education for as long as your child goes to that school and continues to be eligible for special education services. A good working relationship with school staff is important now and in the future. Therefore, when disagreements arise, try to work them out within the IEP team before requesting mediation or due process or before filing a complaint.

How can I support my child's learning?

Here are some suggestions that can help you support your child's learning and maintain a good working relationship with school professionals:

a. Let your child's teacher(s) know that you want to be involved in your child's educational program. Make time to talk with the teacher(s) and, if possible, visit the classroom.

b. Explain any special equipment, medication, or medical problem your child has.

c. Let the teacher(s) know about any activities or big events that may influence your child's performance in school.

d. Ask that samples of your child's work be sent home. If you have questions, make an appointment with the teacher(s) to talk about new ways to meet your child's goals.

e. Ask the teacher(s) how you can build upon your child's school activities at home.

f. Give your child chores at home. Encourage behavior that leads to success in school, such as accepting responsibility, behaving, being organized, and being on time.

g. Volunteer to help in the classroom or school. This will let you see how things work in the school and how your child interacts with others. It will also help the school.

h. Remember that you and the school want success for your child. Working together can make this happen.

What if I still have questions and need more information?

You can contact your state's Parent Training and Information (PTI) center. Your PTI will have a lot of information to share about the special education process in your state.

You can also contact NICHCY. We have information on all aspects of the IEP process. We also have information on other issues that are important to families who have a child with a disability. NICHCY staff can send you more publications (see NICHCY's catalog or visit our Website at: www.nichcy.org), answer questions, and put you in touch with other organizations who can work with you and your family.

It would be our pleasure!

This NICHCY Briefing Paper was reviewed by the U.S. Office of Special Education Programs for consistency with the Individuals with Disabilities Education Act Amendments of 1997, Public Law 105-17, and the final implementing regulations.

APPENDIX D

State Departments of Education

You need to get a copy of your state special education regulations. Appendix D includes contact information for all state departments of education. Addresses, phone numbers, and email addresses change often. For up-to-date numbers, please visit your state page at www.fetaweb.com/

Alabama Department of Special Education
  Services
P.O. Box 302101
Montgomery, AL 36130-2101
334-242-8114
Website: www.alsde.edu

Alaska Office of Special Education/AK
  Department of Education
801 West 10th St, Suite 200
Juneau, AK 99801-1894
907-465-2972
Website: www.eed.state.ak.us/tls/sped

Arizona Exceptional Student Services,
  Department of Education
1535 West Jefferson
Phoenix, AZ 85007
602-542-4013
Website: www.ade.state.az.us

Arkansas Special Education Unit,
  Department of Education
State Education Building C, Room 105
#4 Capitol Mall
Little Rock, AR 72201-1071
501-682-4225

California Special Education, Department of
  Education
515 L Street, Suite 270
Sacramento, CA 95814
916- 445-4729
Website: www.cde.ca.gov/spbranch/sed/
index.htm

Colorado Special Education Services Unit/
  CO Dept. of Educ.
201 East Colfax Avenue
Denver, CO 80203
303-866-6694

Connecticut Bureau of Special Education &
  Pupil Services
25 Industrial Park Road
Middletown, CT 06457-1520
860-807-2025

Delaware Exceptional Children and Early
  Childhood Group
P.O. Box 1402
Dover, DE 19903
302-739-5471
Website: www.doe.state.de.us/
Exceptional_Child/ececehome.htm

District of Columbia Division of Special
  Education
825 Capitol Street, NE, 6th Floor
Washington, DC 20002
202-442-4800
Website: www.k12.dc.us/dcps/home.html

Florida Bureau of Instructional Support &
  Community Services
Division of Public Schools & Community
  Education
325 West Gaines Street, Suite 614
Tallahassee, FL 32399-0400
850-488-1570

Georgia Division for Exceptional Students
1870 Twin Towers East
Atlanta, GA 30334
404-656-3963
Website: www.doe.k12.ga.us/sla/exceptional/
exceptional.html

Hawaii Special Education Section
637 18th Avenue, Room 102
Honolulu, HI 96816
808-733-4990
Website: www2.k12.hi.us/PUBLIC/SPED.nsf

Idaho Bureau of Special Education
P.O. Box 83720
Boise, ID 83720-0027
208-332-6910

Illinois Special Education Coordination
100 North First Street
Springfield, IL 62777-0001
217-782-4826
Website: www.isbe.state.il.us

Indiana Division of Special Education
State House, Room 229
Indianapolis, IN 46204-2798
317-232-0570
Website: http://web.indstate.edu/soe/iseas/
dse.html

Iowa Children, Family and Community
  Services
Grimes State Office Building
Des Moines, IA 50319-0146
515-281-5735
Website: www.state.ia.us/educate/index.html

Kansas Student Support Services
120 East 10th Avenue
Topeka, KS 66612
785-291-3097
Website: www.ksbe.state.ks.us/sss/
specialeducation.html

Kentucky Division of Exceptional Children's
  Services
Capitol Plaza Tower, 8th Floor
500 Mero Street
Frankfort, KY 40601
502-564-4970
Website: www.kde.state.ky.us

Louisiana Division of Special Populations
P.O. Box 94064
Baton Rouge, LA 70804-9064
225-342-3633
Website: www.doe.state.la.us
Office of Special Services
State House, Station #23
Augusta, ME 04333-0023
207-287-5950; 207-287-2550
Website: www.state.me.us/education/
specserv.htm

Maryland Division of Special Education
200 West Baltimore Street
Baltimore, MD 21201-2595
410-767-0238
Website: www.msde.state.md.us

Massachusetts Educational Improvement
   Group
350 Main Street
Malden, MA 02148-5023
781-338-3000; 781-338-3388
Website: www.doe.mass.edu

Michigan Office of Special Education and
   Early Intervention Services
P.O. Box 30008
Lansing, MI 48909-7508
517-373-9433
Website: www.mde.state.mi.us/off/sped

Minnesota Department of Children, Families
   and Learning
Division of Special Education
1500 Highway 36 West
Roseville, MN 55113-4266
651-582-8289; 651-582-8201 (TTY)
Website: children.state.mn.us/speced/
speced.htm

Mississippi Office of Special Education
P.O. Box 771 - Central High School Building
Jackson, MS 39205-0771

601-359-3498
Website: www.mde.k12.ms.us/acad/sped

Missouri Division of Special Education
   Department of Elementary and Secondary
   Education
P.O. Box 480
Jefferson City, MO 65102
573-751-2965
Website: www.dese.state.mo.us/divspeced

Montana Special Education Division
PO Box 202501
Helena, MT 59620 -2501
406-444-4429

Nebraska Special Populations, Department
   of Education
P.O. Box 94987
Lincoln, NE 68509-4987
402-471-2471 (V/TTY);
Website: www.nde.state.ne.us/SPED/
sped.html

Nevada Educational Equity, Department of
   Education
700 E. Fifth Street, Suite 113
Carson City, NV 89701-5096
775-687-9171

New Hampshire Department of Education
101 Pleasant Street
Concord, NH 03301-3860
603-271-1536
Website: www.state.nh.us/educate/index.html

New Jersey Office of Special Education
   Programs
100 Riverview Plaza, P. O. Box 500
Trenton, NJ 08625-0500
609-633-6833
Website: www.state.nj.us/education

New Mexico Special Education
Education Building
300 Don Gaspar Avenue
Santa Fe, NM 87501-2786
505-827-6541
Website: www.sde.state.nm.us

New York Office of Vocational &
    Educational Services
for Individuals with Disabilities
1 Commerce Plaza, Room 1606
Albany, NY 12234
518-474-2714
Website: www.nysed.gov

North Carolina Exceptional Children
    Division
Department of Public Instruction
301 N. Wilmington St, Education Bldg.
Raleigh, NC 27601-2825
919-715-1565

North Dakota Special Education
600 East Boulevard Avenue, Dept. 201
Bismarck, ND 58505-0440
701-328-2277; 701-328-4920 (TTY)
Website: www.dpi.state.nd.us/dpi/speced/
index.htm

Ohio Office for Exceptional Children
933 High Street
Worthington, OH 43085-4017
614-466-2650
Website: www.ode.state.oh.us/SE

Oklahoma Special Education Services
2500 N. Lincoln Boulevard
Oklahoma City, OK 73105-4599
405-521-3351

Oregon Office of Special Education
255 Capitol Street NE
Salem, OR 97310-0203
503-378-3600, ext 2329; 503-378-2892 (TTY)
Website: www.ode.state.or.us/sped/index.htm

Pennsylvania Bureau of Special Education
333 Market Street, 7th Floor
Harrisburg, PA 17126-0333
717-783-6913
Special Education Consultline:
800 879-2301 (V/TTY)
Website: www.pde.psu.edu

Rhode Island Office of Special Needs
Shepard Building
255 Westminster Street, Room 400
Providence, RI 02903-3400
401-222-4600, ext. 2301

South Carolina State Department of
    Education
Office of Exceptional Children
1429 Senate Street, Room 808
Columbia, SC 29201
803-734-8806

South Dakota Office of Special Education
700 Governors Drive
Pierre, SD 57501-2291
605-773-3678; 605-773-6302 (TTY)
Website: www.state.sd.us/deca/special/
special.htm

Tennessee Division of Special Education
Andrew Johnson Tower, 5th Floor
710 James Robertson Pkwy.
Nashville, TN 37243-0380
615-741-2851
Website: www.state.tn.us/education/
msped.htm

Texas Education Agency, Division of Special
    Education
1701 North Congress Avenue
Austin, TX 78701-1494
512-463-9414; 800-252-9668
Website: www.tea.state.tx.us/special.ed

Utah At Risk and Special Education Services
250 East 500 South
Salt Lake City, UT 84111-3204
801-538-7711
Website: www.usoe.k12.ut.us/sars

Vermont Student Support Services
120 State Street, State Office Building
Montpelier, VT 05620-2501
802-828-2755
Website: www.state.vt.us/educ/sped.htm

Virginia Division of Instructional Support
   Services
P. O. Box 2120
Richmond, VA 23218-2120
804-225-3252; 800-292-3820
Website: www.pen.k12.va.us

Washington Special Education Section
P.O. Box 47200
Olympia, WA 98504-7200
360-753-6733; 360-586-0126 (TTY)
Website: www.k12.wa.us

West Virginia Office of Special Education
1900 Kanawha Boulevard East
Bldg. 6, Room B-304
Charleston, WV 25305-0330
304-558-2696

Wisconsin Director of Special Education
   Division for Learning Support: Equity and
   Advocacy
125 South Webster Street, P.O. Box 7841
Madison, WI 53707-7841
608-266-1649; 800-441-4563
Website: www.dpi.state.wi.us/dpi/dlsea/een

Wyoming Department of Education, Special
   Programs Unit
Hathaway Building, 2nd Floor
2300 Capitol Avenue
Cheyenne, WY 82002
307-777-7417
Website: www.k12.wy.us

American Samoa
Special Education Division
Pago Pago, AS 96799
011 (684-633-1323

Guam
GU Department of Education
P.O. Box DE
Hagatna, GU 96932
011-671-475-0552 (V)

Northern Mariana Island
Special Education, Public School System
P.O. Box 501370 CK
Saipan, MP 96950
011-670-664-3730/3731

Puerto Rico
Department of Education
P.O. Box 190759
San Juan, PR 00919-0759
787-759-7228

U. S. Virgin Islands
   Special Education/Department of
   Education
44-46 Kongens Gade
Charlotte Amalie
St. Thomas, VI 00802
340-774-4399

Your Notes Here

APPENDIX E

Parent Training Information Centers

Contact your Parent Training Information Centers to share information and support, and learn how you can get services for your child. Addresses, phone numbers, and email addresses change frequently. For up-to-date information, please visit your state page at our companion site: www.fetaweb.com/

Alabama
Special Education Action Committee Inc.
P.O. Box 161274
Mobile, AL 36616-2274
334-478-1208
Email: seacmobile@zebra.net

Alaska
P.A.R.E.N.T.S. Resource Center
4743 E. Northern Lights Blvd
Anchorage, AK 99508
907-337-7678
Email: parents@alaska.net
Website: www.alaska.net/~parents/
@alaska.net

Arizona
RAISING Special Kids
4750 N. Black Canyon Hwy, Suite 101
Phoenix, AZ 850173621
602-242-4366

Pilot Parents of Southern Arizona
2600 North Wyatt Drive
Tucson, AZ 85712
520-324-3150
Email: PPSA@pilotparents.org
Website: www.pilotparents.org

Reaching Harmony: Native American Family
    Support, Inc
P.O. Box 1420
Window Rock, AZ 86515
520-871-6338
Email: paulas@dns.nncs.ihs.gov

Arkansas
Arkansas Disability Coalition
1123 University Ave., Suite 225
Little Rock, AR 72204-1605
501-614-7020
Email: adc@alltel.net
Website: www.adcpti.org

FOCUS, Inc.
305 West Jefferson Ave.
Jonesboro, AR 72401
870-935-2750; 888-247-3755
Email: focusinc@ipa.net
Website: www.grnco.net/~norre/

California
DREDF
2212 Sixth Street
Berkeley, CA 94710
510-644-2555; 800-466-4232
Email: dredf@dredf.org

Exceptional Parents Unlimited
4120 N. First St.
Fresno, CA 93726
209-229-2000
Email: epu1@cybergate.com

Parents Helping Parents of San Francisco
594 Monterey Blvd.
San Francisco, CA 94127-2416
415-841-8820
Email: sfphp@earthlink.com

Matrix
94 Galli Drive, Suite C
Novato, CA 94949
415-884-3535
Email: matrix@matrixparents.org
Website: www.matrixparents.org

Parents Helping Parents of Santa Clara
3041 Olcott St.
Santa Clara, CA 95054-3222
408-727-5775
Email: info@php.com
Website: www.php.com

Support for Families of Children with
    Disabilities
2601 Mission #710
San Francisco, CA 94110-3111
Email: sfcdmiss@aol.com

TASK
100 West Cerritos Ave.
Anaheim, CA 92805-6546
714-533-8275
Email: taskca@aol.com

TASK, San Diego
3750 Convoy St., Suite 303
San Diego, CA 92111-3741
619-874-2386
Email: tasksd1@aol.com

Exceptional Family Support, Education and
    Advocacy Center
6402 Skyway
Paradise, CA 95969
530-876-8321
Email: sea@sunset.net
Website: www.sea-center.org

Loving Your Disabled Child
4715 Crenshaw Blvd.
Los Angeles, CA 90043
323-299-2925
Email: lydc@pacbell.net
Website: www.lydc.org

Parents Helping Parents of San Francisco
594 Monterey Blvd.
San Francisco, CA 94127-2416
415-841-8820
Email: sfphp@earthlink.com

Loving Your Disabled Child
4528 Crenshaw Boulevard
Los Angeles, CA 90043
323-299-2925
Email: lydc@pacbell.net
Website: www.lydc.org

Vietnamese Parents of Disabled Children
    Assoc., Inc. (VPDCA)
7526 Syracuse Ave

Stanton, CA 90680
310-370-6704
Email: luyenchu@aol.com

Colorado
PEAK Parent Center, Inc.
6055 Lehman Drive, Suite 101
Colorado Springs, CO 80918
719-531-9400
Email: info@peakparent.org
Website: www.peakparent.org

Connecticut
Connecticut Parent Advocacy Center
338 Main Street
Niantic, CT 06357
860-739-3089
Email: cpacinc@aol.com
Website: http://members.aol.com/cpacinc/
cpac.htm

Delaware
Parent Information Center (PIC)
700 Barksdale Road, Suite 16
Newark, DE 19711
302-366-0152
Email: PEP700@aol.com
Website: www.picofdel.org

Florida
Parent to Parent of Miami, Inc.
555 SW 93rd Ave
Miami, FL 33165
305-271-9797
Email: PtoP1086@aol.com

Family Network on Disabilities
2735 Whitney Road
Clearwater, FL 34620-1610
813-523-1130
Email: fnd@gate.net
Website: www.fndfl.org

Georgia
Parents Educating Parents and Professionals
for All Children (PEPPAC)
8318 Durelee Lane Suite 101
Douglas, GA 30134
770-577-7771
Email: PEPPAC@bellsouth.net
Website: www.peppac.org

Hawaii
Palau Parent Network
Center on Disability Studies, University of
Hawaii
1833 Kala Kaua Avenue, #609
Honolulu, HI 96815
808-945-1432
Email: dotty@hawaii.edu
Email: patric@palaunet.com

AWARE
200 N. Vineyard Blvd., Suite 310
Honolulu, HI 96817
808-536-9684
Email: ldah@gte.net

Idaho
Idaho Parents Unlimited, Inc.
4696 Overland Road, Suite 478
Boise, ID 83705
208-342-5884
Email: ipul@rmci.net
Website: http://rmci.net/ipul

Native American Parent Training and
Information Center
129 East Third
Moscow, ID 83843
208-885-3500
Email: famtog@moscow.com

Illinois
Designs for Change
6 North Michigan Ave., Suite 1600
Chicago, IL 60602

312-857-9292; 800-851-8728
Email: dfc1@aol.com
Website: www.dfc1.org

Family T.I.E.S. Network
830 South Spring
Springfield, IL 62704
217-544-5809
Email: ftiesn@aol.com
Website: www.taalliance.org/ptis/fties/

National Center for Latinos with Disabilities
1915-17 South Blue Island
Chicago, IL 60608
312-666-3393
Email: ncld@interaccess.com
Website: www.homepage.interaccess.com/
~ncld/

Family Resource Center on Disabilities‘
20 E. Jackson Blvd., Room 900
Chicago, IL 60604
312-939-3513
Email: fredptiil@ameritech.net

Indiana
IN*SOURCE
809 N. Michigan St.
South Bend, IN 46601-1036
219-234-7101
Email: insourc1@aol.com
Website: www.insource.org

Iowa
Access for Special Kids(ASK)
Des Moines, IA 50309
515-243-1713
Email: ptiiowa@aol.com
Website: www.taalliance.org/ptis/ia/

Kansas
Families Together, Inc.
3340 W Douglas, Ste 102
Wichita, KS 67203

316-945-7747; 888-815-6364
Email: fmin@feist.com
Website: www.kansas.net/~family

Families ACT
555 N. Woodlawn
Wichita, KS 67203
316-685-1821
Email: nina@mhasck.org
Website: www.mhasck.org

Kentucky
Family Training & Information Center
2210 Goldsmith Lane, Suite 118
Louisville, KY 40218
800-525-7746
Email: spininc@aol.com

Council for Retarded Citizens of Jefferson
   Co., KY, Inc.
1146 South Third Street
Louisville, KY 40203
502-584-1239
Email: info@council-crc.org

Louisiana
Project PROMPT
4323 Division Street, Suite 110
Metairie, LA 70124-3179
504-888-9111; 800-766-7736
Email: fhfgno@ix.netcom.com
Website: www.projectprompt.com

Pyramid Parent Training Program
4101 Fontainbleau Dr.
New Orleans, LA 70125
504-827-0610
Email: Dmarkey404@aol.com

Maine
Special Needs Parents Info Network
P.O. Box 2067
Augusta, ME 043382067
207-582-2504

Email: jlachance@mpf.org
Website: www.mpf.org

Maryland
Parents Place of Maryland, Inc.
7484 Candlewood Rd. Suite S
Hanover, MD 21076-1306
410-859-5300
Email: info@ppmd.org
Website: www.mpf.org

Massachusetts
Federation for Children with Special Needs
1135 Tremont Street, Suite 420
Boston, MA 02120-2140
617-236-7210
Email: fcsninfo@fcsn.org
Website: www.fcsn.org/

Urban / PRIDE / IPEST
1472 Tremont
Roxbury Crossing, MA 02120
617-445-3191
Email: cspinkstion@compassinc.com

Michigan
Parents are Experts
23077 Greenfield Road, Suite 205
Southfield, MI 48075-3744
248-557-5070; 800-827-4843
Email: ucp@ameritech.net
Website: www.taalliance.org/ptis/mi-parents/

CAUSE
3303 W. Saginaw, Suite F-1
Lansing, MI 48917-2303
517-886-9167
Email: info-cause@voyager.net
Website: www.pathwaynet.com/cause/

Minnesota
PACER Center, Inc.
4826 Chicago Avenue South
Minneapolis, MN 55417-1098

612-827-2966
Email: pacer@pacer.org
Website: www.pacer.org

Families & Advocates Partnership for
Education
PACER Center
4826 Chicago Ave. S.
Minneapolis, MN 55417-1098
888-248-0822
Email: fape@pacer.org
Website: www.fape.org

Mississippi
Project Empower
136 South Poplar Ave.
Greenville, MS 38701
601-332-4852
Email: empower@tecinfo.com

Parent Partners
1900 North West St. Suite C-100
Jackson, MS 39202
601-714-5707
Email: ptiofms@misnet.com
Website: www.taalliance.org/ptis/ms/

Missouri
Missouri Parents Act
2100 S. Brentwood, Suite G
Springfield, MO 65804
417-882-7434
Email: mpactsm@axs.net
Website: www.crn.org/mpact

Missouri Parents Act (MPACT)
1 West Armour Blvd.
Kansas City, MO 64111
816-531-7070
Email: ptijcj@aol.com
Website: www.crn.org/mpact/

Montana
Parents Let's Unite for Kids
516 N. 32nd Street
Billings, MT 59101
406-255-0540
Email: plukmt@wtp.net
Website: www.pluk.org

Nebraska
Nebraska Parents Center
1941 S. 42nd St. #122
Omaha, NE 68105-2941
402-346-0525
Email: gdavis@neparentcenter.org
Website: www.neparentcenter.org

Nevada
Nevada Parents Encouraging Parents (PEP)
2810 W. Charleston Blvd., Suite G-68 Quail
Park IV
Las Vegas, NV 89102
702-3888-899
Email: nvpep@vegas.infi.net
Website: www.vegas.infi.net/~nvpep

New Hampshire
Parent Information Center
P.O. Box 2405
Concord, NH 03302-2405
603-224-7005
Email: picnh@aol.com
Website: www.taalliance.org/ptis/nhpic

New Jersey
Statewide Parent Advocacy Network (SPAN)
35 Halsey Street, 4th Floor
Newark, NJ 07102
973-642-8100; 800-654-SPAN
Email: span@spannj.org
Website: www.spannj.org

New Mexico
Parents Reaching Out, Project ADOBE
1000-A Main St. NW

Los Lunas, NM 87031
505-865-3700
Southwest Communications Resources
412 Camino Don Thomas, P.O. Box 788
Bernalillo, NM 87004-0788
505-867-3396
Email: epics@swcr.org

New York
The Advocacy Center
277 Alexander St. Suite 500
Rochester, NY 14607
716-546-1700
Email: archie@advocacycenter.com
Website: www.advocacycenter.com

Advocates for Children of NY
151 West 50th Street, 5th Floor
New York, NY 10001
212-974-9779
Email: info@advocatesforchildren.org
Website: www.advocatesforchildren.org

Sinergia/Metropolitan Parent Center
15 West 65th St., 6th Floor
New York, NY 10023
212-496-1300
Email: Sinergia@panix.com
Website: www.panix.com/~sinergia

Resources for Children with Special Needs
200 Park Ave. S., Suite 816
New York, NY 10003
212-677-4650
resourcesnyc@prodigy.net
Website: www.resourcesnyc.org

United We Stand Lourdes Rivera-Putz
728 Driggs Ave.
Brooklyn, NY 11211
718-302-4313
Email: uwsofny@aol.com
Website: www.taalliance.org/ptis/uws/

North Carolina
ECAC, Inc.
P.O. Box 16
Davidson, NC 28036
704-892-1321
Email: ECAC1@aol.com
Website: www.ecac-parentcenter.org

North Dakota
ND Pathfinder Parent Training and
Information Center
Arrowhead Shopping Center
1600d 2nd Ave. SW
Minot, ND 58701
701-837-7500
Email: ndpath01@minot.ndak.net
Website: www.ndcd.org/pathfinder

Ohio
Child Advocacy Center
1821 Summit Road, Suite 303
Cincinnati, OH 45237
513-821-2400
Email: CADCenter@aol.com

OCECD
Bank One Building 165 West Center St.,
Suite 302
Marion, OH 433023741
740-382-5452
Email: ocecd@edu.gte.net
Website: www.taalliance.org/PTIs/regohio

Oklahoma
Parents Reaching Out in OK
1917 S. Harvard Avenue
Oklahoma City, OK 73128
405-681-9710
Email: prook1@aol.com
Website: www.taalliance.ptis/ok/

Oregon
Oregon COPE Project
999 Locust St. NE, Box B

Salem, OR 97303
503-581-8156
Email: orcope@open.org
Website: www.open.org/~orcope

Pennsylvania
Parent Education Network
2107 Industrial Hwy
York, PA 17402-2223
717-600-0100
Email: pen@parentednet.org
Website: www.parentenet.org

Parents Union for Public Schools
1315 Walnut Street, Suite 1124
Philadelphia, PA 19107
215-546-1166
Email: ParentsU@aol.com

Buena Vista Plaza
166 W. Lehigh Ave. Suite 101
Philadelphia, PA 19133-3838
215-425-6203
Email: hupni@aol.com

The Mentor Parent Program
P.O. Box 47
Philadelphia, PA 16340
814-563-3470
Email: gal97@penn.com

Rhode Island
RI Parent Information Network
175 Main Street
Pawtucket, RI 02860
401-727-4144
Email: collins@ripin.org
Website: www.ripin.org

South Carolina
PRO-PARENTS
2712 Middleburg Drive, Suite 102
Columbia, SC 29204
803-779-3859
Email: pro-parents@aol.com

Website: www.community.columbiatoday.com/
realcities/proparents
Advocacy Coalition for Youth with
Disabilities C/O Family Resource Center
135 Rutledge Ave PO Box 250567
Charleston, SC 29425
843-876-1519
Email: mccarthyb@musc.edu

South Dakota
South Dakota Parent Connection
3701 West 49th St., Suite 200B
Sioux Falls, SD 57106
605-361-3171
Email: bpete@dakota.net
Website: www.sdparent.org

Tennessee
Support and Training for Exceptional
Parents, Inc. (STEP)
424 E. Bernard Ave., Suite 3
Greeneville, TN 37745
423-639-0125
Email: tnstep@aol.com
Website: www.tnstep.org

Texas
Partners Research Network Inc.
1090 Longfellow Drive, Suite B
Beaumont, TX 77706-4889
409-898-4684
Email: TXPRN@juno.com
Website: www.partnerstx.org

Arc of Texas in the Rio Grande Valley
Parents Supporting Parents Network
601 N. Texas Blvd.
Weslaco, TX 78596
956-973-9507
Email: dmeraz@gtemail.net
Website: www.thearcoftexas.org

Grassroots Consortium
P.O. Box 61628

Houston, TX 77207-6958
713-734-5355
Email: SpecKids@pdq.net

El Valle Community Parent Resource Center
530 South Texas Blvd, Suite 3
Weslaco, TX 78596
956-969-3611
Email: texasfiestaedu@acnet.net
Website: www.tfepoder.org

Project PODER
1017 N. Main Ave., Suite 207
San Antonio, TX 78212
210-222-2637
Email: poder@world-net.com
Website: www.tfepoder.org

Utah
Utah Parent Center
2290 East 4500 S., Suite 110
Salt Lake City, UT 84117-4428
810-272-1051
Email: upc@inconnect.com.
Website: www.utahparentcenter.org

Vermont
Vermont Parent Information Center
1 Mill Street, Suite A7
Burlington, VT 05401
802-658-5315
Email: vpic@together.net
http://homepages.together.net/~vpic

Virginia
Parent Educational Advocacy Training
Center
6320 Augusta Drive
Springfield, VA 22150
703-923-0010
Email: partners@peatc.org
Website: www.peatc.org

Washington
PAVE/STOMP
6316 South 12th St.
Tacoma, WA 98465
253-565-2266
Email: wapave9@washingtonpave.org
http://washingtonpave.org/stomp.html

Washington PAVE
6316 South 12th
Tacoma, WA 98465-1900
253-565-2266
Email: wapave9@washingtonpave.org
Website: www.washingtonpave.org

Parent to Parent Power
1118 S 142nd St.
Tacoma, WA 98444
253-531-2022
Email: ylink@aa.net

Washington, D.C.
The National Parent Network on Disabilities
(NPND)
1130 - 17th Street, NW, Suite 400
Washington, DC 20036
202-463-2299

Advocates for Justice and Education
2041 Martin Luther King Ave., SE Suite 301
Washington, DC 20020
202-678-8060; 888-327-8060
Email: justice1@bellatlantic.net
Website: www.aje.qpg.com

West Virginia
West Virginia PTI
371 Broaddus Ave
Clarksburg, WV 26301
304-624-1436
Email: wvpti@aol.com
Website: www.iolinc.net/wvpti

Wisconsin
Native American Family Empowerment
Center Great Lakes Inter-Tribal Council
2932 Highway 47N, P.O. Box 9
La du Flambeau, WI 54538
715-588-3324
Email: drosin@newnorth.net

Parent Education Project of Wisconsin
2192 South 60th Street
West Allis, WI 53219-1568
414-328-5520
Email: PMColletti@aol.com
Website: www.members.aol.com/pepofwi/

Wisconsin Family Assistance Center for
Education, Training and Support
2714 North Dr. Martin Luther King Dr.,
Suite E
Milwaukee, WI 53212
414-374-4645
Email: wifacets@execpc.com

Wyoming
Wyoming PIC
5 North Lobban
Buffalo, WY 82834
307-684-2277
Email: tdawsonpic@vcn.com
Website: www.wpic.org

Other

American Samoa
American Samoa PAVE
P.O. Box 3432
Pago Pago, AS 96799
011-684-633-2407
Email: SAMPAVE@samoatelco.com
Website: www.taalliance.org/ptis/amsamoa

American Virgin Islands
Virgin Islands Family Information Network
on Disabilities
V.I.FIND
#2 Nye Gade
P. O. Box 11670
St. Thomas, US VI 00802
340-774-1662
Email: vifind@islands.vi
Website: www.taalliance.org/ptis/vifind

Puerto Rico
APNI Inc., Parents Training Center
P.O. Box 21301
San Juan, PR 00928130
787-250-4552
Email: APNIPR@PRTC.net

APPENDIX F

Disabilities Organizations and Information Groups

You need to learn about your child's disability, and how the disability affects the child's ability to learn. These organizations and groups will provide information and help. Addresses, phone numbers, and email addresses change frequently. For current information, please visit our companion site: www.fetaweb.com/

Alexander Graham Bell Association for the
  Deaf and Hard of Hearing
3417 Volta Place N.W.
Washington, DC 20007
202-337-5220 (Voice); 202-337-5221
(TTY)
Email: info@agbell.org
Website: www.agbell.org

Alliance for Technology Access
2175 East Francisco Boulevard, Suite L
San Rafael, CA 94901
800-455-7970; 415-455-4575 (Voice); 415-455-0491 (TTY)
Email: atainfo@ataccess.org
Website: www.ataccess.org

American Brain Tumor Association
2720 River Road
Des Moines IA 60018
847-827-9910; 800-886-2282 (Patient Services)

Email: info@abta.org
Website: www.abta.org/

American Council of the Blind
1155 15th Street N.W., Suite 720
Washington, DC 20005
800-424-8666; 202-467-5081
Email: ncrabb@erols.com
Website: www.acb.org

American Council on Rural Special
  Education
(ACRES)
Kansas State University
2323 Anderson Avenue, Suite 226
Manhattan, KS 66502
785-532-2737
Email: acres@ksu.edu
Website: www.ksu.edu/acres

American Diabetes Association
1701 N. Beauregard Street

Alexandria, VA 22311
800-342-2383; 703-549-1500
Email: customerservice@diabetes.org
Website: www.diabetes.org

American Foundation for the Blind (AFB)
11 Penn Plaza, Suite 300
New York, NY 10001
800-232-5463; 212-502-7662 (TTY)
Publications available in Spanish
Email: afbinfo@afb.org
Website: www.afb.org

American Occupational Therapy Association
  (AOTA)
4720 Montgomery Lane
P.O. Box 31220
Bethesda, MD 20824-1220
301-652-2682 (Voice)
Website: www.aota.org

American Physical Therapy Association (APTA)
1111 North Fairfax Street
Alexandria, VA 22314
800-999-2782; 703-684-2782 (Voice)
703-683-6748 (TTY)
Email: practice@apta.org
Website: www.apta.org

American Society for Deaf Children
P.O. Box 3355
Gettysburg, PA 17325
800-942-2732; 717-334-7922 (V/TTY)
Email: ASDC1@aol.com
Website: www.deafchildren.org

American Speech-Language-Hearing
Association (ASHA)
10801 Rockville Pike
Rockville, MD 20852
800-498-2071 (V/TTY); 301-571-0457
(TTY)
Publications available in Spanish
Spanish speaker on staff

Email: actioncenter@asha.org
Website: www.asha.org

American Therapeutic Recreation Association
1414 Prince Street, Suite 204
Alexandria, VA 22314
703-683-9420
Email: atra@atra-tr.org
Website: www.atra-tr.org

Angelman Syndrome Foundation
414 Plaza Drive, Suite 209
Westmont, IL 60559
800-432-6435; 630-734-9267
Email: asf@adminsys.com
Website: www.angelman.org

Anxiety Disorders Association of America
11900 Parklawn Drive #100
Rockville, MD 20852-2624
301-231-9350
Email: AnxDis@adaa.org
Website: www.adaa.org

Aplastic Anemia & MDS International
  Foundation
P. O. Box 613
Annapolis, MD 21404-0613
800-747-2820; 410-867-0242
Email: aamdsoffice@aol.com
Website: www.aamds.org

The Arc (formerly the Association for
  Retarded Citizens of the U.S.)
1010 Wayne Avenue, Suite 650
Silver Spring, MD 20910
301-565-3842
Email: Info@thearc.org
Website: www.thearc.org

Asthma and Allergy Foundation of America
1233 20th Street, N.W., Suite 402
Washington, DC 20036
800-727-8462; 202-466-7643

Email: info@aafa.org
Website: www.aafa.org/

Assistive and Adaptive Computing
Technology In Special Education
Resources and Advocacy Information
http://at-advocacy.phillynews.com/index.html

Autism Society of America
7910 Woodmont Avenue, Suite 300
Bethesda, MD 20814-3015
800-328-8476; 301-657-0881
Publications available in Spanish
Website: www.autism-society.org

Brain Injury Association
(formerly the National Head Injury
Foundation)
105 North Alfred Street
Alexandria, VA 22314
800-444-6443; 703-236-6000
Publications available in Spanish
Email: FamilyHelpline@biausa.org
Website: www.biausa.org

CAUSE
3303 W. Saginaw Hwy., Suite F-1,
Lansing, MI 48917
Phone: 517-886-9167 Toll Free: 800-221-
9105 Fax: 517-886-9775
http://www.causeonline.org/

Center for Mental Health Services
Knowledge Exchange Network
P.O. Box 42490
Washington, DC 20015
Publications available in Spanish
800-789-2647; 301-443-9006 (TTY)
Email: ken@mentalhealth.org
Website: www.mentalhealth.org

Children and Adults with Attention-Deficit/
Hyperactivity Disorder (CHADD)
8181 Professional Place, Suite 201

Landover, MD 20785
301-306-7070; 800-233-4050 (To request
information packet)
Email: national@chadd.org
Website: www.chadd.org

Children's Craniofacial Association
P.O. Box 280297
Dallas, TX 75243-4522
800-535-3643; 972-994-9902
Email: contactcca@ccakids.com
Website: www.ccakids.com

Children's Liver Alliance
3835 Richmond Avenue, Suite 190
Staten Island, NY 10312-3828
718-987-6200
Email: Livers4Kids@earthlink.net
Website: http://livertx.org

Chronic Fatigue & Immune Dysfunction
   Syndrome Association
P.O. Box 220398
Charlotte, NC 28222-0398
800-442-3437; 704-365-9755
Email: info@cfids.org
Website: www.cfids.org

Council for Exceptional Children (CEC)
1110 N. Glebe Road, Suite 300
Arlington, VA 22201-5704
703-620-3660 (Voice); 703-264-9446 (TTY)
Email: cec@cec.sped.org
Website: www.cec.sped.org/

Craniofacial Foundation of America
975 East Third Street
Chattanooga, TN 37403
800-418-3223; 423-778-9192
Email: farmertm@erlanger.org
Website: www.erlanger.org/cranio

Disability Statistics Rehabilitation, Research
  and Training Center
3333 California Street, Room 340
University of California at San Francisco
San Francisco, CA 94118
415-502-5210 (Voice); 415-502-5217 (TTY)
Email: distats@itsa.ucsf.edu
Website: http://dsc.ucsf.edu

Easter Seals–National Office
230 West Monroe Street, Suite 1800
Chicago, IL 60606
800-221-6827; 312-726-6200 (Voice); 312-
726-4258 (TTY)
E-Mail: info@easter-seals.org
Website: www.easter-seals.org

Epilepsy Foundation–National Office
4351 Garden City Drive, 5th Floor
Landover, MD 20785-4941
800-332-1000; 301-459-3700
Publications available in Spanish; Spanish
speaker on staff
Email: postmaster@efa.org
Website: www.efa.org

FACES: The National Craniofacial
Association
P.O. Box 11082
Chattanooga, TN 37401
800-332-2372; 423-266-1632
Email: faces@faces-cranio.org
Website: www.faces-cranio.org

Family Resource Center on Disabilities
20 East Jackson Boulevard, Room 900
Chicago, IL 60604
800-952-4199 (Voice/TTY; toll-free in IL
only)
312-939-3513 (Voice); 312-939-3519 (TTY)

Family Village (community of disability-
  related resources)
Waisman Center

University of Wisconsin-Madison
1500 Highland Avenue
Madison, WI 53705-2280
Website: www.familyvillage.wisc.edu/

Family Voices (national coalition for children
  with special health care needs)
P. O. Box 769
Algodones, NM 87001
888-835-5669; 505-867-2368
Email: kidshealth@familyvoices.org
Website: www.familyvoices.org

Father's Network
16120 N.E. 8th Street
Bellevue, WA 98008-3937
425-747-4004, ext. 218
Email: jmay@fathersnetwork.org
Website: www.fathersnetwork.org

Federation of Families for Children's
  Mental Health
1101 King Street, Suite 420
Alexandria, VA 22314
703-684-7710
Publications available in Spanish
Email: ffcmh@ffcmh.com
Website: www.ffcmh.org

Foundation for Ichthyosis & Related
  Skin Types
P.O. Box 669
Ardmore, PA 19003
800-545-3286; 610-789-3995
Email: ichthyosis@aol.com
Website: www.libertynet.org/~ichthyos/

The Genetic Alliance (formerly the Alliance
  of Genetic Support Groups)
4301 Connecticut, N.W., Suite 404
Washington, DC 20008
800-336-4363; 202-966-5557
Email: info@geneticalliance.org
Website: www.geneticalliance.org

Head Start Bureau
Administration on Children, Youth and Families
U.S. Department of Health & Human Services
P.O. Box 1182
Washington, DC 20013
Website: www.acf.dhhs.gov/programs/hsb/

Hydrocephalus Association
870 Market Street #705
San Francisco, CA 94102
415-732-7040
Email: hydroassoc@aol.com
Website: www.hydroassoc.org

Independent Living Research Utilization
 Project
The Institute for Rehabilitation and Research
2323 South Sheppard, Suite 1000
Houston, TX 77019
713-520-0232 (Voice)
Email: ilru@ilru.org
Website: www.ilru.org

International Dyslexia Association
(formerly the Orton Dyslexia Society)
Chester Building #382
8600 LaSalle Road
Baltimore, MD 21286-2044
800-222-3123; 410-296-0232
Email: info@interdys.org
Website: www.interdys.org

International Resource Center for Down
 Syndrome
Keith Building
1621 Euclid Avenue, Suite 514
Cleveland, OH 44115
216-621-5858; 800-899-3039 (toll-free in OH only)
Email: hf854@cleveland.freenet.edu

International Rett Syndrome Association
9121 Piscataway Rd., Suite 2B
Clinton, MD 20735-2561
800-818-7388; 301-856-3334
Email: irsa@rettsyndrome.org
Website: www.rettsyndrome.org

Learning Disabilities Association of
 America (LDA)
4156 Library Road
Pittsburgh, PA 15234
888-300-6710; 412-341-1515; 412-341-8077
Publications available in Spanish
Email: vldanatl@usaor.ne
Website: www.ldanatl.org

Leukemia & Lymphoma Society (formerly
 Leukemia Society of America)
600 Third Avenue
New York, NY 10016
800-955-4LSA; 212-573-8484
Email: infocenter@leukemia-lymphoma.org
Website: www.leukemia-lymphoma.org

Little People of America–National
 Headquarters
P.O. Box 745
Lubbock, TX 79408
888-LPA-2001
Spanish speaker on staff
Email: LPADataBase@juno.com
Website: www.lpaonline.org

March of Dimes Birth Defects Foundation
1275 Mamaroneck Avenue
White Plains, NY 10605
914-428-7100; 888-663-4637
Publications available in Spanish
Email: resourcecenter@modimes.org
Website: www.modimes.org

Muscular Dystrophy Association (MDA)
3300 East Sunrise Drive
Tucson, AZ 85718
800-572-1717; 520-529-2000
Publications available in Spanish
Email: mda@mdausa.org
Website: www.mdausa.org

National Alliance for the Mentally Ill
(NAMI)
Colonial Place Three
2107 Wilson Blvd, Suite 300
Arlington, VA 22201-3042
800-950-6264; 703-524-7600; 703-516-7991 (TTY)
Publications available in Spanish
Email: namiofc@aol.com
Website: www.nami.org

National Association of the Deaf
814 Thayer Avenue, Suite 250
Silver Spring, MD 20910
301-587-1788; 301-587-1789 (TTY)
Email: nadinfo@nad.org
Website: www.nad.org

National Association of Private Schools for
   Exceptional Children (NAPSEC)
1522 K Street N.W., Suite 1032
Washington, DC 20005
202-408-3338
Email: napsec@aol.com
Website: www.napsec.com

National Ataxia Foundation
2600 Fernbrook Lane, Suite 119
Minneapolis, MN 55447
612-553-0020
Email: naf@mr.net
Website: www.ataxia.org

National Attention Deficit Disorder
   Association
1788 Second Street, Suite 200
Highland Park, IL 60035

Email: mail@add.org
Website: www.add.org
National Brain Tumor Foundation
414 13th Street, Suite 700
Oakland, CA 94612
800-934-2873; 510-839-9777
Email: nbtf@braintumor.org
Website: www.braintumor.org

National Center for Learning Disabilities
   (NCLD)
381 Park Avenue South, Suite 1401
New York, NY 10016
212-545-7510; 888-575-7373
Website: www.ncld.org

National Chronic Fatigue Syndrome and
   Fibromyalgia Association (NCFSFA)
P.O. Box 18426
Kansas City, MO 64133
816-313-2000
Email: NCFSFA@aol.com

National Council on Independent Living
1916 Wilson Boulevard, Suite 209
Arlington, VA 22201
703-525-3406; 703-525-4153 (TTY)
Email: ncil@ncil.org
Website: www.ncil.org

National Down Syndrome Congress
7000 Peachtree-Dunwoody Road N.E.
Lake Ridge 400 Office Building 5, Suite 100
Atlanta, GA 30328
800-232-6372; 770-604-9500
Spanish speaker on staff
Email: NDSCcenter@aol.com
Website: www.ndsccenter.org

National Down Syndrome Society
666 Broadway, 8th Floor
New York, NY 10012-2317
800-221-4602; 212-460-9330
Email: info@ndss.org
Website: www.ndss.org

National Federation for the Blind
1800 Johnson Street
Baltimore, MD 21230
410-659-9314
Email: nfb@iam.digex.net
Website: www.nfb.org

National Fragile X Foundation
1441 York Street, Suite 303
Denver, CO 80206
800-688-8765; 303-333-6155
Email: natlfx@sprintmail.com
Website: www.nfxf.org

National Library Service for the Blind &
    Physically Handicapped
The Library of Congress
1291 Taylor Street N.W.
Washington, DC 20542
800-424-8567; 202-707-5100 (Voice)
Publications available in Spanish
E-Mail: nls@loc.gov
Website: www.loc.gov/nls

National Mental Health Association
1021 Prince Street
Alexandria, VA 22314-2971
800-969-6642; 703-684-7722; 800-433-
5959 (TTY)
Publications available in Spanish
Email: nmhainfo@aol.com
Website: www.nmha.org

National Multiple Sclerosis Society
733 Third Avenue
New York, NY 10017
800-344-4867; 212-986-3240
Email: info@nmss.org
Website: www.nmss.org

National Neurofibromatosis Foundation
95 Pine Street; 16th Floor
New York, NY 10005
800-323-7938; 212-344-6633

E-Mail: nnff@nf.org
Website: www.nf.org

National Organization on Fetal Alcohol
    Syndrome (NOFAS)
216 G Street N.E.
Washington, DC 20002
800-666-6327; 202-785-4585
Email: nofas@erols.com
Website: www.nofas.org

National Parent Network on Disabilities
1130 17th Street N.W., Suite 400
Washington, DC 20036
202-463-2299 (V/TTY)
E-Mail: npnd@cs.com
Website: www.npnd.org

National Parent to Parent Support and
    Information System, Inc.
P.O. Box 907
Blue Ridge, GA 30513
800-651-1151; 706-374-3822
Email: nppsis@ellijay.com
Website: www.nppsis.org

National Reye's Syndrome Foundation
P.O. Box 829
Bryan, OH 43506
800-233-7393; 419-636-2679
Email: nrsf@reyessyndrome.org
Website: www.reyessyndrome.org

National Scoliosis Foundation
5 Cabot Place
Stoughton, MA 02072
800-673-6922; 781-341-6333
Email: scoliosis@aol.com

National Spinal Cord Injury Association
8300 Colesville Road, Suite 551
Silver Spring, MD 20910
800-962-9629; 301-588-6959
Email: nscia2@aol.com
Website: www.spinalcord.org

National Stuttering Association
5100 E. La Palma Avenue, Suite 208
Anaheim Hills, CA 92807
800-364-1677; 714-693-7480
Email: nsastutter@aol.com
Website: www.nsastutter.org

National Tuberous Sclerosis Association
8181 Professional Place, Suite 110
Landover, MD 20785-2226
800-225-6872; 301-459-9888
Email: ntsa@ntsa.org
Website: www.ntsa.org

Neurofibromatosis, Inc.
8855 Annapolis Road, Suite 110
Lanham, MD 20706-2924
800-942-6825; 301-577-8984
Email: NFInc1@aol.com
Website: www.nfinc.org

Obsessive Compulsive Foundation, Inc.
337 Notch Hill Road
North Branford, CT 06471
203-315-2190
Email: info@ocfoundation.org
Website: www.ocfoundation.org

Oregon Parents United
22980 Donna Lane
Bend OR 97701
541-389-0004
Website: www.oregonparentsunited.org
Email: OPU@peak.org

Osteogenesis Imperfecta Foundation
804 Diamond Ave., Suite 210
Gaithersburg, MD 20878
800-981-BONE; 301-947-0083
Email: bonelink@aol.com
Website: www.oif.org

Parents Helping Parents:The Parent-Directed
   Family Resource Center for Children with

Special Needs
3041 Olcott St.
Santa Clara, CA 95054
408-727-5775
Publications available in Spanish
Spanish speaker on staff
Email: info@php.com
Website: www.php.com

Pathways Awareness Foundation
123 North Wacker Drive
Chicago, IL 60606
800-955-2445; 312-236-7411 (TTY)
Brochure and video available in Spanish
Website: www.pathwaysawareness.org

Prader-Willi Syndrome Association
5700 Midnight Pass Road, Suite 6
Sarasota, FL 34242
800-926-4797; 941-312-0400
Email: pwsausa@aol.com
Website: www.pwsausa.org

President's Committee's Job
   Accommodation Network
West Virginia University
918 Chestnut Ridge Road, Suite 1
P.O. Box 6080
Morgantown, WV 26506-6080
800-526-7234 (Voice/TTY)
Email: jan@.icdi.wvu.edu
Website: www.jan.wvu.edu

Recording for the Blind and Dyslexic
The Anne T. Macdonald Center
20 Roszel Road
Princeton, NJ 08540
800-221-4792; 609-452-0606
Email: custserv@rfbd.org
Website: www.rfbd.org

Registry of Interpreters for the Deaf
8630 Fenton Street, Suite 324
Silver Spring, MD 20910

301-608-0050 (V/TTY)
Email: info@rid.org
Website: www.rid.org

Sibling Information Network
A.J. Pappanikou Center
University of Connecticut
249 Glenbrook Road, U64
Storrs, CT 06269-2064
860-486-4985

Special Olympics International
1325 G Street N.W., Suite 500
Washington, DC 20005
202-628-3630
Publications available in Spanish and French
Spanish & French speaker on staff
Email: specialolympics@msn.com
Website: www.specialolympics.org/

Spina Bifida Association of America
4590 MacArthur Boulevard, N.W., Suite 250
Washington, DC 20007-4226
800-621-3141; 202-944-3285
Publications available in Spanish
Email: sbaa@sbaa.org
Website: www.sbaa.org

Stuttering Foundation of America
3100 Walnut Grove Road #603
P.O. Box 11749
Memphis, TN 38111
800-992-9392
Email: stuttersfa@aol.com
Website: www.stuttersfa.org

TASH (formerly The Association for Persons
  with Severe Handicaps)
29 W. Susquehanna Ave., Suite 210
Baltimore, MD 21204
410-828-8274 (Voice); 410-828-1306 (TTY)
Email: info@tash.org
Website: www.tash.org

Technical Assistance Alliance for Parent
  Centers
(the Alliance)
PACER Center
8161 Normandale Blvd.
Minneapolis, MN 55437-1044
888-248-0822; 952-838-9000
Spanish speaker on staff
Email: alliance@taalliance.org
Website: www.taalliance.org

Tourette Syndrome Association
42-40 Bell Boulevard
Bayside, NY 11361
800-237-0717; 718-224-2999
Email: tourette@ix.netcom.com
Website: tsa.mgh.harvard.edu/

Trace Research & Development Center
S-151 Waisman Center
1500 Highland Avenue
University of Wisconsin-Madison
Madison, WI 53705-2280
608-262-6966; 608-262-5408 (TTY)
Email: info@trace.wisc.edu
Website: http://trace.wisc.edu/

United Cerebral Palsy Association, Inc.
1660 L Street, N.W., Suite 700
Washington, DC 20036
202-776-0406; 800-872-5827; 202-973-
7197 (TTY)
Publications available in Spanish
E-Mail: ucpnatl@ucpa.org
Website: www.ucpa.org

Williams Syndrome Association, Inc.
P.O. Box 297
Clawson, MI 48017-0297
248-541-3630

Your Notes Here

APPENDIX G

Legal and Advocacy Resources

Amicus for Children, Inc.
1023 Old Swede Road
Douglassville, PA 19518
610-689-4226
Email: amicusforchildren@att.net
Website: www.amicusforchildren.org

Bazelon Center for Mental Health Law
1101 15th Street NW, Suite 1212
Washington, DC 20005-5002
Email: leec@bazelon.org
Website: www.bazelon.org/

Center for Law and Education
1875 Connecticut Avenue, NW Suite 510
Washington, DC 20009
202-986-3000
Email: webmaster@cleweb.org
Website: www.cleweb.org/

Center for Special Education Advocacy
548 Donald Street, Unit 1A
Bedford, NH 03110
603-668-3361
Email: cseadvocacy@msn.com
Website: www.cseadvocacy.com/

Children's Defense Fund
122 C St., N.W., Ste. 400
Washington, DC 20001
202-628-8787
Email: webmaster@childrensdefense.org
Website: www.childrensdefense.org

Council of Parent Attorneys and Advocates
(COPAA)
1321 Pennsylvania Ave., SE
Washington, DC 20003-3027
202-544-2210
Email: copaa@copaa.net
Website: www.copaa.net

G. Emerson Dickman, Esq.
25 E. Spring Valley Avenue
Maywood, NJ 07607
201-909-0404
Email: info@emersondickman.org
Website: www.emersondickman.org

Disability Rights Advocates
449 15th Street, Suite 303
Oakland, CA 94612
510-451-8644
Email: general@dralegal.org
Website: www.dralegal.org

Disability Rights Education and
  Defense Fund
2212 Sixth Street
Berkeley, CA 94710
510-644-2555
Email: dredf@dredf.org
Website: www.dredf.org

The EDLAW Center
P.O. Box 81-7327
Hollywood, FL 33081-1327
954-966-4489
Email: edcenter@edlaw.net
Website: www.edlaw.net

Education A Must
c/o Dorothy French
PO Box 216
East Derry, NH 03041
603-437-6286
Email: Education7@aol.com
Website: www.education-a-must.com

Education Law Center
155 Washington Street, Suite 205
Newark, NJ 07102
973-624-1815
Email: JnPonessa@aol.com
Website: www.edlawcenter.org

Education Law Center - PA
1315 Walnut Street, Suite 400
Philadelphia, PA 19107-4798
215-238-6970
Email: elc@elc-pa.org
Website: www.elc-pa.org/

Families for Early Autism Treatment
P.O. Box 255722
Sacramento, CA 95865-5722
916-843-1536
Email: webmaster@feat.org
Website: www.feat.org

Federation for Children with Special Needs
1135 Tremont Street, Suite 420
Boston, MA 02120
617-236-7210
Email: fcsninfo@fcsn.org
Website: www.fcsn.org

David Ferleger, Esq.
10 Presidential Blvd, Suite 115
Bala Cynwyd, PA 19044
610-668-2221
Email: david@ferleger.com
Website: www.ferleger.com

Fiesta Educativa, Inc.
3939 Selig Place
Los Angeles, CA 90031
323-221-6696
Email: info@fiestaeducative.org
Website: www.fiestaeducativa.org

Galena Parent Advocates
c/o Lynn Gallagher
320 Elk Street
Galena IL 61036
815 777-2796
Email: galenaadvocate@hotmail.com
Website: www.galenaparentadvocates.com

Harbor House Law Press, Inc.
P. O. Box 480
Hartfield, VA 23071
804-758-8400; Orders 877-529-4332 (877-
LAW-IDEA)
Email: Webmaster@harborhouselaw.com
Website: www.harborhouselaw.com

Pat Howey
Special Education Consulting
P.O. Box 117
West Point, IN 47992-0117
765-572-2892
Email: phowey@worldnet.att.net
Website: www.angelfire.com/in2/
spedconsulting/index.html

Kerrlaw
c/o Sonja Kerr, Esq.
5972 Cahill Avenue South Suite 110
Inver Grove Heights, MN 55076
651-552-4900
Email: info@kerrlaw.com
Website: www.kerrlaw.com

Kotin, Crabtree & Strong, LLP
c/o Robert K. Crabtree, Esq.
One Bowdoin Square
Boston, MA 02114-2925
617-227-7031
Email: kcs@kcslegal.com
Website: www.kcslegal.com

Lapeer Foundation for Special Learning
P.O. Box 211
Lapeer, MI 48446
810-245-5606
Email: LapeerFoundation@aol.com
Website: www.iqonline.net/lapeerfoundation

Reed Martin, Esq.
P. O. Box 487
Morgantown, WV 26507
304-598-3406
Email: connie@westco.net
Website: www.reedmartin.com

Monahan & Cohen, Attorneys at Law
225 West Washington Street, Suite 2300
Chicago, Illinois 60606 USA
312-419-0252
Email: mdcspedlaw@earthlink.net
Website: www.monahan-cohen.com

National Association of Protection and
    Advocacy Systems (NAPAS)
900 Second Street N.E., Suite 211
Washington, DC 20002
202-408-9514
Email: napas@earthlink.net
Website: www.protectionandadvocacy.com

National Council on Disability
1331 F St., NW, Suite 1050
Washington, DC 20004-1107
202-272-2004
Email: mquigley@ncd.gov
Website: www.ncd.gov

National Council on Independent Living
1916 Wilson Boulevard, Suite 209
Arlington, VA 22201
703-525-3406
Email: ncil@tsbbs02.tnet.com
Website: www.ncil.org

Brice L. Palmer, Esq.
Research & Advocacy Office
626 Route 4W
Castleton, VT 05735
802-265-8112
Email: education@spedcite.com
Website: www.spedcite.com

Parent Information Center of New Jersey, Inc.
210 Carlton Terrace
Teaneck, NJ 07666
201-692-0898

Edward W. Pepyne, J.D., Ed.D.
P. O. Box 345
Ashfield, MA 01339
Email: pepyne@shaysnet.com
Website: www.pepyne.com/sped.html

Protection & Advocacy, Inc.
100 Howe Avenue, Suite 185N
Sacramento, CA 95825-8219
916-488-9950; 800-776-5746 (In CA)
Email: legalmail@pai-ca.org
Websitew.pai-ca.org

Public Interest Law Center of Philadelphia
    (PILCOP)
125 S. 9th Street, Ste. 700
Philadelphia, PA 19107
215-627-7100

Samford and DePaola, P.C.
One Commerce Street, Suite 601
Montgomery, AL 36104
334-262-1600
Email: ssdp@mindspring.com
Website: http://www.specialedatty.com

Sussan and Greenwald
407 Main Street
Spotswood, NJ 08884
732-251-8585
Email: info@special-ed-law.com
Website: www.special-ed-law.com

Stinson Law Associates, P.C.
c/o Phil Stinson, Esq.
P.O. Box 1340
Bryn Mawr, PA 19010
610-688-7300
Email: info@specialedlaw.net
Website: www.specialedlaw.net

U. S. Department of Education
in cooperation with Council for Exceptional
Children
Toll Free: 877-232-4332 (877-CEC-IDEA)
Website: www.ideapractices.org
See also: www.ed.gov/offices/OSERS/OSEP/
index.html

Wrightslaw
c/o Peter and Pamela Wright
P. O. Box 1008
Deltaville, VA 23043
804-257-0857
Email: webmaster@wrightslaw.com
Website: www.wrightslaw.com

APPENDIX H

Free Publications

Children's Mental Health

Office of the Surgeon General. *Report on the Surgeon General's Conference on Children's Mental Health – A National Action Agenda* (2000).

Download: http://www.surgeongeneral.gov/cmh/default.htm

To order bound copies, contact The National Institutes of Mental Health, Office of Communications and Public Liaison, 6001 Executive Blvd., Room 8184, MSC 9663, Bethesda, MD 20892-9663. Phone: 301-443-4513

Harassment

U. S. Department of Education Office for Civil Rights and National Association of Attorneys General. *Protecting Students from Harassment and Hate Crimes: A Guide for Schools* (1999).

Many children experience sexual, racial and ethnic harassment at school. This Guide provides guidance about protecting students from harassment and violence based on race, color, national origin, sex, and disability.

Download: http://www.ed.gov/pubs/Harassment/

To order bound copies, contact the U.S. Department of Education, Office for Civil Rights at 1-800- 421-3481

High-Stakes Tests

U. S. Department of Education, Office of Civil Rights. *The Use of Tests as Part of High-Stakes Decision-Making for Students: A Resource Guide for Educators and Policy-Makers* (2000).

Standards for standardized tests that are used to make decisions with important consequences for students: tests used for diagnostic and intervention purposes, assessment of academic educational achievement, and alternate assessments for students with disabilities who cannot participate in district-wide academic achievement tests.

Download: http://www.ed.gov/offices/OCR/testing/index.html

Disability Rights Advocates. *Do No Harm – High Stakes Testing and Students with Learning Disabilities*

(2001).

Describes accommodations, alternate assessments, appeals, procedures, and other safeguards that should be implemented for statewide assessment systems to comply with the law and guarantee educationally sound opportunities to students with learning disabilities.

Download: http://www.dralegal.org/

To order bound copies, contact Disability Rights Advocates, 449 15th Street, Suite 303. Oakland, CA 94612-2821

Phone: 510-451-8644

Individualized Education Programs (IEPs)

U. S. Department of Education, Office of Special Education and Rehabilitation Services. *A Guide to the Individualized Education Program* (2000).

Describes how to write IEPs that improve teaching, learning, and educational results. Includes: contents of the IEP; IEP team members; writing the IEP; placement decisions; after the IEP is written; implementing the IEP; revising and revising the IEP; resolving disagreements about the IEP; a sample IEP form, information and resources, the federal regulations for IEPs, and guidance about IEPs.

Download: http://www.ed.gov/offices/OSERS/OSEP/IEP_Guide

To order free copies, contact ED Pubs, Editorial Publications Center, P O Box 1398, Jessup, MD 20794.

Phone: 877-4-ED-PUBS

ERIC Clearinghouse on Disabilities and Gifted Education. *Designing Individualized Education Program (IEP) Transition Plans* (2000).

The Individuals with Disabilities Education Act (IDEA) requires schools to prepare students with disabilities for employment and independent living. Early and meaningful transition planning that involves students and their families has a positive influence on post-school success and independence. This article describes how to design quality IEP transition plans.

Download: http://ericec.org/digests/e598.html

To order bound copies, contact The Council for Exceptional Children, 1110 N. Glebe Rd., Arlington, VA 22201-5704. Phone: 1-800-328-0272

Reading

American Federation of Teachers. Teaching Reading is Rocket Science: What Expert Teachers Should Know and Be Able to Do by Louisa Moats (1999).

Download: www.aft.org/Edissues/downloads/rocketsci.pdf

Moats, Louisa. Whole Language Lives On: The Illusion of "Balanced" Reading Instruction (2000).

Download: http://www.edexcellence.net/library/wholelang/moats.html

National Institutes of Health. Report of the National Reading Panel, Teaching Children to Read: An Evidence-Based Assessment of the Scientific Research Literature on Reading and Its Implications for Reading Instruction (2000).

Download: http://www.nichd.nih.gov/publications/nrppubskey.cfm

To order as NIH Publication Number 00-4769, contact NICHD Clearinghouse at 1-800-370-2943

Retention and Social Promotion

National Association of School Psychologists. Retention and Promotion: A Handout for Parents (1998).

Finds that "research does not support the notion that retention helps children to 'catch up' and that 'social promotion' – sending children on to the next grade regardless of performance –pushes children through the school system without requiring mastery of basic skills."

Download: http://www.nasponline.org/publications/cq268retainpar.html

National Association of School Psychologists. Position Statement on Student Grade Retention and Social Promotion (1998).

"The National Association of School Psychologists promotes the use of interventions that are effective and research-based and discourages the use of practices which, though popular or widely accepted, are neither not beneficial or are harmful to the welfare and educational attainment of America's children and youth. Through many years of research, the practice of retaining children in grade has been shown to be ineffective in meeting the needs of children who are academically delayed."

Download: http://www.nasponline.org/information/pospaper_graderetent.html

Special Education

National Association of Elementary School Principals, *Implementing IDEA: A Guide for Principals* (2001).

Publication from U. S. Department of Education and the Council of Exceptional Children; principals are responsible for educating all students in their schools.

Download: http://www.ideapractices.org/implement.pdf

National Council on Disability, *Back to School on Civil Rights: Advancing the Federal Commitment to Leave No Child Behind.* (2000).

In this report about enforcement of the Individuals With Disabilities Education Act (IDEA), the National Council on Disability found that all states were out of compliance with the law and that " . . . efforts to enforce the law over several Administrations have been inconsistent, ineffective, and lacking any real teeth."

Download: http://www.wrightslaw.com/law/reports/IDEA_Compliance_overview.htm

To order bound copies, contact the National Council on Disability, 1331 F. Street, NW, Suite 1050, Washington, DC 20004-1107. Phone: 202-272-2004

Zero Tolerance and Discipline

Harvard Civil Rights Project. *Opportunities Suspended: The Devastating Consequences of Zero Tolerance and School Discipline Policies* (2000).

Under Zero Tolerance Policies, children from kindergarten through 12th grade receive harsh punishments, often for minor infractions that pose no threat to safety. Compelling research indicates that these "get-tough" disciplinary measures fail to meet sound educational principles. In many cases, their application defies commonsense.

Download: http://www.law.harvard.edu/civilrights/conferences/zero/zt_report2.html

To order bound copies, contact The Civil Rights Project, Harvard University, 124 Mt. Auburn Street Suite 400, South Cambridge, MA 02138. Phone: 617-496-6367

APPENDIX I

Sample Letters to the School

This Appendix includes sixteen sample letters from two hypothetical parents, Mary Parent and Jane Smith. As you read about the purposes of letters in Chapter 23, refer to letters 1-6 from Mary Parent.

Letters 7 through 16 from Jane Smith show you how to use letters to tell your side of the story. When you read these letters, you will see how Jane used letters to document her son's problems and her requests for help. The letters begin with her request for her son's records and include requests for meetings, an evaluation, eligibility, and a Ten-day Notice letter when she announced her intention to withdraw her son from the public school program. You can adapt these letters to fit your circumstances.

1. Sample Letter to Request Information
2. Sample Letter to Request a Meeting
3. Sample Letter to Document a Problem
4. Sample Letter to Express Appreciation and Document Problems
5. Sample Letter to Document an IEP Problem
6. Sample Letter to Decline a Request
7. Letter to Principal to Request Child's Records
8. Letter to Superintendent to Request Child's Records
9. Second Request for Records
10. Letter to Request a Meeting with a Teacher, Includes Educational History
11. Letter to Request a Review of Educational Records
12. Letter to Express Appreciation for Help
13. Letter to Request an Evaluation for Special Education Services
14. Letter to Request Test Scores as Standard Scores and Percentile Ranks
15. Follow-up Letter after IEP Meeting to Document Unresolved Problems
16. Ten-day Notice Letter to Withdraw Child from Public School

#1. Sample Letter to Request Information

Mary Parent
500 Oak Street
Centerville, IN 60010
(899) 555-1234

September 22, 2002

Dr. Ruth Boss, Superintendent
Independent School District #1
1000 Central Avenue
Centerville, IN 60010

Reference: Jennifer Parent
DOB: 01/01/90
School: Stonewall Elementary School

Dear Dr. Boss:

Please send me a complete copy of my child's cumulative and confidential educational records, including medical records, special education records, formal and informal correspondence, discipline records, tests, evaluations, and teacher-to teacher notes. If there is a cost and policy about photocopies, please let me know immediately.

If you have questions about my request, please call me at work (555-9876) or at home (555-1234) after 6 p.m. I appreciate your help and quick response.

Sincerely,

Mary Parent

#2. Sample Letter to Request a Meeting

Mary Parent
500 Oak Street
Centerville, IN 60010
(899) 555-1234

November 8, 2002

Eleanor Randolph
Stonewall Elementary School
1000 Central Avenue
Centerville, IN 60010

Reference: Jennifer Parent
DOB: 01/03/90
School: Stonewall Elementary School

Dear Mrs. Randolph:

I am writing to request an appointment with you on November 15 at 3:30 p.m. I would like to talk with you about Jennifer's behavior problems. As you know, Jennifer is having difficulty with the transition from elementary school to middle school. Two weeks ago, she was suspended again for "inappropriate behavior."

Please call me at work (555-9876) or home (555-1234) after 6:00 p.m. to confirm this date and time or to suggest an alternative date and time. If I am not available, please leave a message on my answering machine.

I appreciate your taking the time to meet with me.

Sincerely,

Mary Parent

#3. Sample Letter to Document a Problem

Mary Parent
500 Oak Street
Centerville, IN 60010
(899) 555-1234

November 15, 2002

John Belcher
Stonewall Elementary School
1000 Central Avenue
Centerville, IN 60010

Reference: Jennifer Parent
DOB: 01/01/90
School: Stonewall Elementary School

Dear Mr. Belcher:

I am writing to ask you to reconsider your decision to suspend Jennifer from school for three days. I do not believe that talking to a classmate during a quiz is an offense that warrants such serious disciplinary action.

As you know, Jennifer has autism. Four years ago, she was unable to communicate with other children. Her social skills deficits were severe. Jennifer has made remarkable progress in these areas. Despite this, her behavior is not always appropriate. The transition from elementary school to middle school has been difficult for her. Suspending Jennifer from school does not teach her how to behave more appropriately.

I am also concerned that this is the third time Jennifer has been suspended for behavior problems this year.

I am requesting a meeting with you to discuss your decision to suspend Jennifer and her needs as a child with autism. Please call me at work (555-9876) or at home (555-1234) after 6:00 p.m. to schedule a meeting. I look forward to your call.

Sincerely,

Mary Parent

#4. Sample Letter to Express Appreciation and Document Problems

Mary Parent
500 Oak Street
Centerville, IN 60010
(899) 555-1234

November 27, 2002

Lee Green Special Education Teacher
Eleanor Randolph, Math Teacher
Stonewall Elementary School
1000 Central Avenue
Centerville, IN 60010

Reference: Jennifer Parent
                DOB: 01/01/90
                School: Stonewall Elementary School

Dear Ms. Randolph and Ms. Smart:

I am writing to thank you for meeting with me on November 25 to discuss Jennifer's progress and grades. As a parent, I sometimes find report cards confusing.

Ms. Randolph, I appreciate your explanation of Jennifer's progress. For example, you explained that her grade of A in math was based on the second grade math book that she has used for two years. I was not aware that her grades were raised because of good attendance.

Ms. Green advised me that Jennifer continues to need an aide 100% of the time. I appreciate the school's attempts to help Jennifer by providing an aide. However, I have serious concerns about this aide. She has received no training about autism and is not being supervised. Instead, of teaching Jennifer to communicate, Ms. Jones speaks for Jennifer. Recently, I learned that Ms. Jones has been doing Jennifer's homework.

If you are interested in learning about Jennifer's type of autism, I have lots of information and will be happy to share this information with you. Thank you again for the meeting and your time. I am glad you enjoyed the cake I brought.

Sincerely,

Mary Parent

#5. Sample Letter to Document an IEP Problem

Mary Parent
500 Oak Street
Centerville, IN 60010
(899) 555-1234
January 2, 2003

Lee Green, Special Education Teacher
Stonewall Elementary School
1000 Central Avenue
Centerville, IN 60010

Reference: Jennifer Parent
Sixth Grade
School: Stonewall Elementary School

Dear Ms. Green:

I am writing to thank you for your telephone call about Jennifer's problems in Mr. Small's class. I appreciate your offer to intervene with Mr. Small on Jennifer's behalf.

I am concerned that Mr. Small is not implementing Jennifer's IEP. As you know, the IEP provides for Jennifer to have a quiet place to go when she is overwhelmed. You assured me that Mr. Small has been advised to follow the IEP. You also advised me that the school would provide a quiet place near Mr. Small's class.

Why does Mr. Small refuse to allow Jennifer to go the quiet place when she is overwhelmed? If she cannot get away when she is overwhelmed, she has behavior problems. She has already been suspended three times this year for behavior problems.

I am confused. The elementary school teachers worked with Jennifer. They taught her communication and social skills. Because of their efforts, she made wonderful progress. We will always feel grateful to these teachers.

The middle school teachers seem to have a "sink or swim" attitude about Jennifer. The IEP team spent hours writing an IEP that would provide Jennifer with an appropriate education. How can a teacher refuse to implement the IEP? Why does Mr. Belcher think he can teach Jennifer to behave appropriately by suspending her?

Please schedule an IEP meeting to address these issues. You can contact me at work (555-9876) or at home (555-1234) after 6:00 p.m. I look forward to meeting with the IEP team.

Sincerely,
Mary Parent

#6. Sample Letter to Decline a Request

Mary Parent
500 Oak Street
Centerville, IN 60010
(899) 555-1234

April 4, 2003

Dr. Alan Brown
Independent School District #1
1000 Central Avenue
Centerville, IN 60010

Reference: Jennifer Parent
                   DOB: 01/03/90
                   School: Stonewall Elementary School

Dear Dr. Brown:

On Thursday evening, April 3, I received a letter from you advising me that an IEP meeting had been scheduled for Monday, April 7, at 2:15 p.m.

I regret that I must ask that this meeting be rescheduled. Unfortunately, I cannot cancel my work obligations on such short notice. I hope this request does not inconvenience the team members. As I advised your secretary, I am available on April 9, 10, and 11.

If you have any questions, please call me at work (555-9876) or at home (555-1234) after 6:00 p.m. I look forward to meeting with the team on one of these dates.

Sincerely,

Mary Parent

#7. Letter to Principal to Request Child's Records

Jane Smith
500 Oak Lane
Centerville, IL 60010
(899) 555-1234

September 18, 2002

George Williams, Principal
Grove Middle School
1000 Main Street
Middleburg, IL 60010

Reference: Michael K. Smith
               DOB: 01/02/90
               School: Grove Middle School

Dear Mr. Williams:

On September 17, I received a letter advising me that a meeting with Michael's teachers has been scheduled for October 2. At this meeting, we will discuss Michaels' educational problems and how we may help him. So that I may be better prepared for the meeting, please send me a complete copy of my son's entire cumulative and confidential records. Please be sure to include copies of all evaluations and actual test scores. If there is a cost and policy about photocopies, please let me know immediately.

I will need time to review Michael's educational records before this important meeting.

If you have questions about my request, please call me at work (555-9876) or at home (555-1234), after 6:00 pm.

Thank you for your assistance and quick response.

Sincerely,

Jane Smith

☑ If you send one letter to the principal and one letter to the superintendent, it is less likely that one person will assume the other person acted on your request.

☑ Do not send letters by certified mail. Hand-deliver important letters to the principal's office. Provide the guidance counselor with copies of important letters.

#8. Letter to Superintendent to Request Child's Records

Jane Smith
500 Oak Lane
Centerville, IL 60010
(899) 555-1234

September 18, 2002

Ruth Meadows, Superintendent
Independent School District #1
10 Main Street
Middleburg, IL 60010

Reference: Michael K. Smith
               DOB: 01/02/90
               School: Grove Middle School

Dear Dr. Meadows:

On September 17, I received a letter advising me that a meeting with Michael's teachers has been scheduled for October 2. At this meeting, we will discuss Michaels' educational problems and how we may help him. So that I may be better prepared for the meeting, please send me a complete copy of my son's entire cumulative and confidential records. Please be sure to include copies of all evaluations and actual test scores.

I will need time to review Michael's educational records before this important meeting.

If you have questions about my request, please call me at work (555-9876) or at home (555-1234), after 6:00 pm.

Thank you for your assistance and quick response.

Sincerely,

Jane Smith

#9. Second Request for Records

Jane Smith
500 Oak Lane
Centerville, IL 60010
(899) 555-1234

October 4, 2002

George Williams, Principal
Grove Middle School
1000 Main Street
Middleburg, IL 60010

Reference: Michael K. Smith
               DOB: 01/02/90
               School: Grove Middle School

Dear Mr. Williams:

I am concerned that I have not received a copy of my son's educational records. I requested these records on September 18, 2001 (copy of letter enclosed). When I did not receive a response from your office, I called on September 25, September 28, and October 1, 2001.

As I mentioned in my earlier letter, a meeting with my son's teachers was scheduled for October 2. I needed to review Michael's educational records before this meeting. Because I did not receive the records in time, the meeting was rescheduled. Michael is still not receiving any help from the school.

I would appreciate your prompt attention to resolve what I view as the beginning of a serious problem. I can come to the school to help photocopy these records. If you need to discuss my request, please call me at work (555-9876) or home (555-1234). Thank you for taking the time to resolve this problem.

Sincerely,

Jane Smith

Enc: September 18 letter requesting records

#10. Letter to Request a Meeting with a Teacher, Includes Educational History

Jane Smith
500 Oak Lane
Centerville, IL 60010
(899) 555-1234

October 15, 2002

Robert Underwood, Teacher
Grove Middle School
1000 Central Avenue
Middleburg, IL 60010

Reference: Michael K. Smith
               DOB: 01/02/90
               School: Grove Middle School

Dear Mr. Underwood:

I am very concerned about Michael's school problems. I would like to meet with you and get your ideas about his problems and how we can help him.

School has been always been difficult for Michael. He repeated first grade. At that time, I asked for special help for Michael. This was denied. In fourth grade, I again asked that he receive special help. The special education staff found him eligible and provided special education services, but felt that he was not far enough behind in reading to receive reading remediation. I told them that he could not read.

In September, 2001, I arranged for Michael to receive private tutoring at our expense. He received tutoring until Christmas when the tutor moved away. Michael was showing improvement, but he needs more help. In the first and second grades, he was happy and energetic. Now he seems sad, depressed, and tells us that children make fun of him because he cannot read. He does not want to go to school.

I understand that you meet with parents on Mondays, Tuesdays, and Thursdays, from 3:15 p.m. to 4:30 p.m. I would like to schedule a meeting with you on Tuesday, October 22 at 3:30 p.m. Please call to confirm this date or suggest an alternative date and time. You can call me at work (555-9876) or home (555-1234) after 6:00 p.m. If I am not available, please leave a message on my answering machine. My job requires me to attend meetings every Monday until 5:00 p.m.

I appreciate your taking time to meet with me. I look forward to your advice about how we can help Michael learn how to read.

Sincerely,

Jane Smith

#11. Letter to Request a Review of Educational Records

Jane Smith
500 Oak Lane, Centerville, IL 60010
(899) 555-1234

November 12, 2002

George Williams, Principal
Grove Middle School
1000 Main Street, Middleburg, IL 60010

Reference: Michael K. Smith
                    DOB: 01/02/90
                    School: Grove Middle School

George Williams, Principal
Grove Middle School
1000 Main Street
Middleburg, IL 60010

Dear Mr. Williams:

On September 18, 2001, I requested a complete copy of my son's educational records. When I did not receive these records, I hand-delivered a second letter to your office on October 4, 2001. (Enclosed are copies of the letters.) I received copies of Michael's educational records on November 8, 2001. I immediately began organizing his file. I found that the records I received from the school appear to be incomplete. He was tested several years ago and that information is missing.

Because Michael's parents and teachers need to have access to the same information, I am requesting that all my son's educational records be brought together in one place for my review. I understand that I may examine all personally identifiable records regarding Michael. This includes medical records, special education records, formal and informal correspondence, discipline records, tests, evaluations, and teacher-to teacher notes.

I appreciate your having a staff member present at this review to certify that these records represent all records held regarding Michael. My friend, Louisa Johnson, will help me to log in records as we review them.

Please call so we can schedule a convenient time to review Michael's educational records. Since Thanksgiving is just around the corner, I would like to finish this task within the next five days. You can reach me at work (555-9876) or at home (555-1234) in the evening. I appreciate your help in this matter.

Sincerely,

Jane Smith

Enc: Letters dated September 18 and October 4, 2001

#12. Letter to Express Appreciation for Help

Jane Smith
500 Oak Lane
Centerville, IL 60010
(899) 555-1234

November 15, 2002

Nathan Weiss, Director of Special Education
School District #10
1001 Main Street
Middleburg, IL 60010

Reference: Michael K. Smith
               DOB: 01/02/90
               School: Grove Middle School

Dear Dr. Weiss:

I greatly appreciate the help your office manager, Joan Patterson, provided during the recent review of my son's educational records.

With Ms. Patterson's help, we were able to locate several records that had been misfiled. Because of Ms. Patterson's suggestions and assistance, we were able to complete the records review more quickly.

You are fortunate to have such a capable office manager.

Sincerely,

Jane Smith

#13. Letter to Request an Evaluation for Special Education Services

Jane Smith
500 Oak Lane
Centerville, IL 60010
(899) 555-1234

November 20, 2002

George Williams, Principal
Grove Middle School
1000 Main Street
Middleburg, IL 60010

Reference: Michael K. Smith
                DOB: 01/02/90
                School: Grove Middle School

Dear Mr. Williams,

I am writing to ask that my son, Michael Smith, be considered for special education services that will teach him how to read. He is in the sixth grade at Grove Middle School.

A brief summary of Michael's educational history follows: Michael was retained in first grade because the teacher felt his problems with reading would improve when he got older. When I asked for special help for Michael, this was denied.

In fourth grade, Michael could not read the labels on cans and boxes at the grocery store. I asked that he receive special education services. He was found eligible and received some services. Although I told your staff that Michael could not read, they said he did not qualify for reading remediation. The special education staff decided to wait to see if his problems improved by the end of the school year. His problems did not improve. I arranged for private tutoring. Michael is now in sixth grade and cannot read labels at the grocery store.

When I met with his teacher last week, I was told that Michael does not read well enough to pass the new state tests. Mr. Underwood explained that Michael's reading skills are at the 2nd to 3rd grade level. He is aware of the severity of Michael's reading problems and is doing all that he can. He suggested that I contact you.

When I first wrote to Mr. Underwood, I told him that in the first and second grades, Michael was happy and energetic. Now he seems sad, depressed, and tells us that several children tease him because he cannot read. He does not want to go to school.

I am afraid that I am losing my child.

Michael needs our help. If you need more information about my request for more reading help for Michael, please call me at home (555-1234) or at work (555-9876). I appreciate your prompt attention to this problem.

Sincerely,

Jane Smith

#14. Letter to Request Test Scores as Standard Scores and Percentile Ranks

Jane Smith
500 Oak Lane
Centerville, IL 60010
(899) 555-1234

February 21, 2003

Nathan Weiss, Director of Special Education
School District #10
1001 Main Street
Middleburg, IL 60010

Reference: Michael K. Smith
              DOB: 01/02/90
              School: Grove Middle School

Dear Dr. Weiss:

I attended an special education meeting for my son on February 20. When I reviewed Mike's test results, I was distressed to find that his scores were reported as "ranges" (i.e. below average, average), not as percentile ranks and/or as standard scores. Because I did not receive his test scores, it was impossible to know where Michael is functioning.

Please send Michael's test scores as standard scores and percentile ranks.

The eligibility team will meet again on **March 20**. To prepare for this meeting, I need the test results no later than **March 13**. If I do not have this information, the team will have to cancel another meeting and waste more valuable time. I understand that your staff is busy. I will pick the information up at the school. If I can do anything to expedite this request or provide any help, please let me know immediately.

Enclosed please find a copy of a comprehensive psycho-educational evaluation of Michael by John Black, Ph.D., NASP, a certified school psychologist, completed on February 12, 2003. I received this evaluation by mail yesterday, while we were at the eligibility meeting.

If you have questions about my request, please let me know. You may call me at work (555-9876) or at home (555-1234). I look forward to receiving these test results no later than **March 13**. Thank you for your assistance.

Sincerely,

Jane Smith

#15. Follow-up Letter after IEP Meeting to Document Unresolved Problems

Jane Smith
500 Oak Lane
Centerville, IL 60010
(899) 555-1234
April 9, 2003

Nathan Weiss, Director of Special Education
School District #10
1001 Main Street, Middleburg, IL 60010

Reference: Michael K. Smith
                  DOB: 01/02/90
                  School: Grove Middle School

Dear Dr. Weiss:

On April 3, I met with you and your staff to develop an appropriate educational program for my son. Michael has received special education services for two years. Before the meeting, I provided you with a comprehensive psycho-educational evaluation of Michael by Dr. John Black, an expert in special education. According to this evaluation, after two years of special education, Michael made no progress learning to read. His self-concept has been damaged.

On April 3, Dr. Black traveled to School District #10 so he could discuss his findings and recommendations with you, your staff, and the IEP Team. At this meeting, he advised you that Michael needs a language arts program that is based on a multi-sensory, sequential approach to reading instruction. Michael learns differently from many children. Michael has dyslexia that was not identified until Dr. Black evaluated him. Dr. Black explained that it is not too late to teach Michael to read, but that he requires intensive services and specialized remediation. I asked the district to provide remediation. You said Michael could attend summer school but advised that the district does not provide reading remediation in summer school.

I am losing confidence in the district's ability to teach Michael how to read and write. The district has provided no remediation. The gap between Michael's ability and achievement is growing. His self-esteem has dropped.

We must find a way to teach Michael to read and write.

I appreciate your taking the time to attend the April 3 meeting. If you can help, please let me know. We are running out of time. You may all me at work (555-9876) or at home (555-1234) after 6:00 p.m.

Sincerely,

Jane Smith

cc: Dr. Black

#16. Ten-day Notice Letter to Withdraw Child from Public School

Jane Smith
500 Oak Lane
Centerville, IL 60010
(899) 555-1234

May 25, 2003

Nathan Weiss, Director of Special Education
School District #10
1001 Main Street
Middleburg, IL 60010

Reference: Michael K. Smith
              DOB: 01/02/90
              School: Grove Middle School

Dear Dr. Weiss:

As you know, my son Michael attends Grove Middle School. Michael has dyslexia. Although he was placed in support classes for two years, he did not learn to read.

Michael has been evaluated by the school psychologist and a private sector school psychologist. Last week, he was evaluated by Dr. Kay, a neuro-psychologist. The enclosed findings are clear and not disputed. Michael has not learned to read. According to the last evaluations, he has fallen further behind. The school personnel blame Michael for his lack of progress.

I advised the team that I may place Michael in private school if the school district will not provide an intensive program of reading remediation. I was told that Michael received the services that were available and that nothing else could be done. The school psychologist said I should not expect Michael to learn to read. Dr. Black, who tested my son in February says that my son will learn to read if he is taught appropriately. Dr. Kay concurs with Dr. Black.

Michael has a right to an appropriate education. I have spent two frustrating years in meetings, trying to educate the district and myself. I have spent thousands of dollars on evaluations that the district ignores.

What can I do? What would you do? Is it unreasonable to expect the school to teach my son to read?

I plan to remove Michael from Independent School District #10 and place him in the Dewey School, a private school that specializes in teaching children like Michael to read. If Michael makes progress in the private program, I will ask the district to reimburse me for the cost of his education.

If you have any questions, you may call me at work (555-9876) or at home (555-1234).

Sincerely,

Jane Smith

cc: Dr. Black
       Dr. Kay

Your Notes Here

APPENDIX J

Glossary of Special Education and Legal Terms

A

Accommodations. Changes in how test is administered that do not substantially alter what the test measures; includes changes in presentation format, response format, test setting or test timing. Appropriate accommodations are made to level the playing field, i.e., to provide equal opportunity to demonstrate knowledge.

Achievement test. Test that measures competency in a particular area of knowledge or skill; measures mastery or acquisition of skills.

Americans with Disabilities Act of 1990 (ADA). Legislation enacted to prohibit discrimination based on disability.

Attention Deficit Disorder/Attention Deficit Hyperactivity Disorder (ADD/ADHD). Child with ADD or ADHD may be eligible for special education under other health impairment, specific learning disability, and/or emotional disturbance categories if ADD/ADHD condition adversely affects educational performance.

Adversarial system. The system of trial practice in which each of the opposing parties has an opportunity to present and establish opposing contentions before the court.

Alternative dispute resolution. See mediation.

Appeal. Procedure in which a party seeks to reverse or modify a judgment or final order of a lower court or administrative agency, usually on grounds that lower court misinterpreted or misapplied the law, rather than on the grounds that it made an incorrect finding of fact.

Appendix A. Appendix to the federal special education regulations that answers questions about IEPs, IEP teams, parental role, transition.

Assessment. Systematic method of obtaining information from tests or other sources; procedures used to determine child's eligibility, identify the child's strengths and needs, and services child needs to meet these needs. See also evaluations.

Assistive technology device. Equipment used to maintain or improve the capabilities of a child with a disability.

Audiology. Related service; includes identification, determination of hearing loss, and referral for habilitation of hearing.

Autism. Developmental disability that affects communication and social interaction, adversely affects educational performance, is generally evident before age 3. Children with autism often engage in repetitive activities and stereotyped movements, resist environmental change or change in daily routines, and have unusual responses to sensory experiences.

B

Basic skills. Skills in subjects like reading, writing, spelling, and mathematics.

Behavior disorder (BD). See emotional disturbance.

Behavior intervention plan. A plan of positive behavioral interventions in the IEP of a child whose behaviors interfere with his/her learning or that of others.

Brief. Written argument that supports a case; usually contains a statement of facts and a discussion of law.

Burden of proof. Duty of a party to substantiate its claim against the other party; in civil actions, the weight of this proof is usually described as a preponderance of the evidence.

Business day. Means Monday through Friday, except for federal and state holidays.

C

Calendar day. (See "day").

Case law. Decisions issued by a court.

Child find. Requirement that states ensure that all children with disabilities are identified, located and evaluated, and determine which children are receiving special education and related services.

C.F.R. Code of Federal Regulations.

Class action. A civil action filed in a court on behalf of a named plaintiff and on behalf of other individuals similarly situated.

Complaint. Legal document that outlines plaintiff's claim against a defendant.

Confidential file. File maintained by the school that contains evaluations conducted to determine whether child is handicapped, other information related to special education placement; parents have a right to inspect the file and have copies of any information contained in it.

Consent. Requirement that the parent be fully informed of all information that relates to any action that school wants to take about the child, that parent understands that consent is voluntary and may be revoked at any time. See also Procedural safeguards notice and prior written notice.

Controlled substance. Means a drug or other substance identified under schedules I, II, III, IV, or V of the Controlled Substances Act; does not include a substance that is legally possessed or used under the supervision of a licensed health care provider.

Counseling services. Related service; includes services provided by social workers, psychologists, guidance counselors, or other qualified personnel.

Cumulative file. General file maintained by the school; parent has right to inspect the file and have copies of any information contained in it.

D

Damages. Monetary compensation that may be recovered by a person who has suffered loss, detriment or injury to his person, property or rights, through the unlawful act or negligence of another; damages are not generally available under the IDEA.

Day. Means calendar day unless otherwise indicated as school day or business day.

Deaf-blindness. IDEA disability category; includes hearing and visual impairments that cause severe communication, developmental and educational problems that adversely affects educational performance.

Deafness. IDEA disability category; impairment in processing information through hearing that adversely affects educational performance.

Disability. In Section 504 and ADA, defined as impairment that substantially affects one or more major life activities; an individual who has a record of having such impairment, or is regarded as having such an impairment.

Discovery. Term for methods of obtaining evidence in advance of trial; includes interrogatories, depositions and inspection of documents.

Due process hearing (impartial due process hearing). Procedure to resolve disputes between parents and schools; administrative hearing before an impartial hearing officer or administrative law judge.

E

Early intervention (EI). Special education and related services provided to children under age of 5.

Education records. All records about the student that are maintained by an educational agency or institution; includes instructional materials, teacher's manuals, films, tapes, test materials and protocols.

Educational consultant/diagnostician. An individual who may be familiar with school curriculum and requirements at various grade levels; may or may not have a background in learning disabilities; may conduct educational evaluations.

Emotional disturbance (ED). Disability category under IDEA; includes depression, fears, schizophrenia; adversely affects educational performance.

EMR. Educable mentally retarded.

ESY. Extended school year services.

Exhibit. Anything tangible that is produced and admitted in evidence during a trial.

F

FERPA. Family Educational Rights and Privacy Act; statute about confidentiality and access to education records.

FAPE. Free appropriate public education; special education and related services provided in conformity with an IEP; are without charge; and meets standards of the SEA.

G

General curriculum. Curriculum adopted by LEA or SEA for all children from preschool through high school.

Guardian ad litem. Person appointed by the court to represent the rights of minors.

H

Hearing impairment. Disability category under IDEA; permanent or fluctuating impairment in hearing that adversely affects educational performance.

I

IDEA. The Individuals with Disabilities Education Act of 1997.

IDELR. Individuals with Disabilities Law Reporter.

IEE. Independent educational evaluation.

IEP. Individualized Educational Plan.

IFSP. Individualized family service plan.

Illegal drug. A controlled substance; does not include substances that are legally possessed or used under the supervision of a licensed health-care professional.

Impartial due process hearing. See due process hearing.

Inclusion. Practice of educating children with special needs in regular education classrooms in neighborhood schools. See also mainstreaming and least restrictive environment.

Interrogatories. Written questions served on a party that must be answered under oath before trial; method of discovery.

ITP. Individual Transition Plan.

J

Judgment. Order by a court.

L

Learning disability. See specific learning disability (SLD).

LRE. Least restrictive environment; requirement to educate special needs children with children who are not disabled to the maximum extent possible.
LEA. Local education agency or school district.

M

Mainstreaming. Practice of placing special needs children in regular classrooms for at least a part of the children's educational program. See also least restrictive environment and inclusion.

Manifestation determination review. If child with disability engages in behavior or breaks a rule or code of conduct that applies to nondisabled children and the school proposes to remove the child, the school must hold a hearing to determine if the child's behavior was caused by the disability.

Mediation. Procedural safeguard to resolve disputes between parents and schools; must be voluntary, cannot be used to deny or delay right to a due process hearing; must be conducted by a qualified and impartial mediator who is trained in effective mediation techniques.

Medical services. Related service; includes services provided by a licensed physician to determine a child's medically related disability that results in the child's need for special education and related services.

Mental retardation. Disability category under IDEA; refers to significantly sub-average general intellectual functioning with deficits in adaptive behavior that adversely affects educational performance.

Modifications. Substantial changes in what the student is expected to demonstrate; includes changes in instructional level, content, and performance criteria, may include changes in test form or format; includes alternate assessments.

Multiple disabilities. Disability category under IDEA; concomitant impairments (such as mental retardation-blindness, mental retardation-orthopedic impairment, etc.) that cause such severe educational problems that problems cannot be accommodated in special education programs solely for one of the impairments; does not include deaf-blindness.

N

Native language. Language normally used by the child's parents.

Norm-referenced test. (See standardized test)

O

OCR. Office of Civil Rights.

Occupational therapy. Related service; includes therapy to remediate fine motor skills.

Opinion. Formal written decision by judge or court; contains the legal principles and reasons upon which the decision was based.

Orientation and mobility services. Related service; includes services to visually impaired students that enable students to move safely at home, school, and community.

Orthopedic impairment. Disability category under IDEA; orthopedic impairment that adversely affects child's educational performance.

OSERS. Office of Special Education and Rehabilitative Services.

OSEP. Office of Special Education Programs.

Other health impairment. Disability category under IDEA; refers to limited strength, vitality or alertness due to chronic or acute health problems that adversely affects educational performance.

P

Parent. Parent, guardian, or surrogate parent; may include grandparent or stepparent with whom a child lives, and foster parent.

Physical therapy. Related service; includes therapy to remediate gross motor skills.

Precedent. A court decision that will influence similar cases in the future.

Prior written notice. Required written notice to parents when school proposes to initiate or change, or refuses to initiate or change, the identification, evaluation, or educational placement of the child.

Pro se. Representing oneself without assistance of legal counsel.

Procedural safeguards notice. Requirement that schools provide full easily understood explanation of procedural safeguards that describe parent's right to an independent educational evaluation, to examine records, to request mediation and due process.

Psychological services. Related service; includes administering psychological and educational tests, interpreting test results, interpreting child behavior related to learning.

Public Law (P.L.) 94-142. The Education for All Handicapped Children Act; enacted into law in 1975.

R

Reasonable accommodation. Adoption of a facility or program that can be accomplished without undue administrative or financial burden.

Recreation. Related service; includes therapeutic recreation services, recreation programs, and leisure education.

Rehabilitation Act of 1973. Civil rights statute designed to protect individuals with disabilities from discrimination; purposes are to maximize employment, economic self-sufficiency, independence, inclusion and integration into society.

Rehabilitation counseling services. Related service; includes career development, preparation for employment, vocational rehabilitation services funded under the Rehabilitation Act of 1973.

Related services. Services that are necessary for child to benefit from special education; includes speech-language pathology and audiology services, psychological services, physical and occupational therapy, recreation, early identification and assessment, counseling, rehabilitation counseling, orientation and mobility services, school health services, social work services, parent counseling and training.

Remediation. Process by which an individual receives instruction and practice in skills that are weak or nonexistent in an effort to develop/strengthen these skills.

S

School day. A day when children attend school for instructional purposes.

School health services. Related service; services provided by a qualified school nurse or other qualified person.

Section 504. Section 504 of the Rehabilitation Act protects individuals with disabilities from discrimination due to disability by recipients of federal financial assistance.

Settlement. Conclusion of a legal matter by agreement of opposing parties in a civil suit before judgment is made.

Special education. Specially designed instruction, at no cost to the parents, to meet the unique needs of a child with a disability.

Specific learning disability (SLD). Disability category under IDEA; includes disorders that affect the ability to understand or use spoken or written language; may manifest in difficulties with listening, thinking, speaking, reading, writing, spelling, and doing mathematical calculations; includes minimal brain dysfunction, dyslexia, and developmental aphasia.

Speech-language pathology services. Related service; includes identification and diagnosis of speech or language impairments, speech or language therapy, counseling and guidance.

Speech or language impairment. Disability category under IDEA; includes communication disorders, language impairments, voice impairments that adversely educational performance.

Statutory rights. Rights protected by statute, as opposed to constitutional rights that are protected by the Constitution.

Statute of limitations. Time within which a legal action must be commenced.

Standardized test. Norm-referenced test that compares child's performance with the performance of a large group of similar children (usually children who are the same age).

State education agency (SEA). State departments of education.

Statutory law. Written law enacted by legislative bodies.

Supplementary aids and services. Means aids, services, and supports that are provided in regular education classes that enable children with disabilities to be educated with nondisabled children to the maximum extent appropriate.

T

Technology (see assistive technology)

Testimony. Evidence given by a person as distinguished from evidence from writings and other sources.

Transcript. Official record taken during a trial or hearing by an authorized stenographer.

Transition services. IEP requirement; designed to facilitate movement from school to the workplace or to higher education.

Transportation. Related service about travel; includes specialized equipment (i.e., special or adapted buses, lifts, and ramps) if required to provide special transportation for a child with a disability.

Traumatic brain injury. Disability category under IDEA; includes acquired injury caused by external physical force and open or closed head injuries that result in impairments; does not include congenital or degenerative brain injuries or brain injuries caused by birth trauma.
Travel training. See orientation and mobility services.

U

U.S.C. United States Code.

V

Visual impairment including blindness. Disability category under IDEA; impaired vision that adversely affects educational performance.

W

Weapon. Means a "dangerous weapon" as defined in the United States Code.

Z

APPENDIX K

Glossary of Assessment Terms

A

Ability. A characteristic that is indicative of competence in a field. (See also aptitude.)

Ability Testing. Use of standardized tests to evaluate an individual's performance in a specific area (i.e., cognitive, psychomotor, or physical functioning).

Achievement tests. Standardized tests that measure knowledge and skills in academic subject areas (i.e., math, spelling, and reading).

Accommodations. Describe changes in format, response, setting, timing, or scheduling that do not alter in any significant way what the test measures or the comparability of scores. Accommodations are designed to ensure that an assessment measures the intended construct, not the child's disability. Accommodations affect three areas of testing: 1) the administration of tests, 2) how students are allowed to respond to the items, and 3) the presentation of the tests (how the items are presented to the students on the test instrument). Accommodations may include Braille forms of a test for blind students or tests in native languages for students whose primary language is other than English.

Age Equivalent. The chronological age in a population for which a score is the median (middle) score. If children who are 10 years and 6 months old have a median score of 17 on a test, the score 17 has an age equivalent of 10-6.

Alternative assessment. Usually means an alternative to a paper and pencil test; refers to non-conventional methods of assessing achievement (e.g., work samples and portfolios).

Alternate Forms. Two or more versions of a test that are considered interchangeable, in that they measure the same constructs in the same ways, are intended for the same purposes, and are administered using the same directions.

Aptitude. An individual's ability to learn or to develop proficiency in an area if provided with appropriate education or training. Aptitude tests include tests of general academic (scholastic) ability; tests of special abilities (i.e., verbal, numerical, mechanical); tests that assess "readiness" for learning; and tests that measure ability and previous learning that are used to predict future performance.

Aptitude tests. Tests that measure an individual's collective knowledge; often used to predict learning potential. See also ability test.

Assessment. The process of testing and measuring skills and abilities. Assessments include aptitude tests, achievement tests, and screening tests.

B

Battery. A group or series of tests or subtests administered; the most common test batteries are achievement tests that include subtests in different areas.

Bell curve. See normal distribution curve.

Benchmark. Levels of academic performance used as checkpoints to monitor progress toward performance goals and/or academic standards.

C

Ceiling. The highest level of performance or score that a test can reliably measure.

Classroom Assessment. An assessment developed, administered, and scored by a teacher to evaluate individual or classroom student performance.

Competency tests. Tests that measure proficiency in subject areas like math and English. Some states require that students pass competency tests before graduating.

Composite score. The practice of combining two or more subtest scores to create an average or composite score. For example, a reading performance score may be an average of vocabulary and reading comprehension subtest scores.

Content area. An academic subject such as math, reading, or English.

Content Standards. Expectations about what the child should know and be able to do in different subjects and grade levels; defines expected student skills and knowledge and what schools should teach.

Conversion table. A chart used to translate test scores into different measures of performance (e.g., grade equivalents and percentile ranks).

Core curriculum. Fundamental knowledge that all students are required to learn in school.

Criteria. Guidelines or rules that are used to judge performance.

Criterion-Referenced Tests. The individual's performance is compared to an objective or performance standard, not to the performance of other students. Tests determine if skills have been mastered; do not compare a child's performance to that of other children.

Curriculum. Instructional plan of skills, lessons, and objectives on a particular subject; may be authored by a state, textbook publisher. A teacher typically executes this plan.

D

Derived Score. A score to which raw scores are converted by numerical transformation (e.g., conversion of raw scores to percentile ranks or standard scores).

Diagnostic Test. A test used to diagnose, analyze or identify specific areas of weakness and strength; to determine the nature of weaknesses or deficiencies; diagnostic achievement tests are used to measure skills.

E

Equivalent Forms. See alternate forms.

Expected Growth. The average change in test scores that occurs over a specific time for individuals at age or grade levels.

F

Floor. The lowest score that a test can reliably measure.

Frequency distribution. A method of displaying test scores.

G

Grade equivalents. Test scores that equate a score to a particular grade level. Example: if a child scores at the average of all fifth graders tested, the child would receive a grade equivalent score of 5.0. Use with caution.

I

Intelligence tests. Tests that measure aptitude or intellectual capacities (Examples: Wechsler Intelligence Scale for Children (WISC-III-R) and Stanford-Binet (SB:IV).

Intelligence quotient (IQ). Score achieved on an intelligence test that identifies learning potential.

Item. A question or exercise in a test or assessment.

M

Mastery Level. The cutoff score on a criterion-referenced or mastery test; people who score at or above the cutoff score are considered to have mastered the material; mastery may be an arbitrary judgment.

Mastery Test. A test that determines whether an individual has mastered a unit of instruction or skill; a test that provides information about what an individual knows, not how his or her performance compares to the norm group.

Mean. Average score; sum of individual scores divided by the total number of scores.

Median. The middle score in a distribution or set of ranked scores; the point (score) that divides a group into two equal parts; the 50th percentile. Half the scores are below the median, and half are above it.

Mode: The score or value that occurs most often in a distribution.

Modifications. Changes in the content, format, and/or administration of a test to accommodate test takers who are unable to take the test under standard test conditions. Modifications alter what the test is designed to measure or the comparability of scores.

N

National percentile rank. Indicates the relative standing of one child when compared with others in the same grade; percentile ranks range from a low score of 1 to a high score of 99.

Normal distribution curve. A distribution of scores used to scale a test. Normal distribution curve is a bell-shaped curve with most scores in the middle and a small number of scores at the low and high ends.

Norm-referenced tests. Standardized tests designed to compare the scores of children to scores achieved by children the same age who have taken the same test. Most standardized achievement tests are norm-referenced.

O

Objectives: Stated, desirable outcomes of education.

Out-of-Level Testing. Means assessing students in one grade level using versions of tests that were designed for students in other (usually lower) grade levels; may not assess the same content standards at the same levels as are assessed in the grade-level assessment.

P

Percentiles (percentile ranks). Percentage of scores that fall below a point on a score distribution; for example, a score at the 75th percentile indicates that 75% of students obtained that score or lower.

Performance Standards. Definitions of what a child must do to demonstrate proficiency at specific levels in content standards.

Portfolio. A collection of work that shows progress and learning; can be designed to assess progress, learning, effort, and/or achievement.

Power Test. Measures performance unaffected by speed of response; time not critical; items usually arranged in order of increasing difficulty.

Profile. A graphic representation of an individual's scores on several tests or subtests; allows for easy identification of strengths or weaknesses across different tests or subtests.

R

Raw score. A raw score is the number of questions answered correctly on a test or subtest. For example, if a test has 59 items and the student gets 23 items correct, the raw score would be 23. Raw scores are converted to percentile ranks, standard scores, grade equivalent and age equivalent scores.

Reliability. The consistency with which a test measures the area being tested; describes the extent to which a test is dependable, stable, and consistent when administered to the same individuals on different occasions.

S

Scaled score. Scaled scores represent approximately equal units on a continuous scale; can convert to other types of scores; can use to examine change in performance over time.

Score. A specific number that results from the assessment of an individual.

Speed Test. A test in which performance is measured by the number of tasks performed in a given time. Examples are tests of typing speed and reading speed.

Standard score. Score on norm-referenced tests that are based on the bell curve and its equal distribution of scores from the average of the distribution. Standard scores are especially useful because they allow for comparison between students and comparisons of one student over time.

Standard deviation (S.D.) A measure of the variability of a distribution of scores. The more the scores cluster around the mean, the smaller the standard deviation. In a normal distribution, 68% of the scores fall within one standard deviation above and one standard deviation below the mean.

Standardization. A consistent set of procedures for designing, administering, and scoring an assessment. The purpose of standardization is to ensure that all individuals are assessed under the same conditions and are not influenced by different conditions.

Standardized tests. Tests that are uniformly developed, administered, and scored.

Standards. Statements that describe what students are expected to know and do in each grade and subject area; include content standards, performance standards, and benchmarks.

Stanine. A standard score between 1 to 9, with a mean of 5 and a standard deviation of 2. The first stanine is the lowest scoring group and the 9th stanine is the highest scoring group.

Subtest. A group of test items that measure a specific area (i.e., math calculation and reading comprehension). Several subtests make up a test.

T

T-Score. A standard score with a mean of 50 and a standard deviation of 10. A T-score of 60 represents a score that is 1 standard deviation above the mean.

Test. A collection of questions that may be divided into subtests that measure abilities in an area or in several areas.

Test bias. The difference in test scores that is attributable to demographic variables (e.g., gender, ethnicity, and age).

V

Validity. The extent to which a test measures the skills it sets out to measure and the extent to which inferences and actions made on the basis of test scores are appropriate and accurate.

Z

z-Score. A standard score with a mean of 0 (zero) and a standard deviation of 1.

Sources: Center for Research on Evaluation, Standards, and Student Testing (CRESST), Graduate School of Education & Information Studies, UCLA; American Guidance Service; Harcourt, Inc.; Office of Special Education and Rehabilitative Services, U. S. Department of Education.

Bibliography

The authors acknowledge the following references used in this book.

Alessi, Galen. "Diagnosis Diagnosed: A Systemic Reaction," *Professional School Psychology* 3 (1988): 145-151.

Allington, Richard L., Anne McGill-Franzel, Ruth Schick. "How Administrators Understand Learning Difficulties," *Remedial and Special Education* 18 (1997): 223-232.

Bramson, Robert M. *Coping with Difficult People.* New York: Dell Publishing, 1981.

Council for Exceptional Children. "Assessments Fail to Give Teachers Relevant Information," *CEC Today* 5 (1998).

Fisher, Roger and William Ury. *Getting to Yes: Negotiating Agreement without Giving In.* New York: Penguin Books, 1991.

Fisher, Roger and Alan Sharp. *Getting It Done: How to Lead When You're Not in Charge.* New York: Harper Business, 1998.

Lake, Jeannie and Bonnie Billingsley. "An Analysis of Factors That Contribute to Parent-School Conflict in Special Education" *Remedial and Special Education* 21 (2000): 240-151.

Mager, Robert F. *Goal Analysis.* Atlanta: Center for Effective Performance, 1997.

Mager, Robert F. *Making Instruction Work.* Atlanta: Center for Effective Performance, 1997.

Mager, Robert F. *Measuring Instructional Results.* Atlanta: Center for Effective Performance, 1997.

Mager, Robert F. *Preparing Instructional Objectives*. Atlanta: Center for Effective Performance, 1997.

National Council on Disability. *Back to School on Civil Rights: Advancing the Federal Commitment to Leave No Child Behind*. Washington, DC, 2000

PEER Project. *Section 504, the Americans with Disabilities Act, and Education Reform*. Boston, MA: The Federation for Children with Special Needs, 1999.

Sattler, Jerome M. *Assessment of Children: Cognitive Applications*. San Diego: Jerome M. Sattler, Publisher, Inc., 2001.

Sattler, Jerome M. *Assessment of Children, 3rd ed*. San Diego: Jerome M. Sattler, Publisher, Inc., 1992.

Spence, Gerry. *How to Argue and Win Every Time*. New York: St Martin's Press, 1995.

Spence, Gerry. *With Justice for None*. New York: Penguin Books, 1989.

Ury, William. *Getting Past No: Negotiating Your Way from Confrontation to Cooperation*. New York: Bantam Books, 1991

Weber, Mark. *Special Education Law and Litigation Treatise*. Horsham, PA: LRP Publications, 1992.

Wright, Peter W. D. and Pamela Darr Wright. *Wrightslaw: Special Education Law*. Hartfield, VA: Harbor House Law Press, 1999.

Index

Symbols

10 Business Day Notice Rule, 133
20 U.S.C. § 1401, 125
20 U.S.C. § 1412, 131
20 U.S.C. § 1414, 141
20 U.S.C. § 1415, 154
29 U. S. C. § 794
   same as Section 504 of the Rehabilitation Act, 175
42 U. S. C. § 12131
   Americans with Disabilities Act, 175
5 Day Rule, 158
5,000 Evaluations, 31
5Ws + H + E Questions, 113, 202, 241, 242
   use to deal with difficult people, 37

A

A Guide to the Individualized Education Program, 328
A Parent's Guide to Special Education and Related Services, 277
ABA/Lovaas Therapy
   one-on-one, 135
   reimbursement for, 137
Academy for Educational Development, 280
Access
   in the general curriculum 123
   to an education, 177
Accommodations and Modifications
   IEP
      additions to meet annual goals, 144
   in statewide assessments, 146
   on high stakes tests, 137
   under Section 504 and ADA, 177, 180

Accountability, 181
   assesssment for, 182
Achievement Tests, 105
Acronyms
   avoid in letters, 214
Action Words
   in SMART IEPs, to be able to, 104
ADA. See Americans with Disabilities Act
Administrative Law Judge, 164
Administrative Remedies
   exhaustion of, required before court, 165
Advocacy
   effective, 248
   groups, 19, 20
   planning, 12
   skills, 5, 6, 12
Advocacy 101, 21
Advocate
   defined, 4
   lay, 4
      at due process hearings, 159
      in IEP, 151
   parent as, 5
Age Equivalent Scores, 78
Age of Majority, 147
Agenda. See Parent Agenda
Alessi, Galen, 31
Alternative Educational Setting
   determined by IEP Team, 166
   placement in, 165
Americans with Disabilities Act
   language of statute, 175
   compared to Section 504, 175
   explained, 179
   high stakes testing, 139
   PEER brief re statewide testing, 179

Annual Goals
    measurable, 107, 144
Appeal
    to Court, 157
    to State Educational Agency, 159
Appendix A
    Appendix A to Special Education Regulations,
        34 C.F.R. Part 300 about IEPs, 249
Appendix B
    Your Rights and Responsibilities Under IDEA,
        277
Appendix C
    Questions Often Asked by Parents About
        Special Education by NICHCY, 281
Appendix D
    State Departments of Special Education, 297
Appendix E
    Parent Training Information Centers, 303
Appendix F
    Disabilities Organizations and Information
        Groups, 313
Appendix G
    Legal and Advocacy Resources, 323
Appendix H
    Free Publications, 327
Appendix I
    Sample Letters to the School, 331
Appendix J
    Glossary of Special Education and Legal Terms,
        351
Appendix K
    Glossary of Assessment Terms, 361
Appropriate
    not most appropriate, not best, 5
ARD
    same as Eligibility and/or IEP meeting, 141
Argument
    if perceived as threat, 247
Assessment
    alternate, 182
    functional behavioral, 171
    glossary of terms, 361
    participation in, 133
    state and district, 137
    state wide and district wide, included in, 133
    techniques, 105
    tools, 142
Assistive Technology
    device defined, 125
    device, school purchased, used at home, 273
    devices and services in IEP, 148
    for communication, 106

    in general, 129
    service defined, 125
Assumptions
    Rules of Adverse, 194
    in worst case scenario, 195
Attitude
    as state of mind, 113
    statements in IEPs, 113
Attorney
    at IEP meetings, 270
    fees
        none if IEP or settlement, 164
        reasonable, settlement exception, 160
Autism, 126
    ABA/Lovaas, 135
    early intervention, 30
    long-range plans, 12
    OSFA programs, 25

B

Back to School on Civil Rights, 330
Balanced Reading Instruction, 329
Basic Skills
    described, 106
    need to acquire, 106
Behavior
    as manifestation of disability, 167
    issues in IEP, 151
Behavior Rating Scales, 99
Behavioral Intervention Plan, 171
Beliefs
    as source of conflict, 42
Bell Curve
    compare scores, 80, 81, 82
    in general, 80
    push-ups, 81
    to measure effectiveness, 80
    to measure progress, 107
    X-axis, 81
    Y-axis, 81
Benchmarks
    defined, 105
    in Appendix A, 106
    in IEP, 146
    legal definition, 106
    used to assess progress, 107
Best
    as obscene four-letter word, 5
    is fatal, 130
    not entitled to, 46

Bibliography, 367
Blame, 228
    in letters, 219
Blind or Visually Impaired
    IEP, special factors in, 148
Board of Education v. Rowley, 130
Body Mass Index (BMI), 109
Bombastic, Bob, 220
Braille
    as accommodation, 182
    instruction in, 148
Brain Injury, 127
Brainstorm
    to prepare for meetings, 232
Brandeis, Justice Louis D.
    Jurist - on passion, 185
Brown v. Board of Education, 119
Bryant, Bear
    football coach - will to prepare, 193
Bullies
    dealing with, 36
Bureaucracy
    schools as, 24
Burlington v. Dept. of Ed. of Mass.
    and reimbursement for private placement, 137
    tuition reimbursement, 100
Burnout, 19
Buros Institute of Mental Measurements, 97

C

Calendar
    as evidence, 204
Carnegie, Dale
    motivational speaker - priorities, 67
Carter. See Florence County Sch. Dist. IV v. Carter
Child Find Requirements, 132
Child with a Disability
    defined, 126
Children Enrolled in Private Schools
    without consent of school, 132
Children's Apperception Test, 99
Children's Mental Health, 327
Circumstantial Evidence, 113
Civil Action, 159
Classification by Disability
    not required, 132
    used to delay, 134
Clinical Evaluation of Language Fundamentals, 99
Closing the Gap, 62

Cluster Scores, 88
Cochlear Implant, 61
Cognitive Tests, 97
Columbo Strategy, 113, 114
Communication
    as basic skill, 106
    mediator's role, 162
    needs must be considered in IEP, 148
    problems, 47
Comparable Benefits and Services
    under 504 and ADA, 179
Compare
    statistics, 78
    with bell curve, 80
Complainers
    dealing with, 39
Complaint Resolution, 157
Complaints and Violations
    laundry lists of, 198
Composite Scores
    in general, 85
    to determine eligibility, 88
Comprehensive Achievement Tests, 98
Comprehensive Evaluation, 57
Confidential File, 68
Confidentiality, 162
Conflict
    beliefs, perceptions, interests, 42
    expense and, 43
    loss of control and, 43
    unresolved, 42
Conflict Avoiders
    dealing with, 37
    peace at any price, 237
Congressional Findings, 121
Conner's Rating Scales, 99
Consultants, 14, 62 (See also Evaluators, Experts)
Contact Log
    as evidence, 197
    in general, 202
Continuum of Alternative Placements, 135
Contractors, 17
Controlled Substance
    defined, 170
    over-the-counter excluded, 172
Conversations and Meetings
    as evidence, 198
Conversion Table
    standard scores and percentile ranks, 94
Council of Exceptional Children, 64
Counselors, 14
Courier font, 215

Crisis
    management, 54
    triggers, 53
Criterion-referenced tests, 90, 105
Criticize, 228
Cumulative File, 68
Current Educational Placement
    stay put, 161, 164
Curriculum
    as reflects standards, 181
    modifications, 181

D

Data
    objective, 110
    used to compare individual to group, 80
Deaf or Hard of Hearing, 148
Decisions
    making, 77
Definitions
    assistive technology device, 125
    assistive technology service, 125
    child find, 132
    child with a disability, 126
    controlled substance, 170
    free appropriate public education, 126
    illegal drug, 170
    individualized education program, 146
    learning disability, specific, 127
    least restrictive environment, 132
    related services, 126
    special education, 127
    statutory, 125
    substantial evidence, 170
    supplementary aids and services, 127
    transition services, 127
    weapon, 170
    Wrightslaw discussion of, 128
Descartes
    on measurement, 73
*Designing Individualized Education Program
    (IEP) Transition Plans*, 328
Destruction of Records, 187
Developmental Aphasia, 127
Developmental Delays, 126
Diagnostic Tests, 110
Difficult People
    dealing with, 34
Direct Instruction, 135
Disability
    learning about, 64

Disability Rights Advocates, 328
Discipline
    suspension, 10 days, 275
    suspension permitted, 274
    under Section 504, 177
    Wrightslaw discussion of, 170
Wrightslaw discussion of, 170
Disclosures of Records, 186
Discrepancy Formulas
    in specific learning disabilities, 129
    when used to deny services, 136
Discrete Trial Therapy, 137
Discrimination
    in education, 182
    protection from, 176
    tests to be free of racial or cultural, 143
Dispute Resolution, 157
District Courts
    jurisdiction of, 160
Do No Harm, 328
Documents
    managing, 67
    master list of, 70
Draw-a-Person, 99
Drugs, illegal, 170
Due Process Hearing
    decision available to public, 159
    discussion, 163
    expedited, 168
    findings of fact, written, 159
    in general, 157
    limitations of actions, 162
    representation by lay advocate, 159
    statute of limitations, 162
    transcript, right to, 159
    under Section 504, 178
Dyslexia, 127
    IEP omits reading and writing, 61
    Orton-Gillingham, 135
    OSFA programs, 25

E

Edelman, Marian Wright
educator - on expertise, 61
Education
    appropriate See Free Appropriate Public
        Education
    reform, 179
*Education for All Handicapped Children Act of
    1975*, 119

Educational
    benefit, not necessary in 504 plan, 177
    history, 67
    measuring change, 75
    opportunity, loss of, 157
    placement, 161
    records, 68, 185
        destruction of, 187
        right to inspect and review, 186
Educational Achievement Tests, 98
Educational Diagnosticians, 14
Effective Educational Practices, 65
Effectiveness
    measuring, 80
Electronic Log, 202
Eligibility, 176
    Child with disability, not eligible, 145, 287
    children with ADD/ADHD, 128
    criteria, 128
        no single procedure, 132
    determination of, 143
    for special education, 176
    Wrightslaw discussion of, 145
Emotions as obstacles, 33
Emotional Disturbance, 126
Emotional Traps
    for parents, 40
English as Second Language (ESL), 148
Equal Educational Opportunity
    in *Brown v. Board of Education*, 119
ESL. See English as Second Language
ESY. See Extended School Year
Evaluation
    advance disclosure, 158
    as evidence, 198
    by school, limitations of, 64
    comprehensive, 57, 61
    functional vocational, 127
    Independent Educational, 154
    learning about, 75
    neuropsychological, 100
    private sector, 145
    obtained by parents, 144
    procedures, 142
    report, given to parent, 143
    in statute, 141
    Wrightslaw discussion of, 145
    Evaluator
    independent, 64
    locating, 62
Evidence
    for due process hearing, 197

preponderance, 160
    right to present, 159
Examples, physical fitness, 80
Excel
    wizard, 100
Exhaustion of Administrative Remedies, 165
Exhibits
    disclosure prior to hearing, 163
    list may include, 163
Expectations
    educational, 13
Expedited Hearing
    discipline, request by school staff, 168
    discipline, requested by parent, 168
Expense
    individualized programs, 43
Experts
    role of, 18
    see also evaluator and consultant, 18
Experts, self-styled
    dealing with, 36
Extended School Year
    in general, 134
    legal right to, 90

F

Face
    importance of, 50
Fair Hearing. *See* Due Process Hearing
Family Educational Rights and Privacy Act
        (FERPA), 185
Family Policy Compliance Office
    FERPA letter
        test protocols, 187
FAPE. See Free Appropriate Public Education
FAQs
    Frequently Asked Questions, NICHCY, 281
Fears
    of parents, 75
    of school staff, 42
Federation for Children with Special Needs, 183
    504 and ADA brief re statewide testing, 178
Feeling Devalued
    as problem, 47
FERPA
    see Family Educational Rights and Privacy Act,
        185
File. *See* Master File
    confidential, 68
    cumulative, 68
    how to organize, 67

Findings and Purposes
  by Congress, 121
  Wrightslaw discussion of, 123
First Impressions
  and simple themes, 198
  overcoming, 222
Fisher, Roger
  Getting to Yes, 162
Five Golden Rules for Negotiators, 50
Five Rules for Successful Negotiating and Problem
    Solving, 228
Five W's + H + E Questions. *See* 5Ws + H + E
    Questions
Florence County Sch. Dist. IV v. Carter
  tuition reimbursement for private placement,
    100, 137
  LRE and mainstreaming, 136
  oral argument, statement by Supreme Court
    Justice, 153
Food, 235
Four Deadly Sins for Negotiators, 50
Four Issues in Special Education Disputes, 43
Franklin, Benjamin
  inventor
    cost of education v ignorance, 3
    persuasion techniques, 219
Free Appropriate Public Education
  defined, 126
  for suspended or expelled children, 131
  not best, not maximized, not most appropriate,
    130
From Emotions to Advocacy,
  The Parent's Journey, 6, 248
Full Participation, 119, 120
Full Scale IQ (FSIQ), 88
Functional Behavioral Assessment, 171

G

Gatekeepers, 24, 25
General Curriculum
  progress in, 146
Getting Past No, 162
Getting to Yes, 162
Glossary of Assessment Terms
  see Appendix K, 361
Glossary of Special Education and Legal Terms
  see Appendix J, 351
Goals
  defined, 105

functional, 13
  in master plans, 11, 12
Good Impressions, 222
Goss v. Lopez, 275
Grade Equivalent Scores, 78
Gray Oral Reading Test, 99
Grieving, 13
Growth
  how to measure educational, 74

H

Handouts and Charts, 234
Harassment, 327
Harbor House Law Press, Inc., 324
Harvard Civil Rights Project, 340
Hearing Impaired, 126, 148
Hearing Officer
  in discipline issues, authority of, 166
  in general, 164
Hidden Issues
  as problem, 46
Hierarchy of Skills
  in SMART IEPs, 116
  three critical, 106
High Stakes Testing, 137, 328
  OCR Report, 137
House-Tree-Person, 99
How to Argue and Win Every Time, 248

I

IDEA, 42
  compared to Section 504 and ADA, 175
  history, 120
  implementation of, 122
  low expectations, 42, 122
IEE. *See* Independent Educational Evaluation
IEP
  annual goals
    not all areas of curriculum, 254
    progress toward, 147
  Appendix A, general IEP questions, 263
  appropriate objective criteria and evaluation
    procedures, 80
  assistive technology device used at home, 273
  behavior issues in, 151
  child placed out of state, responsibility for, 264
  defined, 146, 150
  development of, 148

drafts, dealing with, 242
drafts, full discussion, 272
eligibility, combined with, 265
frequency of meetings, 266
general curriculum requirement, 253
Goals and Objectives
    basic skills, 106
    improved behavior, 114
    measurable, 109
    revising, 110
in effect at beginning of year, 148
lay advocate at meeting, 147
non-Goals, attitude statements, 113
parent input in, 152
placement decisions, 273
preschool, 254
progress reports to parents, 258
required components of, 150
reviewing and revising, 108, 149, 151
right to copy of, 258
SMART IEPS, 103
special factors, 148
tape recording, audio and video, 238, 267
team
    members of, 147, 151, 269
    notification to parents of others invited, 257
    other individuals, 270
    parents are members of, 147
    regular ed teacher, 149, 268
    representative of LEA, 267
    review and revise IEP, 108
    student must be invited, circumstances when, 257
    timelines for development and implementation, 265
    transition
        in Appendix A, 260
        planning in, 151
Illegal Drug
    defined, 170
Impairment, Physical or Mental
    Section 504, 176
Impartial Due Process Hearing. *See* Due Process Hearing
Impressions
first, 198
Improving educational results, 122
Inclusion, 135
Independent Educational Evaluation, 154
Independent Experts
    as witnesses, 198
Individualized Education Program. *See* IEP

Individualized Family Service Plan (IFSP), 148
Individuals with Disabilities Education Act. *See* IDEA
Individuals with Special Knowledge or Training, 159
Integration
    maximum feasible, 181
Intellectual Tests, 97
Interests
    child's, 5, 17, 42
    school staff, 42, 43
    source of conflict, 42
Intimidation, 34
Invisible Strangers, 211, 222
IQ, 88

J

Jefferson, Thomas
    Virginia Gentleman - cost of education, 121
Journals
    as evidence, 197, 204

K

Kaufman Test of Educational Achievement (K-TEA), 98
Kay, Mary, 209
Keller, Helen
    power of one, 248
Kennedy, John F.
    definition of crisis, 53
Keyboarding, 102
KeyMath-Revised, 99
Kinetic Family Drawing, 99
King, Martin Luther
    civil rights activist - obstacles to success, 29
        morality v behavior - legislation or litigation, 175
Know-it-Alls
    dealing with, 36

L

Lack of Information
    as problem, 44
Lack of Options
    as problem, 45
Laundry List
    of complaints, 198

Law Clerk
 impact of your letters on, 214
Law Enforcement
 referral to, 170
Lawyer v Chesterfield County, 134
Lay Advocate
 at Due Process Hearing, 159
 at IEP meeting, 147
LEA. *See* Local Educational Agency
Learning Disability
 defined, 127
 in general, 129
 specific, 126
Least Restrictive Environment, 135
 defined, 132
Left Handed Child
 penalized on WISC-III Coding subtest, 96
Legislative Intent, 119
Leonard, George
 author - on schools and learning, 131
Letter Writing Tips, 213
Letters
 2nd request for records, 340
 angry, 220
 as evidence, 197
 frequently asked questions about, 217
 nuts and bolts of, 216
 persuasive, 224
 pitfalls, 211
 purposes of, 207
 spell checkers, 215
 strategies, 212
 sympathy factor, 222
 ten-day notice of child's withdrawal, 348
 thank you, 245, 343
 threatening, demanding, 212
 tips from Wrightslaw, 212
 to decline a request, 337
 to document a problem, 334, 336
 to express appreciation, 335, 343
 to request action, 333
 to request evaluation, 344
 to request information, 332
 to request meeting, 333, 341, 347
 to request records, 338, 339, 340
 to request records review, 342
 to request test scores, 346
 to superintendent, 339
 to withdraw child from school, 348
Letters to The Stranger, 214
Life Activity, Major
 and Section 504, 176

Limitations of Actions, 162
Limited English Proficiency
 language needs, 148
List
 Master Provider, 68
 of documents, 70
Litigation
 high stakes testing, 137
Local Educational Agency
 school district as, 159
Log, Contact
 as evidence, 202
Loss of Educational Opportunity, 153
LRE. *See* Least Restrictive Environment

M

Mager, Robert, 103
 deal with educator's resistance, 114
 use circumstantial evidence for goal analysis,
  113
Mainstreaming, 135
Manifestation Determination Review, 167
Manners, Mike, 221
Maslow, Abraham, 41
Master Document List
 format of, 71
 sample, 71
Master File, 67, 70
 big picture, 70
 chronological order, 69
 duplicates, 69
 meeting, prepare for, 230
 organizing, 68
 original documents, 69
Master Plan, 9
 comprehensive evaluation in, 61
Master Provider List, 68
Maximum Feasible Integration
 as discussed in PEER Brief, 181
Maximum Potential
 not entitled to, 46
MDT
 same as Eligibility and or IEP meeting, 141
Mean, 90
Measurable, 104
annual goals, 107, 146
Measure Change
 statistics to, 77
Mediation, 157
agreement, 158
cost of, 158

mediator, qualified, impartial, 157
Medical Treatment Plan
    and IEPs, 110
Medications
    as drugs, 172
    over-the-counter, 172
Meetings
    common problems, 240
    dynamics, 240
    food as secret weapon in, 235
    image and presentation, 235
    no resolution, 242
    preparing for, 227
    school meeting anxiety, 237
    strategies, 238
    use of problem resolution worksheet, 242
Mental Retardation, 126
Merriam-Webster Collegiate Dictionary, 106
Millon Adolescent Clinical Inventory, 99
Minimal Brain Dysfunction, 127
Minnesota Multiphasic Personality Inventory for
    Adolescents, 99
Mission
    of public schools, 24, 33
Mission Statement, 11
Moats, Louisa, 329
Modifications. *See* Accommodations and Modifi-
    cations
Myths, 30

N

National Council on Disability, 330
National Information Center for Children and
    Youth with Disabilities. See NICHCY
National Policy, 122
Native Language
    testing in, 136
Negotiate
    Five Rules of, 228
    in general, 49
    in letters, 223
Negotiator
    parent as, 227
Neuropsychological Evaluations, 100
NICHCY
    FAQs for Parents, 281
    Law, excellent overview of, 277
    *Parent's Guide to Special Education and
    Related Services*, 281
        Your Child's Evaluation, 282

        Your Child's Eligibility, 286
        Writing an IEP, 287
        Reevaluation, 293
        Other Special Education Issues, 294
No Single Procedure
    for eligibility or appropriate program, 136
Non-Goals
    states of being, 114
Norm-referenced tests, 90
Normal Distribution Curve
    See Bell Curve, 80
Nuts and Bolts of Letter Writing, 215

O

Objective Personality Tests, 99
Objective Test Data
    in IEPs, 111
    in treatment plans, 111
Objectives
    legal definition, 106
    short-term, 146
    used to assess progress, 107
Observable Behavior
    as circumstantial evidence, 114
Observations
    subjective, 111
Obstacles
    emotions, 33
    in general, 29
    school culture, 31
Occupational Therapist, 14
Office of Civil Rights
    high stakes testing, 137
Office of the Surgeon General, 327
One-Size-Fits-All, 24, 214
One-Tier System, 163
*Opportunities Suspended: The Devastating
    Consequences of Zero Tolerance and School
    Discipline Policies*, 330
Organizations
    source of information, 64
Organize File, 67
Orthopedic Impairments, 126
Orton-Gillingham, 135
Other Health Impairments, 126
Outcomes
    educational, 181
Over-Protectiveness, 34

P

Paper Trails, 201
Parent Agenda
    sample, 45
Parent
    agenda, 45
    as decision-maker, 18
    consent required
        before evaluation, 142
        before re-evaluation, 144
    discipline
        right of appeal, 168
    fathers at meetings, 238
    input at IEP, 152
    mothers at meetings, 238
    notice, ten business day rule, 137
    participation in meetings
        right to, 154
    request to inspect and review records, 45 day
        rule, 186
    role is strengthened, 42
    surrogate, 256
Parent Information and Training Centers, 56, 303
Parent-School
    conflict, 41
    relationship, 40
Parents Engaged in Education Reform
504 and ADA brief re statewide testing, 178
*Parent's Guide to Special Education and Related
    Services* from NICHCY, 281
Part A of IDEA
    findings, purposes, definitions, 118
Part B of IDEA
    eligibility, evaluations, IEPs, hearings, 118
Part C of IDEA
    infants and toddlers with disabilities, 118
Part D of IDEA
    grants, research, and training, 118
Passing Grades, 111
Peabody Individual Achievement Test, 98
Percentile Ranks, 78
Perceptions
    in general, 31
    of school staff, 31-33
    as source of conflict, 42
Perceptual Disabilities, 127
Performance IQ (PIQ), 88
Personal Notes, 186
Personality Styles, 35
Personality Tests, 99

Persuade
    using letters to, 224
Photocopy Fees, 186
Physical Therapists, 14
Pit Bulls
    dealing with, 35
Placement
    continuum of alternative placements, 135
    current educational, 161
    decisions, 151
        made at IEP meeting, 273
        parent member of group, 149
    during appeal of discipline action, 168
    in alternative educational setting, 165
Planning
    for future, 12
    importance of, 13
    Laura and Steve, 12
Plans
    contingency, 13
    long-range, 17
Positive Behavioral Interventions, 148
Powell, Colin
    learning from failure, 207
Pre-Meeting Worksheet, 231
Preparing for Meetings, 227, 230
Preponderance of Evidence, 160
Present Levels of Performance, 105
    for IEPs, 146
    for evaluations, 144
Prevention Model of special education advocacy,
    195
Prior Written Notice
    content of, 155
    Wrightslaw discussion of, 156
Private School Placement
    reimbursement for, 133
    unilateral, 137
Pro-Ed, 97
Problem Report, 205
Problem Solving, 228
Problem-Resolution Worksheet, 242
Procedural Issues, 153
Procedural Safeguards, 41, 132,
    under Section 504, 178
    Wrightslaw discussion of, 156, 161, 170, 173
Procedural Safeguards Notice, 155
    Wrightslaw discussion of, 156
Procedures
    types of, 154
Professional Development
    high quality, intensive, 122

Program Modifications
    for school personnel, 146
Progress
    advising parent about, 107
    apparent progress may be regression, 89
    comparing, 82
    lack of, 108
    measuring, 107, 111
    toward annual goals, 147
Project Manager,
    parent as, 17
Projects,
    reasons for failure, 18
Projective Personality Tests, 99
Proof
    in due process hearing, 197
Protection and Advocacy Office, 56, 325
Proven Methods
    failure to use, 123
Provider List, 68
Psychiatrists, 14
Psychologists, 14
Public Law 94-142, 119
    purpose of, 121-122
Pushy mother, 17

R

Raw Scores, 84
Reading
    oral, 76
    skills, 106
    teaching, 329
Realistic and Relevant
    in SMART IEPs, 104
Reasonable Accommodations
    as discussed in PEER Brief, 180
Recollections
    limitations of, 202
Recording Meetings,
    tips, 239
    law about recording, 239
Records, 68
    disclosures, 186
    right to inspect and review, 186
    right to examine all, 154
    use in advocacy, 201
Reevaluations, 141, 142
Reform, 178
    assessment in, 182
Regression, 82

Regular Education Teacher
    member of IEP team, 149
Rehabilitation Act. See Section 504
Reimbursement
    in general, 137
    limitations on, 133
Related Services, 129
    defined, 126
Relationships
    building, 19
    polarized, 48
    protecting, 49
Remediation
    one-on-one, 135
Removal from Public School, 137
Resistance,
    strategies to deal with, 114
Retention,
    as ineffective and harmful, 138, 329
Review Existing Evaluations
    IEP team shall, 143
Rights and Responsibilities
    overview, 117, 277
Rules
    gatekeepers, 24
    school bureaucracy, 24
Rules of Adverse Assumptions
    in general, 193, 194
    proof and evidence, 197
    letters are the key, 212
Rules of Procedure, 153
Rules of the Game, 23, 26

S

Safeguards, See Procedural Safeguards
Sattler, Jerome
    describes assessment, 87
    coding subtest, 96
    penalty on coding subtest for left-handed
        children, 96
Scale Scores, 84
School
    as factories, 24
    culture, 31
    principals, 32
    using file as evidence, 198
School Personnel
    authority of, 165
    fears of, 49
    information from, 65
    program modifications and supports for, 146

School Climate, 25
School Meeting Anxiety, 237
Schulz, Charles, cartoonist
   on pushy mothers, 17
Screening Tests, 98
SEA. *See* State Educational Agency
Section 504, 175
   compared to IDEA and ADA, 175
   high stakes testing, 139
   impairment, physical or mental, 176
   PEER brief, 178
   statewide testing, 179
Settlement Discussions, 158, 162
Short-term Objectives, 146
Simple Themes
   win cases, 198
Single Procedure
   not sole criterion, 129, 143
Single-Subject Tests, 99
SMART IEPs, 103, 247
SMART Weight Loss Program, 110
Snipers
   dealing with, 39
Social Skills, 106
Special Education
   defined, 127, 128
   eligibility, 128
   individualized programs in, 25
   low expectations in, 42
   rules, 24
Special Education Regulations
   about IEPs, 105
   Appendix A, 249
Specially Designed Instruction, 127
Specific Goals, 104
Speech-Language Tests, 99, 100
Speech or Language Impairments, 126
Speech-Language Pathologists, 14
Spence, Gerry, trial lawyer and writer
   definition of winning, 237
   if perceived as a threat, 247
   on preparing, 248
   research and preparation, 117
Standard Deviation, 78, 90
Standard Scores, 78, 93
Standards-based education reform, 181
Stanford-Binet, 98
State and District Assessments, 137
State Departments of Education, 56, 237
State Educational Agency
   appeal to, 159

State special education regulations
   request and use, 247
Statistics
   common uses of, 74
   to compare, 78
   to describe relationships, 76
   to make decisions, 77
Statute of Limitations, 162
Stay Put, 161, 164
Story-Telling Approach, 220
Stranger
   finds your letter, 214
   identity and description, 214
   writing letters to the, 214
Strategies
   attitude goals, 113
   Columbo, 113
   consultant, finding, 14
   dealing with resistance, 114
   different views of child, 44
   feeling devalued, 47
   hidden issues, 47
   intimidation, 48
   lack of information, 45
   lack of options, 46
   letter writing, 209
   letters, persuasive, 222
   loss of trust, 49
   master plan, 13
   meetings, 238
   parent groups, 15
   post-meeting, 245
   tactics and strategies, 191
   with Complainers, 39
   with Know-it-Alls, 36
   with Pit Bulls, 36
   with Snipers, 39
   with Wet Blankets, 38
Stress
   special education, 19
   tips to deal with, 19
Subjective Observations, 111
Substantial Evidence
   defined, 170
Substantive Issues, 153
Subtest Scores
   explained, 96
   in general, 85
   in parentheses, 96
   on WISC-III, 95
Successful Outcomes, 165
Supplementary Aids and Services

defined, 127
explained, 129
Supplies,
   list of, 7
Support groups, 15
Supports
   for school personnel, 146
Supremacy Clause, U.S. Constitution, 120
Surrogate Parent, 256
Suspensions
   more than 10 days, 171
   up to 10 days, 170

T

Tactics and Strategies, 191
Taking care of yourself, 19
Tape Recording, *see* Recording Meetings
Teacher Opinions, 111
Teams
   invisible members of, 26
   decisions by, 31, 107, 229, 250
Telephone Calls, 206
Ten Business Day Notice Rule, 137
Ten Reasons Why Schools Say No!, 26
Test of Written Language, 87
Testing, High Stakes
   Office of Civil Rights Report, 138
Tests
   as educational records, 185
   categories of, 97
   charting scores of, 100
   Childrens Apperception Test, 99
   Clinical Evaluation of Language Fundamentals, 99
   comprehensive achievement tests, 98
   Conner's Rating Scales,
   criterion-referenced, 90, 105
   Draw-a-Person, 99
   educational achievement, 98
   Gray Oral Reading Test, 99
   High Stakes, 134
   House-Tree-Person, 99
   Intellectual or cognitive, 97
   IQ, 88
   Kaufman Test of Educational Achievement, 98
   KeyMath-Revised, 99
   Kinetic Family Drawing, 99
   learning what they measure, 76
   mean, 90
   Millon Adolescent Clinical Inventory, 99

Minnesota Multiphasic Personality Inventory
   for Adolescents, 99
neuropsychological, 100
non-discrimination in, 132
norm-referenced, 90
objective personality tests, 99
oral reading, 76
Peabody Individual Achievement Test, 98
Peabody Picture Vocabulary Test, 100
projective personality tests, 99
protocols, as education records, 187
scores, to measure educational change, 75
scores, in IEPs, 102
screening tests, 98
single-subject, 99
speech and language, 99, 100
   standard deviation, 90
   sttandard scores, 93
Stanford-Binet, 98
subtest scatter, 96
Subtest Scores, 95
Test of Written Language, 93
Thematic Apperception Test, 99
understanding test results, 62
Vineland Adaptive Behavior Scales, 99
Wechsler Individual Achievement Test, 98
Wechsler Intelligence Scale for Children, 88, 95, 97
Wide Range Achievement Test, 98
Woodcock Reading Mastery Test, 76, 99
Woodcock-Johnson III Tests
   of Achievement, 88
   of Cognitive Abilities, 88
Woodcock-Johnson Psycho-Educational Battery, 88
word identification explained, 76
The Big Picture, 70
Thematic Apperception Test, 99
Thomas v. Davidson Academy,
   first landmark private school ADA case, 183
Time management, 19
Time-limited
   in SMART IEPs, 104
Timelines, 12
Touch-typing, 102
Transcript
   of due process hearing, right to, 159
   of meetings, as evidence, 197
Transition
   planning in the IEP, 151
   service needs in, 147

objectives
  failure to meet, 149
  plans, 259-263
  services, 129
    defined, 127
Traumatic Brain Injury, 126
Treatment Team
  information from, 64
Triggers,
  of crises, 53
Trust
  loss of, 48
Twain, Mark, author
  on school boards, 23
  on loyalty to opinions, 125
Two-Tier System, 163

U

Unilateral Private Placement, 137

V

Verbal IQ (VIQ), 88
Versuslaw, 56
Views. *See also* Perceptions
  as problem, 44
Vineland Adaptive Behavior Scales, 99
Violations
  laundry list of, 198
  loss of educational opportunity, 157
Vision, 12
Visual Impairments, 126
Vocational Training, 127

W

Weapon
  defined, 170
Wechsler Individual Achievement Test, 98
Wechsler Intelligence Scale for Children
  in general, 97
  scores, 95
  subtests, 96
    coding, 96
    Similarities, 96
Weight Watchers, 108

Wet Blankets
  dealing with, 38
Whole language, 329
Wide Range Achievement Test, 98
Win-lose bargaining, 50, 229
Win-win solutions
  goals, 6
  solutions, 27, 161, 229
Witnesses
  disclosure of, 163
  direct and cross examination of, 159
  right to subpoena, 159
Woodcock Reading Mastery Test, 76, 99
Woodcock-Johnson III Tests
  of Achievement, 88, 98
  of Cognitive Abilities, 88
Woodcock-Johnson Psycho-Educational Battery,
  88
Wooden, John, basketball coach
  on preparation, 9
Worst Case Scenario, 195
Wrightslaw: SMART IEPs, 116
Wrightslaw: Special Education Law, 120, 275
Wrightslaw Quick Rules of Tests, 91
Written Prior Notice, 154, 156
www
  ericae.net, 97
  fetaweb.com, 55, 64, 71, 100, 139, 145, 162
  psychcorp.com, 97
  riverpub.com, 97
  smartieps.com, 116
  weightwatchers.com, 109
  wrightslaw.com, 56, 134, 139, 214

Z

Zero Tolerance Policies, 172, 330